Florence

timeout.com / florence

D0861677

247

148

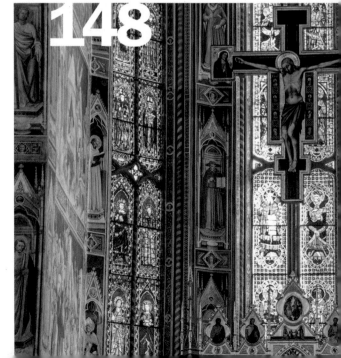

Contents

Introduction

Why Florence? 'For the Renaissance' is the obvious answer.
But, the City of the Lily is so much more than a place to see
Michelangelos and Botticellis. In fact, it boasts two millennia
of history layered and merged into one glorious square mile,
so easily walkable and convenient to navigate that you may
never need to check your bearings on a map. You'll find a
variety of world-class cultural events and performing arts
venues, and a surprisingly fast-growing contemporary art
scene; plus inexpensive food, sublime wine and delicious gelato,
which tradition says was invented here. Florence is also one
of the world's fashion capitals, with museums celebrating its
local designers. It's a cradle of craftsmanship and ingenuity,
with shopping opportunities ranging from artisan studios to
world-class brands. If you can drag yourself away from the city
centre, the surrounding countryside promises unforgettable
days out. As a visitor, there are few downsides to Florence,
and with the help of our insider tips, even the crowds can be
effectively circumvented.

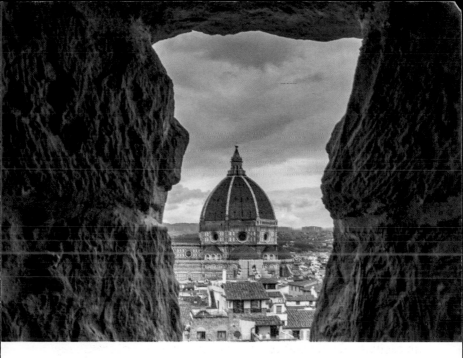

ABOUT THE GUIDE

This is one of a series of Time Out guidebooks to cities across the globe. Written by local experts, our guides are thoroughly researched and meticulously updated. They aim to be inspiring, irreverent, well-informed and trustworthy.

Time Out Florence is divided into five sections: Discover, Explore, Experience, Understand and Plan.

Discover introduces the city and provides inspiration for your visit.

Explore is the main sightseeing section of the guide and includes detailed listings and reviews for sights, museums, restaurants and wine bars ⑩, cafés and gelaterie ⑩, and shops ⑩, all organised by area with a corresponding street map. To help navigation, each area of Florence has been assigned its own colour.

Experience covers the cultural life of the city in depth, including festivals, film, LGBT, music, nightlife, theatre and more.

Understand provides in-depth background information that places Florence in its historical and cultural context.

Plan offers practical visitor information, including accommodation options and details of public transport.

Hearts

We use hearts ♥ to pick out venues, sights and experiences in the city that we particularly recommend. The very best of these are featured in the Top 20 (*see p10*) and receive extended coverage in the guide.

Maps

A detachable fold-out map can be found on the inside back cover. There's also an overview map on *p8* and individual streets maps for each area of the city. All the venues featured in the guide have been given a grid reference so that you can find them easily on the maps and on the ground.

Prices

All our **restaurant listings** are marked with a euro symbol category from budget to blow-out (€-€€€€), indicating the price you should expect to pay for one main dish (*secondo*): € = under €10; €€ = €10-€25; €€€ = €25-€40; €€€€ = over €40.

A similar system is used in our **Accommodation** chapter based on the hotel's standard prices for one night in a double room, mid-week and mid-season: **Budget** = up to €100; **Mid-range** = €100-€200; **Expensive** = €200-€300; **Luxury** = over €300.

Discover

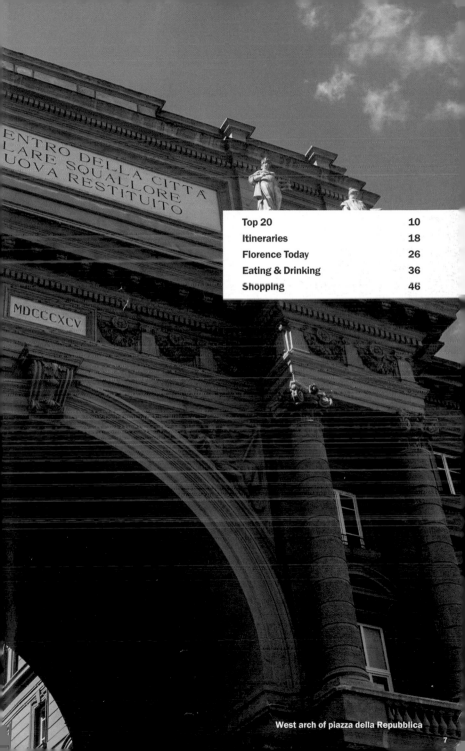

ENTRO DELLA CITTÀ
LARE SQUALLORE
UOVA RESTITUITO

MDCCCXCV

West arch of piazza della Repubblica

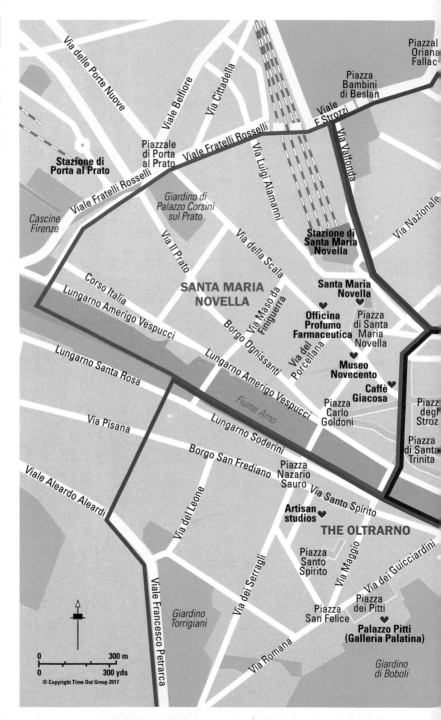

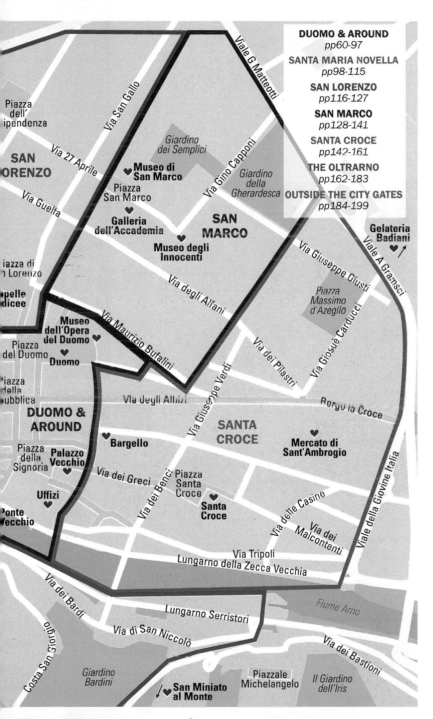

Piazza dell' ipendenza

Via San Gallo

Viale G Matteotti

SAN ORENZO

Via 27 Aprile

Via Guelfa

Giardino dei Semplici

♥ Museo di San Marco

Piazza San Marco

Via Gino Capponi

Giardino della Gherardesca

SAN MARCO

Galleria dell'Accademia ♥

Gelateria Badiani ♥ ↗

Viale A Gramsci

Via Giuseppe Giusti

iazza di
Lorenzo

pelle
dicee

Museo degli Innocenti ♥

Via degli Alfani

Piazza Massimo d'Azeglio

Museo dell'Opera del Duomo ♥

Via Maurizio Bufalini

Piazza del Duomo ♥ Duomo

Via dei Pilastri

Via Giosuè Carducci

iazza
della
ubblica

Via degli Albizi

Via Giuseppe Verdi

Borgo la Croce

DUOMO & AROUND

Piazza della Signoria

Palazzo Vecchio ♥

Bargello ♥

SANTA CROCE

Mercato di Sant'Ambrogio ♥

Viale della Giovine Italia

Uffizi ♥

Via dei Greci

Via dei Benci

Piazza Santa Croce

Santa Croce ♥

Via delle Casine

Via dei Malcontenti

onte ecchio

Via Tripoli

Lungarno della Zecca Vecchia

Via dei Bardi

Lungarno Serristori

Fiume Arno

Via di San Niccolò

Via dei Bastioni

Costa San Giorgio

Giardino Bardini

♥↙ San Miniato al Monte

Piazzale Michelangelo

Il Giardino dell'Iris

Top 20

From Michelangelo's David *to gelato, we count down Florence's finest treasures*

01

Uffizi *p82*

If the queues and the two million visitors each year are any indication, this is the art destination to top all Florentine bucket lists. Once the offices of the local magistrates – hence the name 'Uffizi' (offices) – the Vasari-designed building now houses the world's premier collection of Renaissance art, including masterpieces such as Botticelli's *Birth of Venus* and *Primavera*, each of which has its own wall. Masters like Titian, Fra Filippo Lippi, Michelangelo and Piero della Francesca are all represented, as well as early trailblazers like Cimabue, Giotto and key players in Flemish painting.

02

Galleria dell'Accademia *p134*

This small museum holds numerous noteworthy works, including some lovely examples of Michelangelo's *non finito*, but the main attraction is indisputably his *David,* a statue carrying the technical mastery of the ancient Greeks and all the celebrity power of a rock star. Carved from a Carrara-quarried block of marble, the politically significant sculpture was originally meant to stand atop a protruding portion of Florence's cathedral, and has the confusingly top-heavy proportions to reflect that location.

3

Duomo *p65*

Dominated by Brunelleschi's dome, an engineering feat for the ages, Florence's fairytale-like cathedral complex lives up to its goal. It was commissioned with the aim of proving Florence to be the most important Tuscan city. Built atop the former church of Santa Reparata (the remains of which are in the crypt), the complex also includes Giotto's bell tower. Across from the main church of Santa Maria del Fiore (with a Vasari-frescoed dome interior) stands the Romanesque Baptistery and copies of its fabled bronze doors.

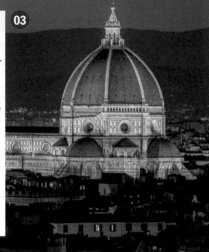

03

4

Museo dell'Opera del Duomo *p70*

This spectacular sculpture museum reopened in late 2015 after a 50 million-euro renovation. Don't let its unassuming entrance deceive you: inside you'll find close to 750 medieval and Renaissance masterpieces, contextualised according to their original roles within the cathedral complex. Heavy hitters include Donatello's *Penitent Magdalene*, Ghiberti's gilded bronze doors (the magnificent Baptistery originals) and a full-scale reconstruction of the original façade by Arnolfo di Cambio.

05

Palazzo Vecchio *p78*

Florence's town hall since medieval times, the imposing Palazzo Vecchio is one of the enduring symbols of the city. Outside, it boasts a 94m (308ft) bell tower; inside are secret passages and the spectacular Salone dei Cinquecento (Hall of the 500) with murals by Vasari and, if rumours are true, Leonardo da Vinci's masterwork *The Battle of Anghiari* hidden beneath.

04

06

Ponte Vecchio *p89*

The Ponte Vecchio is the city's most iconic bridge, and the only one not destroyed during World War II – legend has it that Hitler was so moved by its beauty, he expressly ordered German troops to leave it untouched. Butcher's shops once lined the walkway, but today, the buildings host fine jewellery shops. Rise extra early to cross the bridge sans crowds, or perch next to the central Benvenuto Cellini statue to watch the shopkeepers and street cleaners start their days.

07

San Miniato al Monte *p190*

Conquer the steps above Porta San Niccolò and follow the pathway to the austere San Miniato al Monte. The winding trek to this Romanesque beauty belies its simple interior, where you'll hear monks chanting if you visit in mid-afternoon. Stop at the nearby Piazzale Michelangelo at the day's end to take in an unbeatable Tuscan sunset overlooking the city.

08

Bargello *p146*

Once the chief magistrate's headquarters, this building is now home to a wide-ranging sculpture collection. Mystifyingly, it's rarely crowded, despite must-sees such as Michelangelo's *Bacchus*, Donatello's boyish bronze *David* and Brunelleschi's and Ghiberti's bronze panels depicting the *Sacrifice of Isaac*. In summer, the airy courtyard hosts concerts and dance performances – lively and far more palatable than its past function as an exhibition space for executed criminals' bodies.

09

Galleria Palatina *p167*

A showcase of Medici exhibitionism, this grandiose residential palace, which the Medici purchased in the 16th century, is now home to several museums. The highlight is the lavish Galleria Palatina (Palatine Gallery), which leads into the Appartamenti Reali (Royal Apartments) and pristine White Hall. Titian, Peter Paul Rubens and Raphael are all at home here, and the gilded ceilings are dizzying.

10

Gelato *p194*

Dessert devotees have a built-in excuse for freely indulging their sweet tooth: *gelato* has Florentine roots. Local lore links the treat to Caterina de' Medici, whose kitchen team travelled with her to Paris when she wed Henry II, wowing French nobles with their secret recipe. Today, a fresh cone with a scoop, or three, is Florence's guilty pleasure *par excellence*. Sample the famous Buontalenti at Badiani, salted caramel at La Sorbettiera or the chocolate orange at Vivoli.

11

Santa Croce *p148*

Visiting Santa Croce might inspire an inferiority complex: it's nicknamed the Temple of Italian Glories for a reason. Florence's principal Franciscan church, its 'resting roster' boasts some of the biggest names in the Boot: Michelangelo, Machiavelli and Galileo all have their tombs here. Giotto's floor-to-ceiling frescoes in the Peruzzi and the Bardi chapels are another highlight, but go beyond the basilica: Pazzi Chapel, the complex's hushed former chapter house, is one of the city's most mysterious and architecturally harmonious spaces.

12

Santa Maria Novella *p104*

The Dominican counterpart to Santa Croce, Santa Maria Novella instantly intrigues with its green and white geometric façade, designed by Leon Battista Alberti. More masterpieces include a Giotto crucifix; the *Trinity* by a young Masaccio, and the Strozzi Chapel, frescoed by Filippino Lippi at the end of his career. The city has invested heavily in the complex and square in recent years: Paolo Uccello's Green Cloister frescoes have been restored and the museum has been expanded with the incorporation of the Caserma Mameli complex.

13

Museo di San Marco *p139*

Set aside some quality time with Fra Angelico: this museum, housed in a monastery, is a testament to the leading 15th-century painter's devotion and talent. The few crowds that come here tend to congregate around his *Annunciation*, a commanding introduction at the top of the complex's first staircase. Other must-sees are the amusingly king-size cell Cosimo de' Medici used on his sporadic spiritual cleanses, as well as the bunk of fire-and-brimstone friar Girolamo Savonarola.

14

Museo Novecento *p103*

A refreshing ode to 20th-century Italian art – ideal for when Renaissance fatigue rears its head – this modern museum was born from a tragedy. The 1966 Arno flood destroyed or damaged countless Florentine artworks, prompting the formation of a committee tasked with raising global awareness. Hundreds of artists answered their call to donate work to Florence, with local government promising they'd be featured in a future art museum. These donated works are now part of the museum's 300-piece permanent collection.

15

Officina Profumo-Farmaceutica di Santa Maria Novella *p113*

Antique markets? Check. Scandinavian-inspired concept shops? Check. Flagship boutiques from high fashion's biggest names? Absolutely. Shopping in Florence isn't short on variety: prestigious boutiques from Ferragamo to Pucci line via de' Tornabuoni, while the funkier holes-in-the-wall of via della Spada offer more budget-friendly finds. Save time for a full-blown sensory experience at Officina Profumo-Farmaceutica di Santa Maria Novella, a cosmetic shop with origins dating back to the 13th century, when Dominican friars founded an apothecary in its namesake convent.

16

Mercato di Sant'Ambrogio *p159*

There's no faster lesson in the fundamentals of seasonal eating than shopping at a Tuscan market. The historic Mercato di Sant'Ambrogio is the pulse of its neighbourhood and has stayed unapologetically unfussy through the years. Despite soaring numbers of Florentine supermarkets, you'll find this no-frills space packed with residents each day, picking up fresh produce or grabbing a bite for lunch. Follow their lead and try a *lampredotto* sandwich – a local speciality made from the (gulp) fourth stomach of a cow.

17

Museo degli Innocenti *p136*

Designed by Brunelleschi, the 15th-century Ospedale degli Innocenti was a foundling hospital, notably run by laypeople. The museum's focus is threefold: the history of the institute, tales of its children and highlights from its art collection. The latter includes a striking Domenico Ghirlandaio altarpiece and a smattering of Botticelli and Della Robbia works. Yet it's the touching stories of the institute's children, including 20th-century testimonials, that make this a must-stop.

18

The Oltrarno's artisan studios *p179*

Artisan activity has always been concentrated on Florence's south bank, a traditionally poor district that's taken a controversial turn for the trendy in recent years. This long-time mecca for 'Made in Italy' production – leather and paper, painting and sculpture, silver and gold – continues to face challenges. But handmade crafts and design studios doubling as shops are still part of the neighbourhood fabric, from historic, hidden spots like the silk workshop Antico Setificio Fiorentino to dynamic DIY spaces such as Officine Nora.

19

Cappelle Medicee *p121*

To get a true sense of Medici excess, head to their burial site at San Lorenzo. The almost comically opulent Chapel of the Princes is a domed, marbled home to the grand dukes' sarcophagi, while Michelangelo's New Sacristy is comparatively understated. Downstairs, you might accidentally sidestep the modest tomb of final heir Anna Maria Luisa – a minimal acknowledgment of the woman who, by bequeathing her family's art collections to the Tuscan state, is largely responsible for Florence's continued splendour.

20

Café culture *p111*

No local ritual is more revered than the coffee break in Florence, and residents are fiercely loyal to their corner bars. Amid neighbourhood gossip and days-old newspapers, you'll spot the regulars by how quickly they catch the barista's eye. Soak up the atmosphere at one of the city's historic cafés: Caffè Gilli, founded in 1733 and one of the oldest cafés in Italy; literary hang-outs Giubbe Rosse and Paszkowski; or glitzy Caffè Giacosa, revamped by fashion designer Roberto Cavalli.

Itineraries

Exploring for the weekend, as a family or on a budget; here's how to get the best out of the city

ESSENTIAL WEEKEND

Florence in two days
Budget €100 per person per day
Getting around Walking

▶ *Budgets include transport, meals and admission prices, but not accommodation and shopping. The Accademia, Palazzo Pitti and Uffizi are closed on Mondays. Advance book the Uffizi, Accademia and Cupola to minimise queuing*

DAY 1

Morning

If you haven't done so online, first thing in the morning drop in at one of the Duomo ticket offices (*see p65*) and reserve a same-day slot for climbing the Cupola. Then, head to piazza della Repubblica for breakfast at **Gilli's** (*see p74*) before visiting the **Duomo**, **Baptistery**, **Museo dell'Opera del Duomo** and **Santa Reparata Crypt**: they are all included in your 48-hour Duomo ticket. Stop for a breather at **Grom** (*see p74*), right round the corner. Be careful not to be late for your Cupola booking but, if you miss your slot, you still have the option of climbing the Campanile instead.

Duomo

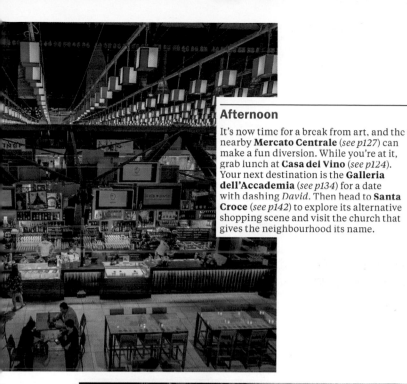

Afternoon

It's now time for a break from art, and the nearby **Mercato Centrale** (*see p127*) can make a fun diversion. While you're at it, grab lunch at **Casa del Vino** (*see p124*). Your next destination is the **Galleria dell'Accademia** (*see p134*) for a date with dashing *David*. Then head to **Santa Croce** (*see p142*) to explore its alternative shopping scene and visit the church that gives the neighbourhood its name.

Evening

The Santa Croce and Sant'Ambrogio areas offer some of the city centre's most attractive dining options, so you'll be spoilt for choice: browse the suggestions on *pp152-160*. Wrap up the evening with drinks at **The William** (*see p241*) or a stroll around the centre.

Palazzo Vecchio

DAY 2

Morning

Kick off the day in style with breakfast at **Caffè Rivoire** (*see p91*). The **Uffizi** (*see p82*) opens at 8.15am and, as long as you're nifty and have worked out a plan of what you want to see, you can get to the *Birth of Venus* long before the tour groups do. Halfway through your visit, squeeze in a quick espresso or a juice on the terrace of the Uffizi cafeteria to admire the exterior of the 13th-century **Palazzo Vecchio** (*see p78*). For lunch, **All'Antico Vinaio** (*see p152*) is almost directly across the road as you exit the gallery.

Afternoon

Now cross the **Ponte Vecchio** (*see p89*) to **Palazzo Pitti**. This sumptuous one-time home of the Medici family is hugely rewarding; topping a long list of must-dos is the **Galleria Palatina** (*see p167*), which houses the world's best collection of Titians and Raphaels. Behind the palace is the **Giardino di Boboli** (*see p168*), one of the city's best-loved green spaces: statues, grottoes and fountains are dotted around the splendidly formal gardens. If you haven't already had lunch this is the perfect stopping-off point for a picnic. Exit the park by the Forte di Belvedere, then use your Boboli ticket to enter the **Giardino Bardini** (*see p182*) across the road for impressive views of the city that beat those from the more celebrated piazzale Michelangelo.

Evening

Exit the gardens on via de' Bardi and browse the amazing jewellery, clothing, shoe and art shops in the narrow streets of the **Oltrarno** (*see p162*), before meandering over to piazza Santo Spirito for drinks and dinner. Lined with bars and restaurants such as **Caffè Ricchi** (*see p173*), this bohemian piazza is pure laidback Italian chic and charm, and guaranteed to make you feel you're living *la dolce vita*.

Giardino di Boboli

Piazzale Michelangelo

FAMILY DAY OUT

The Renaissance, the fun way
Budget €180 for a family of four
Getting around Walking, ATAF family ticket (€6)

▶ *Palazzo Vecchio is closed on Thursday afternoons*

Morning

Breakfast first at **Ditta Artigianale** (*see p155*), a relaxed spot with excellent coffee. Afterwards, catch a bus to **piazzale Michelangelo** (*see p191*) and pinpoint the main sights on a good map; a child's understanding of the city improves dramatically if they can see how it fits together. Older children could climb the **Cupola** (*see p68*) or the **Campanile** (*see p68*) for an unrivalled view over the rooftops. The **Museo Leonardo da Vinci** in via dei Servi (*see p138*), with its da Vinci machines at work, is great fun if you still have some time before lunch.

Afternoon

A five-minute walk from here, the **Caffetteria delle Oblate** (*see p155*), on the roof of the Oblate library, provides a scenic spot for a healthy lunch. The children's section of the library is free to visit and has English-language books and games. The same building is also home to the **Museo Fiorentino di Preistoria** (*see p151*), which will be a hit with any young fossil hunters. Now head to **Palazzo Vecchio** (*see p78*), where family-friendly exhibits will bring the powerful Medici family to life. You can also can hire a Kit for Families for a self-guided visit and take part in activities organised by **Mus.E** (*see p58*). Afterwards, head to **Gelateria dei Neri** (*see p155*).

Evening

It's a ten-minute walk from here to ride the **vintage carousel** in piazza della Repubblica. Opt for supper at an informal spot in the centre such as **Focacceria Bondi** (*see p125*) or catch a minibus (C2 or C3) or tram (T1) to the **Fosso Bandito** (Angolo Viale Fratelli Rosselli and Via del Fosso Macinante, 055365500, www. fossobandito.com), a *pizzeria* with outdoor play area. It's next to the **Teatro dell'Opera** (*see p250*), where you may be lucky enough to catch a family-friendly performance.

BUDGET BREAK

Florence on a shoestring
Budget €30 per person
Getting around Walking

▶ *The state museums (Accademia, Bargello, Medici Chapels, Uffizi, all museums at the Pitti Palace and Medici Villas) are free for all on the first Sunday of each month*

Morning

Pastries at **Sieni** (*see p126*) are great for jumpstarting your day. Stroll through San Lorenzo and by the Duomo to **piazza della Signoria** and the **Loggia dei Lanzi** (*see p86*), a free open-air museum. Nearby are lesser-known gems such as **Orsanmichele** (*see p88*) and the church of **Santa Trinita** (*see p108*) with its Ghirlandaio frescoes, both with free admission. Now follow the Lungarni east to via de' Benci, pass by the church of Santa Croce and peep into the **Scuola del Cuoio** (*see p144*) to see the artisans at work.

Fountain of Neptune on piazza della Signoria (Bartolomeo Ammannati, 1565)

Afternoon

If you're feeling peckish, head to the **Mercato di Sant'Ambrogio** (*see p159*), where the food stalls offer cheap and hearty sustenance: you could be brave and try a *panino col lampredotto* at **Da Rocco** (*see p160*). Just across the **Ponte Vecchio**, the church of **Santa Felicita** (*see p182*) has more amazing free art, including a chapel with some of Pontormo's and Bronzino's finest mannerist works. If you arrive early (the church opens at 3.30pm), idle the time away by wandering the charming streets and alleys of the **Oltrarno** and peeping into the **artisan workshops** (*see p179*). Afterwards, set out for the walk (*see p189)* to the hilltop abbey of **San Miniato al Monte** (*see p190*), where at 5.30pm a Gregorian evensong concert awaits you. Then stroll to the **piazzale Michelangelo** (*see p191*) to take in the grand view, and to the nearby **Giardino delle Rose** (*see p188*) for some free contemporary art.

Cappella del Cardinale del Portogallo, San Miniato al Monte

Evening

In the summer, check www.estate fiorentina. it for free events across town. Otherwise, a safe bet is spending the evening in the lively literary café of the **Murate** complex (*see p150*), where an affordable *apericena* (aperitif with buffet dinner) is served between 6.30pm and 9.30pm.

FLORENCE FASHION

Young designers, innovative boutiques and brand powerhouses
Budget €100 per person
Getting around Walking

▶ *On Fridays, the Gucci Museo (all year) and the Museo Novecento (summer only) are open until 11pm. The Pitti fashion shows are held in January and June*

Morning

After breakfast and people-watching in the café of the **Gucci Museo** (*see p86*), begin your tour of the fashionable side of Florence by visiting the collections of Gucci clothing and accessories from the 1950s to 2000s upstairs. Next, make your way across the Arno while peeking at the glitzy displays of the Ponte Vecchio jewellers. Climbing the costa San Giorgio to **Villa Bardini** and its **Capucci Museum** (*see p182*) is something you may need sensible shoes for, but you'll be rewarded with some amazing views and world-class *couture*.

Museo Ferragamo

Afternoon

Back at river level in Piazza de' Pitti, refuel at the charming **Pitti Gola e Cantina** (*see p172*) before taking in the historic garments and accessories at **Museo della Moda e del Costume** (*see p170*). The same ticket also admits you to the **Tesoro dei Granduchi** (*see p170*), where exhibits include jaw-dropping pieces of jewellery. Now head down via Maggio and across ponte Santa Trinita to the **Museo Ferragamo** (*see p95*); you'll find shoes to die (or kill) for by Italian designer Salvatore Ferragamo, whose flagship store is just around the corner. Stroll down **via dei Tornabuoni** and browse the designer shops of Emilio Pucci, Giorgio Armani, Bulgari, Dior, Fendi, Gucci, Prada, Tiffany, Burberry and Valentino. Thirsty? It's time to order a Negroni cocktail from the Roberto Cavalli-branded **Caffè Giacosa** (*see p110*). You could also squeeze in a visit to the **Museo Novecento** (*see p103*) to learn about the Pitti fashion shows.

Evening

Look for a stylish *aperitivo* spot in the vicinity – perhaps among the fashionable locals at the Ferragamo-owned **La Terrazza Lounge Bar** (*see p237*) in the summer months, or, if it's winter, **Slowly** (*see p237*) is an excellent alternative offering classy cocktails and nibbles.

▶ *For an itinerary touring the Oltrarno's artisan workshops, see p179.*

'Natura morta col giornale' by Renato Guttuso (1943), Museo Novecento

When to Visit

Florence by season

Spring

Spring in Florence is one of the liveliest times of the year, with social life setting up in the city's piazzas, and seasonal gardens opening their gates. Easter celebrations include the flag and firework parade known as the **Scoppio del Carro** (*see p222*). April and May can bring spontaneous showers, but tourist crowds and queues are lighter during this lovely shoulder season. Around the end of May, Tuscany's open-air venues emerge from hibernation.

Summer

Minimal air-conditioning and maximum crowds mean the heat can be more stifling inside than out, so, with the temperatures soaring, it's best to embrace the alfresco lifestyle. Grab an Aperol spritz and see an outdoor film, enjoy open-air bars doubling as music venues, catch a classical concert in a cool church cloister or hit the sandy dancefloor on the Arno 'beach'. However, if you should find yourself in Florence, or many other Tuscan towns, on the **Ferragosto** (Feast of the Assumption; 15 August), the chances are that your only company will be other tourists wandering the baked streets. The Florentines desert the city, and are likely to stay away for several days either side. The sun sets on the Florentine summer with **La Rificolona** (*see p225*), an early September ritual that sees families crowd the streets with paper lanterns.

Scoppio del carro

La Rificolona

Quiet squares in autumn

Nativity scene

Autumn

Tourist crowds tend to thin out once the back-to-school season begins, and prices around town reflect this. Summer is slow to let go (locals frequently talk of *rientro*, or the return to regular work schedules, until late September). Far from falling into a post-summer slump, though, Florence becomes more of its authentic self, and autumn events are more targeted at locals. Restaurants stock up with new oil and wine after the harvest season, and hotels slash their prices when November rolls around.

Winter

Winter in Florence lays the Christmas cheer on thick to make up for all the chill: think outdoor markets, concerts, religious rituals and seasonal treats galore. As Christmas approaches, the Italian tradition of Nativity scenes (*presepi*) is embraced. Many churches set up cribs, the main ones in Florence being in the Duomo, at San Lorenzo, Santa Croce, Chiesa di Dante and Santa Maria de' Ricci. Some country villages in Tuscany also stage *presepi viventi* – live re-enactments of the Nativity. Florence sees a spike in visitors as Christmas Day approaches, but things quieten down again after the Epiphany festivities, making January and February ideal months for museum visits. There's a nip in the air from late November onwards, but temperatures don't typically get too cold until February.

Florence Today

It's not easy to be Florence, and it's possibly even harder to be a Florentine

Florence is, quite literally, trampled by so many visitors that there are suggestions it should be included in UNESCO's list of World Heritage in Danger sites. Like a movie star, the city faces huge amounts of pressure, fanciful stereotypes and even downright misconceptions. The Japanese come to Florence looking for the fine detail and elegance of Botticelli; Americans cannot leave without seeing *David*; Northern Europeans seek the comfort of sun-kissed hills, fine wine and olive oil. All these elements can be found here, but no single one of them is the essence of Florence.

MICHELANGIOLO BUONARROTI

COMPIENDO IL QUARTO SECOLO

DALLA SUA NASCITA

IL MUNICIPIO DI FIRENZE

DEDICATA

A bronze replica of *David* standing in piazzale Michelangelo

The fifth element

Let us start by eradicating a myth: *la dolce vita* is a Roman affair and does not belong in Florence. As our very own Roberto Benigni would say, here life is beautiful – not sweet. And as author Mary McCarthy observed in her classic 1959 essay *The Stones of Florence*, Florence is a city of stone; and Florentines are not mellow either. Like Brunelleschi and Michelangelo, true-blood Florentines are far from sociable, by Italian standards at least: they have a sense of eternity that is much unlike the Roman; a sense of humour that could not be more different from the Neapolitan, and a sense of duty that is not even a distant relation of the Milanese. Self-mockery is fierce, and there is a vein of irreverent irony running straight from Dante's *Divina Commedia* to Benigni's 1997 film *La vita è bella*, via Carlo Collodi's *Pinocchio*. 'Florentines are an element of their own,' as a much-paraphrased remark by Pope Boniface VIII (1235-1303) goes.

Florence is a city of stone; and Florentines are not mellow either

Whose Florence is it anyway? Locals and tourists must find a way to co-exist.

Visitors, by sheer footfall, threaten to damage the works they flock to admire.

Living city or Renaissance theme park?

With approximately 16 million visitors a year against a resident population of little over 380,000, you can guess what every local is thinking when trying to cross a jam-packed piazza del Duomo, or when faced with an exorbitant rubbish-collection bill: 'Whose Florence is it anyway?' Mind you, Florentines are a mercantile lot, and they are perfectly aware of how much their economy relies on the art treasures they have been lucky enough to inherit from their visionary forefathers. Tellingly, they revere the memory of Anna Maria Luisa (1667-1743), the last of the Medici dynasty, an enlightened lady who bequeathed all her family's art treasures to the city.

Florence is under pressure to adapt to modern standards and to cope with mass tourism while preserving its unique assets for generations to come. Pollution and carelessness, not to mention sheer footfall, threaten the delicate artworks that the crowds flock to admire. While UNESCO regulations are invoked to prevent fast-food giant McDonalds from

The city's main attractions lie in a diminutive three square kilometres – that's less than one square mile.

opening next to the Duomo, sadly it's true that this famously human-sized city is at risk of collapsing under its own overgrown popularity. Aside from wondering about the occasional traffic jam around the train station, visitors will probably hardly notice the jungle of building sites and roadworks outside the city gates (especially in the north-western quarters), but the disruption causes a great deal of stress and endless debate among the resident population. Unfortunately, this no-man's land of traffic hysteria has a centrifugal effect on the locals' habits, as they get used to heading further out of town for their work, shopping and entertainment. As a result, the city (and 'city' here actually means the three square kilometres, or little more than one square mile, where the main attractions lie) is becoming more and more an endangered micro-habitat.

This triggers a chain reaction: the few remaining residents are all but evicted by impossible rents and traffic restrictions; historic shops are put out of business by chains; public offices are relocated to more suitable premises in the suburban areas; and, as a result, Florentines have an ever-thinning reason to go into town, with the city centre becoming the realm of old people, poor immigrants, wealthy expats and heaving crowds of careless tourists.

Until a few years ago, most of the vacant spaces in the city centre were ex-convents; more recently, however, the empty shells of large, and often publicly owned, buildings in prime locations have become free, as university departments, law courts, administrative headquarters and military barracks have followed the local population and relocated to purpose-built, state-of-the-art premises outside the city centre. Regrettably, public funds are tight and far too often the highly prized real estate that remains becomes easy prey to speculative ventures.

Incidentally, this process began as an unforeseeable consequence of the catastrophic 1966 *alluvione* (flood; *see below*) of the Arno, when many families and small businesses lost all their belongings and chose to start a new life in more modern, suburban surroundings.

Florence is under pressure to adapt to modern standards and cope with mass tourism, while preserving its unique treasures for generations to come

From makers to restorers

In addition, the 1966 flood forced Florence to develop the skills it now excels at in art diagnostics and restoration. In a desperate bid to save thousands of artworks, books and documents from the aggressive broth of mud, waste and fuel that had drowned the city, the centuries-old Opificio delle Pietre Dure (*see p138*) took on the challenge to combine local expertise with new techniques to clean, restore and preserve not just the stone and marble it had always specialised in, but also paintings, textiles, manuscripts, goldworks, ceramics and everything in between.

It may not be apparent because it's generally taking place behind closed doors, but this skill is now evolving into an ability to reinvent buildings (*see p33* Contemporary Art & Architecture). At the same time, crowdfunding

The 1966 flood forced Florence to develop the skills it now excels at: art diagnostics and restoration.

Locals have ever-thinning reasons to go into the centre of Florence as it becomes the domain of wealthy expats, poor immigrants and tourists.

and fundraising campaigns – such as that recently launched to restore the Pazzi Chapel in Santa Croce (*see p149*) – double as powerful attention-grabbers to foster awareness and advocate the need for a change in art conservation policies.

Rampant politics, bland policies

In recent years, Florence has taken centre stage on the national and international political scene due to the buoyancy of its exuberant ex-mayor Matteo Renzi and his circle. When Renzi became Prime Minister in 2014, his faithful aide Dario Nardella was elected as city mayor for the next five-year term. Although considered by some a mere stand-in for Renzi, Nardella plans to run for re-election in 2019 and constantly features as one of Italy's best-loved citizens in the polls. Regrettably, Nardella's neoliberal politics don't always result in sustainable social and cultural policies, and Florence appears to be at the mercy of ruthless profiteers advocating *grandi opere* (major infrastructure and development projects).

Alerted by a letter signed by a panel of 16 experts earlier that year, in May 2015 ICOMOS (the International Council on Monuments and

The future of Florence as one of the culture capitals of the world cannot rest solely on the shoulders of the Uffizi, the Accademia and the Duomo

Contemporary Art & Architecture

Few changes happen in plain sight, but the city is slowly moving into the 21st century

While some independent cultural institutions – especially **Palazzo Strozzi** (see *p95*) and **Fabbrica Europa** (see *p223*) – have been trail-blazers in acquainting a largely reluctant local scene with contemporary arts, public entities have also started to look ahead. The Civic Museums finally brought most of the city's 20th-century artworks under one single roof with the **Museo Novecento** (see *p103*) and designated the **Forte di Belvedere** (see *p181*) as the venue of choice for a major yearly contemporary art exhibition; the Uffizi signed a three-year agreement with Pitti Immagine Discovery to begin turning the old Galleria del Costume into a much more ambitious **Museo della Moda e del Costume** (see *p170*). There is also scope for using contemporary set-ups to enhance traditional exhibits, as proven by the renovated **Museo dell'Opera del Duomo** (see *p70*) and **Museo degli Innocenti** (see *p137*).

If recognition is easier for the performing arts (see *p244*), it's architecture that Florentines find hard to digest in its latest incarnations. Modernist buildings such as the new Palazzo di Giustizia (law courts) in Novoli are only conceivable well outside the city gates, and controversy still rages over whether the **Teatro dell'Opera project** (expected to swallow up a disproportionate €320 million of public funds by its completion) really was such a good idea.

But it is architectural and functional conversions that Florence has the most scope (and need) for. In the new millennium, successful projects have included reinventing the **Murate** complex (see *p150* In the know), turning the Oblate convent into a user-friendly library, and revamping the upper floor of the industrial-age **Mercato Centrale** (see *p127*) in San Lorenzo as an upscale street-food court. The 1930s **Palazzina Reale** (see *p102*) has been entrusted to the local Architects' Guild and aims to be a permanent House of Architecture with meetings and exhibitions; part of the former **Caserma Mameli** (formerly a military academy for Carabinieri officers), overlooking piazza della Stazione, is set to become a science and technology museum; and the old Law Courts in piazza San Firenze will most likely host a museum dedicated to the film and stage director Franco Zeffirelli. Meanwhile, a publishing entrepreneur has acquired, lovingly restored, thoroughly updated and finally reopened the historic **Teatro Niccolini** (see *p254*).

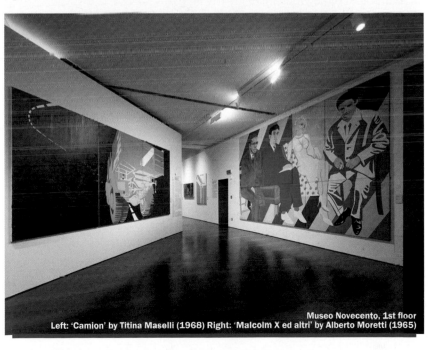

Museo Novecento, 1st floor
Left: 'Camion' by Titina Maselli (1968) Right: 'Malcolm X ed altri' by Alberto Moretti (1965)

Sites, one of the three advisory bodies of the UNESCO World Heritage Committee), issued a warning against some practices they felt were endangering Florence, such as digging tunnels for train and tram lines, building underground parking lots, and selling or dividing listed buildings. Nardella hid the document for several months, and when it finally surfaced, he downplayed its alarming contents by issuing a set of rules against minimarkets and hole-in-the-wall kebab and pizza shops, as though they were what UNESCO meant when denouncing the degeneration of the city.

In the same document, UNESCO also exposed the 'excessive pressure of tourism' and the 'absence of a tourist strategy' in the city. In short, the future of Florence as one of the culture capitals of the world should not rest solely on the shoulders of the Uffizi, the Accademia and the Duomo. That said, the latter has done a great job in redistributing its visitors and revenue among its properties, proving that channelling visitors towards lesser-known sites can greatly help to reduce the strain. Authorities, conservators and tourism professionals agree that another

Florence has been criticised for its 'absence of a tourist strategy'. Which route will it take in the future?

Hills on three sides of the city have limited growth.

viable way to achieve this is to promote longer stays and return visits in order to orient savvier tourists towards a broader range of attractions.

While Florence as an artwork may be fairly well monitored (if unsatisfactorily looked after), Florence as a community is suffering. Hills on three sides have prevented expansion and tall buildings are not allowed in order to preserve the city skyline – Florence continues to struggle as a city too small for its status. So, while the City of the Lily has been prevented from achieving 20th-century urban standards, hopefully it will be more successful at harnessing 21st-century technology to communicate, protect and share its unparalleled heritage.

In its heyday, Florence lifted itself and Europe out of the Dark Ages through a combination of ingenuity and creativity. Can it ever play that role again?

Eating & Drinking

Fresh ingredients, rustic classics and a few contemporary flourishes best define the dining scene in Florence

When it comes to food, Florentines are creatures of habit. Eating at family-owned, unfussy *trattorie* serving up generations-old recipes of standard Tuscan fare is always an enjoyable experience and a safe bet for both visitors and locals. However, in recent years, the city has undergone a culinary Renaissance: Michelin-starred restaurants are offering a far more adventurous (and expensive) experience than the traditional *trattorie*, whether you're dining at lavish three-star Enoteca Pinchiorri or chef Filippo Saporito's La Leggenda dei Frati, inside the spectacular Villa Bardini.

Classics revisited

At mid-level establishments, too, *'rivisitata'* (revisited) is a word that gets thrown around a lot on menus. Many chefs have their own unique ways of infusing local cuisine with more new elements: witness how young star Simone Cipriani (Essenziale, *see p178*) plays with traditional Tuscan soups, creating inventive bites such as the *'pappa al pomodoro* donut' and the *'ribollita* bubble', or how Marco Stabile (Ora d'Aria, *see p91*) adds a splash of raspberry ice-cream to game-based risotto. All of this comes without breaking from the principles that keep foodies flocking to Italy: seasonal eating, fresh, locally sourced ingredients and fair prices.

Restaurants

This guide aims to list the very best eateries in and around town, but it's also worth looking out for windows displaying the recommendation stickers of respected Italian restaurant guides, such as Gambero Rosso's *Ristoranti d'Italia, Veronelli, L'Espresso*, or Slow Food's *Osterie d'Italia*. When in doubt, avoid anywhere that advertises a fixed-price *menù turistico* written in several languages, or places that have staff standing outside trying to reel in passersby. Good restaurants don't need recruiters!

Eating out is a very social affair in Florence, especially in the evenings, and restaurants tend to be informal and lively. You can wear casual dress in all but the very smartest establishments, and children are almost always welcome (it's fairly standard to see children out and about with families long past bedtime hours, which might surprise some visitors). Booking is advisable, especially at weekends or if you want to dine at an outdoor table during the summer months.

In the know
Restaurant price codes

We use the following price codes for restaurant listings throughout the guide; they represent the average cost of one main dish (*secondo*).

€ = under €10

€€ = €10-25

€€€ = €25-40

€€€€ = over €40

❤ **Best traditional Italian joints**

I Brindellone *p177*
No-fuss classics in a workers' area.

Del Fagioli *p153*
Unpretentious Florentine cooking.

Il Chicco di Caffe *p171*
Friendly favourite.

Sergio Gozzi *p125*
Lunch near San Lorenzo.

❤ **Best contemporary cuisine**

Enoteca Pinchiorri *p153*
High-end gastronomy.

Gurdulu *p171*
Inventive cocktails and Balkan-inspired dishes.

Ora D'Aria *p91*
Kitchen artistry not far from the Uffizi.

Il Santo Bevitore *p172*
Reinvented classics.

Florentine Fast Food

Tripe stands are one of the city's must-try food experiences

Once a dying breed, Florence's *trippai* (tripe vendors) are a new generation of 'offalophiles', proud to be carrying on an ancient Florentine culinary tradition.

When faced with a tripe stand, you would be forgiven for not knowing what was brewing. The mobile stalls are laden with bubbling cauldrons and heated trays, the contents of which are not for the faint hearted. *Lampredotto* is probably the scariest item: the lining of the last stomach of the cow is simmered for hours in stock and served either in a *panino* with salt, pepper and maybe a lick of garlicky green *salsa verde* or with its broth in a little dish to be eaten with a plastic fork. Tripe (*trippa*) is served in these parts *alla fiorentina* – in rich tomato sauce topped with a sprinkling of parmesan. It's also eaten cold mixed with pickles and dressed with olive oil, salt and pepper. Other offerings vary from stall to stall, but watch out for such delights as boiled *nervetti* (tendons), stewed *budelline* (intestines) and *lingua* (tongue).

This Florentine-style fast food is cheap (a *panino con lampredotto* and a plastic cup of plonk will only set you back a few euros), healthy and has a fan base that transcends all social boundaries. You're likely to be munching your cow tummy sarnie in the company of factory workers, builders, shop assistants and slick-suited business types; it's a great way to sample Florentine street life.

Trippai normally open from around 8.30am to 7pm Monday to Friday; some also open on Saturdays. You'll find city-centre stalls under the Loggia del Porcellino (*map p63 K8*); on the corner of via de' Macci and borgo La Croce (*map p145 R7*); in piazza dei Nerli (*map p164 D8*) and in Mercato Sant'Ambrogio (*see p159*).

Cafés and bars

Florentine café society isn't just about coffee. Cafés and 'bars', as they are known here, are at the centre of social, work and neighbourhood life. A typical bar serves coffee all day, inexpensive, simple cocktails and house wine, and makes an easy stop for a snack or a simple, if underwhelming, lunch. Most office workers have a corner coffee spot where they pop in for a mid-afternoon pick-me-up; residents are usually on friendly terms with the barista on their home street. Although breakfast is almost always a simple cappuccino and brioche, the 'light lunch' can encompass all manner of buffets, gourmet menus and brunch offerings.

Bear in mind that location is everything when it comes to the bar bill: it usually costs far less if you stand at the bar to drink rather than sit at a table, and you often pay more to sit outside, especially at touristy spots.

Solaria alle Giubbe Rosse by Baccio Maria Bacci (1930-40) is on display at Galleria d'arte Moderna, Palazzo Pitti.

Wine bars

Wine bars encompass tiny street booths (known as *fiaschetterie*, *vinerie* or *vinai*) with virtually no seating, serving basic Tuscan wines and rustic snacks, as well as comfortable, traditional drinking holes. They compete with new, upmarket *enoteche* that offer a huge range of labels from all over Italy and beyond, plus something more sophisticated in the way of food. Just be sure, if you're going to a place that's billed as a wine bar, that you order your food as an accessory to the wine, and not the other way around.

What to eat

An increasing number of more upmarket restaurants now offer some kind of fixed menu (and we're not talking about the ubiquitous *menù turistico* here). Usually called *menù degustazione*, it consists of a series of courses that allow diners to try the house specialities,

or a themed collection of dishes – perhaps a fish-based menu or something more conceptual. Such menus tend to represent the best value at high-end restaurants. For help with sorting through the menu, take a look at Decoding the menu (*see p44*).

How to eat

Most traditional menus are designed for à la carte ordering, beginning with an *antipasto* (starter). *Primi* are first courses, usually pasta, risotto, soups or salads, and are followed by *secondi* (meat, fish or, now and then, a heartier vegetable dish). *Contorni* are side dishes (vegetables, potatoes, smaller salads, perhaps even chips) and are often brought out separately. *Dolci* are desserts, and it's not uncommon to follow them with a coffee or digestif. You're not obligated to order a dish from every section of the menu, and it's not as if Italians all follow this complete cycle every time they sit down, but in general, when dining out in the evening, it's considered bad form to order only a *primo*.

Kid-friendly fare

Bustling family *trattorie* and *pizzerie* that make dishes to order are the best choices for children. Just ask for *pasta al pomodoro* (with tomato sauce), or a half portion (*mezza porzione*) of what you're ordering. Occasionally you'll see a *menu bambini* (kids' menu) in certain restaurants – don't let it scare you off. It's usually just a selection of smaller-portioned classics for not-so-adventurous palates – think chicken and potatoes or simple pastas. For lunch, instead of heading for the ubiquitous fast-food options, try buying picnic goodies at a market (*see p159*) and head for a park (*see p56*). Note: quite a few restaurants offer high chairs (ask for *una seggiolone*).

**In the know
Eat like a native**

The star of the Florentine kitchen is the *bistecca alla Fiorentina* (steak Florentine), which should be at least 5cm thick, a kilo in weight, and served rare: asking for it well done is heresy and any self-respecting Florentine eatery will not serve it that way. Also avoid asking for ketchup, mayonnaise, substitutions or sauces in general. Look for seasonal (*stagionale*) dishes, and remember that *panna* (cream) is not a traditional Florentine ingredient – it's best to steer clear of dishes that use it.

❤ **Best places to eat out with kids**

La Cucina del Garga *p124*
A fun spot with a family-friendly chef.

Mama's Bakery *p174*
Breakfast comforts.

Mercato Centrale First Floor *p127*
Plenty of choices for picky eaters.

Special diets

While there are few strictly vegetarian restaurants in Florence, non meat-eaters, particularly those who eat fish, are better off here than in many parts of, say, France or Germany. Most restaurants offer vegetable-based pasta and rice dishes, as well as plenty of salads and vegetable side dishes (*contorni*), while an increasing number of more upmarket places serve a specifically vegetarian option. Florence is also quite friendly toward gluten-free diners, with a wide variety of restaurants specialising in dishes *senza glutine* (without the wheat-based protein) or simply offering alternative options. And don't think your choices will be restricted to simple vegetables and flavourless salads: gluten-free pastas and pizzas are prevalent. *Celiaco* is the word for someone with Coeliac disease; your concerns will be taken seriously if you speak to a restaurant staffer about your options.

The wine list

Most budget and moderately priced restaurants offer *vino della casa* (house wine) in quarter-litre, half-litre or litre flasks, which is invariably cheaper than buying by the bottle. If you're in the mood for something more elevated, the *liste dei vini* in Tuscany are unsurprisingly dominated by *vini toscani* (Tuscan wines), but other regional varieties – and even the odd non-Italian label – are now being given more cellar space.

Think Tuscany and you normally think Chianti, Vino Nobile di Montepulciano, Brunello di Montalcino... a rich red swirling in the bottom of your glass, the perfect accompaniment to *bistecca fiorentina*. But there are now plenty of options if you're determined to try a Tuscan white. Late-ripening vermentino varieties present subtle floral perfumes, while Fattoria San Donato's 'Angelica' 2013, an aged-in-oak-barrels Vernaccia, goes best with intense

In the know
Pizza

While pizza isn't a typically Florentine dish, *pizzerias* are very popular. Most of the pizzas to be found in the city are of the Neapolitan variety with (ideally) light, puffy bases. Make sure it's baked in a wood oven (*forno a legna*), and you'll want to order it with beer, not wine, for the local seal of approval. Pizza is an evening meal in Florence; very few traditional pizzerias worth their *mozzarella di bufala* serve at lunchtime.

❤ Best pizza in town

Caffè Italiano *p153*
Fewer choices – fresher quality.

Il Pizzaiuolo *p158*
A Sant'Ambrogio standard.

O'Scugnizzo *p180*
Neapolitan noms.

Vico del Carmine *p192*
Light, puffy crusts.

❤ Best wine bars

Casa del Vino *p124*
A San Lorenzo standard.

Fuori Porta *p192*
Around 50 wines available by the glass.

Vivanda *p178*
Organic options.

Le Volpi e L'uva *p183*
Crostini and coveted labels.

First floor, Mercato Centrale

flavours. Even rosé is having a bit of a moment in Tuscany – a frilly, fun-to-drink favourite that makes use of Sangiovese grapes is Bolle di Borro from the Ferragamo family's estate.

Coffee culture

Florence is full of simple corner places with the buzz of local workers throwing back espressos at the bar for a quick hit of caffeine; genteel, gilded affairs where the cutlery is silver and a coffee at a table with a view costs more than the barman's hourly wage; comfy bars with students sitting at the benches with piles of books and a caffè latte; and all the possible combinations in between. If it's quality coffee you're after, avoid any place that looks like a second-rate imitation of Starbucks.

The bill

Bills usually include a cover charge (*pane e coperto*) per person of anything from €1.50 to an outrageous €5; the average is about €2.50. This covers bread and should reflect the standard of service and table settings. There's also a service charge, which must, by law, be included in the bill (though it's sometimes listed separately). Some places now include cover and service in the price of the meal. One consolation is that you're not expected to leave a hefty tip. You can leave ten per cent if you're truly happy with your service and want to make a point of saying so, or, in a modest place, perhaps round up the bill by a euro or so.

❤ **Best snack spots**

Arà: è Sicilia *p140*
Sicilian street food.

L'Ortolano *p141*
Deli delicacies.

Forno Top *p114*
Crackers, sandwiches, cakes.

Procacci *p97*
Tuck into truffles.

Decoding the Menu

A crash course in restaurant Italian

Whether it's haphazard scribbles on a piece of paper, or a volume documenting the eatery's complete family history, Florentine menus are a pleasure to peruse. Translated English versions are often rough and misleading: it's best to arrive with some key words in your arsenal.

Cooking techniques & descriptions

affumicato smoked
al forno cooked in an oven
arrosto roast
brasato braised
disossato deboned
fatto in casa home-made
fritto fried
griglia grilled
nostro prepared our way
ripieno stuffed
vapore steamed

Basics

aceto vinegar
bottiglia bottle
burro butter
focaccia bread made with olive oil
ghiaccio ice
miele honey
olio oil
pane bread
panino sandwich
panna cream
uovo egg

Antipasti

antipasto misto mixed hors d'œuvres
bruschetta bread toasted and rubbed with garlic, sometimes drizzled with olive oil and often topped with tomatoes or white Tuscan beans
crostini small slices of toasted bread (**crostini toscani** are smeared with chicken liver pâté)
crostoni big crostini
fettunta the Tuscan name for *bruschetta*
prosciutto crudo cured ham, either *dolce* (sweet, similar to parma ham) or *salato* (salty)

Primi

acquacotta cabbage soup usually served with a *bruschetta*, sometimes with an egg broken into it
agnolotti stuffed triangular pasta
brodo broth
cecina flat, crispy bread made of chickpea flour
fettuccine long, narrow ribbons of egg pasta
frittata type of substantial omelette
gnocchi small potato and flour dumplings
minestra soup, usually vegetable

panzanella Tuscan bread and tomato salad
pappa al pomodoro bread and tomato soup
pappardelle broad ribbons of egg pasta, usually served with *lepre* (hare)
passato puréed soup
pasta e fagioli pasta and bean soup
pici thick, irregular spaghetti
ribollita literally a twice-cooked soup of bean, bread, cabbage and veg
taglierini thin ribbons of pasta
tordelli/tortelli stuffed pasta
zuppa soup
zuppa frantoiana literally, olive press soup – bean and cabbage soup, distinguished because it's served with the very best young olive oil.

Fish & seafood

acciughe/alici anchovies
anguilla eel
aragosta lobster
aringa herring
baccalà salt cod
bianchetti little fish, like whitebait
bonito small tuna
branzino sea bass
capesante scallops
coda di rospo monkfish tails
cozze mussels
fritto misto mixed fried fish
gamberetti shrimps
gamberi prawns
gefalo grey mullet
granchio crab
insalata di mare seafood salad
merluzzo cod
nasello hake
ostriche oyster
pesce fish
pesce spada swordfish
polpo octopus
ricci sea urchins
rombo turbot
San Pietro John Dory
sarde sardines
scampi langoustines
scoglio shell- and rockfish
seppia cuttlefish or squid
sgombro mackerel
sogliola sole
spigola sea bass
stoccafisso stockfish
tonno tuna
triglia red mullet
trota trout
trota salmonata salmon trout
vongole clams

Meat, poultry & game
agnellino young lamb
agnello lamb
anatra duck
animelle sweetbreads
arrosto misto mixed roast meats
beccacce woodcock
bistecca beef steak
bresaola cured, dried beef,
served in thin slices
caccia general term for game
capretto kid
carpaccio raw beef, served in thin slices
cervo venison
cinghiale wild boar
coniglio rabbit
cotoletta/costoletta chop
fagiano pheasant
fegato liver
lardo pork fat
lepre hare
maiale pork
manzo beef
ocio/oca goose
ossobuco veal shank stew
pancetta like bacon
piccione pigeon
pollo chicken
porchetta roast pork
salsicce sausages
tacchino turkey
trippa tripe
vitello veal

Herbs, pulses & vegetables
aglio garlic
asparagi asparagus
basilico basil
bietola Swiss chard
capperi capers
carciofi artichokes
carote carrots
castagne chestnuts
cavolfiore cauliflower
cavolo nero black cabbage
ceci chickpeas
cetriolo cucumber
cipolla onion
dragoncello tarragon
erbe herbs
fagioli white Tuscan beans
fagiolini green, string or French beans
farro spelt
fave or **baccelli** broad beans (although
fava in Tuscany also means the male
'organ', so use *baccelli*)
finocchio fennel
fiori di zucca courgette flowers
funghi mushroom
funghi porcini ceps
funghi selvatici wild mushrooms
lattuga lettuce
lenticchie lentils
mandorle almonds

melanzane aubergine (UK), eggplant (US)
menta mint
patate potatoes
peperoncino chilli pepper
peperoni peppers
pinoli pine nuts
pinzimonio selection of raw vegetables
piselli peas
pomodoro tomato
porri leeks
prezzemolo parsley
radice/ravanelli radish
ramerino/rosmarino rosemary
rapa turnip
rucola rocket (UK), arugula (US)
salvia sage
sedano celery
spinaci spinach
tartufato cut thin like a truffle
tartufo truffles
zucchini courgette

Fruit
albicocche apricots
ananas pineapple
arance oranges
ciliegie cherries
cocomero watermelon
datteri dates
fichi figs
fragole strawberries
lamponi raspberries
limone lemon
macedonia di frutta fruit salad
mele apples
more blackberries
pere pears
pesche peaches
pompelmo grapefruit
uva grapes

Desserts & cheese
cantuccini almond biscuits
gelato ice-cream
granita flavoured ice
mandorlata almond brittle
panforte cake of dried fruit from Siena
pecorino sheep's milk cheese
ricciarelli almond biscuits from Siena
torta cake
zabaglione egg custard mixed with Marsala
zuppa inglese trifle

Drinks
acqua water **gassata/frizzante** fizzy or
  liscia/naturale still
birra beer
caffè coffee
cioccolata calda hot chocolate
latte milk
succo di frutta fruit juice
tè tea
vin santo dessert wine
vino rosso/bianco/
  rosato red/white/rosé wine

Shopping

Food, fashion and fine fragrances, plus artisan design aplenty

The Florentines' fiercely independent spirit ensures a wonderful array of interesting shops and studios alongside the designer boutiques on via Tornabuoni and the mainstream chains lining via Roma and via Calzaiuoli. From the little leathermakers' ateliers and alternative fashion stores in Santa Croce to the age-old authentic grocers and *salumerie* (delicatessens) around San Lorenzo; from the ancient perfumeries and herbalists of the *centro storico* to the tiny streets across the river that are studded with startlingly original pieces of jewellery, Florence is a shopper's – and browser's – dream.

Officina Profumo-Farmaceutica di Santa Maria Novella

Where to shop

If the most famous names in **fashion** and Florence's flagship stores are what you're after, head to via Tornabuoni, the Renaissance city's runway for well-heeled residents; you'll spot plenty of visitors balancing multiple shopping bags from the world's biggest labels. Via Roma is another high-rolling street for fashionistas. Veer off onto via del Parione for marbled paper and stationery, Tuscan toys and home bric-a-brac, or via della Spada to find elegant, but hardly bank-breaking, boutiques.

For handmade artisan treasures, the best area to explore is still the Oltrarno – backstreets are a safe bet for stumbling on ateliers and workshops (*see p179*), but you'll also find many enticing spots on more popular drags such as Sdrucciolo de' Pitti, Borgo San Frediano and via Santo Spirito.

Vintage bargains pop up sporadically all over the city, but some local favourites lie around Santa Croce and along via dei Fossi (Santa Maria Novella), which also has an array of **antique** shops. As via dei Fossi ends, manoeuvre your way through the roundabout in Piazza Carldoni to cross Ponte alla Carraia for the **delicatessens** and antique shops of via dei Serragli and surrounding streets. **Leather goods** are famously found in the San Lorenzo area, but avoid buying from street vendors if you're after something high-quality. Cosmetics more your bag? Historic **pharmacies** and **perfumeries** are dotted all around the city (*see right*), but you'll find an especially high proliferation in the Santa Maria Novella area.

Markets

Markets abound in Florence. They are a shopping staple for its inhabitants and a treasure trove for visitors looking for great photos, mid-morning nibbles and unusual souvenirs. The annual arrival of February's **Fiera del Cioccolato Artigianale** (Craft

---

In the know
Kids' clothes

Children's clothes can be more expensive than the adult versions in Italy, so check the tags before rushing to the counter. Via il Prato (Santa Maria Novella) and via Gioberti (Outside the City Gates) each have a concentration of children's clothing boutiques or speciality shops.

❤ Best vintage shops

A Ritroso... A Rebours *p156*
Tiny shop, huge deals.

Boutique Nadine *p97*
Curated collection of old and new treasures.

Desii Vintage *p126*
High-end labels.

Street Doing *p141*
One of the city's biggest vintage stashes.

❤ Best gourmet treasures

La Bottega della Frutta *p112*
Grocery store laden with goodies.

La Bottega dell'Olio *p97*
Extra-virgin olive oils to taste.

Osteria de L'Ortolano *p141*
An Aladdin's cave of edible goodies.

Zanobini *p127*
Own-label wine (can be shipped).

Potions, Powders and Perfumes

Florence's herbalists and cosmetic shops are fascinating relics of another time

Step inside many of Florence's beautiful old perfumeries and you're stepping back in time. As far back as the 11th century, when Benedictine monks began making alcoholic elixirs, the city has been renowned for its knowledge of the therapeutic qualities of herbs. Tuscany's fields of lavender and herbs have helped the region to maintain its reputation as a centre for alternative remedies, and many locals call at an *erboristeria* (herbalist's shop) rather than a chemist for minor ailments.

Some of these stores are joys to behold even if you're not shopping, though their products double as gorgeous gifts. **Officina de' Tornabuoni** (*see p97*), housed in the late Renaissance Palazzo Larderel, sells handmade gifts, textile sprays and perfumes. **Spezieria Erboristeria** (*see p93*), a stone's throw from the Palazzo Vecchio, is an old-fashioned and charming frescoed apothecary that specialises in handmade perfumes and floral *eaux de toilette* with such evocative names as Acqua di Caterina de' Medici. Within the shop's 'I Profumi di Firenze' collection, the original scents are inspired by Florentine names or landmarks, should you fancy smelling like the Boboli Gardens, the Medici or the city's flower, the lily (*giglio*).

The **Officina Profumo-Farmaceutica di Santa Maria Novella** (*see p113*), dating back to the thirteenth century and the most famous Florentine herbalist, has such power that it hushes visitors into reverent silence as they walk through its doors. Even if you're not usually cosmetic-crazy and herb-happy, the historic venue is worth a visit for its striking structure and old-fashioned elegance.

Another notable shop is **Bizzarri** (Via della Condotta 32r, Duomo & Around, 055 211580, www.bizzarri-fi.biz), a relic that has shelves of jars filled with substances in every colour. Its herbal concoctions are made to secret, generations-old recipes.

Farmacia del Cinghiale (Piazza del Mercato Nuovo 4-5r, Duomo & Around, 055 282128, www.farmaciadelcinghiale. it), named after the famous wild boar statue in the square opposite, was founded in the 1700s and still makes its own herbal remedies and cosmetics.

A newcomer by comparison, the charming **Münstermann** pharmacy (*see p114*) was opened in 1897 and still has its original shop fittings. As well as stocking pharmaceutical and herbal medicines, the mahogany cabinets are filled with unusual hair accessories, jewellery and toiletries.

Chocolate Fair), the **German Christmas market** in piazza Santa Croce and the **autumn farmers' market** in piazza SS Annunziata are eagerly anticipated events on the city's calendar.

To go where the locals go, head to **Mercato de Sant'Ambrogio** (*see p159*) – it's a foodie's heaven, with the freshest and cheapest farmers' produce in the city. Meanwhile, the **Mercato di San Lorenzo** (7am-6pm Mon-Sat) covers a cobweb of streets around San Lorenzo church, with stalls selling leather goods, clothes and souvenirs. At its centre is the 19th-century covered **Mercato Centrale** (*see p127*), dedicated to fruit, vegetables, meats, fish and cheeses. The market's vibrant first floor is packed with street-food stands, a Roman-run pizzeria, Chianti wine bar and more. It's sleek and commercial – much to the chagrin of some

Mercato Centrale

local shoppers – but it's quite popular and makes a social spot in the centre.

The **Mercato delle Pulci** flea market (piazzas Annigoni and Ghiberti, 9am-7.30pm Mon-Sat) is a great place to browse bric-a-brac in the hope of finding a tiny piece of the Renaissance to take home with you. Better still for browsers is the **Mercato di Santo Spirito** (8am-2pm Mon-Sat), which becomes an antique and flea market on the second Sunday of the month (8am-6pm). The square is also home to a small daily weekday morning market, and plays host to **Fierucola** on the third Sunday of the month (8am-6pm), a market selling organic foods and wines, handmade clothing, cosmetics and natural medicines.

If it's raining, head for the **Mercato Nuovo** (*see p64*); the alabaster chess sets, stationery, leather goods and scarves make for no-fuss souvenirs and gifts. Rubbing the nose of the bronze boar statue that gives the market its more colloquial name, Mercato del Porcellino, is de rigueur if you want a return visit to Florence.

Opening hours

Supermarkets and larger stores in the city centre tend to stay open throughout the day (*orario continuato*), but most shops still operate standard hours, closing at lunchtime and on Monday mornings. The standard opening times are 3.30pm to 7.30pm on Monday, and 9am to 1pm and 3.30pm to 7.30pm Tuesday to Saturday, with clothes shops sometimes opening closer to 10am. Food shops usually open earlier in the morning (perhaps around 8am), close at 1pm and reopen between 3pm and 5pm, and usually have a *giorno di riposo* (which charmingly translates into 'day of rest'). Many of the central shops stay open for at least part of Sunday; several more open on the last Sunday of the month.

Hours alter slightly from mid June until the end of August, when most shops close

♥ Best local jewellery

Angela Caputi *p174*
Bijoux pieces inspired by 1940s Hollywood.

Alessandro Dari *p183*
Conceptual designs by the local goldsmith.

Moneta Traforata *p199*
Accessories made from hand-cut coins.

Sara Amrhein & Scicc'Art *p176*
Polymer clay statement pieces.

In the know
Just popped out... for a while

One delightfully Italian tradition to take in your stride is the frequent posting of '*Torno subito*' signs in shop windows (every so often, this will happen in small bars, too). It literally translates as 'I'll be back immediately', but this should be taken with a pinch of salt: '*subito*' has a wide margin of error. The absent owner might be knocking back an espresso at the corner bar, or they might very well have chosen this time to run some bureaucratic errands. If you're determined to visit one specific shop, stay in the neighbourhood and explore other spots nearby while you wait. Or, as a knowing local might, just head back the next day.

on Saturday afternoons. Small shops tend to shut completely at some point during July or August for anything from a week to a month. Opening times listed in this guide apply most of the year, but they can vary, particularly in the case of smaller shops.

Payment and taxes

While credit and debit cards are generally standard in shops now, count on never using them for purchases below €20, and don't be surprised when shop owners ask if you have any smaller change if paying in cash. They're not being rude, but the obsession with *spiccioli* (small change) can be a bit bewildering to first-timers. Visitors from outside the EU are sometimes entitled to a VAT rebate on larger purchases. Look for the 'tax-free' signs in shop windows.

In the know
Inside the outlets

Florence is known for its out-of-town fashion outlets, but if you only have time to visit one, make it the **Mall** (via Europa 8, Leccio Reggello, 055 865 7775, www.themall.it). Just a half-hour drive from the city, it's home to many designer names, including Alexander McQueen, Ermano Scervino, Fendi, Armani, Gucci, Stella McCartney and Valentino, all of them offering discounts from 30% to 70%. There's also a sprawling Gucci-branded restaurant-café that makes a great cappuccino break when your feet get weary.

Explore

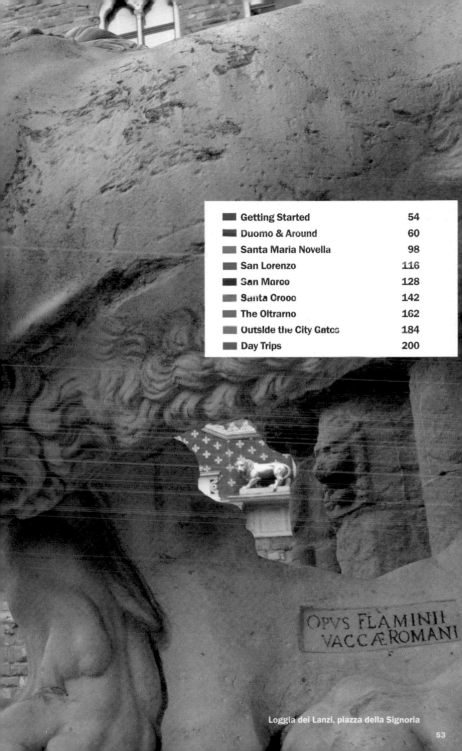

OPVS FLAMINII
VACCÆROMANI

Loggia dei Lanzi, piazza della Signoria

Getting Started

Plan, pre-book and orientate yourself before you start exploring

Every part of Florence is packed with artistic and architectural treasures: Brunelleschi's dome and Giotto's campanile, Botticelli's *Birth of Venus* and Michelangelo's *David*, the incomparable Baptistery doors and the gold shops lining the Ponte Vecchio. If you've chosen to visit the city, there's a high chance you're a lover of the more refined things in life. While there's a lot to be said for just wandering the streets and soaking up the atmosphere – taking in gorgeous, art-studded churches, fascinating museums and gelaterie as you find them – for a truly enjoyable experience it pays to be organised. Florence's virtually unrivalled wealth of artistic highlights – this small 'Renaissance City' has more works per square metre than anywhere else on the planet – attracts in excess of 16 million overnight visitors annually. If you have an itinerary planned, know which sights need pre-booking, and quickly gain a basic knowledge of the city centre, you're a step ahead of the rest.

♥ **Best museums for kids**

Museo di Antropologia e Etnologia *p151*
Ornamental objects, masks, mummies and more.

Museo Galileo *p87*
Scientific tools galore, complete with a sundial outside.

Museo Leonardo di Vinci *p138*
Hands-on reconstructions and interactive machines.

Museo Stibbert *p196*
Ancient weapons, costumes and an impressive cavalcade of lifesize horses and knights in armour.

Museo Zoologico La Specola *p170*
Don't miss the eerie Skeletons' Hall, plus gruesome anatomical waxworks and 24 rooms of taxidermy.

Palazzo Strozzi *p95*
World-class artists and collections, with a focus on family-friendly activities.

Palazzo Vecchio, piazza della Signoria *p78*

Orientation and geography

With a historic centre roughly a fifth the size of Rome's, Florence is easily navigable. Most major sights are in walking distance of any other central point and, with the dome of the Duomo and the River Arno's four central bridges as reference points, it's practically impossible to get lost. The majority of the main sights cluster north of the two central bridges (Ponte Vecchio and Ponte Santa Trinita), around the **Duomo**. Other important sights are in the areas around this rectangle: **Santa Maria Novella**, **San Lorenzo**, **San Marco**, **Santa Croce** and the **Oltrarno**. We use these neighbourhood designations throughout the guide; attractions that lie beyond the historic centre are included in the chapter **Outside the City Gates**.

The main central area of Florence sits in the river valley and is virtually flat, but the surrounding hills rise steeply on both sides, creating challenging walks and rewarding views that are easily accessible on foot or by bus.

The most complex thing about navigating in Florence is the street-numbering system, which has two sets of numbers, in red and black. The red numbers denote a place of business, and run separately from the black, so 16r and 18r may be 100 metres away from each other, separated by a series of black numbers. (Adding to the confusion, red numbers are currently being gradually phased out by local government.)

Public transport

Walking is by far the best way of getting around the city. However, the phrase 'within walking distance' has an ever-expanding meaning, since additions to the pedestrian area have pushed both private and public transport out of the city centre. Until the Duomo and its surroundings became the exclusive realm of strollers in 2009, as many as 19 bus lines passed the cathedral; the 2015 pedestrianisation of the Oltrarno's piazza del Carmine has limited most area traffic to residents and allowed for new outdoor spaces to thrive. While the aesthetic and environmental benefits of such changes are undeniable, the flipside is that buses are now next to useless within the city walls.

Thankfully, the most scenic routes – Lines 7, 12 and 13 – are unscathed. Line 7's terminus is now in San Marco, and it reaches the quaint hilltop village of Fiesole (see p198) in less than 30 minutes. Lines 12 and 13 are circular routes, climbing to piazzale Michelangelo (see p191) from opposite sides.

The cramped C1 and C2 are the only lines that still cut through the heart of the city

❤ Best green spaces

Giardino di Boboli p168
Labyrinths, grottoes, fountains, statues and hiding places make great diversions for children, while parents can enjoy magnificent views.

Giardino dell'Orticultura p193
Home to a famous flower market and striking glasshouse, plus a summer bar and events venue.

Parco delle Cascine p196
Florence's largest park hosts regular fairs and markets.

> Thanks to its river and diminutive centre, Florence is fairly easy to navigate, and walking is by far the best way of getting around

---

In the know
Water on tap

Mindful of Florence's searing summer heat and plastic waste (Italy is the fourth largest consumer of bottled water in the world), the council has installed purified water dispensers, all of them offering the choice of still or sparkling water, for free. The most central is in piazza della Signoria, and you'll spot it by its H20 Gas branding. Other central options include piazza Tasso (the Oltrarno) and via dell'Agnolo (Santa Croce). For all locations, visit www.publiacqua.it/fontanelli/cosa.

(north–south and west–east respectively); D minibuses cover chunks of the Lungarni and much of the Oltrarno, including Santo Spirito. An extensive tram project is underway, set to add two new lines to the existing Santa Maria Novella–Scandicci route by mid-2018. Line 2 will run from Peretola airport to piazza dell'Unità d'Italia, close to the Santa Maria Novella station, while Line 3 will facilitate movement between the station and Careggi hospital.

A few tips. Fines are steep, so always have a valid ticket (look for the ATAF sticker in shop and bar windows, and don't forget to stamp your ticket in the machine on board). In theory, tickets can also be purchased on board at a slightly higher rate, but drivers don't always have them handy. Grab a bus map from the ATAF information office, near the main ticket hall inside the train station. Also, note that much like a maze, bus routes often run in a counter-intuitive direction: check the display on the front of the bus to make sure you are heading where you mean to go. For a map of electric bus routes and timetables, see www.ataf.net.

Museums and galleries

During the summer, around Easter and on public holidays, Florence spills over with visitors: the sights are crowded and huge queues form at the main museums. The quietest times to visit are from January to March (avoiding Easter), and from October to mid December.

Many of Florence's unrivalled museums have private collections at their core, whether that of a mega-family such as the Medici (Uffizi, Palazzo Pitti) or of a lone connoisseur (the Bardini, Horne and Stibbert museums). Other major museums were founded to preserve treasures too precious to expose to the elements (Galleria dell'Accademia, Bargello and Museo dell'Opera del Duomo). The main city-run museums are the Cappella Brancacci, Cenacolo di Santo Spirito, Museo Novecento, Palazzo Vecchio, Museo Bardini and Forte Belvedere, though the latter is open only when hosting exhibitions. State museums are the Pitti museums, Uffizi, Galleria dell'Accademia, Bargello, Museo di San Marco, Opificio delle Pietre Dure, Cappelle Medicee and Museo Archeologico.

Art lovers should be aware that works of art are often loaned to other museums, and restoration can be carried out with little or no notice, so it's wise to call first if you want to view a specific piece.

Temporary exhibitions are regularly held at numerous locations in Florence,

In the know
They don't like Mondays

For non-Italians, it can be a shock to find out that some of Florence's major museums close on Monday. These include the Uffizi, Galleria dell'Accademia and Galleria Palatina in the Palazzo Pitti. If it's the first or third Monday of the month, you could go to the Museo di San Marco; on the second or fourth, try the Cappelle Medicee, the Bargello or certain Palazzo Pitti museums. Exceptions apply: when local or national holidays land on a Monday, many of the major museums open for the occasion. Also note that entry to state-run museums is free on the first Sunday of every month.

Piazzale Michelangelo p191

including designated spaces such as Palazzo Strozzi and Fortezza da Basso, as well as venues such as Palazzo Vecchio, Palazzo Medici Riccardi, the Uffizi, Galleria dell'Accademia, Pitti museums and more. For details, see *The Florentine*, *Firenze Spettacolo*, *Florence is You!* (for all, *see* p302 Newspapers & magazines), events app FirenzeTurismo and local newspapers.

In the know
Musei Eventi Firenze

Mus.e (Palazzo Vecchio, piazza della Signoria, 055 2768224, www.musefirenze. it. Tickets €4 in addition to museum admission. Times vary) is the official organization in charge of promoting Florentine civic museums and the city of Florence as a whole through guided visits, cultural projects, exhibitions, workshops and events. Mus.e (short for museums and events) runs regular activities for children and families as well as guided tours of several museums including Museo Novecento (see p103), with around 20 different programmes in Palazzo Vecchio alone. There's even a *Secrets of Inferno* tour: a guided visit to Palazzo Vecchio in the footsteps of professor Robert Langdon from Dan Brown's novel *Inferno*.

Pre-booking

Firenze Musei (the state-run museums of Florence) strongly recommends booking for the Uffizi and Galleria dell'Accademia, as well as, at busy times of year, the Pitti museums; this could save you a two-hour wait. Reserve as soon as you can (www.b-ticket.com/b-ticket/uffizi is the official online vendor for Firenze Musei or call 055 294883). Advance booking costs €4 for the Uffizi and Accademia; tickets are collected from a window beside the normal ticket office. At Palazzo Pitti's various museums, advance booking costs €3 and tickets can be picked up at an office in the right-hand wing before you reach the main entrance. If you're unable to book ahead, last issuing times for tickets vary (we give closing times, not last admission, in our listings), but try to get to the ticket office at least an hour before the museum closes.

Compared to their state-run counterparts, crowds tend to be (slightly) thinner at Florence's civic museums, but pre-booking is still advisable at heavy hitters such as Palazzo Vecchio and Santa Maria Novella. The civic museums (which also include Museo Novecento, the Bardini Museum and the Brancacci Chapel) have an online ticketing system at ticketsmuseums. comune.fi.it. For most civic museums, there is a fee of €0.80 for pre-booking your ticket, and you'll be allowed direct access upon arrival, skipping the queue.

If you are planning to visit lots of sights, it's definitely worth investing in a €72 **Firenze Card**, which lasts 72 hours from first validation and gives you entry to 72 of the most important museums in Florence, eliminating the need to queue. The card can be used just once in each museum, and on all public transport. Pre-order it online at www.firenzecard.it, or buy it either at one of the tourist information offices or at the ticket offices of museums covered by the card.

Tourist information

Apart from the tourist offices (*see p307*), many of the city's minor sights – churches, *palazzi*, monuments – also have signs posted beside them detailing their histories and distinguishing features, making a DIY tour that much easier. In addition, you'll see large plaques with useful maps in many squares and other strategic positions.

Guided tours

All Florence's tour companies offer a range of itineraries, with English-language options, covering the main monuments and museums on foot or by bus. The highly reputable **AGT Firenze – Florence Associated Tourist Guides** (0574 608254, www.florencetouristguides.com), **Florence Guides** (347 737 8374, www.florenceguides.

it) and **ACG Florence & Tuscany** (055 7877744, www.firenze-guide.com) have a big selection of standard tours; **Florencetown** specialises in American tourism (055 281103, www.florencetown.com).

If you're after a personal touch and something beyond Brunelleschi, **Context Florence** (0158 977508, www.contextflorence.com) uses tour guides who are also Masters or PhD-level scholars, and limits groups to six; Alexandra Lawrence's **Explore Florence** (exploreflorence@gmail.com, www.exploreflorence.net) is another in-depth option, and **Travelability** (055 4684663, www.travel-ability.com) offers customisable, accessible itineraries for those with special needs. **Tuscany Bike Tours** (055 3860253, www.tuscany-biketours.com) provides leisurely and more energetic explorations of Florence on two wheels. Sightseeing buses are another option: try **City Sightseeing Firenze** (piazza Stazione 1, 055 290451, www.firenze.city-sightseeing.it, 8am-6pm daily; €23/1 day, €28/2 days, €33/3 days; €12/1 day, €14/2 days, €17/3 days reductions; no cards for tickets bought on board) runs two lines: Lines A (one hour) and B (two hours). Both depart from Santa Maria Novella train station.

If you prefer to do it yourself, the best ways to see the city – besides on your own two feet – are by bike or moped (*see p297* Moped & bike hire).

Duomo & Around

The centre of Florence showcases the various forces at work on the city at the most crucial moments in its history and is the ideal place to start exploring the Renaissance. The neighbourhood corresponds almost exactly to the ninth-century city walls, stretching from the streets just north of the Duomo to the Arno, with via de' Tornabuoni – famous for its designer shops – marking the western boundary and via del Proconsolo, the eastern one. This area takes in both the religious heartland around the majestic cathedral with its unmistakable red-tiled dome, and the civic and merchant hub surrounding Palazzo Vecchio and piazza della Signoria, with the iconic shop-lined Ponte Vecchio reaching to the Oltrarno at the river's narrowest point.

The district is also home to the Uffizi, Italy's most visited art museum, whose public galleries are to be almost doubled to accommodate an even more diversified display of artworks, including the world's largest collection of self-portraits.

❤ Don't miss

1 Uffizi *p82*
The greatest treasure trove of Renaissance art on the planet.

2 Duomo complex *p65*
Explore the iconic cathedral and its connected monuments.

3 Museo dell'Opera del Duomo *p70*
One of the world's largest collections of devotional art.

4 Palazzo Vecchio *p78*
The city's austere, late 13th-century town hall.

5 Loggia dei Lanzi *p86*
One of the world's most spellbinding open-air museums.

6 Ponte Vecchio *p89*
Laden with shops, Florence's oldest bridge is a fitting symbol of this mercantile city.

In the know
Getting around

This pedestrian area takes no longer than ten minutes to walk from end to end. The main thoroughfares – especially via dei Calzaiuoli between the Duomo and piazza della Signoria – do get overcrowded, but it's a pleasure to get lost in the maze of medieval side streets. Forget your map or GPS and just wander where curiosity takes you: you'll never be more than a couple of turns from the main landmarks anyway.

AROUND PIAZZA DEL DUOMO

Standing in the piazza at the heart of Florence's historic centre, the glorious **Cathedral of Santa Maria del Fiore** (known as the Duomo; *see p65*) is so enormous that there's no spot nearby from which you can see the whole complex, though a walk through the surrounding streets will be punctuated by glimpses of its iconic dome.

Inside the cathedral is the **Crypt of Santa Reparata** (*see p67*), the original church built on this site in the fifth century, while on the north side is the entrance to the 'dome' itself, Brunelleschi's spectacular **Cupola** (*see p68*). The **Campanile** (*see p68*), Giotto's elegant bell tower, is south of the Duomo, level with its façade. Following the curve of the piazza on the north-east side of the cathedral, the recently revamped **Museo dell'Opera del Duomo** (*see p70*) houses many of the Duomo's treasures.

Continuing around the piazza in a clockwise direction, a plaque at the base of a flat column indicates the '*Sasso di Dante*', a stone where the poet allegedly loved to sit. Further west, on the façade of Palazzo dei Canonici, are Luigi Pampaloni's huge 19th-century sculptures of the architects Filippo Brunelleschi and Arnolfo di Cambio, each holding their plans and tools and looking at the parts of the Duomo they worked on.

The octagonal **Baptistery** (*see p69*) of St John the Baptist faces the main doors of the Duomo on piazza San Giovanni. Always thronged with tourists, the square also houses the tiny **Museo del Bigallo** (*see p64*).

To the west of the Baptistery is via de' Cerretani, a busy shopping street and traffic thoroughfare that's home to the 11th-century church of **Santa Maria Maggiore**.

Running down from the south-west corner of the Baptistery is the more upmarket via Roma, which opens into the pompous **piazza della Repubblica**,

In the know
Roman Florence

When, in the 1980s, it was decided that the old paving stones of piazza della Signoria should be taken up and restored, the ruins of several private and public buildings from 12th-century Florence were discovered, built over the thermal baths of Roman Florentia. The ancient Roman theatre can now be seen below Palazzo Vecchio, and the remains of the Roman walls are visible on the corner of via del Proconsolo with via Dante Alighieri.

DUOMO & AROUND

Restaurants & wine bars

1. Cantinetta di Verrazzano
2. Coquinarius
3. Dei Frescobaldi Ristorante & Wine Bar
4. Fashion Foodballer
5. Fiaschetteria-Osteria Nuvoli
6. Fishing Lab Alle Murate
7. Fusion Bar
8. The Goose
9. Irene
10. Ora d'Aria
11. Osteria I Buongustai
12. Trattoria Le Mossacce

Cafés, bars & gelaterie

1. Boulangerie del Rifrullo
2. Caffè Giubbe Rosse
3. Caffè Rivoire
4. Carapina
5. Edoardo
6. Gilli
7. Grom
8. I Due Fratellini
9. Ino
10. Move On
11. Paszkowski
12. Perchè No!
13. Procacci
14. Seven Brothers
15. La Terrazza Rinascente

Shops

1. A Piedi Nudi nel Parco
2. Alessi
3. Bartolucci
4. La Bottega dell'Olio
5. Bottega Quattro
6. Boutique Nadine
7. Bramada
8. Flow
9. Luisa Via Roma
10. Maledetti Toscani
11. Migone
12. Officina de' Tornabuoni
13. Paperback Exchange
14. Patrizia Pepe
15. La Rinascente
16. Sartoni
17. Spezierie-Erboristerie
18. VIAJIYU

— — — Duomo Walking Tour
See p94

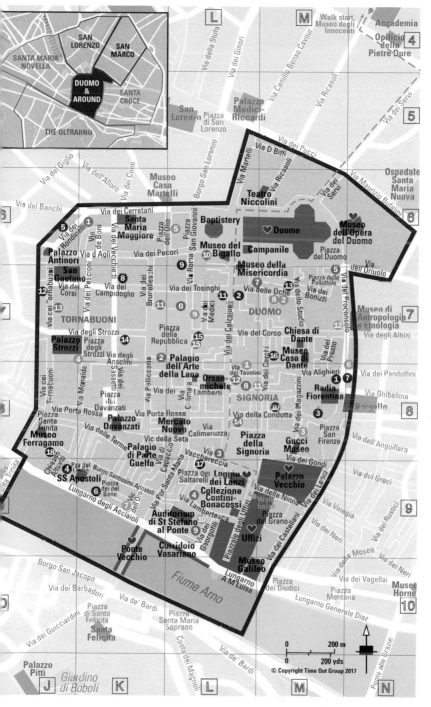

San Lorenzo

SAN LORENZO

SAN MARCO

SANTA MARIA NOVELLA

DUOMO & AROUND

SANTA CROCE

THE OLTRARNO

Walk start, Museo degli Innocenti

Accademia

Opificio delle Pietre Dure

Via della Stufa

Via dei Ginori

Via Camillo Benso Cavour

Via Ricasoli

Via dei Servi

San Lorenzo

Piazza di San Lorenzo

Palazzo Medici-Riccardi

Ospedale Santa Maria Nuova

Via dei Pucci

Via D Biffi

Via del Giglio

Via dei Banchi

Via dei Cerretani

Museo Casa Martelli

Via dell'Alloro

Via dei Conti

Borgo San Lorenzo

Via Martelli

Via Ricasoli

Teatro Niccolini

Via dei Servi

Via Maurizio Bufalini

Baptistery

♡ Duomo

Museo dell'Opera del Duomo

Santa Maria Maggiore

Piazza dell'Olio

Piazza San Giovanni

Museo del Bigallo

Campanile

Piazza del Duomo

Via dell'Oriuolo

Palazzo Antinori

Via d'Agli

Via dei Pecori

Museo della Misericordia

Piazza delle Pallottole

San Gaetano

Via dei Vecchietti

Via dei Brunelleschi

Via Roma

Via dei Tosinghi

Via delle Oche

Via dello Studio

Via dei Bonizzi

Via del Proconsolo

TORNABUONI

Via dei Corsi

Via del Campidoglio

Via dei Medici

Via dei Calzaiuoli

DUOMO

Museo di Antropologia e Etnologia

Via degli Alhizi

Palazzo Strozzi

Piazza degli Strozzi

Via degli Strozzi

Piazza della Repubblica

Via del Corso

Chiesa di Dante

Via del Presto

Via degli Anselmi

Palagio dell'Arte della Lana

Orsanmichele

Via dei Cerchi

Museo Casa di Dante

Via Alighieri

Via dei Pandolfini

Via dei Sassetti

Via Pellicceria

Via dei Lamberti

Via dei Tavolini

SIGNORIA

Badia Fiorentina

Via Ghibellina

Via dei Magazzini

Bargello

Piazza Davanzati

Palazzo Davanzati

Via Porta Rossa

Mercato Nuovo

Via Calimaruzza

Via della Condotta

Piazza San Firenze

Via dell'Anguillara

Via Porta Rossa

Via delle Terme

Palagio di Parte Guelfa

Via di Capaccio

Via Vacchereccia

Piazza della Signoria

Gucci Museo

Via dei Gondi

Via dei Greci

Piazza Santa Trinita

Museo Ferragamo

Chiasso Altoviti

Borgo Santissimi Apostoli

Piazza del Limbo

SS Apostoli

Piazza del Bene

Via Por-Santa Maria

Piazza dei Saltarelli

Loggia dei Lanzi

♡ Palazzo Vecchio

Via della Ninna

Via dei Leoni

Via dei Rustici

Lungarno degli Acciaioli

Via Lambertesca

Collezione Contini-Bonacossi

Auditorium di St Stefano al Ponte

Piazzale degli Uffizi

Walk finish

Piazza del Grano

Via Vinegia

Via della Mosca

Via dei Neri

Ponte Vecchio

Corridoio Vasariano

Via dei Georgofili

Uffizi

Via dei Castellani

Borgo San Jacopo

Via dei Barbadori

Fiume Arno

Museo Galileo

Lungarno A M'Luisa

Piazza dei Giudici

Piazza Mentana

Via dei Vagellai

Museo Horne

Via de' Bardi

Piazza di Santa Felicita

Piazza Santa Maria Soprano

Lungarno Generale Diaz

Via della Stufa

Santa Felicita

Palazzo Pitti

Giardino di Boboli

Costa dei Magnoli

Via de' Bardi

Ponte alle Grazie

0   200 m
0   200 yds

© Copyright Time Out Group 2017

flanked by pavement cafés, and dominated at night by street artists and strollers. This ungainly square was built in 1882, when the so-called Mercato Vecchio ('old market') was demolished and rebuilt in a massive clean-up after a cholera outbreak. Vasari's delightful **Loggia del Pesce** – now in piazza de' Ciompi in Santa Croce (*see p156*) – was once the meeting place of the square. The only remnant from before the redevelopment is now the huge **Colonna dell'Abbondanza**, marking the spot where the two principal Roman roads crossed.

Sights & museums

Museo del Bigallo

Piazza San Giovanni 1 (055 288496, www. museicivicifiorentini.comune.fi.it). Open 10.30am-4.30pm Mon-Sat, 9.30am-12.30pm Sun & hols. Admission free. Map p63 L6.

The city's smallest museum is housed in a beautiful Gothic loggia built in 1358 for the Misericordia, a charitable organisation that cared for unwanted children and plague victims. The loggia was later renovated for another fraternity, the Bigallo, and the Misericordia moved to piazza del Duomo (no.19), from where it still works as a voluntary medical service. The main room has frescoes depicting the two fraternities at work, though the two scenes on the left wall as you enter were damaged in the 18th century. The *Madonna della Misericordia*, a fresco of 1342 from the workshop of Bernardo Daddi, a pupil of Giotto, has the Virgin suspended above the earliest known depiction of Florence. The fresco shows the Baptistery, the original Arnolfo façade to the domeless Duomo, the original Santa Reparata with its two bell towers, and an incomplete Campanile.

Museo della Misericordia

Piazza del Duomo 20 (055 239393, www. misericordia.firenze.it). Open Sept-June 10am-noon, 3-5pm Mon, Fri; 10am-noon Sat. July-Aug by appt only. Admission by donation. No cards. Map p63 L6.

The 750-year-old Misericordia museum provides a great opportunity to learn the fascinating history of this 13th-century almshouse, infirmary and poor house. Guided tours in English may be arranged by writing to info@misericordia.firenze.it.

Museo del Bigallo

❤ Time to eat & drink

Coffee break
Caffè Giubbe Rosse *p73*
Caffè Rivoire *p91*
Paszkowski *p75*

Top paninis
Procacci *p97*

A classy lunch
Ora D'Aria *p91*

Traditional gelato
Perchè No! *p92*

Seafood on the go
Fishing Lab alle Murate *p90*

Beer and vinyl
Move On *p75*

❤ Time to shop

Concept boutique
Bottega Quattro *p97*

English books
Paperback Exchange *p75*

Fabulous vintage
Boutique Nadine *p97*

Olive oil goodies
La Bottega dell'Olio *p97*

Scented gifts
Spezierie-Erboristerie
Palazzo Vecchio *p93*
Officina de' Tornabuoni *p97*

❤ Time well spent

Mercato Nuovo
Between via Calimala and via Porta Rossa. **Open** *9am-6.30pm daily.* **Map** *p63 L8. Market*
Often referred to as the *Mercato della Paglia* (straw market), its stalls now sell leather and straw goods and cheap souvenirs, but in the 16th century it was erected for silk and gold merchants. The market is also known as the *Porcellino* (Piglet), after the bronze statue of a boar, a copy of a Pietro Tacca bronze that was, in turn, a copy of an ancient marble now in the Uffizi. It's thought to be good luck to rub the boar's nose and put a coin in its mouth: proceeds go to charity and legend says the donor is assured a return trip.

💗 Duomo complex

Piazza del Duomo (055 2302885, www. ilgrandemuseodelduomo.it). **Admission** *€15, 48-hr ticket incl the Museo dell'Opera del Duomo (see p70).* **Map** *p63 M6.*

Florence's cathedral complex is a truly awe-inspiring sight which dominates the city's skyline from all sides. The octagonal Romanesque Baptistery, Giotto's free-standing Campanile and the huge Duomo of Santa Maria del Fiore, topped with the iconic cupola and hiding the underlying Crypt of Santa Reparata, bear witness not only to the city's wealth and devotion, but also to the visionary genius of its artists.

💗 Don't miss

1 Climbing Brunelleschi's Cupola
The most rewarding 463 steps you'll ever take.

2 The Baptistery's mosaic ceiling
With a depiction of Hell that is thought to have inspired Dante's *Inferno.*

3 The Last Judgement on the underside of the Dome
Vasari's and Zuccari's decoration is one of the largest frescoed surfaces in the world.

Cattedrale di Santa Maria del Fiore (Duomo)
Open *10am-5pm Mon-Wed, Fri; 10am-4.30pm Thur; 10am-4.45pm Sat; 1.30-3.30pm Sun.*

The result of work spanning more than six centuries, the Duomo not only dominates the skyline but also represents the geographical, cultural and historical centre of the city.

The building was commissioned by the Florentine Republic as an opportunity to affirm its status as the most important

4 Giotto's bell tower at midday
More steps – 414 this time. Make it to the top by noon for a close encounter with the Campanile's chimes.

5 The Funerary Monument to Sir John Hawkwood
A daring treatment of perspective makes Paolo Uccello a visionary forerunner of Cubism.

The Duomo from the top of the Campanile

💙 Duomo complex *continued*

Tuscan city. The competition to find an architect was won by Arnolfo di Cambio and the first stones were laid on 8 September 1296 around the exterior of Santa Reparata. Building continued for the next 170 years – despite the 1348 plague that killed half of Florence's 90,000 population – with guidance and revision from three further architects. When it was finally consecrated in 1436, Santa Maria del Fiore was the largest cathedral in Europe, and it's still the world's third largest after St Peter's in Rome and St Paul's in London.

The rich exterior in white Carrara, green Prato and red Maremma marbles, reflects the 170 year-long building period, with a huge variation in the styles of the inlaid patterns. The last significant change came in the 19th century, when Emilio de Fabris designed a neo-Gothic façade that was added to the Duomo between 1871 and 1887. After Emilio's death, Luigi del Moro was left to crown the façade.

The Duomo's bronze doors (1899-1903) are decorated with scenes from the life of the Virgin. Each door is complemented by a mosaic lunette by Barbarino. These represent (*right to left*): local artists, merchants and Humanists honouring Christ; Christ with Mary and John the Baptist; and Charity among the Florentine noblemen who had established the city's charitable foundations. An appearance on the façade was a vital status symbol, ensuring these nobles would be remembered and venerated for their generosity. Above them are the 12 Apostles.

After the splendid exterior, the interior is somewhat underwhelming. It is full of fascinating peculiarities, however: notably, Paolo Uccello's clock on the inner façade, which marks 24 hours, operates anti-clockwise and starts its days at sunset (it's between four and six hours fast). The clock is surrounded by the so-called Heads of the Prophets, peering out from four roundels and showing the distinct influences of Ghiberti and Donatello.

Also by Uccello is the *Monument to Sir John Hawkwood*, painted in 1436 as a tribute

La Porta del Paradiso (Lorenzo Ghiberti, 1425–52)

to the English soldier who led Florentine troops to victory in the Battle of Cascina of 1364. The fresco has given rise to debate about whether the movement of the horse's right legs are wrong, or an original treatment of perspective construction, considered by some to be visionary – even a forerunner to Cubism. Beyond Andrea del Castagno's 1456 monument to Niccolò da Tolentino, illustrating the heroic characteristics of a Renaissance man, is Domenico di Michelino's *Dante Explaining the Divine Comedy*, featuring the pink-clad poet and the new Duomo vying for prominence with the Mountain of Purgatory.

When it was consecrated in 1436, Santa Maria del Fiore was the largest cathedral in Europe; it is still the world's third largest

A couple of strides put you directly underneath the dome, the size of which is even more breathtaking inside than out. The lantern in the centre is 90m (295ft) above you and the diameter of the inner dome is 43m (141ft) across, housing within it one of the largest frescoed surfaces in the world. Brunelleschi had intended the decoration of the inner cupola to be mosaic in order to mirror the Baptistery ceiling. However, interior work only began some 125 years after his death in 1572, when Cosimo de' Medici commissioned Giorgio Vasari to carry out the work; together with Don Vincenzo Borghini, who chose the iconographic subjects, they decided to fresco the surface instead.

The concentric rows of images were started by Vasari, whose subtle treatment of colour and form drew inspiration from Michelangelo's Sistine Chapel, but he died two years later, before completing the project. Vasari was succeeded by Federico Zuccari, who worked for a further five years until its completion. Zuccari had a much more flamboyant dry-painting style, believing that the distance from which the visitor would view the Cupola wasted the delicacy of Vasari's wet fresco technique.

Zuccari's most crucial contribution to the cycle is the rendering of Dante's vision of Hell, which was inspired by Signorelli's frescoes in Orvieto Cathedral.

Crypt of Santa Reparata

Open 10am-5pm Mon-Wed, Fri; 10am-4.30pm Thur; 10am-4.45pm Sat; 1.30-3.30pm Sun.

Excavations carried out between 1965 and 1973 unearthed the medieval ruins of Santa Reparata, which are now on view for visitors. The entrance to the crypt is inside the Duomo itself.

The church's foundation date is unknown, but it must be between the fifth and seventh centuries. By the late 13th century, however, Santa Reparata had become too small for the rapidly expanding population and desperately needed to be replaced. So, in 1293 it was decided that a new cathedral should be built on the site of the original church. Local legend has it that some of the land needed for the building of the much bigger Duomo was occupied by the Florentine Bischeri family, who, when they continued to refuse the ever-bigger sums of money they were offered to relocate, were unceremoniously kicked out of their *palazzo* without compensation. This led to the Florentine term *bischero* (a gullible fool).

The intricate mosaic floor of the church was built only 30cm above the Roman remains of houses and shops, some of which surface in the crypt. Also here is the tomb of Brunelleschi, although no trace has been found of those of Arnolfo di Cambio and Giotto. Burials were not normally allowed in the cathedral, but these great fathers of the Duomo were supposedly buried here in recognition of their work.

**In the know
Tour prices**

General guided tours (€20 including admission) and special themed tours (€30 including admission) are available. Try *A glimpse of Florence*, which offers exclusive access to the north terrace of the cathedral for extraordinary views of the city and Brunelleschi's dome.

💜 Duomo complex *continued*

Cupola

Accessed via the Porta della Mandorla on the north side of the cathedral.
Open *8.15am-7pm daily.*

Containing four million bricks and weighing 37,000 tonnes, the Cupola isn't just visually stunning: as the first octagonal dome built without a wooden supporting frame, it is also an incredible feat of Renaissance engineering. As Alberti put it, it is 'a structure so immense, rising above the skies [that it is] broad enough to cover with its shadow all the peoples of Tuscany'.

Filippo Brunelleschi won the commission in 1418 – following two years of fierce debate over his design – together with the more experienced Lorenzo Ghiberti, who was riding on the back of his success with the Baptistery doors.

Brunelleschi first considered designing a classic semi-spherical dome like those in existing churches around Italy, but the sheer size of the structure precluded the traditional method of laying tree trunks across the diameter in order to build around them. In the end, he made the dome support itself by building two shells, one on top of the other, and by laying the bricks in herringbone-pattern rings to integrate successive self-supporting layers. The design risked becoming a victim of its own success: the ribs around the dome were in danger of 'springing' open at the top, so a heavier lantern than normal was designed to hold them in place. The gilt copper ball and a cross containing holy relics that topped the lantern were hoisted up using machinery designed by Leonardo da Vinci. The original ball was hit by lightning in 1600 (*see p73* Thunderstruck) and replaced.

The Cupola provides fantastic views over the city centre and the surrounding hills. And while the 463 steps (about 20 minutes up and down) are not for the faint-hearted or those with limited mobility, climbing the curve between the Cupola's two shells is a truly unforgettable experience.

Campanile

Open *8.30am-7pm Mon-Fri; 8.30am-5pm Sat; 1-4pm Sun. Booking required. Restrictions may apply in adverse weather conditions.*

The cathedral's three-floor, 414-step Campanile (bell tower) was designed by Giotto in 1334, though his plans weren't followed faithfully (the original drawing can be seen in Siena's Museo dell'Opera del Duomo, *see p213*). Andrea Pisano, who continued the work after Giotto's death in 1337, took the precaution of doubling the thickness of the walls, while Francesco Talenti, who saw the building to completion in 1359, inserted the large windows high up the tower. Inlaid with pretty pink, white and green marble, the Campanile is decorated with 16 sculptures of prophets, patriarchs and pagans (the originals are in the Museo dell'Opera del Duomo, *see p70*), and bas-reliefs designed by Giotto and artfully executed by Pisano that recount the *Creation and Fall of Man* and *Redemption*

Brunelleschi's Cupola

through Industry; you can make out Eve emerging from Adam's side and a drunken Noah. The steps to the top are steep and narrow, but great views await.

Baptistery

Open 8.15-10.15am, 11.15am-7.30pm Mon-Fri; 8.15-6.30 Sat; 8.15am-1.30pm Sun.

For centuries, the likes of Brunelleschi and Alberti believed that the Baptistery of St John the Baptist – the patron saint of Florence – had been converted from a pre-existing Roman temple dedicated to Mars. In fact, it was built to an octagonal design between 1059 and 1128 as a remodelling of a sixth or seventh-century version. In between, it also functioned for a period as the cathedral for Florence (then Florentia) in place of Santa Reparata (*see p67*).

The striped octagonal building is best known for its doors (*see below*), but the interior is worth visiting for the dazzling *Last Judgement* mosaic that lines the vault ceiling: an 8m-high (26ft) mosaic figure of *Christ in Judgement* dominates the apse (1225), and the mosaics of Hell are thought to have inspired Dante's *Inferno*. The geometrically patterned marble mosaic floor showing oriental zodiac motifs was begun in 1209, around the same time that the western side of the Baptistery was enlarged. Squeezed between two columns, the tomb of Antipope John XXIII (Baldassare Coscia) was designed by Donatello and his student Michelozzo in the 1420s.

The octagon is also the shape of the remains of the original font where children, including many of the Medici family and Dante, were brought for a double baptism: as both Christian and Florentine. The font, which you can see near the exit, was installed in 1658, and its relief decorations are attributed to Andrea Pisano or his school.

The Renaissance started on this spot when, in the winter of 1400, the Calimala guild of cloth merchants held a competition to find an artist to create a pair of bronze doors for the north entrance. Judging works by seven artists, Brunelleschi among them (you can compare two of the finalists' entries in the Bargello; *see p146*), they gave the commission to the 20-year-old Ghiberti; Brunelleschi later got revenge with superior work on the Cupola, but never sculpted again. The 28 relief panels on the three-tonne, 6m-high (20ft) doors tell the story of Christ from the Annunciation to the Crucifixion; the eight lower panels show the four evangelists and four doctors of the Church. The deep pictorial space and emphasis on figures have led many scholars to consider these doors to be the very first signs of Renaissance art.

No sooner had the north doors been installed, than the Calimala commissioned Ghiberti to make another pair: the even more remarkable east doors – described by Vasari as 'undeniably perfect in every way'. These took the artist and his workshop (including Michelozzo and Benozzo Gozzoli) 27 years to complete. They're known, since Michelangelo coined the phrase, as the 'Gate of Paradise' (although 'paradise' is, in fact, what the area between a baptistery and its church was called in medieval times). The doors you see here are copies (the originals are in the Museo dell'Opera del Duomo; *see p70*), but the casts are good enough to appreciate Ghiberti's amazing work.

The very first set of Baptistery doors were those on the south side, completed by Andrea Pisano in 1336, after only six years of work. Their 28 Gothic quatrefoil-framed panels show stories from the life of St John the Baptist and the eight theological and cardinal virtues. The Latin inscription on top of the door translates as 'Andrea Pisano made me in 1330'.

In the know
Pioneering high-rise techniques

Trained as a goldsmith and clockmaker, Brunelleschi employed his expertise with gears and weights to devise the mechanical cranes and hoisting machines that were used to build the Cupola. He also proved to be a problem-solver with unorthodox methods: tradition has it that he even arranged a canteen to be set up on the scaffolding for labourers working on the dome in order to save time and reduce risks. Although there are no extant written records of this arrangement, it's a well documented fact that the safety of his workers was a primary concern for Brunelleschi: amazingly, only one fatal accident is recorded in the 16 years of building work (1420-1436).

❤ Museo dell'Opera del Duomo

Piazza del Duomo 9 (055 2302885, www. ilgrandemuseodelduomo.it). **Open** *9am-7.30pm daily (or later in summer). Closed 1st Tue of mth.* **Admission** *€15 combined with Duomo (see p65).* **Map** *p63 M6.*

Built on the site of the 15th-century cathedral workshop where Michelangelo carved his famous *David (see p133)*, the Museum of the Cathedral Works is billed as the second largest collection of devotional art in the world after the Vatican museums in Rome.

Much expanded and imaginatively reorganised between 2012 and 2015 at a cost of €45 million to the design of Adolfo Natalini and Guicciardini & Magni Architetti, the museum now showcases over 750 works of art covering 720 years of history in 25 rooms over three floors, making a total display area of about 6,000sq m (almost 65,000sq ft).

Every single piece in its unique collection has some kind of direct link with the Duomo complex; from the early basilica of Santa Reparata to the 19th-century façade. There are works by the greatest medieval and Renaissance artists, including Arnolfo di Cambio, Andrea Pisano, Lorenzo Ghiberti, Donatello, Luca della Robbia, Antonio Pollaiuolo, Andrea del Verrocchio, Michelangelo Buonarroti and, of course, the visionary genius of Filippo Brunelleschi, who created the iconic Cupola; find their names engraved on the north wall of the museum's entry corridor.

As well as housing original, restored pieces taken from the Duomo to protect them from the ravages of pollution and time, the museum continually searches for new pieces as they surface on the antiquarian market. In 2016 it paid almost €3 million to acquire three long-lost pieces from the medieval cathedral: a marble Apostle by Arnolfo di Cambio from the original façade and two smaller angels by Tino da Camaino (from the funeral monument of bishop Antonio d'Orso).

The most impressive room is the skylit **Salone del Paradiso**, spanning three floors

❤ Don't miss

1 The original Porta del Paradiso
Salone del Paradiso
Lorenzo Ghiberti's 27-year labour of love for the east side of the Baptistery.

2 Donatello's Penitent Saint Mary Magdalene *Sala della Maddalena*
An extreme example of the artist's unprecedented use of naturalism.

3 Michelangelo's Pietà Bandini
Tribune de Michelangelo
With the artist's self-portrait as the elderly Nicodemus.

4 Arnolfo di Cambio's Madonna with the Glass Eyes *Salone del Paradiso*
The central figure over the main door in the cathedral's medieval façade.

5 Brunelleschi's wooden models and original tools *Galleria della Cupola*
A precious insight into the building process of the iconic Cupola.

Pietà Bandini (Michelangelo, 1547-55)

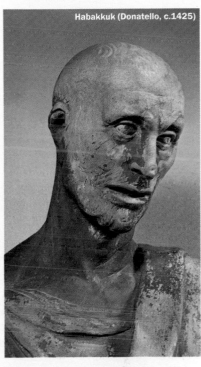

Habakkuk (Donatello, c.1425)

Reliefs and statues from the Campanile

and obtained by taking over the former site of the 18th-century Teatro degli Intrepidi. It recreates the space between the Duomo and the Baptistery with the earliest façade of Santa Maria del Fiore – never completed and finally dismantled in 1587 – on one side, and the three doors of the Baptistery facing it. The highlights of this room are Arnolfo di Cambio's mesmerising *Madonna with the Glass Eyes* and monumental statue of *Pope Boniface VIII*. A must-see is also the original ten gilt-bronze panels of the recently restored east door of the Baptistery, the so-called *Porta del Paradiso* (Gate of Paradise), sculpted by Lorenzo Ghiberti over 27 years between 1425 and 1452. The realism of its pictorial reliefs and an effective use of perspective mark a clean step into the Renaissance, compared to the two earlier doors to the left and right (Andrea Pisano's 1336 south door and Ghiberti's 1403-24 north door). Left to right starting from

above, the panels depict several scenes in one relating to the following figures from the Old Testament: Adam and Eve; Cain and Abel; Noah; Abraham and Isaac; Esau and Jacob; Joseph and Benjamin; Moses; Joshua; David; and finally, Solomon and the Queen of Sheba. Notice Ghiberti's own self-portrait in high relief in the centre-left of the door frame, between the second and third rows of panels counting from the bottom.

Habakkuk is a work of such realism that Donatello himself is said to have gripped it and screamed, 'Speak, damn you, speak!'

💜 Museo dell'Opera del Duomo *continued*

Donatello was the first artist to free sculpture from its Gothic limitations. In the **Sala della Maddalena** is an extreme example of the artist's unprecedented use of naturalism: the emotive wooden *Penitent Saint Mary Magdalene*. Dishevelled and ugly, with coarse, dirty hair so realistic you can almost smell it, the sculpture provoked a mix of outrage and awe when it was placed in the Baptistery in 1456.

In the **Tribuna di Michelangelo**, the *Pietà Bandini* (c1547-55) is a heart-rending unfinished piece intended by Michelangelo for his own tombstone: he sculpted his own features on the face of elderly Nicodemus, revealing how his obsession with the story had become too much to bear. In true tortured-artist style, frustrated with the piece, he smashed Christ's left arm. The obviously much inferior and out of proportion Mary Magdalene on the left is the later work of a pupil.

The **Galleria della Cupola** displays period and modern wooden models and sections of Brunelleschi's dome, alongside tools such as brick moulds, compasses and the pulleys and ropes used to winch building materials (and workers) up inside the cupola. There is also Filippo Brunelleschi's death mask.

The originals of Donatello's *Prophets* from the exterior of the bell tower are upstairs in the **Galleria del Campanile**, notably *Habakkuk* (affectionately called *Lo Zuccone* by Florentines, meaning 'marrow head'), a work of such realism that Donatello himself is said to have gripped it and screamed, 'Speak, damn you, speak!'. Beyond are bas-reliefs for the Campanile, most carved by Andrea Pisano and his assistants to Giotto's designs. This floor also houses the **Sala delle Cantorie** with two enormous and joyful choir galleries. One is by Donatello, with cavorting *putti* (small, angelic boys); the other, by Luca della Robbia, is full of angel musicians.

The **Sala del Tesoro** contains two stunning silver pieces: a 250kg (550lb) processional cross and a 400kg (880lb) altar front worked on by the likes of Michelozzo, Verrocchio, Antonio del Pollaiolo and Bernardo Cennini. Also on the first floor is a five-room gallery illustrating the façade made for the cathedral in the 19th century.

Other displays include pieces from **Santa Reparata** (*see p67*), a collection of relics, some fine illuminated books and liturgical vestments. A multi-purpose area houses temporary exhibitions and special events, while the panoramic terrace offers a remarkable view of Brunelleschi's dome.

The Penitent Magdalene (Donatello, 1453-1455)

Restaurants & wine bars

Coquinarius €€
*Via delle Oche 11r (055 2302153,
www.coquinarius.com).* **Open** *12.30-3pm,
6.30-10.30pm Mon-Sun.* **Map** *p63 M7* ②
Traditional Italian

Tucked away behind the Duomo, this cosy
little restaurant-wine bar is great for a quiet
lunch or an informal evening meal. The wine
list is ever-changing as the owners discover
new producers worth spotlighting. But it's
not all about the grapes: mouth-watering first
courses are enough to satisfy on their own
(go for the *pici*, a thick Sienese pasta, served
with roast beef sauce and rosemary), but
you'll probably want to save room for seconds
like the tuna tartare with avocado, mango,
lime and ginger. Imaginative appetisers are
another strength, and for those with a sweet
tooth, the home-made cakes are truly divine.

Fiaschetteria-Osteria Nuvoli €
Piazza dell'Olio 15 (055 2396616). **Open**
9.30am-3pm Sun; 8am-9pm Mon-Sat.
Map *p63 L6* ⑤ *Traditional Italian*

There aren't many spots in Duomo territory
where you'll find Florentines in droves, but
this delightfully traditional, two-part eatery is
one of the few. Grab a hefty sandwich upstairs
if you want a satisfying quick bite – the salty
schiacciata bread topped with any of the cold
cuts or *sott'oli* (pickled vegetables) is lovely,
and you can people-watch on the wobbly
chairs outside or squeeze in at the countertop
if it's not too crowded. For a more leisurely
meal (and a longer menu), make your way
downstairs to dine on no-frills, filling fare (the
meatballs and potatoes work wonders when
you're weary post-sightseeing).

The Goose €€
*Via delle Oche 15r (055 2654511,
www.thegoosefirenze.wordpress.com).*
Open *noon-midnight Sun-Thurs,
noon-1am Fri, Sat.* **Map** *p63 M7* ⑧ *Bistro*

With a name inspired by its home street,
the Goose looks more like a snug mountain-
town tavern than an international Florentine
bistro. The menu takes as many cues from
Scotland as it does from Tuscany. You'll find
a friendly, multinational staff serving up
tasty Chianina and Tuscan lamb burgers,
homemade soups and bountiful salads,
including one of the few appealing Caesar
varieties in town. There's live music on Friday
nights and a quiet downstairs room with
comfy seating, perfect for plotting out the
finer points of your trip, beer in hand.

Irene €€€
*Piazza della Repubblica 7 (055 2735891,
www.roccofortehotels.com/hotels-and-
resorts/hotel-savoy/restaurant-and-bar/
irene).* **Open** *12.30-10.30pm daily.* **Map**
p63 L7 ⑨ *Contemporary Italian*

The aesthetic at the Hotel Savoy's popular
bistro-style eatery and cocktail bar is retro,
but the food and service are far from old-
fashioned. Steered by food director Fulvio
Pierangelini and head chef Giovanni Cosmai,
Irene flaunts an eclectic menu inspired – but
never inhibited – by the tenets of Tuscan
dining. With fresh first courses (try the
octopus salad), it'd be easy to stop at a light
lunch, but Irene is the kind of place where
you'll want to indulge. A tip: the risotto made
with San Gimignano saffron, shrimp tartare
and pistachio is heavenly.

Trattoria Le Mossacce €€
*Via del Proconsolo 55r (055 294361,
www.trattorialemossacce.it/en).* **Open**
noon-2.30pm, 7-9.30pm Sun-Fri.
Map *p63 M7* ⑫ *Traditional Italian*

Run by the friendly and hospitable Fantoni-
Mannucci family, this rustic haunt offers
inexpensive, fresh and traditional Florentine
fare in one of the city's most touristy areas.
The team is particularly proud of their
classic comfort foods, such as *ribollita*
(Tuscan vegetable soup), best paired with a
glass of house Chianti. Its location between
the Bargello and Duomo make Mossacce a
strategic stop en route.

Cafés, bars & gelaterie
♥ Caffè Giubbe Rosse
*Piazza della Repubblica 13/14r (055 212280,
www.giubberosse.it).* **Open** *10am-2am daily.*
Map *p63 K7* ② *Café*

This historic haunt is something of a
local legend: once a hub for 20th-century
Florentine literati, it's believed to be the
birthplace of the Futurist movement. Past
regulars included the poet-painter Ardengo

In the know
Thunderstruck

Near the main entrance to the Museo
dell'Opera del Duomo is a round marble
slab embedded in the pavement, with no
inscription to identify it. It marks the exact
spot where the gilt copper ball and cross –
made by Verrocchio in 1469 and containing
holy relics – fell from the top of the dome's
lantern after being struck by lightning on 17
July 1600. It was replaced by an even larger
bronze ball two years later.

Soffici, and the café's intellectual ties are well-documented in its decor today. Food here is rather forgettable, but stopping in for a fairly-priced coffee or Campari-based cocktail, a perusal of the newspaper stack and a lively discussion of current events is a must for all lovers of literary cafés.

Edoardo

Piazza del Duomo 45r (055 281055, www.edoardobio.it). **Open** *11am-11.30pm daily.* **Map** *p63 M7* ❺ *Gelateria*

Hidden in the back corner of Florence's busiest piazza, this organic gelateria offers some of the city's most memorable flavours (the red wine or hazelnut-laden Gianduia varieties are popular choices). Sorbets are made strictly with seasonal fruits, and the homemade cones add another layer of goodness to each treat. There's nowhere to sit inside, and the queue frequently snakes around the street corner, but Edoardo is a reliably good sweet stop, especially on evening strolls.

Gilli

Piazza della Repubblica 36-39r (055 213896, www.gilli.it). **Open** *7.30am-12.30am daily.* **Map** *p63 L7* ❻ *Café*

With the continual closing of many of the city centre's most beloved shops and bars to make room for international designers and mass-market chains, murmurings abound about the future of the historic Gilli. Its closure would be a blow to its loyal clientele and to its many impressed visitors. Gilli's belle époque interior is original, its seasonally themed sweet window displays are wickedly tempting and its rich, flavoured hot chocolates legendary. Service is hit or miss, but Gilli's institutional status endures. Outside seating year-round.

Grom

Via del Campanile 2 (corner of via delle Oche), (055 216158, www.grom.it). **Open** *Summer 10.30am-11.30pm Sun-Fri; 10.30am-midnight Sat. Winter 10.30am-10.30pm Sun-Thurs; 10.30am-11:.0pm Fri-Sat.* **No cards.** **Map** *p63 L7* ❼ *Gelateria*

It may be a franchise but from the limestone flagging and the metal jars to the gelataio's apron, everything about Grom says traditional. Flavours of the month may be the refreshing milk and fresh mint in the summer, or zingy ginger in the winter. Fortunately, the sensational *Crema di Grom,*

Paszkowski

made with organic egg, soft cookies and *Valrhona Ecuadorian* chocolate, is served all year round.

❤ Move On
Piazza San Giovanni 1/r (055 219251, www. moveonfirenze.com/en). Open 10am-1am daily. Map p63 L6 ❿ *Italian pub/record shop*

With a variety of Italian beers on tap, this hybrid pub-shop in the shadow of the Duomo makes a great stop for an afternoon brew-with-a-view. Music junkies are drawn in by the rotating vinyl selection up for sale. The sounds aren't just vintage, either: you're as likely to find Solange Knowles as you are King Crimson. If you get hungry, the menu offers a Tuscan twist on pub food, serving cold cuts and cheeses as well as burgers and frankfurters from the nearby Mugello area.

❤ Paszkowski
Piazza della Repubblica 35r (055 210236, www.paszkowski.it). Open 7am-2am daily. Map p63 K7 ⓫ *Café*

Among Florence's elegant historic cafés, this corner place stands out for its modestly priced and genuinely delicious lunch options. Regulars and intrigued passers-by queue up by the glass display in the back, scoping out the daily specials and rhythmically reciting their orders to the expedient staff (he who hesitates is lost). Generally, there's at least one hearty soup and tasty pasta on offer, with a range of roasted veggies and other sides to choose from. By night, the venue regularly hosts live musicians, mini orchestras and DJ sets on its outdoor terrace.

La Terrazza
Rinascente, piazza della Repubblica 1 (055 283612, www.rinascente.it/rinascente/it/barcufe/202). Open 9am-8.30pm daily. Map p63 L7 ⓯ *Café*

The rooftop terrace café at this department store (*see p76*) affords some of the most stunning views of the city; the splendour of Brunelleschi's Cupola at such close quarters is unforgettable, especially at sundown, when the city is bathed in pink light. Come for cocktails or coffee rather than the mediocre food; you're paying for the quality of the view, not the menu.

Shops

Alessi
Via delle Oche 27r (055 214966, www. enotecaalessi it/en). Open 9am-7.30pm Mon-Sat. Map p63 L7 ❷ *Wine and food*

This fabulous, family-run *enoteca* is piled high with cakes, biscuits and chocolates. Coffee is ground on the spot. Organising a tasting in its spacious wine cellar is well worth it for the engaging talk with the friendly staff and generous sampler platters served with the sips.

Flow
Via Vecchietti 22r (055 215504, www.flow-store.it). Open 10am-7.30pm Mon-Sat; 2.30-7.30pm Sun. Map p63 K7 ❽ *Fashion*

Exposed brick arches, large flexible space and old-fashioned display cases make this a pleasant space in which to browse a great range of collections by up-and-coming designers and independent young brands from Italy and beyond, among them Department 5, Collection Privée, Soho de Luxe, Daniela Pancheri, Tela, PT01, Citizens of Humanity, and Giuliette Brown. Expect on-trend clothing for men and women, attentive staff and a great range of accessories.

Luisa Via Roma
Via Roma 19-21r (055 217826, www. luisaviaroma.com). Open 10am-7.30pm Mon-Sat; 11am-7.30pm Sun. Map p63 L7 ❾ *Fashion*

Renowned for its inventive, multimedia window displays, and now an online shopping giant, this multi-level supershop is almost museum-like, bordering on cartoonish in certain sections. It features the latest from Issey Miyake, Marc Jacobs, Mulberry, Chloé and others. Scoop up a pair of signature sparkly flats by Italian power blogger Chiara Ferragni (The Blonde Salad) or just soak up all the visual stimulation.

Migone
Via de' Calzaiuoli 85r (055 214004). Open 9am-7.30pm daily. Map p63 L7 ⓫ *Food*

Lydia Migone's sweet shop is a delight to spend time in, admiring the lovely cardboard Duomos filled with chocolates or sweets, the pretty cellophane bags of sweets and *biscottini*, the slabs of *torrone*, as well as traditional Tuscan bites such as *panforte* (a sugar-dusted fruit and nut bread) and *ricciarelli* (Siena-style macaroons). Prices aren't cheap but the instant charm of a Baptistery-shaped package is pretty tough to deny.

❤ Paperback Exchange
Via delle Oche 4r (055 293460, www.papex.it). Open 9am-7.30pm Mon-Fri; 10.30am-7.30pm Sat. Closed 2wks Aug. Map p63 M7 ⓭ *Books*

Cross-cultural pair Maurizio and Emily are the winning twosome behind this old favourite, which stocks thousands of new and used English-language fiction and non-fiction titles, specialising in art, art history and Italian culture and lifestyle, from medieval

Paperback Exchange

times up to Frances Mayes and her myriad copycats. You'll also find children's books, buzzed-about bestsellers and new releases – the team can usually place an order for you if you can't find what you're looking for. The noticeboard has information about courses, accommodation and language lessons, and the shop – a hub for the local Anglo-American community and internationally minded Florentines – regularly hosts its own readings, author talks and special events. Second-hand books can be exchanged.

La Rinascente

Piazza della Repubblica 1 (055 219113, www.rinascente.it). **Open** *9am-9pm Mon-Sat; 10.30am-8pm Sun.* **Map** *p63 L7* **⑮** *Department store*

This classic department store has casual and designer clothes, accessories by Furla, Coccinelle and other mid-range brands, the most extensive cosmetics and perfume department in the city, a decent lingerie section and smart bedding supplies. The rooftop café **La Terrazza**, reached via the top floor, has fantastic views (*see p75*).

THE CIVIC CENTRE

Via de' Calzaiuoli, a heaving, pedestrianised shopping street flanked by self-service restaurants, shops and gelaterie, links the Duomo with piazza della Signoria. This area represents the city's medieval centre which grew on top of the Roman City. On via del Proconsolo, just north of piazza San Firenze with its imposing ex-law courts building, is the entrance to the **Badia Fiorentina** (*see p77*) with its elegant stone bell tower. Opposite, on the corner with via Ghibellina, is the sculpture-laden **Bargello** (*see p146*). We're now in Danteland; just behind the Badia is the **Museo Casa di Dante** (*see p87*), while opposite the house is the **Chiesa di Dante**, the delightful church where the poet's beloved Beatrice is buried.

West of via de' Calzaiuoli is the portico-and-ramparts grandeur of **Palagio dell'Arte della Lana** (*see p90*), connected by an arched overpass to the church of **Orsanmichele** (*see p87*).

Piazza della Signoria

Despite being lined with tourist-trap restaurants and cafés, Florence's civic showpiece piazza della Signoria is delightful, especially in the early morning before the tour groups arrive or late in the evening. One of the most recognisable squares in the world and a true open-air museum, piazza della Signoria started life in 1268 when the Guelphs regained control of the area from the Ghibellines. They demolished their rivals' houses, but left the neighbouring buildings intact: hence the asymmetrical shape of the square.

It was here that the religious and political reformer Girolamo Savonarola lit his 'Bonfire of the Vanities' in 1497 (*see below*), and whenever Florence was threatened by an external enemy, the bell of Palazzo Vecchio (known as the *vacca*, or cow, after its mooing tone) was tolled to summon the citizens' militia. Part of their training included playing *calcio storico* on the piazza, a version of football that's still played in piazza Santa Croce every June (*see p225*).

The piazza is dominated by **Palazzo Vecchio** (*see p78*). Completed at the end of the 13th century, the crenellated and corbelled building looms over the piazza and is visible from almost any point in the city. Its front gate is guarded on one side by a copy of Michelangelo's *David* (on the spot previously occupied by the original before it was transferred to the Galleria dell'Accademia; *see p134*), and on the other side by Baccio Bandinelli's *Hercules and Cacus*, much ridiculed by the exacting Florentines and described by rival sculptor

Benvenuto Cellini as a 'sack of melons'. Behind it, on one of the cornerstones at the edge of Palazzo Vecchio nearest the open-air gallery of **Loggia dei Lanzi** (*see p86*), is the etched graffiti profile of a hawk-nosed man – this is reputed to be a portrait of a prisoner by Michelangelo.

The 14th-century Palazzo della Mercanzia on the east side of the square is home to the corporate **Gucci Museo** (*see p86*).

Dominating this longer side of the *piazza* is an equestrian bronze of Cosimo I by Giambologna notable mainly for the horse, which was cast as a single piece.

Giambologna also created sexy nymphs and satyrs for Ammannati's Neptune fountain (nicknamed *il Biancone* or 'big whitey'), a Mannerist monstrosity about which Michelangelo is reputed to have wailed: 'Ammannati, what beautiful marble you have ruined!' Even Ammannati admitted it was a failure, in part because the block of marble used for Neptune lacked width, forcing him to give the god narrow shoulders and keep his right arm close to his body.

Beyond the fountain are copies of Donatello's *Marzocco* (the original of this heraldic lion, one of Florence's oldest emblems, is in the Bargello; *see p146*) and *Judith and Holofernes* (the original is in Palazzo Vecchio; *see p78*). Like David, Judith was a symbol of the power of the people over tyrannical rulers: a Jewish widow who inveigled her way into the camp of Holofernes, Israel's enemy, she got him drunk and cut off his head.

From the Uffizi to the Arno

Leading down to the river from piazza della Signoria, the daunting piazzale degli Uffizi is home to the world-renowned **Uffizi** (*see p82*) art gallery. Also here are the separate entrances to the currently inaccessible **Corridoio Vasariano** (*see p81*) and, halfway down the *piazzale* on the right, in via Lambertesca, to the **Collezione Contini-Bonacossi** (*see right*) and the Georgofili Library, where a Mafia bomb exploded in 1993.

Turning left from the riverbank east of the Uffizi leads you to the **Museo Galileo** (*see p87*). On the pavement outside the museum on the Arno side, a monumental sundial was built in 2007. Via dei Castellani heads north from the museum to piazza San Firenze.

Back at the river, but to the west of the Uffizi, is the **Ponte Vecchio** (*see p89*), north of which is the mainly modern architecture of via Por Santa Maria, a busy shopping street rebuilt after German bombing in World War II. In a *piazza* just off the east side of the street is the **Auditorium di Santo Stefano al Ponte** (*see below*) housed in a former church.

At the top of via Por Santa Maria is the **Mercato Nuovo** (new market), a fine stone loggia erected between 1547 and 1551 on a site where there had been a market since the 11th century (*see p64* Time well spent).

Sights & museums

Auditorium di Santo Stefano al Ponte
Piazza di Santo Stefano 5 (055 217418, www.santostefanoalponte.it). Show times and ticket prices vary. **Map** *p63 L9.*

Overlooking a small square off via Por Santa Maria, just north of the Ponte Vecchio, this unexpectedly large deconsecrated church is a multifunctional venue and a multimedia space for interactive immersive exhibitions. It also hosts regular concerts and theatre shows. Next door, the namesake museum of devotional art is closed until further notice.

Badia Fiorentina
Via Dante Alighieri (055 264402). **Open** *3-6pm Mon. Donations.* **Map** *p63 M8.*

A Benedictine abbey founded in the tenth century by Willa, the mother of Ugo, Margrave of Tuscany, the Badia Fiorentia was the richest religious institution in medieval Florence. Willa had been deeply influenced by Romuald, a monk who travelled around Tuscany denouncing the wickedness of the clergy, flagellating himself and urging the rich to build monasteries; it was Romuald who persuaded Willa to found the Badia in 978.

When Ugo was a child, his exiled father returned to Florence and invented a novel paternity test: asking the boy to recognise the father he'd never seen in a room of men. Happily for his mother, Ugo succeeded. The people decided he must have had divine guidance, and he was considered a visionary leader. Ugo lavished money and land on

💗 Palazzo Vecchio

Piazza della Signoria, (055 2768325, www.museicivicifiorentini.comune.fi.it). **Open** *Apr-Sept 9am-11pm Mon-Wed, Fri-Sun; 9am-2pm Thur. Oct-Mar 9am-7pm Mon-Wed, Fri-Sun; 9am-1pm Thur. Shorter opening times apply to the tower and ramparts.* **Admission** *€4 to €18 depending on ticket combinations.* **Map** *p63 M9*

Florence's austere and commanding town hall was built to Arnolfo di Cambio's late 13th century plans to represent the immense strength of the city at the time. Despite the Mannerist makeover of the interior carried out by Vasari between 1555 and 1574, the rustic stone exterior of the building and Arnolfo's tower, the highest in the city at 94m (308ft), remained largely intact. The tower is set just off-centre in order to incorporate a previous tower and to fit in with the irregularity of the square, and is topped by two of the main symbols of Florence (a lion holding a lily). Savonarola and Cosimo il Vecchio were both imprisoned here, in a room euphemistically called the Albergaccio ('bad hotel').

It became known as Palazzo Vecchio ('old') when Cosimo I moved his family to the 'new' Palazzo Pitti (*see p167*) in 1565. At this time, Palazzo Vecchio also lost some of its administrative exclusivity to the Pitti Palace and the Uffizi. However, it became the seat of the Italian government's House of Deputies from 1865 to 1871, when Florence was the first capital of the Kingdom of Italy.

The **Salone dei Cinquecento** (Hall of the Five Hundred), where members of the Great Council met, should have been decorated by Michelangelo and Leonardo, not with the zestless scenes of victory over Siena and Pisa by Vasari that cover the walls. Leonardo abandoned the project, while Michelangelo had only finished the cartoon for the Battle of Cascine when he was summoned to Rome by Pope Julius II. Many believe da Vinci's sketches lie beneath the Vasari mural (*see p80 Lost da Vinci*). One of Michelangelo's commissions did end up here, however: *Genius of Victory*, a statue thought to have been carved, along with the better-known *Slaves* (*see p134*), for the Pope's never-finished tomb. The *palazzo's* other meeting room, the smaller Hall of the Two Hundred, is the seat of the city council and is not part of the museum.

Off the Salone is the **Studiolo di Francesco I**, the office where Francesco hid away to practise alchemy. Also decorated by Vasari, it includes a scene from the alchemist's laboratory and illustrations of the four elements. From the vaulted ceiling, Bronzino's portraits of Francesco's parents, Cosimo I and Eleonora, look down.

On the opposite side of the Salone, the **Quartiere di Leone X** is almost entirely occupied by the mayor's offices. Upstairs are the **Quartiere degli Elementi** in the east wing, and the apartments of Cosimo I's wife Eleonora da Toledo on the west side. Bronzino used intense pastel hues to depict

---

In the know
Associazione Mus.e

For an insight into Palazzo Vecchio's workings and to see private rooms not usually open to the public, such as the roof space above the wood-panelled ceiling of the Salone dei Cinquecento, join one of the informative guided tours offered by Associazione Mus.e (*see p58*).

a surreal *Crossing the Red Sea* in Eleonora's private chapel off the Green Room. On the outer wall of the same room, a perennially closed door marks the beginning of the **Vasari Corridor** (*see p81*).

Further ahead, the more sedate **Cappella dei Priori** is decorated with fake mosaics and an idealised *Annunciation*. Beyond is the garish **Sala dell'Udienza** ('Hearing room'), with a carved ceiling dripping in gold; more subtle is the **Sala dei Gigli**, so named because of the gilded lilies that cover the walls. Decorated in the 15th century, it has a ceiling by Giuliano and Benedetto da Maiano, and some sublime frescoes of Roman statesmen by Ghirlandaio opposite the door. Donatello's original *Judith and Holofernes*, rich in political significance, is also here. Finally, go through into the **Map Room** for the gigantic 16th-century globe by Egnazio Danti and, from the same period, 53 hand-decorated maps of countries and continents hiding cabinets where the Medici ceremonial costumes and family treasures were stored.

Up another steep flight of stairs, visitors reach the ramparts and, weather permitting, can climb the tower for fabulous views of the city. On the way down, the Loeser

Alchemist's Workshop (Giovanni Stradano, 1570)

collection with its 30 works of art has shorter opening hours. The *Tracce di Firenze* (Traces of Florence) exhibition near the ticket office is free for all. Plus, archaeological excavations underneath Palazzo Vecchio have brought to light the remains of the Roman theatre of ancient Florentia, which can be visited separately or by purchasing a joint ticket with the museum.

Frescoes (Giorgio Vasari, 1565) Cortile di Michelozzo

High-tech Hunt for a Lost da Vinci

A wiped-out Leonardo is causing controversy, centuries after its creation

Between 1503 and 1504, the Republic of Florence commissioned two mural paintings that might have proved the zenith of Renaissance art. The plan would have had Leonardo da Vinci and Michelangelo Buonarroti working back to back in the Salone dei Cinquecento in Palazzo Vecchio (see p78). Leonardo would portrait *The Battle of Anghiari*, while Michelangelo's subject would be The Battle of Cascina.

The latter's progress stopped at the preparatory cartoon stage when Michelangelo was summoned to Rome in 1505 by the Pope. Yet Leonardo began his mural and worked on it with several assistants, probably completing 15 to 20sq m (160 to 200sq ft) of the centrepiece, *The Fight for the Standard*. However, the upper parts of his experimental take on the ancient Roman encaustic technique dripped, and the painting was left unaccomplished when da Vinci relocated to Milan in 1506. The unfinished mural was still visible in 1563 when the reinstated Medici asked Vasari to remodel the hall and wipe out anything celebrating the Republic, including Leonardo's aborted *Battle*.

But Maurizio Seracini, a Florentine biomedical engineer whose reputation rests on his ability to repurpose non-invasive medical and military technology for art diagnostics, believes that Vasari was too fine a connoisseur to destroy a masterpiece, and he has been trying to prove the survival of Leonardo's mural since 1975. Funding this quest isn't the only concern, since the debate is fierce: to what lengths should we threaten Vasari's work in order to search for the lost da Vinci, and what to do if faced with one masterpiece topped by another?

At first, Seracini was convinced that Leonardo had worked on the western wall. Then, in 2002, researchers from the University of Florence detected a 2cm gap behind Vasari's *eastern* mural. Maybe – Seracini reasoned – Vasari had built a new wall parallel to the original, in order to protect Leonardo's work? After all, Vasari also saved Masaccio's *Holy Trinity* in Santa Maria Novella (see p104) by screening it with an altar. Seracini also noticed that a green flag in Vasari's *Battle of Marciano* bore two tiny words in white paint: '*Cerca trova*' ('Seek, and you shall find'). Could it be a clue? Since then, all efforts have concentrated on the eastern wall.

Following this, at an astrophysics congress, Professor Raymond DuVarney suggested that neutron-activation analysis might reveal traces of paint chemicals by measuring their gamma rays, so in 2011, Seracini and his team were allowed to bore several holes into Vasari's work and insert an endoscopic probe in the gap. The six points were chosen by Florentine restorers to cause the least damage to the Vasari mural and did not match Seracini's desired search areas. However, in a statement issued in March 2012, Seracini and his *National Geographic* backers claimed to have found manganese- and iron-based black pigment compatible with Leonardo's black paint from taken from his other works. The results were certified by two private laboratories – one Seracini's own – and apparently, the samples gathered were too small to allow a third opinion from a public institute.

The latest chapter in the saga dates from August 2012, when a jurisdiction feud broke out between local powers (in the form of the then city Mayor Matteo Renzi) and central government. In the end, permission was denied by the Ministry of Culture to allow further investigation. Is a mystery better marketing material than a flop? Some conspiracy theorists think so.

Study for the Battle of Anghiari (Leonardo da Vinci, 1503-1505)

what was then known as the Badia Florentia, and was eventually buried there in a Roman sarcophagus (later replaced by a tomb made by Renaissance sculptor Mino da Fiesole) that's still housed in the abbey.

It was here in 1274, just across the street from his probable birthplace, that the eight-year-old Dante fell in love at first sight with Beatrice Portinari. He was devastated when her family arranged her marriage, at the tender age of 17, to Simone de' Bardi, and absolutely crushed when she died seven years later. Poor Dante attempted to forget his pain and anguish by throwing himself into war.

The Badia has been rebuilt many times since then, but retains a graceful Romanesque campanile and exquisite carved ceiling. The Chiostro degli Aranci dates from 1430 and is frescoed with scenes from the life of San Bernardo. Inside the church, Bernardo is celebrated once again in a Filippino Lippi painting. The Cappella dei Pandolfini is where Boccaccio held the first public reading of the works of Dante.

Collezione Contini-Bonacossi
Uffizi, entrance from via Lambertesca 6 (055 2388693, www.uffizi.it). **Admission** *free.* **Map** *p63 L9.*

An impressive collection donated to the state by the Contini-Bonacossi family in 1974. Exhibits include renderings of the *Madonna and Child* by Duccio, Cimabue and Andrea del Castagno, and a roomful of artistic VIPs such as Bernini and Tintoretto. El Greco, Velázquez and Goya are among the foreigners considered prestigious enough for the collection.

Corridoio Vasariano
Between Palazzo Vecchio and Palazzo Pitti (www.uffizi.it). **Open** *From May 2018, hours and ticket prices to be confirmed.*

If you look up from the Ponte Vecchio, you'll see a neat row of small round windows running on top of the jewellery shops on the east (upstream) side of the bridge: it's the Corridoio Vasariano (Vasari corridor). Commissioned by Cosimo I de' Medici to

Corridoio Vasariano

❤ Uffizi

Piazzale degli Uffizi 6 (055 23885, www.uffizi. it). **Open** *8.15am-6.50pm Tue-Sun; June-Sept until 10pm Tue only. Ticket office closes at 6.05pm.* **Admission** *€8; €4 reductions. Small extra charge for special exhibitions. Free on 1st Sun of every month. Advance booking B-ticket (www.b-ticket.com/b-ticket/ uffizi); booking charge €4. Audio tours €6 (single headset) or €10 (double headset).* **Map** *p63 L9.*

The 28 mid 19th-century statues outside the Uffizi commemorating eminent Florentines lend an air of gravitas to the entrance to this temple of Renaissance art. The museum is Italy's most visited art gallery by far, receiving over two million visitors yearly, and about 2,000 to 9,000 visitors daily.

The building was designed by Vasari in the 16th century as a public administration centre for Cosimo I; hence 'Uffizi' meaning 'offices'. To make way for the *pietra serena* and white plaster building inspired by Michelangelo's Biblioteca Medicea Laurenziana (Laurentian Library; *see p124*), most of the 11th-century church of San Piero Scheraggio was demolished. By 1581, Francesco I had already begun turning the top floor into a home for his art collection; a succession of Medici added to it, culminating in the bequest to the city of the family's artworks by the last dynasty member, Anna Maria Luisa, in 1743.

Since there cannot be more than about 1,000 people in the building at any given time, booking in advance is the best way to skip the ticket lines, but beware of (deceptively official-looking!) secondary ticketing websites and apps – and of course of illegal touts on the spot – reselling tickets with unreasonable markups up to four times the original price. The busiest days

In the know
Find your favourites

Renovation of the main gallery on the ground floor and the reorganisation of the first and second floor exhibits mean that famous works are not always where you expect them to be: pick up a current plan of the gallery at the entrance on arrival to locate what is where at the time of your visit, and note that paintings may be moved or go on loan at any time.

are weekends and Tuesdays (the gallery is closed on Mondays) and the peak hours are mid morning and early afternoon, so be smart and schedule accordingly, setting aside at least two hours for your visit. Needless to say, the gallery is at its all-time busiest on the first Sunday of the month, when admission is free for all. In the summer, one pleasant option is to take advantage of the late opening hours on Tuesdays, when free entertainment (called *Uffizi Live* and ranging from string quartets to *commedia dell'arte*, see website for programme) is on offer.

Since 2015, the Uffizi Galleries, comprising the **Uffizi**, **Corridoio Vasariano** (*see p81*) and **Palazzo Pitti** (*see p167*), have been under the single directorship of German-born art historian Eike Schmidt – the first non-Italian Uffizi director, whose stated aim is to make the collections as widely accessible as possible. This is in the spirit of Pietro Leopoldo's original enlightened intention to make the Medici private art treasures available to visitors in 1765. Significantly, one of Schmidt's first

---

❤ Don't miss

1 Botticelli's Birth of Venus & Allegory of Spring *Sale Botticelli*
The undisputed Uffizi icons. Americans prefer *Venere*, Asians the *Primavera*. Which one is your favourite?

2 Giotto's Maestà di Ognissanti
Sala delle Maestà
Compare it with Duccio's and Cimabue's enthroned *Madonnas* in the same room: for the first time, a Maestà becomes 3D.

3 Michelangelo's Doni Tondo
Sala Michelangelo
A fascinating precursor to the Sistine Chapel. Even the frame was designed by Michelangelo.

4 Titian's Venere di Urbino
Sala di Tiziano
Languid Venus is one of the most alluring women in the history of art.

5 Caravaggio's Head of Medusa
Sala di Caravaggio
A genius trick: Medusa as reflected in the mirrored shield that finally defeated her.

💙 Uffizi *continued*

steps was to organise special guided tours of the Uffizi for the visually impaired on Friday mornings (booking required) and for disabled people on Mondays, when the gallery is otherwise closed to the public.

The Uffizi has a number of world-class statuary pieces, nowadays often overlooked even though they were the pride of the collection in the late 18th and early 19th century

The Uffizi has undergone massive changes in recent years, with cranes and scaffolding blighting the *loggiato* since 2006 with work expected to finish in 2022. But, on the plus side, exhibition space has doubled, with no fewer than 56 new rooms made available between 2011 and 2015. Temporary exhibitions have also finally found a dedicated space since the **Aula Magliabechiana** (Magliabechi Hall) at the south end of the east wing, opened in

December 2016. Accessed independently, it reduces congestion in the main gallery. The bulk of the work is funded with public money, but smaller projects, such as the rearrangement of the Botticelli rooms, have been sponsored by non-profit organisations such as the Friends of Florence (www. friendsofflorence.org) or the Amici degli Uffizi (www.amicidegliuffizi.it).

The Uffizi collections hold a total of around 5,400 artworks, 2,900 of which are currently on display. The return of Leonardo da Vinci's *Adoration of the Magi* in the spring of 2017 after a five-year restoration, meant that all of the gallery's 'non-lendable and unmovable works' were finally on permanent display again. The list of these 21 paintings and seven sculptures includes artworks considered too delicate or too unique to travel and was compiled following the loan of Leonardo's *Annunciation* and Titian's *Venus* to Japan in 2007/8 for temporary exhibitions. These 28 masterpieces are what define the Uffizi as a museum and what people travel from all corners of the globe to see; in other words, they are the ultimate shortlist of Uffizi artworks that you shouldn't miss.

In chronological order, the 'unmovable' paintings are Cimabue's, Duccio's and Giotto's three *Maestàs*; Simone Martini's *Annunciation*; Ambrogio Lorenzetti's

Allegory of Spring (Sandro Botticelli, c. 1482)

Tribuna room (Bernardo Buontalenti, 1581-83)

Presentation at the Temple; Gentile da Fabriano's *Adoration of the Magi*; Masolino and Masaccio's *Virgin and Child with St Anne*; Paolo Uccello's *Battle of San Romano*; Domenico Veneziano's *Pala di Santa Lucia de' Magnoli*; Piero della Francesca's *Duke and Duchess of Urbino*; Botticelli's *Birth of Venus* and *Allegory of Spring*; Leonardo's *Annunciation*; *Adoration of the Magi* and *Baptism of Christ* (with Verrocchio); Michelangelo's *Doni Tondo*; Raphael's *Pope Leo X with Two Cardinals* and *Madonna of the Goldfinch*; Titian's *Venus of Urbino*; Parmigianino's *Madonna with the Long Neck*; and Caravaggio's *Medusa* (with his *Bacchus* rumoured to be a forthcoming addition to the exclusive club).

The list also highlights that the Uffizi (whose full name is, significantly, 'Galleria delle Statue e delle Pitture degli Uffizi') has a number of world-class statuary pieces, nowadays often overlooked by the public, even though they were the pride of the collection in the late 18th and early 19th centuries. Take the life-size *Medici Venus*, a first-century BC Greek original that Napoleon wanted for the Louvre. Interestingly, pigment traces found during the 2012 restoration suggest that, originally, Venus would have had red lips and gold-flecked hair, while the holes in her ear lobes show that she used to wear real dangling earrings.

A curated anthology from the Uffizi's unparalleled collection of self portraits is taking over a dozen rooms in the west wing on the first floor of the gallery in November 2017. The display will showcase around 300 pieces, made up of a permanent selection of the most representative works and a rotating pick of the rest. Formerly housed in the Corridoio Vasariano (*see p81*), the collection was started by cardinal Leopoldo de' Medici in the mid 18th century and boosted in 2005 with the acquisition of 295 self-portraits by contemporary artists from Raimondo Rezzonico's private collection. The Uffizi self-portraits now consist of almost 1,800 pieces in a variety of techniques; recent additions include a watercolour by Jean Michel Folon, a video self-portrait by Bill Viola, a self-photograph by Oliviero Toscani and a Lego self-portrait by Chinese artist Ai Weiwei.

In the know
The Mafia bombing

In May 1993, a Mafia-related car bomb exploded outside the west wing of the Uffizi. Several paintings were damaged or destroyed in the blast; ironically, most of the damage came from the shattering of the protective glass screens, which ripped the canvases to shreds.

court architect Giorgio Vasari and completed in five months in 1565, the corridor was a quick and safe private walkway between the administrative offices at Palazzo Vecchio (*see p78*) north of the river and the new Grand Ducal residence, Palazzo Pitti (*see p167*), on the left bank.

Until recently the corridor housed the Uffizi collection of self-portraits, which are soon to be relocated to the main gallery (*see p85*). At the time of writing, the corridor was closed to the public for the installation of suitable safety measures, air conditioning and improved lighting, but from May 2018 the corridor will display the Uffizi collection of Greek, Roman and Etruscan stone inscriptions, as well as providing an optional direct link for visitors between the Uffizi gallery and the Palazzo Pitti museums. Regardless, you can follow the route of this ingenious passage at street level from Palazzo Vecchio (watch for the little bridge joining Palazzo Vecchio and the Uffizi) to the little door next to Buontalenti's grotto in the Giardino di Boboli (*see p168*).

Gucci Museo
*Piazza della Signoria 10 (055 75927010, www.guccimuseo.com). **Open** 10am-8pm daily; Fri until 11pm. **Admission** €7 (€5 Fri 8-11pm). **Map** p63 M8.*

Together with fellow local designers Pucci, Ferragamo, Cavalli, Coveri and up-and-coming Patrizia Pepe, Gucci belongs in the Olympus of fashion megabrands. Located in the 14th-century Palazzo del Tribunale della Mercanzia overlooking piazza della Signoria, the Gucci Museo opened in 2011 to celebrate the 90th anniversary of the company founded by Guccio Gucci in 1921.

Nine rooms over three floors house the permanent exhibits showcasing the signature designs of the Gucci brand including the iconic travel cases, the horse-bit loafer (1952) and bamboo-handle handbags (1947). Fashionistas will swoon before Gucci's evening gowns, worn by the stars on red carpets or featured in the leading fashion glossies. Two more rooms house two exhibitions of contemporary art and design.

The bookshop and café-restaurant – both free to visit – display a series of terracotta crests of the historic trade guilds of Florence, formerly on the façade of the building. Visit on a Friday night to take advantage of reduced tickets that are partly devoted to restoring the city's art treasures.

♥ Loggia dei Lanzi
*Piazza della Signoria. **Open** always. **Admission** free. **Map** p63 L9.*

This 14th-century loggia derives its name from the *lanzichenecchi*, a private army of

Loggia dei Lanzi
showing Perseus (Benvenuto Cellini)

Cosimo I that used to be stationed here. Built in the late 1300s to shelter civic bigwigs during ceremonies, by the mid 15th century it had become a favourite spot for old men to gossip and shelter from the sun.

Since the late 18th century, the loggia has been used as an open-air museum, best enjoyed at night after the crowds dissolve. Cellini's fabulous *Perseus* stands victorious holding the snaky head of Medusa. The bronze is testament to the artist's pig-headed determination: most considered it impossible to cast, but after several failed attempts, Cellini finally succeeded by burning even his family furniture to fan the furnace. Also in the loggia is Giambologna's spiralling marble *Abduction of a Sabine Woman* (1582), a virtuoso attempt to outdo Cellini, and Agnolo Gaddi's *Seven Virtues*.

Museo Casa di Dante

Via Santa Margherita 1 (055 219416, www.museocasadidante.it). **Open** *Oct-Mar 10am-5pm Tue-Sun. Apr-Sept 10am-6pm daily.* **Admission** *€4. No cards.* **Map** *p63 M7.*

A medieval pastiche built in the early 1900s where the Alighieri properties once were, this museum dedicated to the father of the Italian language offers extensive information about the political, economic and cultural environment of Dante's time, mostly in the form of brightly coloured factual posters lining the walls on all three floors. There are miniature-model reconstructions of battles and of ancient Florence, an example of a medieval bedroom, costumed mannequins and clear illustrations of Heaven, Hell and Purgatory taken from *The Divine Comedy*. However, if you go expecting to see the poet's belongings, original works or in fact anything original at all, you'll be disappointed.

Museo Galileo

Piazza dei Giudici 1 (055 265311, www.museogalileo.it). **Open** *9.30am-6pm Mon, Wed-Sun; 9.30am-1pm Tue.* **Admission** *€9. No cards.* **Map** *p63 L10.*

Spanning 18 rooms on two floors, the new exhibition layout presents more than 1,000 instruments and devices of major scientific importance and exceptional beauty, placing them in the historical and cultural setting in which the Medici and Lorraine collections were assembled.

The only surviving instruments designed and built by Galileo Galilei are the big draw here, notably two of his original telescopes and the objective lens of the telescope with which he discovered Jupiter's moons. A morbid reliquary in the shape of his middle right finger is also on display, offering unintentionally ironic echoes to the honour more usually bestowed on saints.

In the other rooms are a collection of prisms and optical games, armillary spheres, globes, nautical devices, a selection of electromagnetic and electrostatic instruments and a mix of machines, mechanisms and models including a 19th-century clock (*pianola*) that writes a sentence with a mechanical hand.

Orsanmichele & Museo di Orsanmichele

Via dell'Arte della Lana (church 055 210305, museum 055 284944, www.bargellomusei. beniculturali.it). Open church 10am-5pm daily, museum 10am-5pm Mon. Admission free. Map p63 L8.

Most famous for the statues in the 14 niches that surround the building, Orsanmichele has become a relic of the extreme dedication and pride of Florentine trades, and a reminder that a competitive climate often heralds the greatest art. There's no spire and no overt religious symbols: Orsanmichele may not look much like a church, but it is – although one with a difference, melding as it does the relationship between art, religion and commerce.

In 1290, a loggia intended as a grain store was built to a design by Arnolfo di Cambio, the original architect of the Duomo, in the garden (*orto*) of the Monastery of San Michele (hence, 'Orsanmichele'). The loggia burned down in 1304, along with a painting of the Madonna that, from 1292, had been said to perform miracles. Such was the effect of her miracles that people flocked from across Tuscany to worship her. When the building was reconstructed in the mid 1300s by Talenti and Fioravante, the painting was replaced and honoured by the creation of a marvellously elaborate glass and marble tabernacle by Andrea Orcagna. This was replaced in 1347 by Bernardo Daddi's *Coronation of the Madonna with Eight Angels*, which is still here today.

During reconstruction of the building, two upper floors were added for religious services. From the outset, the council

Interior of Orsanmichele

🖤 Ponte Vecchio

Between lungarno Acciaioli and via Guicciardini. **Map** *p63 K9.*

Crossing Florence's oldest bridge must be on any visitor's checklist of things to do in Florence. The 14th-century shop-lined – or rather shop-laden – Ponte Vecchio may lack the charm of Venice's Bridge of Sighs, but it is the busiest pedestrian thoroughfare between the two banks of the Arno and an apt symbol of this mercantile city. Head for one of the two neighbouring bridges (ponte alle Grazie or ponte Santa Trinita; *see p150*) to take mandatory pictures – with the right light, it's as pretty as they come!

A series of bridges has occupied the narrowest spot on the river for more than 1,000 years, but the builders of the current one remain unknown, although Vasari attributes the project to Taddeo Gaddi. Bridges with shops on them were common in medieval times, but by 1593 the original tenants of this one, a lively mix of butchers, fishmongers, tanners and blacksmiths, were deemed too smelly and loud to stay, and were evicted on the orders of Ferdinando I. The shops and workshops were given over to the gold- and silversmiths, whose descendants still occupy them. A sharp rise in rents led to many of the 17th-century shopkeepers adding the back shops (*retrobotteghe*) that still hang precariously over the bridge's sides.

This was famously the only bridge in the city to be spared from destruction during the German army's retreat in 1944 – supposedly on Hitler's orders, but certainly thanks to the efforts of Gerhard Wolf, German consul in Florence during World War II. Against all the odds, its low arches also survived the massive impact of water and debris in the catastrophic 1966 flood.

The bust topping the fountain in the centre of the bridge is of Benvenuto Cellini, put up by the goldsmiths of Florence in 1901 to mark the fourth centenary since the birth (3 November 1500) of their illustrious colleague. For a time, love padlocks were attached to the railing around the monument, putting its stability at risk. As a consequence, the city council started routinely removing them, and a hefty fine is now in store for anyone caught in the act of attaching anything to Ponte Vecchio.

intended the building to be a magnificent advertisement for the wealth of the city's guilds, and in 1339 each guild was instructed to fill one of the loggia's 14 niches with a statue of its patron saint. Only the wool guild obliged, so in 1406, after the building's conversion into a church, the council handed the guilds a ten-year deadline.

Six years later, the Calimala cloth importers, the wealthiest of all the guilds, commissioned Ghiberti to create a life-sized bronze of John the Baptist. It was the largest statue ever cast in Florence, and its arrival spurred the other major guilds into action. The guild of armourers was represented by a tense *St George* by Donatello (now in the Bargello; *see p146*), one of the first psychologically realistic sculptures of the Renaissance, while the Parte Guelfa guild had Donatello gild their bronze, a *St Louis of Toulouse* (later removed by the Medici in their drive to expunge all memory of the Guelphs).

All the statues in the external niches today are copies. However, the originals can be found on the first floor of the museum, displayed on a platform in their original order. And on the second floor is a collection of statues of 14th-century saints and prophets in Arenaria stone. They were on the external façade of the church until the 1950s.

The church and museum do not always stick to the opening hours posted, so it's advisable to phone to check the hours before making a special trip.

Palagio dell'Arte della Lana

Via Arte della Lana 1 (055 287134, www.dantesca.org). Open by app only. Map p63 L8.

The medieval seat of the filthy-rich Calimala guild of clothmakers and wool merchants was built in the late 13th century and miraculously survived the 19th-century 'cleansing' of the area. In 1905, architect Enrico Lusini restored it in neo-Gothic style to house the Società Dantesca Italiana. On the corner of the *palazzo* facing Orsanmichele (*see p87*) is the stunning Gothic *Madonna of the Trumpet* tabernacle, complete with spiral columns, a pointed arch, family crest decorations, and a long and complex history. The tabernacle started life in the 13th century on the corner of the old market and Calimala, housing the miracle-working Madonna painting (later destroyed by fire). The painting was replaced in 1335 by *Enthroned Madonna and Child, Saint John the Baptist* and *John the Evangelist and Angels* by Jacopo di Casentino; *Coronation of the Virgin and Saints* by Niccolò di Pietro Gerini was added in 1380. The interior is normally closed to the public, but private visits may occasionally be arranged.

Restaurants & wine bars

Cantinetta di Verrazzano €€

Via dei Tavolini 18r (055 268590, www.verrazzano.com/en). Open 8am-9pm Mon-Sat; 10am-4.30pm Sun. Map p63 L8 ① *Wine bar*

The wood-panelled rooms of this *cantinetta* are continually crowded with smartly dressed Florentines and discerning tourists. Owned and run by the historic Castello di Verrazzano, one of the major wine estates in Chianti, this locale features a bakery with a wood oven and coffee shop (serving the excellent Piansa coffee blend) on one side, and a wine bar serving (very good) estate-produced wines by the glass or bottle on the other (the ruby-red Chianti Classico Riserva DOCG is sure to please). Snacks include *focaccia* straight from the wood oven, *sbrisolona* (fennel seed salami) and other specialities from Greve in Chianti's best butchers, plus an unusual selection of *crostini*.

Dei Frescobaldi Ristorante & Wine Bar €€€

Via dei Magazzini 2-4r (055 284724, www.deifrescobaldi.it). Open noon-3.30pm and 7-11.30pm daily. Map p63 M8 ③ *Wine bar-restaurant*

Located on a side street off piazza della Signoria, this wine bar offers top-quality wines from the formidable Frescobaldi estates of Tuscany, Friuli and the Veneto. The wines range from Sangiovese-based Tuscan favourites to several crisp Pinot Grigio options if you fancy transporting your taste buds to northern Italy. Most can be ordered by the glass as well as the bottle. Snacks at the wine bar include decadent Burrata (creamy mozzarella) from Apulia, as well as thoughtfully selected Tuscan salamis, veggies and cheeses with spicy chutney. You can also choose from the full menu offered in its adjoining restaurant.

❤ Fishing Lab Alle Murate €€

Via del Proconsolo 16r (055 240618, www.fishinglab.it/en). Open 10am-midnight daily. Map p63 N8 ⑥ *Seafood*

Call it contrived (many have), but this cool concept restaurant has a beguiling mix of old and new, best seen not on its menu, but in its design. Fishing Lab's bar is spacious, its main floor sleek and clean-lined, contrasting with the frescoed ceiling vaults upstairs and Roman Florence ruins on the cosy lower level. The menu offers snack and meal-size portions of street seafood (think mixed fried fish or mini sandwiches), as well as pastas, sampling platters and raw selections. Rather than strictly adhering to a lunch and dinner schedule, the kitchen and bar stay open all

Il Porcellino, Mercato Nuovo p64

day; pop in for an afternoon pick-me-up, grab an early lunch before most spots are open or indulge in the four-person raw tasting menu. Wash it all down with a crisp Vermentino or any of the other whites and bubblies on the extensive wine list.

♥ Ora d'Aria €€€€
Via de' Georgofili 11r (055 2001699, www.oradariaristorante.com). Open 12.30-2.30pm Tues-Sat and 7.30-10pm Mon-Sat. Map p63 L9 ⑩ *Experimental Italian*

Marco Stabile, the young Tuscan chef in charge of the kitchen at this stylish Michelin-starred eatery, has impeccable credentials and his dishes are executed with skill. His changing seasonal menus – usually rife with seafood and game options – are based on fresh, understated ingredients, all carefully researched and winningly assembled. If you're ready to indulge, try one of the pricy but bountiful tasting menus (at €90 per person, plus a €5 cover charge, they deliver). À la carte options are also available. Stabile fuses traditional practices with more innovative ideas: you'll find beef ragu-topped polenta and Florentine steak alongside game-stuffed tortellini with foie gras and liquorice cream. Everything is beautifully presented, and there's a substantial wine

list, though some of the prices per bottle are rather inflated.

Osteria I Buongustai €€
Via dei Cerchi 15r (055 291304, www.facebook.com/ibuongustaifirenze). Open 8am-4pm Mon-Fri; 8am-11pm Sat. Map p63 M8 ⑪ *Traditional Italian*

Just turning around in this tiny lunch favourite can be a challenge: its foyer and main dining room overflow with neighbourhood workers, in-the-know visitors and intrepid staff wriggling their way through narrow spaces. The cheap prices, local crowd and efficient service make all the manoeuvring well worth it. You won't find better prices in the town centre for hearty *primi* such as *spaghetti all'amatriciana* (pasta with a pork cheek-based sauce) and *tagliolini al tartufo* (truffle pasta).

Cafés, bars & gelaterie
♥ Caffè Rivoire
Piazza della Signoria 5r (055 214412, www.rivoire.it). Open Summer 7.30am-midnight Tue-Sun. Winter 7.30am-9pm Tue-Sun. Map p63 L8 ③
Café and chocolatier

Founded in 1872 as a chocolate factory with ties to the Savoy royals, Rivoire later became a bohemian haunt before morphing into the most famous and best loved of all Florentine cafés. Its chocolates – also available in gift boxes – are divine and its house-brand coffee and seasonal hot chocolate beverage are among the best in the city. The outside tables have unmatched views of Palazzo Vecchio and the Loggia dei Lanzi. One downside: your wallet will be hit hard for the privilege. Knock back an espresso at the bar to sample some of the glamour without the hefty price tag.

Carapina

Via Lambertesca 18r (055 291128, www.carapina.it). **Open** *8am-midnight Tue-Sun. Closed Jan.* **Map** *p63 L9* ❹ *Gelateria*

This artisanal gelato maker, spearheaded by Simone Bonini, prides itself on seasonality and keeping flavours to a minimum (16 at a time), offering a largely fruit-based selection. Of course, when you operate in a country where fruit ranges from figs, chestnuts and almonds to apricots, peaches and pine nuts, you've a pretty good selection to choose from. The place is also noted for its cheese-based tastes, made with varieties ranging from Gorgonzola to Grana Padano. **Other location:** piazza Guglielmo Oberdan 2r (Campo di Marte, Outside the City Gates).

I Due Fratellini

Via de' Cimatori 38r (055 2396096, www. iduefratellini.com). **Open** *10am-7pm daily.* **No cards.** **Map** *p63 L8* ❽ *Sandwich bar*

Florence was once brimming with these hole-in-the-wall *vinai* (wine merchants) but today I Due Fratellini, founded back in 1875, is one of very few left in the city. The focus has shifted to its sandwiches, a fast and fresh lunch option that will only set you back €4. Don't dilly dally or fret about making substitutions as you place your order: most sandwiches have only a couple of ingredients and the combinations on offer are dependably delicious (goat's cheese and fennel salami, anyone?). There's nowhere to sit down: join the locals standing in the road or squatting on the pavement for a glass of cheap and cheerful plonk or something a bit more special.

'Ino

Via de' Georgofili 3r-7r (055 214154, www.inofirenze.com). **Open** *11am-5pm daily.* **Map** *p63 L9* ❾ *Gourmet sandwich bar*

At this classy, contemporary sandwich bar and deli – behind the Uffizi, near where the Mafia placed its bomb in 1993 – they've perfected the art of the *panino*, and most choices will set you back around €8. It's higher than the local average for

sandwiches, but so is the quality of these ingredients. Fillings are sourced from all over the country by owner Alessandro Frassica. Sandwiches (to be enjoyed seated at a barrel table, perched at the counter, or to take away) are made to order and filled according to seasonal availability, with plenty of vegetarian-friendly options as well as mouth-watering meats. The deli/shop (*see p93*) is stocked with tempting goodies, and there's a range of sweets that make excellent gifts (you can't go wrong with *biscotti* by Fratelli Lunardi).

❤ Perchè No!

Via de' Tavolini 19r (055 2398969, www. percheno.firenze.it). **Open** *noon-8pm Wed-Mon.* **No cards.** **Map** *p63 L8* ⓬ *Gelateria*

This is a favourite with the locals – many have been coming for generations. Not by chance, it is often cited as the best gelateria for the more traditional flavours – *crema* (sweet egg custard), pistachio and chocolate. It's narrow and the one or two benches haphazardly stuck inside are hardly adequate seating, so prepare to take a scenic walk with your ice-cream in hand.

Seven Brothers

Via della Condotta 61 (055 051 6656, www.sevenbrothers.eu). **Open** *Summer 11am-11pm daily. Winter 12-7pm Sun-Fri; 12pm-midnight Sat.* **Map** *p63 L8* ⓮ *Gelateria*

A new contender in gelato-land, at Seven Brothers you serve yourself and add your own toppings. The idea is innovative and certainly fun to try, but add-ons are addictive and since your cup is weighed at checkout, sticking to a budget is impossible and you end up spending way more than you would in any old-fashioned gelateria. That said, the concept is thriving and the owners are even planning to franchise it.

Shops

A Piedi Nudi nel Parco

Via del Proconsolo, corner of via Dante Alighieri (055 218099, www.pnp-firenze.com). **Open** *noon-7.30pm Sun; 10.30am-7.30pm Mon-Sat.* **Map** *p63 M8* ❶ *Avant-garde fashion*

These sister shops take their name from the 1960s play-turned-film *Barefoot in the Park*, but the style is not for the timid, and is barely evocative of a Neil Simon rom-com. Black is the dominant colour and edge is the common thread: you'll find harsh military jackets, floor-length 19th century-esque dresses, futuristic fabrics, goth-chic looks and asymmetrical styles with a decorative twist. PNP's wide range of forward-charging international brands (Issey Miyake, Vic

Matiye, If Six Was Nine) make it a popular stop among the fashion elite when the Pitti trade shows are in town. **Menswear location** behind the via del Proconsolo shop at via Santa Margherita 2r (055 280179).

Bartolucci
Via della Condotta 12r (055.211773, www.bartolucci.com). **Open** *10am-7.30pm daily.* **Map** *p63 M8* ❸ *Toys*

Individually crafted pinewood rabbit-clocks and cat-lamps, spring guns and rocking horses, as well as Vespa replicas and Pinocchio puppets, all the result of three generations' worth of Bartolucci expertise. **Other location** Borgo de' Greci 11r, Santa Croce (055 2398596).

Bramada
Via del Proconsolo 12r (055 2399982, www.bramada.it/en). **Open** *10.30am-7.30pm daily.* **Map** *p63 N8* ❼ *Fashion and homeware*

Softly lit and impeccably curated, this shop sporting clothing, jewellery and home accessories is a pleasure to browse. Most of the items for sale are handcrafted by Florentine and Tuscan artisans and designers: think silky scarves and pillows, eye-catching ceramics, cashmere accessories and hand-painted clothing.

'Ino
See p92 **Map** *p63 L9* ❾ *Food*

A gourmet's dream kitchen-cupboard shop, with wines, fresh tomato sauce, *biscotti* from famed Pistoia-based brand Fratelli Lunardi (the chocolate ones are to die for), artfully-shaped pastas, chutneys and jams in unusual flavours. Everything comes beautifully packaged, of course. There's also a few options for the eager cookbook hoarder or foodie literature lover, including the shop's own colourful, gorgeously photographed books on crafting the perfect *panino*.

Maledetti Toscani
Via della Condotta 36r (055 211981, www.maledettitoscani.com). **Open** *11am-7.30pm Tues-Sun; 1.30-7.30pm Mon.* **Map** *p63 M8* ❿ *Leather goods*

From its cheesy Western-style exterior and faux-rustic decor, it'd be easy to write this place off, but look a little closer at the quality of the leather. Maledetti Toscani ('Damn Tuscans') has longstanding roots in leatherwork, traceable back to Montepulciano in 1848, when the first location opened. This Florence shop is well stocked with fine vegetable-tanned leather goods for men and women, from boots and Oxfords to wallets and jackets. Styles range from classic and refined to wearably edgy (picture

zany colours or a strategically placed snakeskin patch).

Sartoni
Via de' Cerchi 34r (055 212570, www.fornosartonifirenze.it). **Open** *7.30am-8pm Mon-Sat.* **Map** *p63 M7* ⓰ *Food*

A central pit-stop stocking slices of delicious hot pizza, filled *focaccia*, biscuits and traditional Tuscan sweets.

♥ Spezierie-Erboristerie Palazzo Vecchio
Via Vacchereccia 9r (055 2396055, www.spezieriepalazzovecchio.it). **Open** *10am-7.30pm Mon-Sat.* **Map** *p63 L9* ⓱ *Herbs & perfumes*

A beautiful frescoed interior selling herbal products made to centuries-old recipes and, supposedly, original Florentine perfumes commissioned by the Medici family. Charmingly, many of the scented products have fragrances inspired by Florentine locations or characters from history: dab on a little perfume and you'll give off the air of Caterina de' Medici, or buy an air freshener that'll ensure your living room evokes the Giardino di Boboli.

AROUND VIA DE' TORNABUONI

The elegant shopping hub of via de' Tornabuoni sweeps down from piazza Antinori to **Ponte Santa Trinita** (*p108*). It's crowned by **Palazzo Antinori**, an austere mid 15th century palace of neat stone blocks that's been inhabited by the

Spezierie-Erboristerie Palazzo Vecchio

A Walk Through Fictional Florence

Step into other worlds, from Portrait of a Lady *to* Hannibal

Start from the **Spedale degli Innocenti** in **piazza della SS Annunziata**, San Marco. The courtyard of the foundling hospital sets the scene for Joan Plowright's Mary Wallace to rescue the illegitimate Luca from an orphanage fate in Franco Zeffirelli's *Tea with Mussolini*. Meanwhile, Giambologna's Grand Duke Ferdinand I statue is the starting point from which Judi Dench's Eleanor Lavish whisks Maggie Smith's Charlotte Bartlett to see the sights in *A Room with a View*. The exquisite *piazza* also has a cameo role in Jane Campion's *Portrait of a Lady*, based on the novel by Henry James.

Follow via de' Servi down to **piazza del Duomo**, where in the same film Nicole Kidman's independently minded Isabel Archer rides in her carriage with John Malkovich's Gilbert Osmond.

Skirt round the north of the Duomo and reach the octagonal **Baptistery** (*see p69*) with its dazzling mosaics depicting the *Last Judgement*. It's here in Ron Howard's *Inferno* that Tom Hanks's Robert Langdon fishes the missing death mask of Dante Alighieri from the baptismal font. Back outside, between the Baptistery and the Duomo, Charlton Heston's Michelangelo lovingly contemplates the cathedral's carved images in *The Agony and the Ecstasy*. Continue down via de'

Calzaiuoli to **via de' Tavolini**: in Irving Stone's source novel, Michelangelo is seconded to Ghirlandaio's studio here. Then make your way south to **piazza della Signoria** (see p76).

Filmmakers seem to consider the *piazza* and **Palazzo Vecchio** (*see p78*) to be the perfect backdrop for gruesome scenes: in *A Room with a View*, Helena Bonham-Carter's young aristo Lucy Honeychurch swoons in the square after witnessing a murder; while on the balcony of Palazzo Vecchio, Anthony Hopkins' Dr Hannibal Lecter brings a whole new meaning to 'letting it all hang out' – at the expense of police inspector Rinaldo Pazzi's innards – in the *Silence of the Lambs* sequel *Hannibal*.

It's now time to enter Palazzo Vecchio and visit the **museum**. This was the main filming location in Florence for *Inferno* – in the film, Langdon claims to have learned of the palace's secret passages through a guided tour years earlier. Not only does this tour actually run – but a new, intriguing *The Secrets of Inferno Tour* (see p58) is also available, and every film buff should give it a go.

Finish at the **Uffizi** (*see p82*), where Asia Argento's detective Anna Manni suffers a bout of artistic overkill in the 1990s horror *The Stendhal Syndrome*. ▶*The route of this walk is shown on the map on p63.*

A Room With a View (James Ivory, 1985)

Antinori winemaking family since 1506. The rather garish **San Gaetano** opposite is one of the only completely Baroque churches in Florence.

Heading south towards the river, it is the gargantuan stones of fortified **Palazzo Strozzi** (*see p95*) that dominate. The walls of the building (up to and around the main entrance in piazza Strozzi) are set with horse-tethering rings and torch holders and embellished with the three crescent-moon motifs of the Strozzi family, who were banking rivals of the more famous Medici.

Continuing south, and passing all manner of designer names, you'll come to piazza Santa Trinita. Just before the square via Porta Rossa runs east; the Renaissance house museum **Palazzo Davanzati** (*see p95*) is on the south side. South-east of here is the 13th-century **Palagio di Parte Guelfa** (*see p95*). Running parallel to via Porta Rossa is borgo Santissimi Apostoli, a narrow street in the middle of which is piazza del Limbo, so called because it occupies the site of a graveyard for unbaptised babies. The tiny church is **Santissimi Apostoli** (*see p96*), one of Florence's oldest.

Piazza Santa Trinita is little more than a bulge dominated by the curved ramparts of Palazzo Spini Feroni, home to the shoetastic **Museo Ferragamo** (*see p95*), and by an ancient column from the Baths of Caracalla in Rome, given to Cosimo I by Pope Pius I in 1560. The statue of Justice on top is by Francesco del Tadda. The first *palazzo* after via de' Tornabuoni is Palazzo Bartolini Salimbeni by Baccio d'Agnolo.

Sights & museums

Museo dell'Antica Casa Fiorentina

Palazzo Davanzati, via Porta Rossa 13 (055 2388610, www.bargellomusei.beniculturali.it). Open 8.15am-1.50pm daily. Closed 1st, 3rd & 5th Mon, 2nd & 4th Sun of mth. Admission €6. Free 1st Sun of every month. Map p63 K8.

On the first floor of the Ancient Florentine House Museum within Palazzo Davanzati are the painted **Sala dei Pappagalli**, the **Salone Madornale** and the **Studiolo**, displaying carved Renaissance furniture, paintings, tapestries, an incredible 16th-century strongbox and a permanent exhibition about spinning, weaving, embroidery and lace. The building itself is a wonderful example of a 14th-century *palazzo* for well-to-do Florentines; the little *cortile* with a view up to all the levels has a stone staircase leading to the first floor (as high as the noble guests would be visiting) and wooden stairs thereafter. There is a well beneath the building accessed by buckets that were lowered down a hollow column (like a dumb-waiter) from the kitchens; the kitchens themselves were

hidden high up on the (inaccessible) third floor to keep smoke and smells out of the way. Access to the second and third floors is only by guided group, by request at 10am, 11am and noon when the museum is open.

Museo Ferragamo

Piazza Santa Trinita 5r (055 3562846, www. museoferragamo.it). Open 10am-7.30pm daily. Admission €6. Map p63 J8.

Down some steps from the eponymous shop and into the medieval basement, this corporate museum is as elegant and stylish as the shoes on display. In the first chamber, you can see order forms signed by famous actors and actresses, including John Wayne, and wooden 'lasts' (foot shapes) for Ava Gardner and Drew Barrymore. The rest of the museum is filled with a choice selection of the company's 10,000 shoes. Exhibits change periodically and there are pairs created for Marilyn Monroe, Judy Garland and Audrey Hepburn, affording an opportunity for shoe lovers to drool over some of the world's most beautiful footwear.

Palagio di Parte Guelfa

Piazzetta di Parte Guelfa. No set times. Admission free. Map p63 K8.

Once the headquarters of the Guelph Captains, this crenellated building with Gothic leaded windows dates back to the 13th century. The outside staircase was modified by Giorgio Vasari, while Filippo Brunelleschi is credited by some sources with designing the large first floor hall (normally closed, but if you are in luck it may be hosting a meeting or an exhibition).

Palazzo Strozzi

Piazza Strozzi (055 2645155 info, 055 2469600 bookings, www.palazzostrozzi.org). Open 10am-8pm daily; 10am-11pm Thur. Admission €12. CCC Strozzina exhibitions vary. Map p63 J7.

Flanked by Florence's most stylish shopping streets, Palazzo Strozzi is one of the most magnificent of the 100 or so palaces built in the city during the 15th century. In 1489, work began on the construction of the *palazzo* by order of Filippo Strozzi, whose family had been exiled from Florence in 1434 for opposing the Medici. However, they'd made good use of the time, moving south and becoming bankers to the King of Naples; by the time they returned to Florence in 1466, they'd amassed a fortune. Filippo began buying up property in the centre of Florence eight years later, until he had acquired enough real estate to build the biggest palace in the city.

An astrologer was asked to choose an auspicious day to lay the foundation stone; 6 August 1489 tied in nicely with a new law that tax-exempted anyone who built a house on an empty site. When Filippo died in 1491, he left his heirs to complete the project, which eventually bankrupted them, but the palace remained in the family up until 1937, when it became the seat of an insurance company. It was finally handed over to the state in 1999.

Behind the imposing rusticated stone walls lie a few cultural institutions including the *Gabinetto Vieusseux*, the Humanist Institute's Renaissance book and manuscript collection. A pleasant café and a bookshop open onto the *palazzo's* Renaissance courtyard (admission free), which also hosts concerts, contemporary art installations, theatrical performances and events.

For over a decade, the independent public-private *Fondazione Palazzo Strozzi* has been hosting the most important and talked-about exhibitions in Florence in the *piano nobile* of the *palazzo*, ranging from ancient art (Hellenistic sculpture) via the Renaissance (Botticelli) to international modern (Picasso) and contemporary artists (Bill Viola). Shows run for approximately four to six months at a time, and you are strongly advised to check the current programme at the time of your stay because it may well be worth a visit.

Also managed by the Fondazione Palazzo Strozzi, the Centro di Cultura Contemporanea Strozzina, or **CCC Strozzina** (www.strozzina.org), is a modern space in the *palazzo's* cellar which holds imaginatively curated international contemporary events and shows with works by the likes of Cindy Sherman, Andreas Gursky and Gerhard Richter and emerging artists.

Santissimi Apostoli

*Piazza del Limbo 1 (055 290642). **Open** 4-7pm Tue-Fri. **Admission** free. **Map** p63 K9.*

The design of Santissimi Apostoli, like that of the early Christian churches of Rome, is based on a Roman basilica. It's one of the oldest churches in Florence, retaining much of its 11th-century façade. The third chapel on the right holds an *Immaculate Conception* by Vasari; in the left aisle is an odd glazed terracotta tabernacle by Giovanni della Robbia. The church holds pieces of flint reputed to have come from Jerusalem's Holy Sepulchre, awarded to Pazzino de' Pazzi for his bravery during the Crusades: he was the first to scale the walls of Jerusalem, though his nickname, 'Little Mad Man of the Mad Men', suggests his actions may have been more foolish than brave. These flints were used on Easter Day to light the 'dove' that set off the fireworks display at the Scoppio del Carro (*see p222*). Note that the church has a tendency to close in the afternoon without notice.

Restaurants & wine bars

Fashion Foodballer €€

*Piazza degli Strozzi 14r-15r (055 0454529, www.fashionfoodballer.com/en). **Open** noon-1am daily. **Map** p63 K7* ❹ *Traditional Italian*

It's a shrine to Italy's favourite sport but don't mistake Fashion Foodballer for a standard sports bar. The family-friendly, yet fashionable, venue mostly serves hearty dishes (the house special is meat and potatoes), and you can order a half portion of most main courses. Live football matches air in the background, but if you're not particularly invested in the teams facing off, you can explore the locker room-style gift shop or Hall of Fame-esque memorabilia wall by the bar.

Fusion Bar €€

*Gallery Hotel Art, vicolo dell'Oro 2 (055 27266987, www.lungarnocollection.com/the-fusion). **Open** noon-midnight daily. **Map** p63 K9* ❼ *International fusion & cocktails*

This stylish-bordering-on-snobby local is a good option for a quiet, light lunch, or an adventurous evening cocktail accompanied by tapas or a sushi dinner. Fitting in beautifully with the East-meets-West design ethos of the hotel that hosts it, this bar-restaurant serves safe yet innovative lunchtime dishes (sliced tuna with sesame and quinoa offers a refreshing break from meaty *trattoria* staples). Things get really interesting by night, with a full sushi menu and a plethora of Nikkei specialities, a niche-y Japanese-Peruvian cuisine. The ship is steered by starred executive chef Peter Brunel and resident chef Gilberto Vannini. Order à la carte with a cool lemongrass cocktail (this isn't the place to stick with your old standby) or try the fixed price Fusion Path sushi menu, paired with a signature cocktail for €48.

Cafés, bars & gelaterie

Boulangerie del Rifrullo

*Via de' Rondinelli 24r (055 281658, www.facebook.com/laboulangeriedelrifrullo). **Open** 8am-6.30pm Mon-Sat. **Map** p63 K6* ❶ *Café*

Owned by the people behind Rifrullo (*see p183*) and with the same combination of great food served in a clean, relaxed atmosphere, the boulangerie justly describes itself as a cross between a New York café and a Paris bistro. In an elegant, modern space that's all white walls and wood panelling, staff serve a huge range of breakfasts, as well as crisp baguettes, small Mediterranean dishes and scrumptious pastries and coffee throughout the day – perfect for an energy injection before indulging in a little fashion shopping on nearby via de' Tornabuoni.

❤ Procacci
Via de' Tornabuoni 64r (055 211656, www.procacci1885.it/en/florence). **Open** *10am-9pm Mon-Sat; 11am-8pm Sun. Closed Aug.* **Map** *p63 J7* ⑬ *Bar & shop*

One of the few traditional shops to survive the onslaught of international designer names on this thoroughfare, the small wood-lined wine bar and shop is a favourite with nostalgic Florentines and is famous for its truffle-based specialities. In season (Oct-Dec), truffles arrive daily at around 10am, filling the room with their soft musty aroma. Try a melt-in-your-mouth sandwich filled with *prosciutto crudo* and truffled artichoke cream.

Shops
❤ La Bottega dell'Olio
Piazza del Limbo 4r (055 2670468, www. labottegadellolioflrenze.it). **Open** *Mar-Sept 10am-7pm Mon-Sat. Closed 2wks Jan. Oct-Feb 2.30-6.30pm Mon; 10am-1pm, 2-6.30pm Tue-Sat.* **Map** *p63 J9* ❹ *Gifts & souvenirs*

Fans of the 'green gold' will go wild for La Bottega dell'Olio, which stocks all things olive oil, from soaps and delicacies to olive-wood breadboards, oil dispensers and pestles and mortars.

❤ Bottega Quattro
Via dei Rondinelli 9/11/13 (055 8736290, www.shopbottegaquattro.com). **Open** *10am-7.30pm Mon-Sat; 2.30-7.30pm Sun.* **Map** *p63 J6* ❺ *Men's and women's concept boutique*

With a rustic wooden floor, repurposed antique decor and colourful walls to match its inventory (a welcome change from Florentine fashion's usual palette, where neutrals tend to reign supreme), this spacious shop is a favourite among young local tastemakers. Bottega Quattro offers a varied selection of fashion-forward international brands (Scotch & Soda is its show pony) and mid-range designers, and its expertly styled window displays will capture the attention of even the least style-conscious.

❤ Boutique Nadine
Lungarno degli Acciaiuoli 22r (055 287851, www.boutiquenadine.it). **Open** *2.30-7.30pm Mon; 10am-7.30pm Tue-Sat, noon-7pm Sun* **Map** *p63 K9* ❻ *Vintage*

This mood-brightening boutique boasts a varied selection of vintage and lovely contemporary pieces from owner Irene's brand, Orette. Gucci bags, Louis Vuitton trunks, Pucci dresses and Yves Saint Laurent

shoes are all standard finds, but the costume jewellery and household knick-knacks are easily as fun to browse through as the illustrious labels. You'll also find plenty of old but unused stock, probably dug out from dusty storerooms and still in the original packaging. A second shop in via de' Benci 32r (055 2478274) also stocks menswear.

❤ Officina de' Tornabuoni
Via de' Tornabuoni 19 (055 217481, www.odtskincare.com/en). **Open** *10.30am-8pm daily.* **Map** *p63 J7* ⑫ *Herbs & perfumes*

Housed in the 15th-century Palazzo Larderel, this is a fragrant wonderland of handmade gifts, perfumes and candles, herbal remedies, intensive facial masks and treatments, toiletries and cosmetics. You can even take a piece of the Palazzo with you: in 2015, Officina de' Tornabuoni created a home fragrance inspired by the building, characterised by notes of rose, Florentine iris and violet, among others. There's no main shop window so look for the raised entrance set off the street.

Patrizia Pepe
Via Strozzi 11/19r (055 2302518, www.patriziapepe.com). **Open** *10am-7.30pm daily.* **Map** *p63 K7* ⑭ *Fashion*

This Florentine brand is an international powerhouse steered by creative director Patrizia Bambi. The 11 stores in Florence all sell the brand's signature womenswear, which is known for being both sophisticated and playful, but the via Strozzi location is one of the most 'user-friendly' and central options. Prices are upper-end high street.

VIAJIYU
Borgo Santi Apostoli 45r (055 290380, www.viajiyu.com, www.VIAJIYU.setmore. com for apps). **Open** *by app.* **Map** *p63 J8* ⑱ *Women's shoes*

#NoHighHeels is the official hashtag and working motto of this colourful shoe boutique founded by a globetrotting American entrepreneur with no patience for impractical footwear. Catering to professional, worldly women-on-the-go (AKA 'trailblazers', as the brand puts it), VIAJIYU is a stone's throw from the flagship Ferragamo store and rents its space directly from the legendary family. Shoes are all handmade in Italy and there are countless customisable options: the pointed-toe Milano flat is a bestseller, but you'll also find tasselled loafers and low wedges. Visits are by appointment only and price points are reasonable (starting at about €445) for the level of craftsmanship and personalised customer care involved.

Santa Maria Novella

Santa Maria Novella church, the heart and namesake of this district west of the Duomo, was one of two significant buildings (the other being Santa Croce) that lay immediately outside the city walls in the 13th century. Many visitors think of the Santa Maria Novella area in functional terms – mostly because of the main railway station (named after the church). There's a bus terminal, tram and large car park all within a few short steps of each other, and the station is a stop-off point for nearly all airport shuttles or coaches into central Florence. Most car-hire firms and tour companies can be found in the neighbourhood too.

But it's not all about coming and going: plenty of people stick around for the artistic treasures, including the church and the Museo Novecento, which has increased the main square's modern and contemporary appeal since it opened in 2014. Stepping away from piazza Santa Maria Novella, you'll find a series of vibrant streets, each with an increasingly distinct identity. With a hotbed of ethnic eateries, quick lunch stops, antique shops and more, this is no longer the token 'dirty district' around the train station.

♥ Don't miss

1 Santa Maria Novella p104

Florence's definitive Dominican structure, with masterworks by Masaccio, Giotto and more.

2 Museo Novecento p103

The 20th-century art treasure house that hits 'refresh' on the Renaissance city.

3 Officina Profumo-Farmaceutica di Santa Maria Novella p113

Cosmetic products and treatments from this age-old friar-run pharmacy.

4 Caffè Giacosa p110

Stylish Roberto Cavalli-connected café and cocktail bar: the birthplace of the Negroni.

5 Ponte Santa Trinita p108

A bridge unrivalled in its elegance, originally commissioned by the Frescobaldi family.

6 Museo Marino Marini p106

Horse-and-rider sculptures by the late Pistoiese artist, flanked by hip contemporary exhibitions.

Superarchitettura (Archizoom and Superstudio, 1966-7), Museo Novecento

♥ Time to eat & drink

Pastries, cakes and more
Forno Top *p114*

Designer coffee
Caffè Giacosa *p110*

Authentic Japanese ramen
Bar Galli & Banki Ramen
p110

Classy cocktails
Uva Nera *p109*

♥ Time to shop

Books with a coffee
Todo Modo *p115*

Foodie gifts
La Bottega della Frutta *p112*

Genteel menswear
Frasi di Simone Righi *p114*

Handmade marbled paper
Alberto Cozzi *p112*

To-die-for kids' stuff
Baby Bottega *p112*

♥ Time well spent

San Paolino
*Via San Paolino 8 (off via
Palazzuolo) (055 216996).
Map p101 G6.*

From its unfinished
Romanesque façade, this
hidden church doesn't look
like much, but step inside
for a wonderful surprise.
The gilded Baroque interior
is sumptuous enough to
sit and observe at length,
and you'll probably have
the place to yourself
(Boccaccio's mention of the
church in his *Decameron*
notwithstanding).

**In the know
Getting around**

This neighbourhood hosts
Florence's transportation
hub, so options abound, but
most take you *out* of the
area rather than through
the thick of it. Much of the
district is best seen on foot,
but bus 23 will take you
from the station down via
della Scala; it has plenty of
interesting stops but is not
the most inspiring street for
an aimless wander.

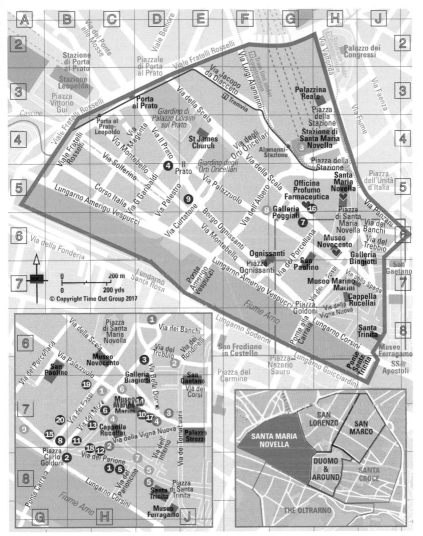

SANTA MARIA NOVELLA

Restaurants & wine bars

1 Buca Mario
2 Cantinetta Antinori
3 Fratelli Cuore
4 Il Latini
5 Rose's
6 La Spada
7 Trattoria Coco Lezzone
8 Trattoria Giorgio
9 Uva Nera

Cafés, bars & gelaterie

1 Bar Galli & Banki Ramen
2 Caffè Amerini
3 Caffè Giacosa
4 Caffè Megara
5 Mariano Alimentari

Shops

1 Alberto Cozzi
2 Anichini
3 Babele
4 Baby Bottega
5 Il Bisonte
6 La Bottega della Frutta
7 Dolceforte
8 Epoca Vintage
9 Fashion Room
10 Forno Top
11 Frasi di Simone Righi
12 Letizia Fiorini
13 Mercatino dei Ninni
14 MIO Concept Store
15 Münstermann
16 Officina Profumo-Farmaceutica
17 Otto d'ame
18 Patti & Co.
19 Peter's Tea House
20 Todo Modo

EXPLORING SANTA MARIA NOVELLA

Santa Maria Novella station (*see p107*) has a bold form that's not to everyone's taste, but the building is regarded as a masterpiece of modernism. The station has also seen a revival in recent years, with an expanded and smartened-up shopping gallery both on the main floor and downstairs, the introduction of a 24-hour restaurant-café-*pizzeria* and an international bookshop. Adjacent to the station stands the sleek, white marble **Palazzina Reale**, originally built to house the royal family on their Florentine visits, and now home to an eatery and chic outdoor venue during the summer months.

A short walk south, Leon Battista Alberti's exquisite, precision-built façade for the church of **Santa Maria Novella** (*see p104*) looks out on to the increasingly pristine piazza of the same name, which held annual chariot races on the feast day of Florence's patron saint, John the Baptist, from 1563 to 1852. The course was marked by two obelisks for the chariots to lap, both restored and still standing in the piazza, resting on turtles sculpted by Giambologna. Opposite the church, on the southern side of the square, is the **Loggia di San Paolo**, a late 15th-century arcade modelled on Brunelleschi's loggia of the Ospedale degli Innocenti in San Marco (*see p136*). Its building – the Leopoldine complex – is now home to 20th-century art hub the **Museo Novecento** (see *p103*), a colourful respite from Renaissance Florence.

In recent years, cleanup efforts, expanded pedestrianisation and key investments by city officials have gradually transitioned this square away from its once-grimy reputation. Smart, sophisticated hotels have spruced things up, and local and foreign event firms frequently organise lively pop-up markets for days, or even weeks, at a time. By night, this means the square feels more social than seedy. By day, it's always a reliably bright and pretty tourist mecca.

Walk a little south of the piazza to the triangle formed by **via dei Fossi**, **via della Spada** and **via della Vigna Nuova**. This is not just a friendly, lively area during the day, but also a well-lit, densely populated spot for night-time window-shopping. The area is cluttered with antiques emporia, designer clothes shops, cafés and *trattorie*. Next to each other in the centre of the triangle are the fine 15th-century townhouse Palazzo Rucellai (not open to the public), the **Cappella Rucellai** and the adjacent modern art museum, the **Museo Marino Marini** (*see p106*).

Workaday via Palazzuolo leads north-west from here, cutting through the heart of the district. At no.17 is the **Oratorio dei Vanchetoni**, a beautiful 1602 building that occasionally hosts free concerts. Parallel to via Palazzuolo is traffic-heavy via della Scala, location of the famous **Officina Profumo Farmaceutica di Santa Maria Novella** (*see p113*) and the **Giardino di Palazzo Corsini sul Prato**: a hidden green space lined with 16th-century sculptures, which is also the venue for the famous Artigianato e Palazzo craftsmanship showcase every spring.

The district meets the river at the exquisite **Ponte Santa Trinita** (*see p108*), named after the church on the west side of via de' Tornabuoni, opposite the iconic Palazzo Spini Feroni. Beyond piazza Carlo Goldoni, lungarno Amerigo Vespucci and borgo Ognissanti lead north-west, opening out onto piazza Ognissanti, flanked by swanky hotels and topped by the church of **Ognissanti** (*see p106*), the cloister of which houses the **Cenacolo di Ognissanti** (*see p106*). Further up, elegant residential roads lead towards Porta al Prato, part of the old city walls.

Sights & museums

Cappella Rucellai

*Via della Spada (055 216912). **Open** 10am-1pm Wed-Fri; 10am-7pm Sat-Mon. **Admission** €6 (includes Museo Marino Marini). **Map** p101 H7.*

Once part of the church of San Pancrazio (now the Museo Marino Marini, see *p106*), the chapel retains the church's charming bell tower and contains the tombs of many members of the extended family of 15th-century wool magnate Giovanni Rucellai, including that of his wife Iacopa Strozzi. It's worth a visit to see Alberti's Temple of the Santo Sepolcro: commissioned in 1467 by Giovanni, it was built to the same proportions as the Holy Sepulchre of Jerusalem in an attempt to ensure his salvation. On occasion, it hosts can't-miss concerts.

In the know
The borrowers

Join the Children's Lending Library of Florence (St James Church undercroft, via Bernardo Rucellai 9, www.childrenslibrary.altervista.org, Map *p101 E4*) and you can borrow English language books and DVDs during your stay, as well as take part in kids' activities run by the English-speaking, volunteer-run library. It's open from mid September to the end of June.

❤ Museo Novecento

Piazza Santa Maria Novella 10 (055 286132,
*www.museonovecento.it). **Open** 1 Apr-30 Sept*
9am-7pm Mon-Wed & Sat, Sun; 9am-2pm
Thur; 9am-11pm Fri. 1 Oct-31 Mar 9am-
6pm Mon-Wed, Fri-Sun; 9am-2pm Thur.
***Admission** €8.50. **Map** p101 H6.*

'Everything might be different' is the cryptic
proclamation of Maurizio Nannucci's blue
neon installation affixed above the arcades
of this museum's courtyard. Though not a
site-specific piece, Nannucci's work is fitting
in this venue, evoking how incomplete
one's experience of Florence might be
without an understanding of its more
recent artistic evolution.

Literally translating to the 'Museum of
the 1900s', this long-awaited 20th-century
art space injected much-needed fresh
energy into Florence immediately upon
its 2014 opening. The Museo Novecento's
story began with a promise made after one
of the city's most memorable disasters, the
flooding of the Arno river in November 1966
(*see p266*). With support from then-mayor
Piero Bargellini, art historian Carlo Ludovico
Ragghianti appealed to artists all over the
world to donate their works to Florence, to
replace the thousands of priceless pieces
that had been damaged or destroyed by
the waters. Those who responded – some
200 do-gooders dubbed the '*Artisti per
Firenze*' (Artists for Florence) – were told
that their work would be displayed in a
dedicated space. It took a while, but a
promise is a promise: two years shy of
the 50th anniversary of the tragedy, the
Museo Novecento opened its doors inside
the Leopoldine complex.

Italian artworks (around 300 of them, to
be exact) are placed in reverse chronological
order across 15 rooms, taking you back in
time from the 1990s to the beginning of the
20th century. Heavy hitters such as Giorgio

Italian artworks are placed in reverse chronological order, taking you back in time from the 1990s to the beginning of the 20th century

de Chirico and still life master Giorgio
Morandi are represented, along with lesser-
known figures. The selection is far from
comprehensive, but it's impressively varied,
vaunting paintings, installations, video
work, sound devices and beyond.

The Museo Novecento hosts intriguing
temporary exhibitions too (Gaetano Pesce's
gaudy *Majesty Betrayed* sculpture caused
quite a stir when it was juxtaposed with the
basilica façade for several months in late
2016 and early 2017). It is also a popular
events venue and concert space, particularly
for edgy, experimental 'sound artists'.
Numerous collaborations with local arts
and entertainment festivals take place
throughout the year; check the website for
an updated programme ahead of your visit.
One thing's for sure: this museum routinely
challenges Florence to look beyond its
Renaissance glory days.

**Album Dantesco
(Alberto Martini)**

In the know
Kids' stuff

Frequent children's activities are put on
by the organisation Mus.e. Firenze; they're
usually in Italian but English tours or
educational activities, usually centred on the
current exhibition, are offered when demand
is high. Call 055 2768224 or send an email
to info@muse.comune.fi.it to enquire.

💜 Santa Maria Novella

Piazza Santa Maria Novella (055 219257, www.smn.it). **Open** *Apr-Sept 9am-7pm Mon-Fri. Oct-Mar 9am-5.30pm Mon-Fri. Sept-June 9am-5.30pm Sat; 1-5.30pm Sun. July, August 9am-6.30pm Sat; noon-6.30pm Sun.* **Admission** *€5.* **Map** *p101 H5.*

Called Novella ('New') because it was built on the site of the ninth-century Santa Maria delle Vigne, the church dominates the piazza with its huge, geometrical façade. Santa Maria Novella was the Florentine seat of the Dominicans, an order fond of leading street brawls against suspected heretics. The piazza outside was enlarged in 1244-45 to accommodate the crowds that came to hear St Peter the Martyr, a fervent preacher of orthodox Catholicism.

The pièce de résistance of the church is the magnificent Alberti façade. In 1470, the architect incorporated the Romanesque lower storey into a refined Renaissance scheme, adding the triangular tympanum and the scrolls that mask the side nave exteriors in an exercise of consummate classical harmony. The church interior, however, was designed by the order's monks and is fittingly severe.

The church houses the *Crocifisso* by Giotto, a simple wooden crucifix that was finally returned to the church in 2001 after a 12-year restoration. It was placed in the centre of the basilica where the Dominicans had originally positioned it in 1290.

Until Vasari had them whitewashed in the mid 16th century, the church walls were covered with frescoes. Fortunately, Masaccio's *Trinità* of 1427 remains on the left nave, a triumph of trompe l'œil, with God, Christ and two saints appearing to stand in a niche watched by the patrons Lorenzo Lenzi and his wife. The sinister inscription above the skeleton on the sarcophagus reads: 'I was what you are and what I am you shall be.'

In 1485, the Dominicans let Ghirlandaio cover the walls of the **Cappella Tornabuoni**, behind the altarpiece, with scenes from the life of John the Baptist, featuring lavish contemporary Florentine interiors and a supporting cast from the Tornabuoni family, all wearing beautiful clothes – effectively making the work part-advertisement, as the family were cloth merchants. Ghirlandaio also found time to train a young Michelangelo while working on the chapel. At about the same time, Filippino Lippi was at work next door in the Cappella di Filippo Strozzi, painting scenes from the life of St Philip. A wooden crucifix by Brunelleschi, the envy of Donatello, is to the left of the altarpiece.

To compare Masaccio's easeful use of perspective with the contorted struggles of Paolo Uccello, visit the **Chiostro Verde** (green cloister) to the left of the church (via a separate entrance). Uccello's lunettes can be considered either visionary experiments of modern art or a complete perspectival mess, depending on your tolerance of artistic licence. Off the Chiostro you'll find the **Cappellone** (or **Cappella**) **degli Spagnoli**, named after the Spanish wife of Cosimo I, Eleonora di Toledo, and decorated with vibrant scenes by Andrea di Bonaiuto. Look out for the odd-looking cupola on the Duomo fresco: it's the artist's own design for the dome, ultimately rejected in favour of Brunelleschi's plan.

Uccello's lunettes can be considered either visionary experiments of modern art or a complete perspectival mess, depending on your tolerance of artistic licence

Peek inside the **Caserma Mameli** and its spectacular **Grand Cloister**, which previously served as a training centre for the Italian military police force but is soon to be incorporated into the museum complex (along with Capella del Papa and the former dormitories). Its glorious 14th-century arcaded walkway is a real treasure, lined by a fresco cycle carried out by painters of the 16th-century Florentine school. But truthfully, the way the natural light touches the sprawling green enclosed by the cloister and spills into the former dormitory, teeming with towering pillars, is far more visually striking.

Don't skip the upper level: the tiny **Cappella del Papa** (Pope's Chapel) was designed for Pope Leo X's 1515 visit to Florence – a quiet place for morning reflection and prayer prior to his meetings with city officials. The captivating *Coronation of the Virgin* scene on the north wall was painted by Ridolfo del Ghirlandaio, while a young Pontormo contributed frescoes.

Giotto: From Sheep To Great Heights

According to legend, the Florentine painter and architect Giotto di Bondone (1266-1337) was seen by the medieval master Cimabue sketching sheep on stones and was immediately apprenticed to his studio. Giotto was the first artist to break from Byzantine art with its elongated faces and heavily stylised clothes by introducing an inkling of humanism, real emotion and three-dimensional space.

Often credited as the father of the Renaissance, Giotto was well regarded by Dante, his contemporary, and in 1334 was named *Magnus Magister* (Great Master) and appointed as head Florentine architect and chief of public works. For prime examples of his work, see his *Crocifisso* in Santa Maria Novella (*see below*) frescoes of St Francis in the Bardi/Peruzzi chapels in Santa Croce (*see p148*) and his *Maestà* at the Uffizi (*see p82*). Oh, and climb his impeccably-designed bell tower in piazza del Duomo while you're at it (*see p68*).

Crocifisso (Giotto, c1290)

Cenacolo di Ognissanti

*Borgo Ognissanti 42 (055 2398700,
055 2396802). **Open** 9am-12.30pm,
4-7.30pm daily. Cenacolo and Last Supper
9am-noon Mon, Tue, Sat. **Admission** free.
Map p101 F7.*

The church of Ognissanti ('All Saints')
was founded in the 13th century by the
Umiliati, a group of monks from Lombardy.
The monks introduced the wool trade
to Florence, bringing with them great
prosperity; without them, perhaps, there
would have been no Florentine Renaissance.
The Umiliati were so rich by the 14th century
that they commissioned Giotto to paint
the *Maestà* for their high altar; 50 years
later, they got Giovanni da Milano to create
a flashier altarpiece. Both are now in the
Uffizi (*see p82*). Ognissanti was also the
parish church of the Vespucci, a family
of merchants that included 15th-century
navigator Amerigo, who sailed to the
Venezuelan coast in 1499 – and had two
continents named after him.

The church has been rebuilt numerous
times and is now visited mainly for paintings
by Ghirlandaio: among them *St Jerome*
and a *Madonna della Misericordia* that
incorporates a portrait of Amerigo Vespucci:
he's the young boy dressed in pink. To see
Ghirlandaio's masterful *Last Supper* you
have to go back outside and through the next
door. Other frescoes include a *St Augustine*
by Botticelli. In the Chapel of St Peter of
Alcantara, look for Botticelli's tomb, marked
with his family name of Filipepi.

Cenacolo di Ognissanti, the Ognissanti's
lovely cloister, accessed via a separate
entrance on borgo Ognissanti, is painted with
frescoes illustrating the life of St Francis. The
cloister's main point of interest, however,
is Ghirlandaio's most famous *Last Supper*,
dated 1480, housed in the refectory. There's
also a museum of Franciscan bits and bobs.

Galleria Biagiotti Arte Contemporanea

*Via delle Belle Donne 39r, Santa Maria
Novella (055 214757, www.artbiagiotti.com).
Open 3-7pm Tue-Fri or by appt. Closed Aug.
Map p101 J7.*

American Carole Biagiotti runs this
stunning 15th-century converted atrium
gallery like a fairy godmother, supporting
young international artists. Installations
are a favourite, and have previously featured
elephants in 'un-gilded' cages and even
the artists themselves in 'live' works. The
gallery also collaborates with leading
international institutions and universities,
as seen through past exhibitions such as
the provocative *ReSignifications* show,
which subverted the prevailing tropes

in the representation of black bodies in
the Western art canon. Pieces often sell
to collectors unseen.

Galleria Poggiali

*Via della Scala 35a (055 287748,
www.galleriapoggiali.com). **Open**
10am–7pm Tue-Sat. **Map** p101 G6.*

This structurally stark gallery, a series
of arched spaces, showcases the works of
some of Italy's best-known young artists, as
well as those of emerging and established
international figures. Past exhibitions have
touched on heady philosophical themes
(Zhivago Duncan's *Faith and Fathom*). The
space also partners with local associations to
host one-of-a-kind events for hip arty types:
collaborators have included experimental
music enthusiasts Tempo Reale.

❤ Museo Marino Marini

*Piazza San Pancrazio (055 219432,
www.museomarinomarini.it). **Open**
10am-7pm Sat-Mon; 10am-1pm Wed-Fri.
Admission €6 (includes Cappella Rucellai).
No cards. **Map** p101 J7.*

The original Albertian church on this
site, San Pancrazio, was redesigned to
accommodate the works of prolific sculptor
and painter Marino Marini (1901-80),
who hailed from nearby Pistoia. It's now
a huge, bright and modern space filled
predominantly with sculptures on the
theme of horse and rider; the central exhibit
is the 6m (20ft) *Composizione Equestre*. The
second floor has a series of other bronze
and polychrome plaster pieces, including
the hypnotic *Nuotatore* (Swimmer) and
some fabulous colourful paintings and
sculptures of dancers and jugglers created
during the early 1950s. The Marini is also
a trendy and experimental events venue,
frequently hosting public symposiums,

In the know
Station savvy

Gone are the days when grumpily waiting
for a delayed train meant dawdling in a dirty
station. Florence's main railway hub, the
Santa Maria Novella station, has undergone
a revival. Shopping on both the main
floor and the lower gallery has increased
considerably with the addition of many
mass market shops (Sephora, Tiger, Mango).
Instead of twiddling your thumbs, put them
to work on the ground floor public piano, or
head to the 24-hour *pizzeria*-bar-restaurant
Fratelli Cuore, a welcoming, well-lit venue
ideal for relaxing and refueling pre-night
train departure (*see p108*).

Santa Maria Novella Station

Florence's fabulous example of modernist architecture

Florence doesn't do modern architecture terribly well. Amid Brunelleschi's and Michelangelo's marvels in the centre, the city is wary of introducing anything that could upset the Renaissance rhythms. Outside the gates, however, architectural anomalies such as the ultra-harsh Palazzo di Giustizia or the bizarre 1970s Condiminio in San Jacopino (piazza San Jacopino 5b) are often viewed as overcompensation for the long tradition of architectural reticence. So, it's rather surprising that in the heart of the historic centre, in Santa Maria Novella station, the city can boast at least one glorious example of Italian modernist architecture – albeit one with unpleasant associations.

Designed in 1932 by a group of architects called the Gruppo Toscano (Tuscan Group), overseen by lead architect Giovanni Michelucci, the sleek, low lines of the building, constructed between 1932 and 1935, belie their origins. The Gruppo's plans, submitted as part of a competition to design a replacement for ageing Leopolda station, had to be approved by Benito Mussolini, who understandably was rather taken with the idea of a building that, viewed from above, was based on the *fascio littorio*, the logo of his National Fascist Party. The plans won the competition, but with hindsight, it's plain they deserved to. View it from any angle, and it looks beautiful. Not only a key piece of Italian modernism and one of the country's finest examples of the Functionalist style, Santa Maria Novella station – thanks to Mussolini's approval of the design – also ushered in an acceptance of modernity in Italy that has had a huge impact on the country's design and architecture.

The station's influences clearly lay outside the country – in the work of Frank Lloyd Wright, and the Viennese architecture of Adolf Loos and Josef Hoffman – but it's a wholly original design whose exterior scale and brickwork respond to Leon Battista Alberti's gorgeous façade for the Santa Maria Novella church it sits opposite, and whose predominantly glass and metal interior is so light and airy that, despite its 59 million annual passengers, it always feels spacious. This feeling is heightened by the horizontal planes of the concourse, making the most of the station's width and filling it with light that streams through angled skylights.

The interior, including the benches and platforms, was designed by Angiolo Mazzoni, an architect from the Ministry of Communication, but it echoes the exterior's determinedly modern stance and use of materials, and in its 1930s feel can't help but draw you into pondering what horrendous, tragic scenes must have been played out here. If you're in any doubt, find the plaque near Platform 8: a moving memorial to the thousands of Jews who were deported from the station to Nazi concentration camps during World War II.

concerts and the like, as well as VIP parties now and then. Temporary exhibitions are unlike anything else in Florence: the museum's high-energy administration breathes new life into the space with the annual appointment of a visiting director, Italian or foreign, whose vision shapes the following year's programming.

❤ Ponte Santa Trinita
Accessed via lungarno Corsini or lungarno Guicciardini. **Map** *p101 J9.*

Considered by many to be the most beautiful bridge in the world, Ponte Santa Trinita's elliptical arch links piazza Santa Trinita with the Oltrarno. Built in 1252 on the initiative of the Frescobaldi family, it was rebuilt in 1346 and again in 1567. It's this version, by Ammannati (but perhaps to a design by Michelangelo) that stands today. The statues at each end represent the four seasons, and were placed there in 1608 to celebrate Cosimo II's marriage to Maria of Austria. Bombed on the night of 3 August 1944 by retreating Germans, the bridge was rebuilt in 1955 in the same position and to the same design.

The head of the most famous statue, *Spring*, by Pietro Francavilla, on the north-east side of the bridge, remained lost until 1961, when a council employee dredged it up during a routine clean-up and claimed the reward offered by a US newspaper for its return.

Santa Trinita
Piazza Santa Trinita (055 216912). **Open** *8am-noon, 4-6pm Mon-Sat; 4-6pm Sun.* **Admission** *free.* **Map** *p101 J8.*

This plain church was built in the 13th century over the ruins of two earlier churches belonging to the Vallombrosans. The order was founded in 1038 by San Giovanni Gualberto Visdomini, who spent much of his life attempting to persuade pious aristocrats to surrender their wealth and live a life of austerity. The order became extremely wealthy and powerful, reaching a peak in the 16th and 17th centuries, when its huge fortress abbey at Vallombrosa, in the Casentino countryside north of Arezzo, was built. Santa Trinita's façade was made at the end of the 16th century by Bernardo Buontalenti (who created the Giardino di Boboli's Grotta Grande; *see p169* Walk), but the church is well worth a visit for the Cappella Sassetti alone.

This chapel was luminously frescoed in 1486 by Ghirlandaio with scenes from the life of St Francis: one, set in the piazza della Signoria, features Lorenzo il Magnifico and his children.

Restaurants & wine bars

Buca Mario €€€
Piazza degli Ottaviani 16r (055 214179, www.bucamario.com). **Open** *from 7pm daily.* **Map** *p101 H7* ❶ *Traditional Italian*

Housed in a 16th-century cellar, this traditional Tuscan eatery gets a lot of attention, particularly for its Florentine steak. Apart from said *bistecca*, Buca Mario doesn't prepare many dishes notably better than its competitors, but there's something truly special about its walk-down location and homely ambience (a nice touch is the discreet private dining room, which requires booking three days in advance). The homemade gnocchi are a top choice for a first course.

Cantinetta Antinori
Piazza degli Antinori 3 (055 292234, www.cantinetta-antinori.com). **Open** *noon-2.30pm, 7-10.30 pm Mon-Sat. Closed 3wks Aug.* **Map** *p101 J6* ❷ *Wine bar*

Continuing to attract well-dressed tourists and classy locals since its opening in 1965, this upscale wine bar occupies an elegantly vaulted ground-floor room of the 15th-century Palazzo Antinori, the historic home of one of Tuscany's foremost wine-producing families. Expect a wide variety of wines (including selections from Piedmont, Apulia and Lombardy, as well as Tuscany), plus *grappa* and spirits. The food menu features seasonal, simple items meant to complement the wine, not the other way around. There are textbook versions of Florentine classics, such as *pappa al pomodoro*, along with a few worthwhile desserts (pear pie with mascarpone or the chestnut-flour cake, especially in autumn).

Fratelli Cuore €
Piazza della Stazione (attached to SMN station) (055 2670024, www.fratellicuore.it). **Open** *24hrs daily.* **Map** *p101 G4* ❸ *Pizzeria, bar & grill*

Quality dining options in the station's immediate vicinity were scarce before Fratelli Cuore entered the scene in 2015. Neapolitan-style pizzas are the speciality here: the five made-fresh varieties are prepared in a wood-fired oven. Simple, classic pastas (*carbonara, amatriciana* and so forth), salads (go for the fennel-topped *Cuore*) and burgers (named after major Italian train stations) are also available. Though there's not much ambience to speak of, this place is priceless for those in transit, particularly at odd hours. It's always open, saving the red-eyed train travellers from sloppy chains and offering a safe haven if you're stuck waiting for late-night airport shuttles and the like.

Il Latini €€

Via de' Palchetti 6r (055 210916, www.illatini.com). **Open** *12.30-2pm, 7-10.30pm Tue-Sun. Closed last wk Dec.* **Map** *p101 H7* ④ *Traditional Italian*

Run by the Latini family since 1950, this rustic eatery has become a Florence classic. Rather hidden, yet overrun by tourists and the odd Florentine, what keeps people coming back to Latini is the *ciccia* (meat) – and great hunks of it too. Queues are inevitable after 8pm when reservations are no longer taken and, once inside, it'll be noisy and you'll probably be sharing a table with other customers, but that's all part of the fun. Skip the mediocre *primi*, and dive into the hefty *secondi*: this is a good place to order *salsicce e fagioli* (sausage and beans, a Tuscan classic) or, of course, Florentine steak. Il Latini also produces a fine, sludgy green olive oil, and some decent wines: the house red is very drinkable.

Rose's €€

Via del Parione 26r (055 287090, www.roses. it). **Open** *noon-3.30pm, 7pm-1.30am Mon-Sat.* **Map** *p101 J8* ⑤ *Traditional Italian*

Born as a bar, this restaurant has some quirky tendencies, and the cornflower-blue velvet décor proves it. It's often busy with a young crowd from local offices. Lunch specialities are burgers, chicken curry over rice and mixed salads; dinner brings standard and not-so-ordinary pasta dishes (*taglierini* with Porcini mushrooms, ragu-topped *pappardelle*, *pici* with dried tomatoes and fava beans).

La Spada €€

Via della Spada 62r (055 218757, www. laspadaitalia.com). **Open** *noon-10.30pm daily.* **Map** *p101 H7* ⑥ *Traditional Italian*

A low-cost option for lunch or a snack, this centrally located *rosticceria* has been selling delicious dishes to go for many years (the entrance to the *rosticceria* is on the via del Moro side of the building). You can also eat inside the spacious restaurant: the menu is more or less the same whether you choose to sit in or take away, but you'll pay about 50% less if you do the latter. *Primi* change daily, but most of them are good (the *pici* with chickpeas is a favourite), and you can always find a bounty of roast meats and grilled vegetables. The rosemary roast potatoes are simply delicious. On Fridays, you can usually find fish and seafood specials, including sumptuous *spaghetti alle vongole* (spaghetti with clams).

Trattoria Coco Lezzone €€

Via del Parioncino 26r (055 287178, www. cocolezzone.it). **Open** *noon-2.15pm, 7-10.15pm Mon-Sat. Closed 3wks Aug & Tue for dinner.* **No cards.** **Map** *p101 F5* ⑦ *Traditional Italian*

Respect for tradition, hand-selected prime ingredients and a centuries-old wood-burning stove mark out this authentic *trattoria*, in one of Florence's few medieval towers still standing. Open since the 1800s, current owner Gianfranco Paoli has brought this temple of Tuscan tastes back to the limelight, serving simple, well-made classics on the long, family-style tables. Dishes on the menu are thoroughly Tuscan, including traditional soups, home-made pastas and a range of wild game cooked (often for hours on end) in the early 20th-century oven. You'll find a wide variety of roast meats, seafood on Fridays and if you want to try Coco's Florentine steak, you'll have to order it in advance. It's hidden on a backstreet surrounded by parking garages, and you may get lost looking for it. Tip: don't give up.

Trattoria Giorgio €

Via Palazzuolo 100r (055 284302, www.trattoriadagiorgio.it). **Open** *noon-2.30pm & 6-10pm Mon-Sat.* **Map** *p101 F5* ⑧ *Traditional Italian*

There's nothing touristy or ironic about this family-run, modest *trattoria*, not even the giant *Mona Lisa* reproduction on the wall. The D'Amico family hail from Abruzzo and on Thursdays offer a special menu showcasing their regional specialities. The rest of the time, there's a sizeable selection of simple first courses (four-cheese penne pasta, sage and butter ravioli) and tasty mains (Roman-style *saltimbocca*, peppery beef stew). You can order à la carte, but you'll come out way ahead if you opt for the generous fixed menus: €13 at lunchtime, €15 at dinner, or €28 if you're in the mood for Florentine steak, all with wine and water included.

♥ Uva Nera

Borgo Ognissanti 25r (055 0121189, www. uvaneraenoteca.it). **Open** *11.30am-10pm Mon-Sat.* **Map** *p101 G7* ⑨ *Wine bar*

The wines at this place are never set in stone: 'blame' it on passionate young owner-manager Costanza, who can hardly contain her enthusiasm for researching, then spotlighting, the producers she discovers. She personally visits each of her suppliers before serving their sips or snacks, trusting her own taste and staying firmly committed to small and mid-size companies, with a particular affinity for biodynamic and organic producers. Tuscans are always front and centre, but you'll occasionally find options from Piedmont and further afield. At *aperitivo* time, there's either a generous buffet or a custom-prepared platter, typically filled with scrumptious cold cuts, fresh cheeses with well-matched marmalades and other high quality snacks. The cherry on top is the place's look and feel: retro, but never forced. Antique furnishings are peppered throughout (the chairs are repurposed seats from a former cinema).

Cafés, bars & gelaterie

♥ Bar Galli & Banki Ramen

Via de' Banchi 14r (055 213776). **Open** *7am-7pm Sun-Mon; 7am-6.30pm Tue-Sat. Japanese food served 7-10pm Tue-Fri; 12.30-2.30pm, 7-10pm Sat.* **Map** *p101 J6* ❶ *Bar*

This is one of the most delightfully bizarre hybrids you'll come across in downtown Florence: a traditional, family-run Florentine bar by day, morphing into a Japanese ramen joint by night (and at the lunch hour on Saturdays). Early in the day, it's a friendly spot for a bite of breakfast before you visit Santa Maria Novella; at lunchtime, family matriarch Piera is the lady of the house, taking orders for *primi* that are above-average bar standard, if not particularly memorable, save for the *paccheri* (southern Italian tube pasta) dishes. When the ramen hour arrives, many of the bar staff stay on, helping the Japanese cooks and waiting staff serve the hungry masses. The setting in the bar's back room is spartan (Formica-topped tables and ugly strip lighting) and the choice is limited to ramen noodles and soups, plus *gyozo* (dumplings) and rice dishes, but it's very good and it's cheap. A steaming bowl of noodles costs from €7; the best deal is the combined menus, from €10 to €15. Chase the saltiness with a bottle of crisp, cold Asahi beer.

Caffè Amerini

Via della Vigna Nuova 63r (055 284941). **Open** *7.30am-8.30pm Mon-Sat. Closed 2wks Aug.* **Map** *p101 H7* ❷ *Café*

Smart but cosy, Amerini gets so crowded at lunchtime that you might be seated with unknown companions at your small table. The simple sandwiches and pastas are nothing special, but the ambience is lovely for a morning cappuccino or afternoon dessert (stop by after the lunch rush to sample luscious lemon tart relatively undisturbed).

♥ Caffè Giacosa

Via della Spada 10r (055 2776328, www.caffegiacosa.it). **Open** *7.45am-8.30pm Mon-Fri; 8.30am-8.30pm Sat; 12.30-8.30pm Sun.* **Map** *p101 J7* ❸ *Café*

Adjacent to Florentine fashion legend Roberto Cavalli's prestigious shop it'd be easy to mistake this café as being strictly for the style set. Don't fall for it: it's chic, but it's hardly snooty, routinely attracting a clientele that defies categorisation by age, nationality or even fashion sense. Staff members are always congenial, particularly the handsome baristas serving up arguably the city's best cappuccino (it's drizzled in chocolate, if you weren't daydreaming about it already). The tiny space is often packed at peak breakfast hour (around 9am usually), and scoring a seat is next to impossible on weekend afternoons. What keeps the people coming? The flaky pastries, decadent cakes, pralines and cream-filled delights, high fashion portraits and banquette seating (sit down indoors at no extra charge in the mornings) are all solid starts.

Caffè Megara

Via della Spada 15-17r (055 211837, www.facebook.com/Caffe-Megara-122993461108158). **Open** *7am-1am daily (lunch noon-3pm).* **Map** *p101 J7* ❹ *Café*

An atmospheric stop for a morning coffee – with plenty of seating – Megara is always full at lunchtimes with tourists and loyal regulars who know about the inexpensive daily specials. Pasta dishes (tortellini with prosciutto and mushrooms, trofie with pesto) or salads (Greek, Caprese) are always a safe bet. It gets even busier when big matches are on, and retro pop music plays onscreen when there's no big game to speak of.

> **In the know**
> **Birthplace of the Negroni**
>
> Caffè Giacosa's original site is said to be the birthplace of the Negroni, a broody concoction of gin, Campari and red vermouth. Between 1919 and 1920, count Camillo Negroni was among the illustrious regulars, and bartender Fosco Scarselli often served him an unusual spin on the standard Americano cocktail by adding a splash of gin. When other customers caught on, the new cocktail was called Negroni, after the count. Today's Caffè Giacosa serves the refreshing Negroni *Sbagliato*, prepared with prosecco instead of gin, lifting a little of the cocktail's 'dark cloud'.

❤ Café culture

Florentines, like many Italians, are fiercely loyal to their neighbourhood bars. It's not uncommon for a friend to ask '*Dove fai colazione?*' (Where do you have breakfast?) or '*Qual è il tuo bar?*' (What's your bar?) when they discover where you live. Offices generally have an established afternoon coffee stop where the barista is likely to offer discounts, as well as friendly banter, perhaps even the occasional free espresso.

So, the gilded historic cafés lining piazza della Repubblica and scattered throughout the Duomo-Signoria area are rare entries in the routines of many Florentines. However, on Sundays or special occasions it's not uncommon to spot well-coiffed locals leafing through the newspaper at **Giubbe Rosse** (*see p73*) or knocking back an espresso at **Caffè Rivoire** (*see p91*) during a shopping break. What you will hardly ever see, however, is a Florentine paying to sit on a covered terrace looking out onto a *piazza*.

Despite the fact that a cappuccino with a view will cost you at least twice as much as it will at your corner bar, the refined bars, tea rooms and chocolate shops dotting the centre have a long history that makes many of them well worth visiting. Giubbe Rosse, named after Garibaldi's 'Red Shirts', was an important hub for the Futurist movement in the early 20th century. It also drew poets such as Ardengo Soffici, Eugenio Montale and their bohemian brethren; today's wall art still attests to this legacy. Across the piazza stands **Paszkowski** (*see p75*), a 19th-century institution that was originally a Polish-owned brewery. Now, it's better known for its stiff coffee, inexpensive takeaway lunches and live music in the evenings; the sound often dominates the square, as if to remind the Hard Rock Café across the way that this historic haunt isn't going anywhere.

For underwhelming service, but opulent seating areas and general grandeur, scoot to the nearby **Gilli** (*see p74*), with its eye-catching trifles in the window. Equally elegant, but noticeably friendlier, is **Caffè Giacosa** (*see opposite*) in Santa Maria Novella. In the morning, the baristas make mouthwatering *cappuccini* topped with chocolate. Giacosa is now an extension of the Roberto Cavalli boutique, but its original location is believed to be the spot where the Negroni cocktail was invented (*see opposite*), so try something bitter or Campari-based come *aperitivo* hour.

For a homely vibe, make for piazza Santo Spirito and enjoy an espresso at **Caffè Ricchi** (*see p173*), one of the Oltrarno's old standbys. The restaurant leaves much to be desired, but the bar has a delightful back room where you can sit amid eclectic depictions of the nearby Basilica of Santo Spirito. Or why not steal away to **Caffè Pasticceria Serafini** (*see p197*), near to piazza Beccaria, if you're in the mood for well-crafted sweets; the selection of biscuits, pastries, eclairs and other treats is a delight.

Mariano Alimentari

Via del Parione 19r (055 214067). **Open**
*8am-3pm, 5-7.30pm Mon-Fri; 8am-3pm
Sat. Closed 3wks Aug.* **Map** *p101 J8* ❺
Sandwich bar

Tucked out of the way on via del Parione,
this walk-in place is tough to beat for a quick
sandwich break when you're out exploring.
Tuscan bread is filled with delicious
ingredients such as marinated aubergines,
artichokes or oil-preserved pecorino, and an
array of other delicacies. Have a coffee at the
bar or in the vaulted wine cellar.

Shops

❤ Alberto Cozzi

*Via del Parione 35r (055 294968, www.
facebook.com/AlbertoCozzi1908).* **Open**
*3-7pm Mon; 10am-1pm, 3-7pm Tue-Fri; Sat
by appt.* **Map** *p101 H8* ❶ *Gifts & souvenirs*

Part bookbinder's workshop and showroom,
part Florentine gift paradise, this
generations-strong shop has been working
with libraries to restore books since the
turn of the 20th century. If you're lucky, the
bookbinders will be at work in the adjacent
lab as you shop. Browse through a wonderful
selection of marbled stationery, gold-flecked
paper and leather-bound journals, which
can all be personalised when you purchase.

Anichini

*Via del Parione 59r (055 284977,
www.anichini.net).* **Open** *3.30-7.30pm
Mon; 9.30am-1.30pm, 3.30-7.30pm Tue-
Sat. Closed 1wk Aug.* **Map** *p101 G8* ❷
Children's clothing

Ridiculously cute kids' clothing has been
the mainstay of this shop, housed in the
15th-century Ricasoli Palace, for 100 years,
and some of the styles have barely changed.
Christening and ceremonial gowns plus
clothing for newborns are as traditional
as they come, featuring hand-smocking,
embroidery and lace. Older girls will
adore the frilly frocks and the little boys'
suits are to die for.

Babele

*Via delle Belle Donne 41r (055 283312, www.
babelefirenze.com).* **Open** *3.30-7.30pm Mon;
10am-1pm, 3.30-7.30 pm Tue-Sat.* **Map**
p101 J6 ❸ *Bookshop & gallery*

A delightful art bookshop and gallery
stocking mainly limited editions, numbered
prints and handmade stationery. The small
and delightfully disordered venue also
regularly hosts events and exhibitions.

❤ Baby Bottega

*Via il Prato 53-55r (055 286091,
www.babybottega.com).* **Open** *10am-1pm,
2.30-7.30pm Mon-Sat.* **Map** *p101 D5* ❹
Children's interiors and toys

Owner and chief curator Daisy Diaz bridges
her identities as an American interior
designer and an in-the-know Italian *mamma*
at this playful and punchy concept boutique.
The focus is on children's interiors, with
cool furnishings, light fixtures, accessories
and room accents from all the hippest
international brands. The shop also teems
with toys, party supplies, and practical,
foldable, flight-friendly pushchairs by
trailblazing brand Bugaboo. To top it off,
Baby Bottega's a fab place to find out about
kids' events and activities about town.

Il Bisonte

*Via del Parione 31r (055 215722,
www.ilbisonte.com).* **Open** *10am-7pm Mon-
Sat; 11am-6.30pm Sun.* **Map** *p101 H8* ❺
Leather

A renowned, long-established
outlet for top-tier soft leather bags,
accessories and rugged cases.

❤ La Bottega della Frutta

*Via de' Federighi 31r (055 2398590,
www.facebook.com/La-Bottega-della-
Frutta-393945310670529/).* **Open**
8.30am-7.30pm Mon-Sat. Closed Aug. **Map**
p101 H7 ❻ *Groceries*

Your neighbourhood supermarket will never
look the same after you see the smörgåsbord
of fruits, veggies, and novelty items in this
hidden foodie nook. Sift through the wines,
vintage balsamic vinegars, truffle-scented
oils and speciality sweets, and if you need
tips, look to Elisabetta and Francesco, the
dynamic duo running the show.

Dolceforte

*Via della Scala 21 (055 219116,
www.dolceforte.it).* **Open** *10am-1pm, 3.30-
7.45pm Mon and Wed-Sat; 3.30-7.45pm Tue.*
Map *p101 G6* ❼ *Chocolate*

Connoisseur chocolates, plus novelty-
shaped treats such as chocolate Duomos. In
hot months, melting stock is replaced with
jams, sugared almond flours and jars of
gianduja, a chocolate hazelnut spread. It's
not just for those with a sweet tooth: truffle
sauces, balsamic vinegar and PGI extra
virgin olive oil all feature.

Epoca Vintage

*Via dei Fossi 6r (055 216698,
www.epocavintage.it).* **Open** *3.30-7.30pm
Sun; 10am-1.30pm, 3.30-7.30pm Mon-Sat.*
Map *p101 G7* ❽ *Vintage*

♥ Officina Profumo-Farmaceutica di Santa Maria Novella

Via della Scala 16 (055 216276, www. smnovella.it). **Open** *9am-8pm daily.* **Admission** *free.* **Map** *p101 G5* ⑯ *Herbs & fragrances*

A beautiful 13th-century frescoed chapel in Santa Maria Novella is home to one of the world's oldest herbal pharmacies – now a global brand. The Officina Profumo-Farmaceutica di Santa Maria Novella was officially founded in 1612 by Fra' Angiolo Marchissi, though its origins date back as far as 1221, to the time of the Dominican friars. As you reach the entrance, the scent of the *antica farmacia's* potpourri fills the air, a mix of locally grown flowers and herbs, macerated in terracotta jars.

A domed marble passageway leads to the main hall, which was turned into the shop in 1848. It's lined with mahogany and glass cabinets, and filled with the pharmacy's signature soaps (reputed to be the best in the world), delicate glass bottles of pure oils and perfume essences, and scented paper. Through a gilded archway is the apothecary, a grand antechamber decorated with Medici portraits, where herbal concoctions are still weighed up on brass scales. A back room, dotted with ancient apothecary tools, is where jams, sweets and soaps are packaged in lovely cream vellum boxes.

The pharmacy's serenity and beauty stand in stark contrast to the bloodthirsty nature of some of its past patrons. The pharmacy must have its roots in the gentler side of Florence's torture-loving Dominican monks. Perfumes – including the original Eau de Cologne – were also created here for the notorious Caterina de' Medici. And more recently, the olfactory powers of Thomas Harris's *Hannibal* the cannibal led him to the Officina Profumo-Farmaceutica when it came to choosing a scent for his paramour.

But it's the contemporary boom for luxury natural products that has transformed the *farmacia* from local icon into internationally coveted brand with branches in New York, Tokyo, Miami and more, as well as numerous global retailers. The original lavender-smelling salts, 'anti-hysteria' Acqua di Santa Maria Novella, 14th-century Acqua di Rose and powder produced from the ground rhizomes of irises are practically unchanged formulas. Other renowned items include orange-blossom water and pomegranate perfume. However, with globalisation comes the march of modernity: you can now find parabens in the rose cream and tan-prolonging shower gel alongside the medieval ladies' favourite: skin whitening powder. If perusing all the many different products feels too overwhelming, numerous prepackaged gift sets can help streamline your shopping.

History buffs and those curious about the finer points of the monks' production should step inside the dedicated museum space. It offers a look at work tools used in ages past, as well as the collections of copper and bronze objects and Maiolica ceramic pharmaceutical containers.

A back room, dotted with ancient apothecary tools, is where jams, sweets and soaps are packaged In lovely cream vellum boxes

Owner Valentina Ferroni's grandfather ran the first second-hand clothing stall at the San Lorenzo market, so it's safe to say vintage is in her genes (and vintage jeans are found in her shop every now and then). Epoca has an array of top-tier garments, typically organised by colour rather than label (Chanel, Gucci, Ferragamo, Hermes and Celine aren't hard to spot).

Fashion Room
Via il Prato 7r (055 213270, www.fashionroom.it). **Open** *9.30am-7.30pm Mon-Fri, 10am-1pm, 3-7pm Sat.* **Map** *p101 E5* ❾ *Books*

An unrivalled collection of books, catalogues and magazines on interior design, architecture and fashion, including hard-to-find limited editions and coffee-table tomes. It's no coincidence that this shop is a stone's throw from Villa Favard, which houses premier fashion institute Polimoda.

❤ Forno Top
Via della Spada 23r (055 212461, www. fornotop.it). **Open** *7.30am-7.30pm Mon-Sat.* **No cards.** **Map** *p101 J7* ❿ *Bakery*

Delcious sandwiches, hot focaccia and other flatbreads, fabulous carrot or chocolate and pear cakes, and seasonal specialities, including traditional Tuscan sweets, in this stylish bakery beloved by locals. Pop by in the morning for a decadent croissant.

❤ Frasi di Simone Righi
Via de' Federighi 7r (055 211015, lnx.upper. simonerighi.it). **Open** *3.30-7.30pm Mon; 9.30am-1pm, 3.30-7.30pm Tue-Sat.* **Map** *p101 H7* ⓫ *Menswear*

Well-coiffed, ultra-cool Simone Righi is a local fashion icon who's been serially snapped by the likes of Scott Schuman, also known as pioneering street style photographer The Sartorialist. His shop is a must-stop for stylish men looking to stay one step ahead of the crowd in impeccably fitted blazers, coats, suits and more. Bespoke shirts generally take one month to complete and are shipped all over the world.

Letizia Fiorini
Via del Parione 60r (055 216504). **Open** *11am-7pm Tue-Sat.* **Map** *p101 H8* ⓬ *Toys & gifts*

This shop's namesake owner is a character and a half, happy to make colourful conversation about her handmade puppets, dolls, pillows and other gift items, all crafted in-house (in the back room of the tiny shop, in fact). You'll find fairytale favourites (and villains), milkmaids and witches, conniving cats and characters from Italian fables.

Mercatino dei Ninni
Via dei Federighi 11r (055 291604, www.facebook.com/Mercatino-di-Ninni-1690313241195199). **Open** *10.30am-1pm Tue-Sun; 2:30-7pm daily.* **Map** *p101 H7* ⓭ *Vintage & contemporary clothing*

This well-curated vintage and contemporary womenswear shop is run by a former model whose stylish daughter also makes frequent appearances in-house. Items stocked are fairly priced, but hardly inexpensive, since the standard rack on a random day might include a vintage Chanel jacket, Narciso Rodriguez dress, Yves Saint Laurent blouse and other one-of-a-kind finds. Beyond investment pieces for your wardrobe, there are usually a hotchpotch of bags, from boxy Kelly-inspired classics to trendy backpacks, along with shoes from hip contemporary and diffusion lines such as See by Chloe.

MIO Concept Store
Via della Spada 34r (055 2645543, www.mio-concept.com). **Open** *3-7pm Mon; 10am-1.30pm, 2.30-7pm Tue-Sat.* **Map** *p101 J7* ⓮ *Design & gifts*

A veritable cabinet of curiosities, this tiny shop teems with design objects for the home and has an ongoing collaboration with Florence's famous French street artist CLET. Finely crafted items, from statement necklaces and mood rings to journals, bric-a-brac, scarves and wall art, are carefully chosen by charismatic German owner-founder Antje d'Almeida, a self-professed globetrotter with a Zen vibe and a knack for pinpointing exactly what her customers want. The inventory is in constant flux, but a reliable favourite is the colourful paper hunting trophies handmade in Ravenna. Emerging local designers are also given space.

Münstermann
Piazza Goldoni 2r (055 210660, www.munstermann.it). **Open** *10am-1pm, 2-7pm Tue-Sat.* **Map** *p101 G7* ⓯ *Herbs & perfumes*

This charming shell-shaped corner icon was opened in 1897, a stone's throw from Ponte alla Carraia, and still has its original shop fittings. Along with potpourri and perfumes, it stocks pharmaceutical and herbal medicines, toiletries, silver pillboxes, hair accessories, skincare products, sun protection cream and bathroom oddities. The house brand products all use high quality, natural ingredients and follow tried and tested recipes.

Otto d'ame

Via della Spada 19r (055 2654100, www.ottodame.it). Open noon-7.30pm Sun; 10am-7.30pm Mon-Sat. Map p101 J7  *Womenswear*

This ultra-feminine flagship boutique (with branches in Paris and Milan) is heavy on the blush hues, ethereal dresses and Mary Janes, yet it never flits too far into Manic Pixie Dream Girl territory. Otto d'Ame has its own brand, displaying velvet sandals to practical city-proof boots and smart knitwear to embellished purses. The setup of the shop's light-filled interior changes every two weeks, so the stylish staff always has a fresh perspective on what's in stock.

Patti & Co.

Via dei Federighi 10r (055 0464897, www.facebook.com/PATTI-Co-282940415200008). Open 3.30-7pm Mon, 11am-7pm Tue-Sat. Map p101 H8 ⓲ *Design & fashion*

This self branded cabinet of curiosities is run by a true 21st-century bohemian, a lady named Patti who's inspired by all things Japan. She's also got a penchant for World War II military gear, which hangs, unassumingly, alongside splashy kimonos and plaid pieces that seem culled from a stylish grandparent's attic. Beyond the clothes, you'll find kitschy wall art, candelabras, tea and kitchen sets, knobs,

pulls and countless design items you couldn't dream up if you tried, yet you'll know you need them when you see them.

Peter's Tea House

Via de' Fossi 57r, Santa Maria Novella (055 215913, www.peters-teahouse.com). Open 3-7pm Mon; 10am-1.30pm, 3-7pm Tue-Sat. Closed 3wks Aug. Map p101 H7 ⓳ *Teahouse*

Hundreds of different types of tea from around the world, with biscuits to dunk in them and a range of tea-themed gift sets.

❤ Todo Modo

Via dei Fossi 15r (055 2399110, www.todomodo.org). Open noon-8pm Mon; 10am-8pm Tue, Wed, Sun; 10am-9pm Thurs-Sat. Map p101 G7 ⓴ *Bookshop/café*

The selection of reading material here is great, but this expansive, independent bookshop-café looks made with first romantic meetings in mind. It's a popular study space and work spot for freelancing locals, and its spacious back room often hosts presentations and events. The café food is nothing to write home about, but you can enjoy a coffee, tea or glass of wine as you leaf through a (purchased) book and people-watch. The majority of the shop's books are in Italian, but there's a sizeable English section where you'll find novels, coffee table treasures and a limited selection of 'airport bestsellers'.

Todo Modo

San Lorenzo

Teeming with life, San Lorenzo is loved and hated in equal measure: adored for the bustle of Mercato Centrale and its boisterous traditional lunch spots, and disliked for its overcrowded tourist traps. This is a neighbourhood of contrasts: the incongruously unfinished façade of San Lorenzo church itself and the chapels of the Medici family are rather serious affairs, but the district is also marked out by the fun and frenetic activity generated by the huge market, the high number of tourists, and the plethora of shops, delis, cafés and doughnut stands.

The market of San Lorenzo is the hub of the area, spreading over a swathe of *piazze* north of the church of San Lorenzo. Tacky street stalls are what keep the district ticking, selling everything from University of Florence hoodies to aprons decorated with *David*'s nether regions. However, the stalls are not as sprawling as they once were, thanks largely to the efforts of then-mayor and now ex-premier Matteo Renzi. In 2014, in an attempt to declutter the district and to bring a little more dignity to its namesake basilica, local officials cleared all the stalls out of piazza San Lorenzo and tidied up the clusters of them on piazza del Mercato Centrale and its adjacent streets.

♥ **Don't miss**

1 Cappelle Medicee *p121*
The Medici family's grand mausoleum.

2 Palazzo Medici Riccardi *p120*
A stately Renaissance palace, home to Benozzo Gozzoli's frescoed chapel.

3 San Lorenzo *p122*
A basilica with a touch of Brunelleschi and an unfinished façade.

4 Mercato Centrale *p127*
Florence's traditional market and hip first-floor food court.

In the know
Getting around

The main shopping area around the Mercato Centrale, as well as the pedestrian-packed pockets around the Medici chapels, are best explored on foot. But as you move west of via Panicale on to the more traffic-heavy via Nazionale and surrounding areas, you may want to hop on a bus. The 11 and 23 lines stop in piazza dell'Indipendenza, while the 36, 37, 13, 11, 10 and 14B are just a few of the main lines moving up and down via Nazionale.

Orfeo e Cerbero (Baccio Bandinelli, 1519), Palazzo Medici Riccardi *p120*

EXPLORING SAN LORENZO

The vast basilica of **San Lorenzo** sprawls, heavy and imposing, between piazza di San Lorenzo and piazza di Madonna degli Aldobrandini, with a dome almost as prominent as that of the Duomo. The highlight of the complex is the unmissable **Cappelle Medicee**, where members of the dynasty were interred.

Roads lead off piazza di San Lorenzo in a star shape. Heading north-west up via dell' Ariento, you can stop for a snack and to soak up the atmosphere at the bustling **Mercato Centrale** (*see p127*), a lively hub for shopping and socialising. The downstairs is still famous for its fresh produce, meats, cheeses and lunch bites, even though shrinking numbers of local residents shop here. A revival came with the 2014 opening of an upstairs gourmet food-and-drink court that spawned a spin-off in Rome at its main railway station. The busy 'first floor', as it's known, stays open until midnight and is probably central Florence's most popular spot for an all-purpose pit stop.

Alternatively, from piazza di San Lorenzo, head north-east up via dei Ginori, which runs alongside the gardens at the rear of Palazzo Medici Riccardi, and past craft shops up to the corner of via San Gallo and via Ventisette Aprile. At this crossroads, turn left for the Benedictine refectory of **Cenacolo di Sant'Apollonia** (*see p120*), or right then first left for the **Chiostro dello Scalzo** (*see p120*), decorated with frescoes by the Mannerist painter Andrea del Sarto.

Coming south back down via Cavour, you'll pass **Palazzo Medici Riccardi** (*see p120*); its beautiful Chapel of the Magi was painted by Benozzo Gozzoli and is famous for inspiring the costumes in Florence's largest-scale parade, **La Cavalcata dei Mag**i (*see p229*). Following the walls of the *palazzo* round to the right, you'll once more find yourself in piazza San Lorenzo.

Travelling south from the *piazza* will lead you past busy shoe and clothes shops in borgo San Lorenzo directly to the historic house of the wealthy Martelli family, **Museo Casa Martelli** (*see p120*). From here, turn north towards piazza di Madonna degli Aldobrandini and then continue up via Faenza and cross dingy via Nazionale to reach the **Cenacolo del Conservatorio di Fuligno** (*see below*) on the right, home to a year-round theatre production on the Medici family (*see p248*). Heading north-east up via Nazionale, the roads widen into **piazza dell'Indipendenza**, where grand *palazzi* herald the beginnings of a more genteel area.

Sights & museums

Cenacolo del Conservatorio di Fuligno

Via Faenza 42 (055 286982, www. polomusealetoscanwa.beniculturali.it). **Open** *by appt.* **Admission** *free.* **Map** *p119 J3.*

The harmonious fresco on the refectory wall of the ex-convent of St Onofrio was discovered in 1845. It was at first thought to

---

❤ Time to eat & drink

Traditional Florentine lunch
Sergio Gozzi *p125*

Street food, beers and snacks
Mostodolce *p126*
Mercato Centrale First Floor *p127*

Wine break
Casa del Vino *p124*

Florentine-NYC fusion dinner
La Cucina del Garga *p124*

❤ Time to shop

Bric-a-brac treasures
UB Firenze *p127*

Fine wine and liquors
Zanobini *p127*

High-end vintage
Desii Vintage *p126*

Moka pots and more
Gioia della Casa *p127*

❤ Time well spent

Fonticine tabernacle
Intersection of via dell'Ariento and via Nazionale. **Map** *p119 J3.*
The restored Fonticine tabernacle is one of those uniquely Florentine oddities that makes strolling through the city such a pleasure. The top portion is a blue-yellow-green terracotta masterwork of the Madonna and child by one of the della Robbia brothers – sons of Italian Renaissance sculptor-potter Andrea della Robbia. Its strange name – which translates as 'little fountains' – comes from the cherub-shaped water spouts found on the sizeable marble basin below the tabernacle.

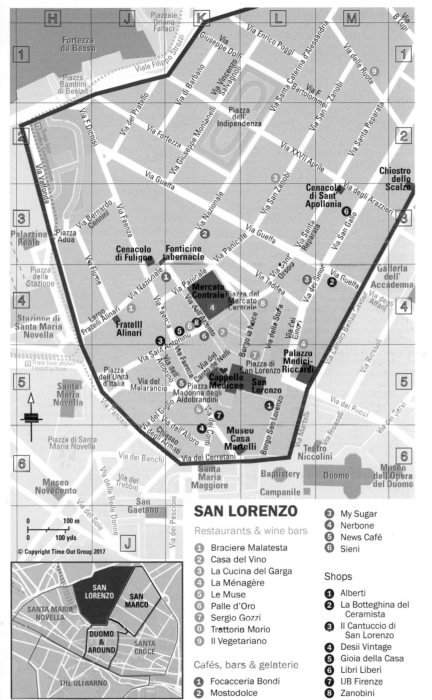

SAN LORENZO

Restaurants & wine bars

1. Braciere Malatesta
2. Casa del Vino
3. La Cucina del Garga
4. La Ménagère
5. Le Muse
6. Palle d'Oro
7. Sergio Gozzi
8. Trattoria Mario
9. Il Vegetariano

Cafés, bars & gelaterie

1. Focacceria Bondi
2. Mostodolce
3. My Sugar
4. Nerbone
5. News Café
6. Sieni

Shops

1. Alberti
2. La Botteghina del Ceramista
3. Il Cantuccio di San Lorenzo
4. Desii Vintage
5. Gioia della Casa
6. Libri Liberi
7. UB Firenze
8. Zanobini

© Copyright Time Out Group 2017

be the work of Raphael, but is, in fact, one of the best of Perugino's works: a *Last Supper* from about 1490. In the background is a representation of the Oration of the Garden set in a characteristically Umbrian landscape, giveaway evidence of the Perugian-born painter's roots. The best way to visit is to take in an evening performance of *The Medici Dynasty Show* (see p248 Performing Arts), a theatre production in English that runs year-round inside the still-consecrated Baroque church of St Onofrio. Generally, the friendly production team will take curious audience members around to the highlights after the show.

Cenacolo di Sant'Apollonia

*Via XXVII Aprile 1 (055 2388607, www.polomusealetoscana.beniculturali.it). **Open** 8.15am-1.50pm Sat-Wed; 10am-1pm Thur, Fri; 2nd, 4th Sat & Sun of mth. **Admission** free. **Map** p119 M3.*

The works in this Benedictine refectory, such as the frescoes of the Passion of Christ, were covered over during the Baroque period and only came to light in 1866. The most important is Andrea del Castagno's *Last Supper* (1445-50). In this depiction, del Castagno reverts to a 14th-century seating plan: Judas is alienated on our side of the table, a dark figure breaking the pure white of the tablecloth and symbolically portrayed to resemble a satyr, a Catholic symbol of evil. The colours and enclosed space intensify the scene. Above the *Last Supper* are a Crucifixion, Deposition and Resurrection, also by del Castagno. Ring the bell for entry to see these masterpieces.

Chiostro dello Scalzo

*Via Cavour 69 (055 2388604). **Open** 8.15am- 1.50pm Mon, Thur, Sat, or by appt. **Admission** free. **Map** p119 N3.*

The 'Cloister of the Barefoot' (so-called because the monk holding the Cross in the re-enactments of the Passion of Christ traditionally went shoeless) is frescoed with monochrome chiaroscuro episodes from the life of St John the Baptist by Andrea del Sarto. Built around a double courtyard with spindly Corinthian columns to a design by Sangallo, the cloister is a must-see epitome of delicacy and understatement.

Fratelli Alinari

*Largo Fratelli Alinari 15 (055 23951, www.alinari.it). **Open** by appt. **Map** p119 J4.*

Fratelli Alinari is the world's oldest photographic company. This fascinating archive dating back to the 19th century contains over 4 million photographs and once had a dedicated museum in the Leopoldine complex, which now houses the Museo Novecento (see p103). Occasional exhibitions are now held at this address, drawing on the archive or focusing on related artwork.

Museo Casa Martelli

*Via Ferdinando Zannetti 8 (055 216725, www.bargellomusei.beniculturali.it). **Open** 2-7pm Thur; 9am-2pm Sat; 1st, 3rd & 5th Sun of mth. Free admission and guided visits. **Map** p119 K6.*

One of Florence's hidden gems, this frescoed residential palace turned museum offers a glimpse into the lives of the wealthy Martelli family who lived here from the 15th to the mid 18th century. The family's most prominent members included 18th-century Archbishop of Florence, Giuseppe Maria Martelli, who enlisted the help of architect Bernardino Ciurini, painters Vincenzo Meucci and Bernardo Minozzi and many others in restructuring the palace into what we see today. The family's prolific art collection contains significant pieces that most visitors to Florence don't see: Piero di Cosimo's *Adoration of the Child*, works by Luca Giordano and Salvator Rosa, as well as numerous antique furnishings and decorative elements.

♥ Palazzo Medici Riccardi

*Via Cavour 1 (055 2760340, www.palazzo-medici.it). **Open** 9am-7pm Mon, Tue, Thur -Sun. **Admission** €4. No cards. **Map** p119 L5.*

In true Medici fashion, the family's 15th-century palace is strategically placed. They bought a string of adjacent houses on via Larga (now via Cavour) in the mid 14th century, when it was a fairly broad

💜 Cappelle Medicee

*Piazza di Madonna degli Aldobrandini 6
(055 2388602, www.firenzemusei.it).* **Open**
*8.15am-2pm Tue-Sat; 1st, 3rd, 5th Mon & 2nd,
4th Sun of mth.* **Admission** *€8; free on 1st Sun
of every mth. No cards.* **Map** *p119 K5.*

The spectacular Medici mausoleum is the
most splendid and fascinating part of the
basilica of San Lorenzo. Up the curling
stairs at the back of the entrance chamber
(which contains the family's reliquaries and
memorial plaques) is the grand **Cappella
dei Principi** (Chapel of the Princes),
constructed from huge hunks of porphyry
and ancient Roman marble hauled into the
city by Turkish slaves. The chapel houses
six sarcophagi of the Medici Grand Dukes.
The floor plan of the chapel was based on
that of the Baptistery and, possibly, the
Holy Sepulchre in Jerusalem – it had been
hoped that the supposed tomb of Christ
would reside here, but the authorities in
Jerusalem refused to sell it. This mausoleum
was commissioned in 1602 but, amazingly,
the beautifully intricate inlay of marble
and precious stones wasn't completed
until 1962, when workers from the Opificio
delle Pietre Dure finished the last external
pavement; by then, the Medici dynasty had
been over for 220 years.

In 1994 the entrance to the **crypt** was
discovered beneath a stone under the
chapel's altar. This sensational revelation
was followed by the exhumation of 49
Medici bodies, and scientists were able to
determine the manner in which many of
them had died. It was originally thought
that Francesco I de' Medici and his
mistress Bianca Cappello, who died within
hours of each other, had suffered from
malaria but tests showed they had in fact
been killed by acute arsenic poisoning
– probably at the hand of Francesco's
jealous brother Ferdinando.

Out of the Cappella dei Principi, a
passage to your left leads to Michelangelo's
Sagrestia Nuova (New Sacristy). This
chamber, begun in 1520, is in stark contrast
to the excesses of the chapel. It's dominated
by the tombs of Lorenzo il Magnifico's
relatives: grandson Lorenzo, Duke of Urbino,
and his son Giuliano, Duke of Nemours, who
grew up alongside Michelangelo. The tombs
incorporate the figures of *Night and Day,*
and, opposite, *Dawn and Dusk,* reclining on
top; their gaze directs the visitor's eyes to
a sculpture of a *Madonna and Child* on the

facing wall. Also here, under the sacristy, is
the incomplete tomb of Lorenzo il Magnifico
and his brother Giuliano. The Sagrestia
Nuova was finished by Giorgio Vasari, after
Michelangelo was hauled off to Rome to work
on the Sistine Chapel. The great man was
furious at having to leave the city – 'I cannot
live under pressure from patrons, let alone
paint' – but he'd worked long enough on the
project to leave it as one of his masterpieces.

SAN LORENZO

In the know
Michelangelo's secret room

Underneath the New Sacristy in the Medici
Chapel is a room, hidden for centuries,
where Michelangelo hid in fear for his life.
Michelangelo owed his career to the Medici
family but in a coup against them in 1530
he joined the Florentines who had grown
weary of their rule. When they returned to
power and to escape their wrath, he hid for
three months in this small room and, with
time on his hands, sketched around 50
charcoal 'doodles' on the wall. Some appear
to be work he had already completed, such
as *David* and images from the ceiling of the
Sistine Chapel. Hidden by a white stucco the
drawings remained a secret until they were
discovered in 1975. Unfortunately, visitors
breathing in this tiny, unvented space are
found to cause the drawings to deteriorate,
so you can no longer visit the hideaway, but
you can take a virtual tour.

Palazzo Medici Riccardi p120

road in a peaceful residential area – but in close proximity to the Duomo and merely a few steps from their favoured church, San Lorenzo (*see right*). The Medici thereby made sure their home (until they moved into Palazzo Vecchio in 1540) was in a position of power and would subtly intimidate any opposition with its strongbox-like appearance. Not wishing to appear too ostentatious, however, Cosimo il Vecchio rejected Brunelleschi's design as too extravagant and plumped for one by Michelozzo, who had recently proved his worth as a heavyweight architect in the rebuilding of the San Marco convent complex. Michelozzo designed a façade with a heavily rusticated lower storey (in the style of many military buildings), but a smoother and more refined first storey and a yet more restrained second storey.

The building was expanded and revamped in the 17th century by the Riccardi, its new owners, but retains Michelozzo's charming chapel. Almost entirely covered with frescoes by Benozzo Gozzoli, a student of Fra Angelico, this chapel features a vivid *Procession of the Magi* that is actually a portrait of 15th-century Medici. (In one of the most thoroughly Florentine rituals of the year, an elaborate parade passes from piazza Pitti to piazza del Duomo on Epiphany, re-enacting the wise men's journey to Jesus and costumed as Gozzoli's characters, *see p229*). In another room, off the gallery, is Fra Filippo Lippi's winsome *Madonna and Child*.

❤ San Lorenzo

Piazza San Lorenzo (055 214042, www.operamedicealaurenziana.it). **Open** *Winter 10am-5.30pm Mon-Sat. Summer 10am-5.30pm Mon-Sat; 1.30-5.30pm Sun.* **Admission** *€7. No cards.* **Map** *p119 L5.*

Built where Florence's cathedral stood from the end of the fourth to the ninth century – and thus right on the site of Florence's oldest church – San Lorenzo's sheer size more than compensates for its very plain exterior. San Lorenzo was built between 1419 and 1469 to a design by Brunelleschi (but largely completed by Manetti, his erstwhile assistant, who made several design alterations), and was the first church to which the architect applied his theory of rational proportion.

Despite the fortune spent on the place, the façade was never finished, hence the digestive biscuit-coloured bricks. In 1518, the Medici Pope Leo X commissioned Michelangelo to design a façade and ordained that the marble should be quarried at Pietrasanta. Michelangelo disagreed, preferring high-quality Carrara marble. In the end, it didn't matter: the scheme was cancelled in 1520 (*see p123* The Unfinished Façade).

A couple of artworks in the church merit a closer look. Savonarola snarled his tales of sin and doom from Donatello's bronze pulpits, but the reliefs are also powerful: you can almost hear the crowds scream in the *Deposition*. On the north wall is a *Martyrdom*

The Unfinished Façade

Michelangelo's marble finish to San Lorenzo lives on

In 1516, Michelangelo won a competition called by Pope Leo X (a son of Lorenzo il Magnifico) to erect a monumental marble façade for the basilica of San Lorenzo (*see left*), beating Andrea and Jacopo Sansovino, Raphael, Baccio d'Agnolo and Giuliano da Sangallo.

A wooden model in the Casa Buonarroti museum (*see p151*) shows how grand Michelangelo's design was. The commission was signed in 1518, and documents attest to Michelangelo having personally supervised every detail of the project until, to his great frustration, two years later the pope shifted his funds to the New Sacristy (*see p121*) and the Biblioteca Medicea Laurenziana (Laurentian Library, *see p124*). The façade was left unfinished; its architectural elements were dispersed, and the marble was relocated elsewhere.

In recent years, interest in the project was reignited by the discovery of three columns in a marble warehouse near Pietrasanta that might be the set quarried by Michelangelo for San Lorenzo's façade: the height, size and marble type match perfectly. In 2007, the Teseco Foundation for Art Pisa, which

had purchased the three columns, sent one of them to Florence to be displayed by the church, with a 'virtual façade' projected on to San Lorenzo's bare brick front.

Later, in July 2011, then-mayor Matteo Renzi came up with the kind of coup de théâtre typical of his style: why not build Michelangelo's façade the way the artist meant it, in solid marble? He argued that sponsors would flock to the initiative, and he called for a referendum, inviting Florentines to vote on whether or not the project should be carried out. However, the steep price tag meant that his plans met with strong resistance, and it was decided to leave the church as Michelangelo's unfinished work.

Interest in the façade hasn't disappeared, however, and a compromise of sorts has come about through the annual Settimana Michelangiolesca (Michelangelo Week), launched in 2014. For one week in July, San Lorenzo is lit up nightly with projections recreating Michelangelo's intended façade; concerts and lectures take place and contemporary replicas or reinterpretations of *David* or other artworks are installed around town.

San Lorenzo's unfinished façade

of St Lawrence by Mannerist painter par excellence Bronzino. In the second chapel on the right is another Mannerist work, a *Marriage of the Virgin* by Rosso Fiorentino, while the north transept holds an *Annunciation* by Filippo Lippi with a clarity of line and a depth of perspective that make it perfect for this interior.

Opening off the north transept is the **Sagrestia Vecchia** (Old Sacristy): another Brunelleschi design, it has a dome segmented like a tangerine and proportions based on cubes and spheres, along with a fabulous painted *tondo* by Donatello. The doors, also by Donatello, feature martyrs, apostles and Church fathers; to the left of the entrance, an elaborate tomb made by Verrocchio out of serpentine, porphyry, marble and bronze contains the remains of Lorenzo il Magnifico's father and uncle.

Reached via the door to the left of the façade is Michelangelo's architectural classic, the **Biblioteca Mediceo-Laurenziana**, built to house the Medici's large library. It still contains priceless volumes, papyri, codices and documents, though not all of them are on permanent display. The entrance corridor has a stunning red and cream inlaid mosaic floor, while the library itself displays Michelangelo's predilection for the human form over any classical architectural norms. However, it's in the vestibule leading into the reading room that the true masterpiece of the library is found. The highly original three-sweep stairwell in *pietra serena* was a ground-breaking design, the first example ever of the expressive Mannerist style in architecture and one of the most elegant staircases ever built.

▶ *For details of the Cappelle Medicee, see p121.*

Restaurants & wine bars

For quick lunches and tasty snacks, head to the first floor of the refurbished **Mercato Centrale**, *see p127.*

Braciere Malatesta €€
Via Nazionale 36r (055 215164, www.facebook.com/bracieremalatesta). **Open** *noon-10.30pm daily.* **Map** *p119 J4* ❶ *Grill*

Serving up mouth-watering grilled meats at reasonable prices is the modus operandi here. The venue smartly mixes a traditional menu (wood oven-fired pizzas, vegetables and grilled meat-based classics) with a fresh design aesthetic spread over their sprawling space. One of the great guarantees about this spot – besides that you're bound to find something you like on its long menu – is that you'll always find a seat (try to snag one out

on the quaint little garden). And whatever you're ordering, try one of the tasty mixed *taglieri* (Tuscan sampling platters) first.

♥ Casa del Vino €
Via dell'Ariento 16r (055 215609, www.casadelvino.it). **Open** *9.30am-3.30pm Mon-Fri; 9.30am-8pm Sat. Closed Aug.* **Map** *p119 K4* ❷ *Wine bar*

Hidden behind the stalls of the San Lorenzo market, this wine bar has very limited seating on a few benches and stools backed up against the wine cabinets. No matter: punters continue to pile in for a glass of good plonk and some delicious *panini, crostini* and Florentine-style salads (hint: that means tripe) to accompany it. Bottles for all budgets sit on lovely old carved wooden shelves that line the room; you'll find fairly priced wines from all over Italy, plus labels from further afield and plenty of choice by the glass. In addition to the vast selection of wines, you can purchase Tuscan extra virgin olive oil, balsamic vinegar and Prato's famed Mattei *biscotti*.

♥ La Cucina del Garga €€
Via San Zanobi 33r (055 475286, www.garga.it). **Open** *7.30-10.30pm Mon-Sat.* **Map** *p119 L2* ❸ *Contemporary Italian*

Chef Alessandro Gargani is a bona-fide Florentine who inherited his parents' kitchen prowess. His father, the late Giuliano Gargani, was well known in local art circles and fused his passions for food and painting at the whimsically decorated restaurant he ran with his Canadian wife, Sharon. Sharon's still a big part of proceedings, running cooking classes and picking up ingredients at the market, while Ale oversees kitchen operations, staying faithful to most of his dad's original recipes but also adding his own twists, having lived and cooked in New York City. Think comfort Italian food with a bit of saucy American style thrown in, such as *tagliatelle del magnifico*, a citrus cream pasta with a hint of mint, or the truffle and avocado chicken. Don't skip dessert: Sharon's famous cheesecake won her favour with the Florentines when she first arrived as a young, foreign chef, and the flourless chocolate tart with rosemary and olive oil is unreal.

La Ménagère €€
Via de' Ginori 8r (055 0750600, www.lamenagere.it). **Bistro and bar** *7am-2am daily.* **Restaurant** *noon-11pm daily.* **Map** *p119 L4* ❹ *Concept restaurant*

Cynics say this ultra-chic, combination bistro-bar-restaurant-florist-kitchenware shop has already worn out its welcome since opening in 2015. Presentation tends to win out over quality here, but some find it worth it simply for the experience of sitting inside the beautifully designed space, which was completed in less than three months. Flowers are abundant, furnishings are unfinished, columns unplastered and a single rustic table spans nearly the entire length of the room. The main restaurant is in the back and serves a €55 tasting menu, as well as inventive mains including filled calamari with persimmon mayonnaise. A budget-friendly option is the bistro and coffee bar out at the front, which offers free Wi-Fi, fun seating and a chance to enjoy the ambience without the price tag.

Le Muse €€
Via dei Conti 9 (055 2937730, www.lemusefirenze.com). **Open** *7am-10.30pm daily.* **Map** *p119 K5* ⑤
Contemporary Italian

You wouldn't know it if you simply walked in, but elegant Le Muse is a hotel restaurant, attached to boutique gem Firenze Number Nine. Its experimental dishes mean it often draws in more curious food bloggers than guests. Cocktail hour is another strength: stop by for an aperitif on the shady terrace, knowing you can stay for dinner if you like.

Palle d'Oro €
Via Sant'Antonino 43/45r (055 288383, www.trattoriapalledorofirenze.com). **Open** *noon-3pm, 6-11pm Mon-Sat.* **Map** *p119 K4* ⑥ *Traditional Italian*

Long a favourite with local workers, Palle d'Oro – which cheekily translates to 'Golden Balls' – cooks up classic Tuscan fare that isn't fancy or particularly innovative, but satisfying, hearty and served by a staff that cares. One of its big strengths is *pranzo al balcone*, or counter lunches, a chance to enjoy a fresh, fast lunch seated at the marble tabletops lining the walls: you'd be hard-pressed to find anything that costs more than €10. By night, it's a place where budget travellers can afford a full feast – start with an antipasto plate of *coccoli* (Tuscan fried dough) and *prosciutto* and then dig into simple *primi* and mains such as roast chicken and potatoes or *peposo* (a peppery Tuscan beef stew).

❤ Sergio Gozzi €
Piazza San Lorenzo 8r (055 281941). **Open** *noon-3.45pm Mon-Sat. Closed Aug.* **Map** *p119 L5* ⑦ *Traditional Italian*

An authentic, old-fashioned Florentine *trattoria*, this family-run eatery has only hit the tourist radar since the stalls of the San Lorenzo market were cleared out of the church area. Thankfully, its unassuming door still keeps all but the most serious away, making it a less frantic alternative to Trattoria Mario (*see right*) as a place to sample simple and genuine home cooking. Perhaps

begin with *minestrone di verdura, ribollita* or *minestra di farro* (spelt soup), before moving on to a roast or *bistecca alla fiorentina*. On Fridays, you can sample their superb *seppie in inzimino* – sweet tender squid stewed with Swiss chard.

Trattoria Mario €
Via Rosina 2r (055 218550, www.trattoria-mario.com). **Open** *noon-3.30pm Mon-Sat. Closed 3wks Aug.* **No cards.** **Map** *p119 L4* ⑧ *Traditional Italian*

Reservations are not taken and the long queue for a table may not seem worth the wait, but you'll be glad you stuck it out. Run by four generations of the Colsi family, you'll be eating elbow-to-elbow with your fellow lunchers on long bare-wood tables inside this chaotic and cramped eaterie, which draws an egalitarian mix of people who are all interested in the simple yet excellent Florentine home cooking. Try the earthy *ribollita* (Tuscan vegetable and bread soup), a terrific *bollito misto* (mixed boiled meats) served with a biting garlic and parsley *salsa verde* and, for a supplement, the tasty *bistecca* (steak) or mouth-watering *lombatina* (veal chop). It doesn't get much better for the price.

Il Vegetariano €€
Via delle Ruote 30r (055 475030, www.il-vegetariano.it). **Open** *12.30-2.30pm Mon-Fri, 7.30-10.30pm Fri-Sun & hols. Closed 3wks Aug.* **Map** *p119 M1* ⑨ *Vegetarian*

Il Vegetariano was one of the first vegetarian restaurants in Florence, although more rivals are popping up. The menu offers plenty of variety, including a choice of ethnic dishes, and generous portions for excellent prices. There's a fabulous salad bar and the wines are all organic.

Cafés, bars & gelaterie

Focacceria Bondi
Via dell'Ariento 85r (055287390). **Open** *11.30am-12am daily.* **Map** *p119 K4* ①
Sandwiches

By day, this is not just a tasty sandwich shop, but a calm respite from the busy tourist crowds of via dell'Ariento. At lunch, its wooden benches are mostly filled with neighbourhood workers feasting on low cost *focaccine* (triangular *focaccia* bread-based sandwiches). By night, you'll find young Florentines and internationals squeezing in a post-dinner snack before hitting some of the nearby watering hotels. Best to keep your sandwich simple at a place like this: the fresh mint, goat's cheese and tomato combo is heavenly.

♥ Mostodolce
Via Nazionale 114r (055 2302928). **Open**
11.30am-2am daily. **Map** *p119 K3* ❷
Gastropub

Mostodolce is a must for any craft-beer enthusiasts – or, really, for anyone who appreciates a good beer and a fried snack. Walking by, you could easily mistake it for little more than a dive bar, and while it does swing that way, it's also an excellent stop for a full meal at lunch or dinner (quality burgers with unexpected ingredients are the house speciality, although there are pizzas, salads and a substantial selection of *crostini*). If you're looking for something a little more Tuscan, pop by mid-afternoon for an original beer (opt for the Melissa, with hints of honey) and *coccoli* (Tuscan fried dough balls), served with a savoury, addictive hot sauce.

My Sugar
Via de' Ginori 49r (393 0696042). **Open**
1-9pm daily. **Map** *p119 L4* ❸ *Gelateria*

Run by charming young couple Alberto and Julia, this hole in the wall doesn't look like much from the outside, but it's one of the most buzzed-about gelaterie in Florence, offering a mix of inventive and traditional flavours, including some that show up for a limited time only (in the past, custom-made tastes have been inspired by everything from a major airline to a local news magazine). Ingredients are reliably fresh and flavours are all made on-site.

Nerbone
Mercato Centrale (055 219949). **Open**
7am-2pm Mon-Sat. Closed Aug. **No cards.**
Map *p119 K4* ❹ *Market stall*

Opened way back in 1872, this food stall/ *trattoria* has a strategic location on the ground floor of the covered central market in San Lorenzo. A great place to find local colour, it's packed from breakfast time with market workers: even if you can't face a *lampredotto* (cow's intestine) sarnie and a glass of rough red plonk at 7am, the locals can, and with the low-price tags, who could blame them? Plates of simple pasta and soups, as well as less adventurous *panini*, are on offer at lunchtime; seating (generally elbow to elbow) is available.

News Café
Via del Giglio 59r (055 2654310, www.facebook.com/newscafefirenze). **Open**
7.30am-10.30pm Mon-Sat. **Map** *p119 K5* ❺
Café

Don't go for the food – go for the cappuccino art. The head barista here has won over the hearts (and Instagram likes) of legions of international students in Florence with his intricate depictions of Brunelleschi's dome-atop-the-foam. (If he doesn't draw it for you, don't be offended: it means you're doing a convincing job of seeming like a smug local or skeptical tourist.) It's a spacious and friendly place to stop before or after your visit to the nearby Medici chapels, and the free Wi-Fi and reading material are welcome bonuses.

Sieni
Via Sant'Antonino 54r (055 213830, www.pasticceriasieni.it). **Open** *7.30am-7.30pm daily.* **No cards.** **Map** *p119 K4* ❻ *Café*

With its turn-of-the-century decor, this 1909 café and *pasticceria* is the real deal, serving up a great range of sweet and savoury breakfast pastries and snacks to a very local crowd, some of them taking a coffee break from their market shopping. Try yours with a hefty slice of perfect polenta cake.

Shops
Alberti
Borgo San Lorenzo 45r-49r (055 294271). **Open** *9am-7.30pm Mon-Sat; 3-7pm Sun.* **Map** *p119 L5* ❶ *Music & entertainment*

The oldest record shop in the city has a vast repertoire of pop, dance, jazz and indie CD recordings, some vinyl, a variety of DVDs and a great selection of portable DVD and CD players. **Other locations** Via Nazionale 80-82r, San Lorenzo (055 285476).

La Botteghina del Ceramista
Via Guelfa 5r (055 287367, www.labotteghinadelceramista.it). **Open** *Winter 11am-7.30pm Tue-Sat; Summer 10.30am-7.30pm Mon-Sat. Closed 2wks Aug.* **Map** *p119 M4* ❷ *Ceramics*

Superb hand-painted ceramics in intricate designs and vivid colours.

Il Cantuccio di San Lorenzo
Via Sant'Antonino 23r (055 290034, www.ilcantucciodisanlorenzo.it). **Open** *8.30am-7.30pm Mon-Sat; 9.30am-6.30pm Sun. Closed Aug.* **Map** *p119 J5* ❸ *Bakery & sweets*

The scent of this place will pull you in off the street. It's a relatively new shop serving up old Tuscan favourites, from Prato-style *cantucci*, a special type of Tuscan almond biscuit, to special variations made with orange and chocolate, as well as seasonal sweets and cakes. Grab a quick counter-to-belly biscuit, or splash out on an elaborate gift pack.

♥ Desii Vintage
Via dei Conti 17 (055 2302817). **Open** *10.30am-1pm, 2.30-7.30pm Mon-Sat.* **Map** *p119 K6* ❹ *Vintage fashion*

This sleek, well-curated boutique carries a large variety of vintage items, from Chanel suits to Louis Vuitton luggage to more affordable finds such as Salvatore Ferragamo flats. With all the combat boots and catchy window displays, it tends to draw trendsetters, particularly during the Pitti Immagine trade show season.

❤ Gioia della Casa
*Via Sant'Antonino 31r (055 216020, www.gioiadellacasa.it). **Open** 3.45-7.30pm Mon; 9.30am-1pm, 3.45-7.30pm Tue-Sat.* **Map** *p119 K4* **5** *Kitchen supplies*

You'll find a smörgåsbord of kitchen supplies at this expansive shop, one of the largest of its type in the area and offering some of the lowest prices. Souvenir favourites such as Italian Bialetti Moka pots are standard, but there's also a plethora of international products and brands, with biscuit tins and cake sheets as well as ceramics and silverware.

Libri Liberi
*Via San Gallo 25r (055 0517670, www.libriliberiofficine.it). **Open** 8am-8.30pm daily.* **Map** *p119 M4* **6** *Books*

Although the English language selection at this shop isn't huge, popping in for a poke around is well worth it. Besides being a bookshop, it's a co-working space that offers breakfast, comfortable seating and an outdoor garden – you can rent a desk by the hour, day, week or even longer, depending on your stay. They also organise **Teatro del Gallo**, a children's theatre programme that takes place 'behind the scenes' of the bookshop itself – out in the garden and in its hidden building, to be precise.

❤ Mercato Centrale
*Piazzale Mercato Centrale (055 2399798, www.mercatocentrale.it). **Ground floor** 7am-2pm Mon-Fri; 7am-5pm Sat. **First floor** 10am-midnight daily.* **Map** *p119 K4.*

The Mercato Centrale has undergone quite a makeover in recent years – and there's debate over whether or not it's changed for the better. The traditional produce, meat, cheese and fish market on the ground floor is worth exploring for the colours, sights and scents, but if it's a 'local' shopping experience you're looking for, you'll find more Florentines at the less tourist-tracked Mercato Sant'Ambrogio (see p159). Upstairs, the chic 'first floor' has become a popular pit stop for both travellers and locals. It's a dynamite dining option if you're wandering in a group and can't all agree on what to eat, or if you're itching for a sit-down snack. The *pizzeria* is particularly noteworthy, if not Florentine: it's run by Roman *pizzaiuolo*, Stefano Callegari, and

features a short menu of standard classics, as well as a seasonal and Rome-inspired options (think unconventional toppings taken from traditional Roman cuisine – such as *carbonara*, featuring egg, cheese, pancetta and black pepper).

❤ UB Firenze
*Via dei Conti 4r (055 214884, www.ubfirenze. it). **Open** 10.30am-7.30pm Mon-Sat.* **Map** *p119 K5* **7** *Vintage homeware*

This grab-bag of vintage treasures, strange antiques and old prints is difficult to define. Owner (and namesake) Ubaldo says it best: 'If you don't come inside, you won't understand.' Browsing through the faded posters, art prints and cards is a pleasure, and you never know what you might stumble on here – from garden gnomes to dolls' houses. Here, it's about exploring and conversing as much as it is shopping.

❤ Zanobini
*Via Sant'Antonino 47r (055 2396850, www.lelame.com/enoteca). **Open** 9am-2pm, 4-8pm Mon-Sat.* **Map** *p119 K5* **8** *Wine*

Gino and Silvano Zanobini opened their wine shop here in 1944, and it's barely changed since, still selling an astonishing range of wines and liqueurs with the help of their trained sommelier sons, Mario and Simon. The shop has a stand-up bar serving wine by the glass (including its own label), and a great range of Tuscan wines, as well as a careful selection of wines from further afield.

Mercato Centrale

San Marco

When it comes to famous attractions, San Marco wins hands-down over all the other districts of Florence, principally because Galleria dell'Accademia houses Michelangelo's iconic *David*, perhaps the most famous statue in the world. While throngs of tourists flock daily to admire this monument to libertarian principles, there are plenty of other museums in the San Marco district to divert you, containing fascinating displays of weird and wonderful things, and they're among the most family-friendly in town. From Egyptian mummies and Leonardo's flying machines to prehistoric gems and Renaissance masterpieces, each collection vies for the attention of the visiting masses. The newly revamped museum of the charitable Istituto degli Innocenti provides an interesting compendium of Renaissance art; or for quiet contemplation, try the mystical pleasures of the San Marco museum, a shrine to the intimate art of Dominican friar Beato Angelico.

However, the district of San Marco is far from just a tourist hub: head to the nigh-on perfect porticoed square of Santissima Annunziata and it's apparent that the area thrives on crowds of artsy students from nearby faculties, including the Luigi Cherubini Music

❤ Don't miss

1 Galleria dell'Accademia *p134*
Home to Michelangelo's original *David* since 1873.

2 Museo degli Innocenti *p136*
Art and social history from the world's earliest institution for children.

3 Museo di San Marco *p139*
The mystical paintings that earned Fra'Angelico the title of Blessed.

4 Opificio delle Pietre Dure *p138*
Marvel at the traditional Florentine art of stone inlay.

5 Museo Archeologico & Museo Egizio *p136*
Etruscan masterpieces and a remarkable collection of Egyptian antiquities.

In the know
Getting around

San Marco is most easily explored on foot. Piazza San Marco is the city's second largest bus hub. The 7 bus to Fiesole (see *p198*) leaves from via Giorgio La Pira around the corner.

View of the Duomo from piazza della Santissima Annunziata *p132*

Fountain with Sea Monsters (Pietro Tacca, 1627-1641), piazza Santissima Annunziata *p132*

Conservatory and the Academy of Fine Arts. The dining and nightlife scenes are still underdeveloped here, but piazza Santissima Annunziata provides an appropriate backdrop for summer festivals and occasional markets, featuring the stalls of local artisans and food producers.

The San Marco neighbourhood was the most affected by the decision to pedestrianise the Duomo area in 2009. On the one hand, the via Martelli–via Cavour thoroughfare – one of the grandest within the city walls – looks and feels deserted since piazza Duomo became off limits to city buses; but on the other hand, the already busy piazza San Marco has taken on the burden as Florence's second largest bus hub, and is hardly recognisable as the quiet convent area it must have been in centuries past.

❤ **Time to eat**

Sicilian street food
Arà: è Sicilia *p140*

Fresh paninis
Un Caffè da I' Sardo *p140*

Post-David dinner
Osteria de L'Ortolano *p140*

❤ **Time to shop**

Charming homewares
Bartolini *p141*, Frette *p141*

Picnic supplies
L'Ortolano *p141*

The ultimate vintage find
Street Doing *p141*

❤ **Time well spent**

Giardino dei Semplici
Via Micheli 3 (055 2756444, www.msn.unifi.it). **Open** *Winter 10am-4pm Sat-Sun. Summer 10am-7pm daily.* **Admission** *€3 (€10 combined for University science museums). No cards.* **Map** *p131 O2.*
Explore Europe's third oldest botanical garden (after those at Pisa and Padua). It was planted in 1545 by landscape gardener Il Tribolo for Cosimo I to cultivate and research exotic plants, extract essential oils, distil perfumes, seek cures for a variety of ailments and find antidotes for poisons. The garden opened to the public in the mid 19th century and contains an estimated 9,000 plant specimens including five monumental trees.

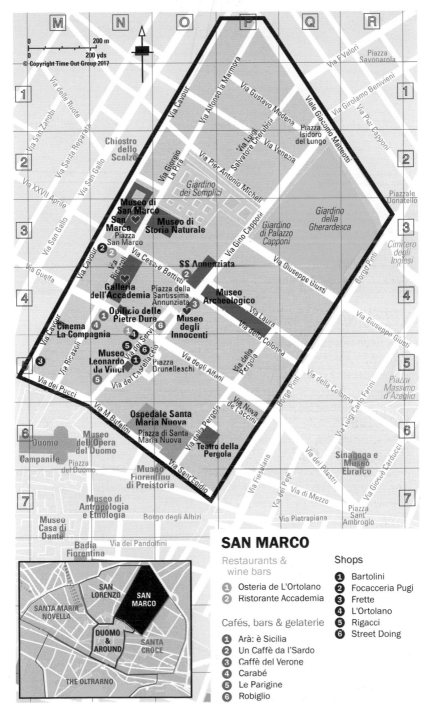

SAN MARCO

Restaurants & wine bars

1 Osteria de L'Ortolano
2 Ristorante Accademia

Cafés, bars & gelaterie

1 Arà: è Sicilia
2 Un Caffè da l'Sardo
3 Caffè del Verone
4 Carabé
5 Le Parigine
6 Robiglio

Shops

1 Bartolini
2 Focacceria Pugi
3 Frette
4 L'Ortolano
5 Rigacci
6 Street Doing

Putti (Andrea della Robbia, 1487) on the façade of the Spedale degli Innocenti

EXPLORING SAN MARCO

Piazza della Santissima Annunziata
(abbreviated to SS Annunziata) is dominated
by the powerful equestrian statue of Grand
Duke Ferdinando I by Giambologna and his
pupil Pietro Tacca. Try counting the bees on
the bronze plaque attached to its base: if you
succeed – without pointing at or touching
them – there's good luck in store for you!

The church of **Santissima Annunziata**
(*see p138*) is to the north. On the eastern
side of the square is the **Spedale degli
Innocenti**, opened in 1445 as the first
foundling hospital in Europe. It was
designed by Filippo Brunelleschi and marks
the advent of Renaissance town planning:
Brunelleschi had designed it to fit into his
greater plan for a perfectly symmetrical
piazza, but died before realising his dream.
The glazed terracotta medallions in the
spandrels, each showing a swaddled baby,
are by Andrea della Robbia. The building
houses an impressive collection of artworks
in the recently revamped **Museo degli
Innocenti** (*see p136*).

Heading southeast under the
northernmost arch of the Spedale is via
della Colonna, flanked by the **Museo
Archeologico** (*see p136*). Alternatively,
walking south down via de' Servi towards
the Duomo will bring you to the privately-
owned **Museo Leonardo da Vinci** (*see p138*)
and a clutch of shops and cafés where you
can take a break from sightseeing.

West takes you to piazza San Marco,
the site of the Dominican church of **San
Marco** (*see p138*) and the rector's offices
of the University. Beside the church is the
Museo di San Marco (*see p139*). North of
the piazza are some of the University's
scientific institutions, such as the mineral
department of the city's **Museo di Storia
Naturale** (*see p136*) and the **Giardino dei
Semplici** (*see p130*).

Stretching south from the square along
Via Ricasoli is the **Galleria dell'Accademia**
(*see p134*), housed in the former Ospedale
di San Matteo, whose 14th-century loggia
can still be seen on the corner of piazza San
Marco. Make your way past the queues and
around the corner to reach the **Opificio
delle Pietre Dure** (*see p138*), dedicated to
the art of inlaying semi-precious stones
in mosaics.

Tourists hardly ever venture outside
the via Ricasoli–San Marco–Santissima
Annunziata–via dei Servi quadrangle, and
it speaks volumes that the best shops in
this district (*see p141*) are definitely not
visitor-oriented. Still, the area is worth
exploring further, as it is also home to
some of the most important cultural
venues in town, namely the historic opera
house **Teatro della Pergola** (*see p250*),
recently appointed a National Theatre,
and the newly reinvented **Cinema La
Compagnia** (*see p233*), a picture house
devoted to non-commercial and art films
that hosts several interesting film festivals
throughout the year.

Michelangelo's David

From an imperfect block of marble, the sculptor created a Renaissance masterpiece

The largest freestanding marble nude since classical antiquity started life as a religious symbol but promptly became a political icon as soon as it was unveiled. Portraying strength and resolve, it was chosen to encourage Florentines to support their fledgling republic against the Medici tyranny.

The biblical story of David and Goliath had long been a popular theme in Florentine art, but Michelangelo's innovative take on the subject marked a clean break from the tradition exemplified by Donatello's and Verrocchio's graceful bronzes (now both in the Bargello; see p146). Michelangelo's *David* is no longer a boy, but a youth on the verge of manhood; and he is portrayed in the tense, purposeful, defiant pose of a hero ready for combat rather than, as he was usually depicted, after the battle with Goliath's head at his feet. His deliberately oversized head and hands are the symbols of his deadly weapons: reason and strength.

Of course, another reason for *David's* top-heavy shape is that it was intended to stand high up on the Duomo: the head and hands would look well proportioned from the beholder's viewpoint down below. However, by the time the statue was completed in 1504, a committee of city officials and fellow artists had decided to place it by the entrance of Palazzo Vecchio instead, where a copy now stands (see p76 Piazza della Signoria).

Michelangelo was commissioned to make the statue in 1501, when he was 26, and worked frantically and secretly at it for nearly three years. He achieved the enormous feat of creating a seemingly perfect figure from an unusually tall, impossibly shallow, dangerously fractured and – worse still – previously hacked-at block of Carrara marble, which had lain abandoned for nearly 25 years in a courtyard of the Opera del Duomo before Michelangelo started work on it. The marble had defeated the efforts of other sculptors over the preceding four decades (notably, Agostino di Duccio in 1463-6 and Antonio Rossellino ten years later).

Over the centuries, a few minor injuries have affected *David* – most recently in 1991, when a frustrated Italian artist smashed the (now skilfully restored) second toe of his left foot with a hammer. Still, it's the micro fractures in the ankles, caused by the slightly off-balance position in which the statue stood for over 350 years, which cause the greatest worries for its future, especially in the event of earthquakes or other tremors; to prevent this, a shock-proof base is being planned.

❤ Galleria dell'Accademia

Via Ricasoli 58-60 (055 294883, www.
accademia.org (unofficial info site), www.
firenzemusei.it (official ticket booking).
Open *8.15am-6.50pm Tue-Sun.* **Admission**
€8 (€12.50 with special exhibitions); €6.25
reductions. Free on 1st Sun of every mth. No
cards. **Map** *p131 N4.*

The gallery was founded in 1784 when Grand Duke Pietro Leopoldo di Lorena decided to merge all the existing fine art academies of Florence into a single institution. At the time, the collection included old masters' paintings, drawings, casts and plaster models that art students could study, copy and restore. Among them were the original plaster cast of Giambologna's *Abduction of a Sabine Women (see p86)* and Pontormo's *Venus and Cupid*, based on a sketch by Michelangelo. The collection was further enriched by works from religious institutions suppressed in 1786 by Pietro Leopoldo and in 1810 by Napoleon, some of which were later moved to the Uffizi. At one time, the gallery even housed Botticelli's *Primavera (see p82)*.

Galleria dell'Accademia first became a public museum in the years when Florence was capital of Italy (1865-71). Then, in 1872, a crucial decision was reached: the original *David* by Michelangelo would be moved here from piazza della Signoria where it had been since 1504. It took several days and a purpose-built cart on tracks to move *David*, which remained hidden from view while the neoclassical *tribuna* (alcove), surmounted by a glass dome created by architect Emilio De Fabris (who also designed the Duomo façade, *see p66*), was completed. The Museo Michelangiolesco, as it became known, opened in July 1882.

Today, Galleria dell'Accademia is Italy's secondmost visited museum after the Uffizi (*see p82*), with over 1.4 million visitors yearly. Despite the fact that it contains a huge number of magnificent and historic works in its 11 rooms over two floors, the queue snaking around the block is usually here for one attraction only: Michelangelo's monumental *David (see p133)* .

Michelangelo was convinced that figures were encased by God inside the stone, and that it was the artist's task to let them emerge

Other Michelangelo works line the walls of the long hall leading to the *David* salon; among them are four slaves, formerly in Buontalenti's Grotto in Boboli (*see p168*). They were intended for Pope Julius II's tomb in Rome, a project that Michelangelo was forced to abandon in order to paint the Sistine Chapel. They are masterly but unfinished sculptures, called *schiavi* (slaves) or *prigioni* (prisoners) because it seems as if the figures are struggling to escape from their marble constraints. As such, they provide a precious insight into the Master's *non finito* (unfinished) sculpting technique. Michelangelo was convinced that figures were encased by God inside the stone, and that it was the artist's task to let them emerge. The (also unfinished) *Palestrina Pietà*, once attributed to Michelangelo, is now widely considered the work of a pupil instead.

In the know
Behind closed doors

If you find the Accademia's Monday closure annoying, think twice: it's when essential routine maintenance takes place. In the case of *David* this means regular soft-brush dusting and low-pressure vacuum cleaning, carried out by expert hands every couple of months. This is thanks to generous donations by Friends of Florence, a charitable American organisation that also co-funded his €400,000 clean-up in 2003: *David*'s first 'bath' for 130 years was given to him on his 500th birthday.

Bearded Slave (Michelangelo, 1519–1534)

Atlantis (Michelangelo, 1519–1534)

Highlights of the Accademia collections also include Michelangelo's bronze bust by his pupil Daniele da Volterra; a remarkable anthology of Florentine late Gothic paintings; the elegant bridal scene depicted by Masaccio's brother Lo Scheggia on a wedding chest for the Adimari family (c1450), and some fine Renaissance paintings, such as Botticelli's *Madonna of the Sea* (c1477; attributed by some to Filippino Lippi).

Finally, music lovers should not overlook the fabulous collection of around 50 musical instruments on permanent loan here from the **Luigi Cherubini Music Conservatory** next door, including a remarkably well-preserved tenor viola built by Antonio Stradivari (1690) for the Medici string quintet.

❤ Don't miss

1 David *Tribuna del David*
Michelangelo's monumental sculpture.

2 The Slaves *Galleria dei Prigioni*
Magnificent examples of Michelangelo's sculpting technique.

3 Madonna of the Sea *Sala del Colosso*
Sandro Botticelli's sweet painting.

4 Cassone Adimari *Sala del Colosso*
The painted panels of a 15th-century wedding chest.

5 Antonio Stradivari's 1690 tenor viola *Museo degli Strumenti musicali*
Used by the Medici quintet.

Sights & museums

💗 Museo Archeologico & Museo Egizio

Piazza della SS Annunziata 9b (055 23575, www.archeotoscana.beniculturali.it). **Open** *8.30am-2pm Sat-Mon; 8.30am-7pm Tue-Fri.* **Admission** *€4; €2 reductions. No cards.* **Map** *p131 P4.*

It's easy to come to Florence and get completely submerged in the Renaissance, but the archaeological museum, housed in Palazzo della Crocetta, explains what happened before the Golden Age. The museum has an impressive entrance hall, an enormous temporary exhibition space and the largest collection anywhere of Etruscan coins. Exhibits include jewellery, funerary sculpture, urns and bronzes dating from the fifth century BC, as well as the fabulous *Chimera*, a mythical beast that's part lion, part goat and part snake. Also present is the first-century BC Etruscan bronze *Orator*, famous and historically important because the speaker in question is wearing a Roman toga. The first rooms house Egyptian artefacts (including sarcophagi complete with creepy shrivelled bodies) from prehistoric eras through to AD 310. Outside, the beautiful garden lined with Etruscan tombs and monuments opens only on Saturday mornings, weather conditions allowing.

Museo di Storia Naturale – Sezione Mineralogia

Via la Pira 4 (055 2756444, www.msn.unifi. it). **Open** *Oct-May 9.30am-4.30pm Mon, Tue, Thur, Fri; 10am-4.30pm Sat, Sun. June-Sept 10.30am-5.30pm daily.* **Admission** *€6; €3 reductions (€10 combined ticket for University science museums). No cards.* **Map** *p131 O3.*

This clearly explained collection makes gem-lovers drool. It's packed full of strange and lovely stones, including 12 huge Brazilian quartzes.

In the know
Wheel of misfortune

Once you've explored the Museum degli Innocenti, take a look along the outside walls of Brunelleschi's Spedale; in the far left-hand corner of the loggia you'll find a medieval version of the 'baby hatch', a little square window once equipped with a revolving hatch and a rotating horizontal wheel, designed for people anonymously to leave their unwanted babies for the nuns to collect. The system was in operation for more than 400 years, from 1445 until the hospital's closure in 1875.

💗 Museo degli Innocenti (MUDI)

Piazza della SS Annunziata 12 (055 2037308, www.istitutodeglinnocenti.it). **Open** *10am-7pm daily.* **Admission** *€5. No cards.* **Map** *p131 O4.*

Europe's first foundling hospital opened here in 1445 thanks to a 1,000-florin bequest by Francesco Datini, a rich merchant from Prato. Although it no longer operates as an orphanage, the Istituto degli Innocenti continues to pursue its mission to care for the well-being of children, and hosts an important UNICEF research centre. However, to the visitor its importance lies first and foremost in the artistic value of the building itself and in the artworks it contains.

The gallery suffered a substantial blow in 1853, when several important works were auctioned off to raise money for the hospital

💗 Don't miss

1 Adoration of the Magi
Sala del Ghirlandaio
A splendid altarpiece by Domenico Ghirlandaio.

2 Madonna with Child and an Angel
Main gallery
An early work by Sandro Botticelli.

3 Madonna with Child *Main gallery*
Luca della Robbia's glazed-terracotta high-relief masterpiece.

4 The Swaddled Babies *Façade*
Andrea della Robbia's iconic medallions of infants.

5 Caffè del Verone
Rooftop terrace
The new café in the top-floor loggia affords fantastic views.

Following a €12.8 million, three-year overhaul, the thoroughly redesigned museum opened in June 2016 and is now one of the city's most innovative exhibition spaces, deserving to attract more visitors than ever before. Andrea della Robbia's powder-blue medallions, each featuring a white glazed terracotta Swaddled Baby, grace the elegant Brunelleschi façade and were restored as part of the renovation project. On the flip side, two ultra-modern brass doors have been added, sparking fierce debate.

The museum aims to be child-friendly and fully accessible for disabled visitors, and the new set-up certainly fulfils this promise: there are plenty of engaging multimedia displays, the captions are positioned at a child-friendly eye level, and La Bottega dei Ragazzi – the Institute's own children's workshop and recreational area, providing

activities for schools and families – has teamed up with Associazione MUSE (see pxx) to offer a free Family Tour kit (and matching app), available in Italian and English from the reception desk.

The visit spans three different sections and starts from the newly reclaimed basement, where documents and objects recount the history of the institution and the stories of some of the children it saved and raised over the centuries. The second section showcases the building's architectural features, while the second-floor gallery displays the Institute's art collection, which – although it suffered a substantial blow in 1853, when several important works were auctioned off to raise money for the hospital – includes outstanding pieces such as Domenico Ghirlandaio's Adoration of the Magi, commissioned for the main altar of the hospital's church.

Adoration of the Magi (Domenico Ghirlandaio, c. 1485)

Museo Leonardo da Vinci

*Via de' Servi 66-68r (055 282966, www.mostredileonardo.com). **Open** Apr-Oct 10am-7pm daily. Nov-Mar 10am-6pm daily. **Admission** €7; €5 reductions. **Map** p131 N5.*

The painter, sculptor, musician, engineer, inventor, scientist and all-round genius Leonardo da Vinci justly has a museum to himself. The museum offers an attractive, interactive insight into the machines that featured in da Vinci's codes. Several of his most extraordinary inventions have been built from studies taken from his drawings: flying machines, a hydraulic saw, a printing machine and even a massive tank – it measures 5.3m by 3m (17ft by 10ft) and weighs two tonnes. Most of the exhibits can be touched, moved and even dangled from, making this place immensely popular with kids.

❤ Opificio delle Pietre Dure

*Via degli Alfani 78 (055 26511, www.opificiodellepietredure.it). **Open** 8.15am-2pm Mon-Sat. **Admission** €4; €2 reductions. No cards. **Map** p131 N4.*

In all the grandest palaces and most expensive shops in town, you'll see fine examples of the Florentine craft of inlaying *pietre dure* (semi-precious stones) in intricate mosaics. The Opificio (workshop) was founded by Grand Duke Ferdinando I in 1588. It's now an important restoration centre, but also provides a fascinating insight into this typically Florentine art, with its mezzanine exhibitions of tools and stones, and its displays of the methods used for cutting and polishing the stones, through to inlaying and mosaic techniques.

Opificio delle Pietre Dure
The restoration of Dwarf Morgante
(Bronzino c. 1553)

San Marco

*Piazza San Marco (055 2388608). **Open** 8.15am-1.50pm Mon-Fri; 8.15am-4.50pm Sat, Sun. Closed 2nd, 4th Mon and 1st, 3rd, 5th Sun each mth. **Admission** €4; €2 reductions. **Map** p131 N3.*

The amount of money lavished by the Medici family on San Lorenzo (*see p122*) is nothing compared with that spent on the church and convent of San Marco. After Cosimo il Vecchio (*see p263* A Medici Who's Who) returned from exile in 1434, he organised the transfer of San Marco from the Silvestrine monks to the Dominican friars from Fiesole. Cosimo went on to fund the renovation of the decaying church and convent by Michelozzo, and also founded a public library that greatly influenced Florentine Humanists; Florentine Humanist Academy meetings were held in the gardens. Ironically, later in the 15th century San Marco became the base of religious fundamentalist Fra Girolamo Savonarola, who burned countless Humanist treasures in his notorious Bonfire of the Vanities (*see p77*).

Inside the church, see Giambologna's 16th-century nave with side chapels. In 1589, he completed the Cappella di Sant'Antonino, where you can now, creepily, see the whole dried body of the saint.

The altarpiece *Madonna and Child* (1440s) is by Fra Angelico, whose other more famous works can be seen next door in the Museo di San Marco (*see opposite*). Two missing panels from the painting were discovered, curiously enough, in Oxford, behind the door of an elderly Englishwoman's house in 2006.

Santissima Annunziata

*Piazza della SS Annunziata (055 266181). **Open** 7.30am-12.30pm, 4-6.30pm daily. **Admission** free. **Map** p131 O4.*

Despite Brunelleschi's perfectionist ambitions for the square it crowns, Santissima Annunziata – the church of the

---

In the know
Not an artist, but an inspired saint

Fra Angelico was a friar who carried out his most spiritual work during his redecorations at San Marco. Masaccio and Alberti influences are evident in his treatment of linear perspective, and his pioneering use of light and colour to depict movement and expression guarantee him a place in the Renaissance hall of fame. Described by Ruskin as 'Not an artist... but an inspired saint', he is the only *beato* (blessed) in the history of Catholicism to have earned his beatification on the grounds of purely artistic merits.

❤ Museo di San Marco

Piazza San Marco 1 (055 2388608, www.polomuseale.firenze.it). **Open** *8.15am-1.50pm Tue-Fri, 1st, 3rd & 5th Mon of mth; 8.15am-4.50pm Sat, 2nd & 4th Sun of mth.* **Admission** *€4; €2 reductions; free on 1st Sun of every mth. No cards.* **Map** *p131 N2.*

The Museo di San Marco is not only a fascinating coming-together of religion and history, but a wonderful place to rest and take in the general splendour. Housed in the Dominican monastery where he worked, the museum is largely dedicated to the ethereal paintings of Fra Angelico (aka Beato Angelico), one of the most important spiritual artists of the 15th century, a man who would never lift a brush without a prayer and who wept whenever he painted a crucifixion.

You're greeted on the first floor by one of the most famous images in Christendom: an other-worldly *Annunciation,* but the images Fra Angelico and his assistants frescoed on the walls of the monks' white-vaulted cells are almost as impressive. Particularly outstanding is the lyrical *Noli Me Tangere,* which depicts Christ appearing to Mary Magdalene in a field of flowers, and the surreal *Mocking of Christ,* in which Christ's torturers are represented simply by relevant fragments of their anatomy (a hand holding a whip, a face spitting).

The cell that was later occupied by Fra Girolamo Savonarola is adorned with portraits of the rabid reformer by Fra Bartolomeo. You can also see his black wool cloak and his cilice, which was tied around the thigh to cause constant pain in reminder of the suffering of Christ. Near the cells reserved specially for Cosimo the Elder is the beautiful library designed by his favourite architect, Michelozzo, in 1441.

On the ground floor, in the Ospizio dei Pellegrini (pilgrims' hospice), are more works by Fra Angelico. The recently restored *Tabernacle of the Madonna dei Linaiuoli,* his first commission from 1433 for the guild of linen makers, is here – painted on wood carved by Ghiberti – and contains some of his best-known images: the multi-coloured musical angels. You can also see a superb *Deposition* and a *Last Judgement.* The Small Refectory (or Guest Refectory) is dominated by a Ghirlandaio *Last Supper* (1486) in which the disciples pick at a repast of bread, wine and cherries against a symbolic background of orange trees, a peacock, a Burmese cat and flying ducks. You may want to compare this with Ghirlandaio's earlier fresco of the same subject in the Cenacolo di Ognissanti (*see p106*).

❤ Don't miss

1 Annunciation fresco *at the top of the staircase to the first floor*
Fra Angelico's finest version of this traditional theme.

2 Michelozzo's Library *first floor, off the western corridor (to the right of the entrance stairs)*
One of the most pleasing Renaissance spaces in the city.

3 Fra Angelico's Madonna dei Linaioli *Hospice (ground floor)*
Recently restored to its former splendour.

4 Last Supper *Small Refectory (ground floor)*
Domenico Ghirlandaio's large fresco in the Small Refectory.

5 Girolamo Savonarola portrait *Room of Fra Bartolomeo paintings (ground floor)*
A haunting profile by fellow Dominican Fra Bartolomeo.

Library (Michelozzo, 1442-4)

Servite order – is a place of popular worship rather than perfect proportion. Highlights include a frescoed Baroque ceiling and an opulent shrine built around a miraculous Madonna, purportedly painted by a monk in 1252 and, as the story goes, finished overnight by angels. Surrounding the icon are flowers, silver lamps and pewter body parts, ex-votos left in the hope that the Madonna will cure the dicky heart or gammy leg of a loved one.

Michelozzo was the directing architect and built the Villani and Madonna chapels, and the oratory on the left side of the church. In 1453, after almost ten years of work and not much progress, directorship was handed to Antonio Manetti. When Manetti ran into financial difficulty, the governing priests ceded the venture to the Gonzaga family. Finally, in 1477, Leon Battista Alberti completed the church with slight modifications. The atrium was frescoed early the following century by Pontormo, Rosso Fiorentino and, most strikingly, Andrea del Sarto, whose *Birth of the Virgin* is set within the walls of a Renaissance palazzo that has cherubs perched on a mantelpiece.

Restaurants & wine bars

♥ Osteria de L'Ortolano €€
Via degli Alfani 91r, (055 2396466, www. osteriafirenze.com). Open 10am-3pm Mon-Sat, 6-10pm Wed-Sat. Closed Aug. Map p131 N4 ① Osteria

In an area historically devoid of great dining options, Osteria de L'Ortolano (deli by day, restaurant by night) is a refreshingly fair-priced spot for a sit-down dinner, managed by a lovely couple serving seasonal, often unexpectedly rich dishes, from guinea fowl to bitter chicory. There's a thoroughly Tuscan vin santo risotto (made with the region's famous dessert wine), as well as inventive seconds like the beer-based veal meatballs with sweet potatoes. Simpler, kid-friendly fare such as chicken and chips ensures no one in the family will go hungry.

Ristorante Accademia €€
Piazza San Marco 7r (055 217343, www. ristoranteaccademia.it). Open noon-3pm, 7-11pm daily. Map p131 N3 ② Italian

Attracting a mix of local Florentines, resident foreigners and tourists, Ristorante Accademia is a useful spot in an area where there is a dearth of good eating choices. With a few exceptions (fillet steak cooked in an intense *brachetto* wine sauce with glazed shallots, for example), the more ambitious options on the menu are the least successful. Go for more reliable staples such as traditional pastas (try the homemade pasta with lamb meat sauce and roasted almonds). Pizzas are a decent

choice too. The wine list is surprisingly comprehensive, prices are reasonable and the Iacovitti brothers are cheerful hosts.

Cafés, bars & gelaterie

♥ Arà: è Sicilia
Via degli Alfani 127r (328 6117029, www. araesicilia.it). Open 10am-10pm daily. Map p131 N4 ① Café

Specialising in tasty Sicilian street food and desserts, this simple café attracts local workers and students and makes for a welcome break from Florentine staples. Apart from gelato, Tuscany isn't exactly known for its desserts, but here you can indulge in Sicilian sweets: think *cannoli, granite, cassate* (cream gelato pyramid blocks with candied fruit) and praline-based treats, as well as savoury snacks including popular *arancini*, the region's lip-smacking stuffed rice balls.

♥ Un Caffè da l' Sardo
Via Cesare Battisti 2 (347 3734307, www. facebook.com/DaISardo). Open 8am-1am Mon-Fri; 9am-2am Sat; 10am-7pm Sun. No cards. Map p131 O4 ② Café

This Sardinian-owned hole-in-the-wall off piazza Santissima Annunziata is inexpensive and unpretentious, staffed by friendly young faces and popular for being a picturesque *aperitivo* destination. It's one of those rare spaces that seamlessly moves between being a breakfast spot, coffee-break option, lunch hideaway and nightlife haunt. Come for the generous *schiacciate* (Tuscan flat bread) stacked with fresh ingredients and paired with house wine; stick around for frequent live music and priceless views of the sprawling square.

Caffè del Verone
MUDI See pp136-137 Map p131 O4 ③ Café

A sleek bonus to Museo degli Innocenti (MUDI) created in the rooftop loggia (originally a laundry-drying place), Caffè del Verone affords beautiful views, with Filippo Brunelleschi's red-brick dome on one side and the green dome of the Synagogue at the opposite end. In keeping with the Institute's protection of children, the café offers a 50% discount to children under 12.

♥ Carabè
Via Ricasoli 60r (055 289476, www. parcocarabe.it). Open Summer 9am-1am daily. Winter 9am-8pm daily. Closed mid Dec-mid Jan. No cards. Map p131 N4 ④ Gelateria

The Sicilian owners of this gelateria near the Accademia are third-generation ice-cream makers and proud of their heritage. They excel in the island's specialities – one crunchy granita is flavoured with almond milk, fresh lemons are brought in weekly from Sicily to make a tangy ice-cream/sorbet crossbreed and the *cremolata* is made with the pulp of seasonal soft fruits. Along with Arà: è Sicilia (*see left*), it's one of the few places in the city to offer authentic *cassate* and *cannoli* (the round ricotta-filled snaps immortalised as weapons in *The Godfather III*).

Le Parigine
Via de' Servi 41r (055 2398470, www. facebook.com/leparigine). Open noon-8pm daily. Map p131 N5 ❺ *Gelateria*

Le Parigine (named after those old-fashioned ice-cream and biscuit sandwiches, which are served here in three sizes) stands out to sweet-toothed travellers and locals in an area that doesn't have enough really good *gelaterie*. Flavours are seasonal and unusual – pink grapefruit, anyone? – and ingredients are fresh and natural, with great provenance (pistachios from Bronte in Catania, cocoa powder from Madagascar). Sit in or outside on little benches to eat your cone. With all ice-creams made on-site, you'll be hard pressed to find a better gelato this close to the Duomo.

Robiglio
Via de' Servi 112r (055 214501). Open 7.30am-7.30pm Mon-Sat. Closed 3wks Aug. Map p131 O4 ❻ *Café and pasticceria*

The sublime hot chocolate served here is so thick that the spoon stands up in it, and the delicious pastries are a Florentine institution. Pietro Robiglio began his mini *pasticceria* empire in Florence in 1928, since which time he has opened five shops selling deliciously light brioches, galette biscuits, meringues, crème-filled pastries and celebration cakes. **Other locations** viale Spartaco Lavagnini 18r, Fortezza da Basso area, Outside the City Gates (055 490886) and via dei Tosinghi 11r, Duomo & Around (055 215013).

Shops
❤ Bartolini
Via de' Servi 72r (055 211895, www. bartolinifirenze.it). Open 3.30-7.30pm Mon; 10am-1pm, 3.30-7.30pm Tue-Sat. Closed 2wks Aug. Map p131 N5 ❶ *Kitchenware*

This charming kitchen shop has extensive selections of cutlery and crockery, plus beautiful gadgets, appliances and unusual and interesting accessories.

Focacceria Pugi
Piazza San Marco 10 (055 280981, www. focacceria-pugi.it). Open 7.45am-8pm Mon-Sat. Map p131 N3 ❷ *Food*

An institution since 1924, and justly famed for its *schiacciata* – a delicious flatbread served with olive oil or grapes.

❤ Frette
Via Cavour 2r (055 211369, www.frette. com). Open 3-7pm Mon; 10am-7pm Tue-Sat; 11am-6pm Sun. Closed 3wks Aug. Map p131 M5 ❸ *Homeware*

The full range of bedding, towels and robes so beloved of boutique hotels the world over. **Other locations** Via San Gallo 62r, San Lorenzo (055 475975); via Orsini 63/65, Outside the City Gates (055 689763)

❤ L'Ortolano
Via degli Alfani 91r (055 2396466, www. osteriafirenze.com). Open 10am-3pm Mon-Sat. Closed Aug. Map p131 N4 ❹ *Food*

This excellent grocery shop is a great place to pick up gourmet gifts, from fruit-infused honey to a huge selection of cheeses from Tuscany and beyond; the Caciocavallo is incredible. Ortolano produces its own range of lovely little jars of bruschetta toppings too, among them cream of artichoke and cream of asparagus, and the *salumi* (Italian cold cuts) include the rich and intense *cinta senese prosciutto* – get some made up into a *panino* and enjoy a very special lunch. By night, the shop transforms into a tasty osteria (*see left*).

Rigacci
Via de' Servi 71r (055 216206, www. rigaccifirenze.it). Open 8.30am-7pm Mon-Fri; 8.30am-12.30pm Sat; 3-7pm Sun (Dec only). Map p131 N5 ❺ *Art*

This historic art supply store is a one-stop shop for established or aspiring artists, and is regularly packed with students of all nationalities stocking up on fine art supplies. Uncover pastels, oil and acrylic paints, canvases, textured papers and other materials. Occasionally the back room displays work by emerging local artists.

❤ Street Doing
Via de' Servi 88r (055 5381334, www. streetdoingvintage.it). Open 10.30am-7.30pm Mon-Sat, 2.30-7.30pm Sun. Map p131 N5 ❻ *Vintage fashion*

With multiple rooms and an impressive collection of designers, from Florentine favourites to the biggest names in the fashion business, Street Doing requires the most serious vintage shoppers to set aside some time for it. The front room contains artfully arranged accessories and most of the prime stock, but venture toward the back for winter coats, bargain-bin finds and even a full gallery of ballgowns.

Santa Croce

Like much of the city centre, Santa Croce has a heady air of history and learning. Here you'll find the city's synagogue, the national library and fascinating art: the Bargello museum contains a wealth of incredible Renaissance pieces, while the church of Santa Croce itself – besides being the focal point of the neighbourhood and a pantheon where several of Italy's illustrious dead are buried or honoured – has some of the finest 14th-century frescoes in Florence.

Still fairly authentic, working-class Santa Croce borders the Duomo along its western edge, yet it is a very different beast – especially in the Sant'Ambrogio district, peopled largely by locals who wouldn't trade shopping at the wonderful *mercato* for all the glitzy supermarkets in the world. A fair number of artisan workshops – mostly leather crafters and wood gilders – still survive, alongside the ubiquitous new stores filled with tourist wares.

In terms of new openings and general buzziness, Santa Croce comes in a close second to the boho-chic Oltrarno for the title of Florence's most exciting area; so if you don't have time to venture across the Arno, this lively district makes a good alternative.

❤ Don't miss

1 Bargello *p146*
A unique collection of Renaissance sculpture in one of the city's oldest buildings.

2 Santa Croce *p148*
The largest Franciscan church in the world is a temple of Italian glories.

3 Mercato Sant'Ambrogio *p159*
Try Florentine specialities and enjoy the local vibe at the stalls of this indoor food market.

4 Museo Horne *p152*
A remarkable art collection bequeathed to the Italian state by an English expat.

5 Casa Buonarroti *p151*
Michelangelo's early works and his wooden model for the San Lorenzo façade.

In the know
Getting around

The neighbourhood is best explored on foot, but a few bus routes cross it on their way between piazza della Stazione and piazza Beccaria, either through San Marco and piazza d'Azeglio (bus 14, 23) or via the old centre (minibus C1, C2, D).

View of Santa Croce *p148*

PIAZZA SANTA CROCE & AROUND

Just north of the river, piazza Santa Croce with its imposing Gothic basilica of **Santa Croce** (*see p148*) and attached museum and cloisters is a natural meeting spot where children play and adults rest their feet. The suicidal/homicidal game *calcio storico* (historic football; *see p225*) is played here every June, and from the end of November there's a German-style Christmas market. Lining the square is a mix of shops and restaurants with outside tables. On the south side is the frescoed sepia façade of **Palazzo d'Antella**: decorated in 1620, it now houses smart rental apartments. Outside the church is Enrico Pazzi's 1865 statue of Dante, formerly in the middle of the square.

♥ Time to eat & drink

Coffee with a view
Caffetteria delle Oblate *p155*

Tuscan classics
Del Fagioli *p153*

Divine gelato
Vivoli *p155*

Perfect pizza
Caffè Italiano *p153*
Il Pizzaiuolo *p158*

Once-in-a-lifetime splurge
Enoteca Pinchiorri *p153*

♥ Time to shop

Cutting-edge fashion
Société Anonyme *p161*

Florentine artisan gifts
Signum *p156*

Rare vinyl and 'lost' tracks
Data Records 93 *p156*

Indulgent cakes
Dolci e Dolcezze *p160*

Vintage fashion bargains
A Ritroso... A Rebours *p156*

♥ Time well spent

Scuola del Cuoio
Via San Giuseppe 5r (055 244533, www. scuoladelcuoio.com). **Open** *Apr-Oct 10am-6pm daily. Nov-Mar 10am-6pm Mon-Fri; 10.30am-6pm Sat.* **Map** *p145 Q9.*
Regardless of whether or not you intend to purchase the quality leather goods handmade on site (how about a photo album or a travel journal?), at the leather school in the cloisters of Santa Croce you can watch skilled craftspeople busy at their workbenches making bags and accessories with traditional techniques and passing their expertise from master to apprentice.

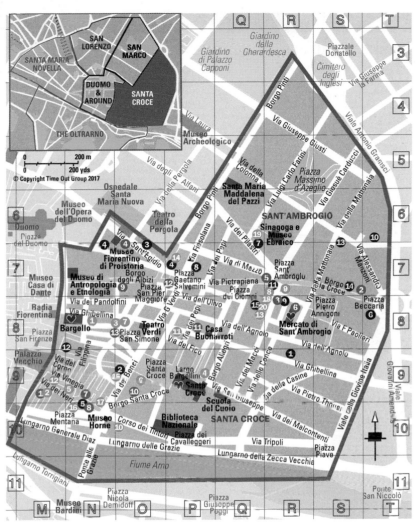

SANTA CROCE

Restaurants & wine bars

1. Acqua al 2
2. All'Antico Vinaio
3. Ara è Sud
4. Baldovino
5. Beijing8
6. Boccadama
7. Caffè Italiano
8. Cibrèino
9. Cibrèo
10. Del Fagioli
11. Enoteca Pinchiorri
12. La Fettunta
13. Ganzo
14. La Giostra
15. Kome
16. Libreria Brac
17. Osteria de' Benci
18. Il Pizzaiuolo
19. Ruth's
20. Teatro del Sale

Cafés, bars & gelaterie

1. All'Antico Vinaio
2. L'Arte del Sogno
3. Caffè Cibrèo
4. Caffetteria delle Oblate
5. Caffè Sant' Ambrogio
6. Da Rocco
7. Ditta Artigianale
8. Gelateria dei Neri
9. La Loggia degli Albizi
10. Quelo
11. Le Vespe
12. Vestri
13. Vivoli

Shops

1. A Ritroso... A Rebours
2. La Bottega dei Cristalli
3. Casa della Cornice
4. Cup of Milk
5. Data Records 93
6. Dolci e Dolcezze
7. Lady Jane B Vintage Boutique
8. Libreria delle Donne
9. Lisa Corti Home Textiles Emporium
10. La Raccolta
11. Sandra Dori
12. Signum
13. Société Anonyme
14. Il Sole nel Borgo
15. Teatro del Sale

❤ Bargello

Via del Proconsolo 4 (055 2388606, www. bargellomusei.beniculturali.it). **Open** *8.15am-5pm daily. Closed 1st, 3rd & 5th Mon of mth, 2nd & 4th Sun of mth.* **Admission** *€8; €4 reductions. Free on the 1st Sun of every month. No cards.* **Map** *p145 N8.*

This imposing, fortified structure has had so many functions over the years that, although it now contains Florence's most important sculpture collection, the history of the building itself is as fascinating as the exhibits. The Bargello started life as the Palazzo del Popolo in 1250 and soon became the mainstay of the chief magistrate, or *podestà*. The bodies of executed criminals were displayed in the courtyard during the 14th century; in the 15th century, law courts, prisons and torture chambers were set up inside. The Medici made it the seat of the *bargello* (chief of police) in the 16th century.

Officially called Museo Nazionale del Bargello, the museum opened in 1865 to celebrate Florence becoming the capital of Italy. It now holds the city's most eclectic and prestigious collection of sculpture.

Upon entering, the first room you enter on the ground floor is the Sala di Michelangelo with such famous pieces as his *Drunken Bacchus* and *Brutus* (the only bust he ever sculpted), and Giambologna's fleet-footed *Mercury*. Works by Andrea Sansovino, Baccio Bandinelli, Bartolomeo Ammannati, Benvenuto Cellini and Giambologna are also in this room.

The Salone Donatello on the first floor contains the artist's two triumphant *Davids* and a tense *St George*, the original of which once stood outside the Orsanmichele church. Also fascinating are the two bronze panels of the *Sacrifice of Isaac*, sculpted by Brunelleschi and Lorenzo Ghiberti for a competition to design the north doors of the Duomo's Baptistery. Back out on the grand loggia you can see Giambologna's bronze birds – they used to spout water in the grotto of the Medici Villa di Castello, and include a madly exaggerated turkey. On this floor, you can also find the little frescoed Magdalen Chapel, which contains the oldest confirmed portrait of Dante, painted by Giotto.

The easily missed second floor has a fascinating selection of bronze statuettes

and a fine collection of Florentine busts, including Andrea del Verrocchio's elegant *Lady with Primroses* (1474), perhaps carved in collaboration with his student Leonardo da Vinci.

The rest of the museum contains a variety of collections, including Della Robbia glazed terracottas, Scandinavian chess sets and Egyptian ivories, European clocks, reliquary caskets, Islamic art, Medici arms and armours and a huge collection of medals. There is also a ground-floor wing reserved for temporary exhibitions, while in the summer, the Bargello courtyard provides a striking backdrop for a much-loved evening festival unimaginatively called *Estate al Bargello*. The programme offers a pleasant mix of theatre, music, dance and literary readings between June and July, sometimes followed by a few more shows in September (*see p247* Performing Arts).

❤ Don't miss

1 The 'other' Davids *Salone di Donatello & Sala del Verrocchio*
Donatello's and Verrocchio's predecessors of Michelangelo's iconic work.

2 Mercury *Sala di Michelangelo*
Giambologna's fleet-footed, swirling bronze masterpiece.

3 Sacrifice of Isaac panels *Salone di Donatello*
Brunelleschi's and Ghiberti's entries for the Baptistery door competition.

4 Tondo Pitti *Sala di Michelangelo*
A Madonna and Child bas-relief that was Michelangelo's commission just after the *David*.

5 Lady with Primroses *Sala del Verrocchio*
A graceful full bust del Verrocchio, particularly admired for its delicate hands.

6 Portrait of Dante as a young man *Cappella di S. Maria Maddalena*
Once attributed to Giotto, but now widely considered the work of his school.

Mercury (Giambologna, c1580)

❤ Santa Croce

Largo Bargellini (left side of the church) (055 2466105, www.santacroceopera.it). **Open** *9.30am-5.30pm Mon-Sat; 1-5.30pm Sun.* **Admission** *€8; €4 reductions (incl museum & chapel); free for under 11s.* **Map** *p145 P9.*

The richest medieval church in the city, Santa Croce has a great deal to offer, even to visitors long tired of church-hopping. The Museo dell'Opera di Santa Croce is housed here, along with the delightful chapter house known as the Cappella dei Pazzi and two beautiful cloistered courtyards; not to mention the church itself, which is crammed with illustrious tombs and cenotaphs.

Although impressive, the white, pink and green marble façade was only created between 1853 and 1863 by architect Niccolò Matas in the neo-Gothic style. Before that, the façade had been a bare stone front not unlike today's San Lorenzo (*see p122*). Most of the project was funded by Sir Francis Joseph Sloane, an Italian-born Briton who contributed a whopping 400,000 *scudi* (Italy's currency until 1857) out of the total 580,000 *scudi* it eventually cost.

At first sight the interior seems big and gloomy, with overbearing marble tombs clogging the walls. Not all of them contain bodies: Dante's, for example, is simply a memorial to the poet, who is buried in Ravenna. In the niche alongside Dante's is the tomb of Michelangelo, by Vasari. The artist had insisted on burial here when the time came, as he wanted 'a view towards the cupola of the Duomo for all eternity', and to adorn his tomb had worked obsessively on the *Pietà* (now in the Museo dell'Opera del Duomo; *see p70*). It is said that he would have disliked the finished tomb because, despite being an impressive mixture of painting, sculpture and architecture, the whole is too ostentatious and complicated for a memorial tomb (unlike his own serene Sagrestia Nuova in the Cappelle Medicee; *see p121*). Further into the church are the tombs of Leonardo Bruni (by Bernardo Rossellino), Vittorio Alfieri and, best known for eating brains in the *Divine Comedy*, Ugolino della Gherardesca. Back at the top of the left aisle is Galileo's tomb, a polychrome marble confection created by Foggini more than a century after the astronomer's death, when the Church finally permitted him a Christian burial.

It may seem something of a paradox that, while the church is filled with the tombs of the great and the grand, it belongs to the Franciscans, the least worldly of the religious orders. They founded it in 1228, ten years after arriving in the city. But by the late 13th century, their vow of poverty eroded,

Cappella dei Pazzi (The Pazzi Chapel), Basilica di Santa Croce

the old church was felt to be inadequate and a new building was planned: intended to be one of the largest in Christendom, it was designed by Arnolfo di Cambio, architect of the Duomo and Palazzo Vecchio. The building was financed partly by confiscated Ghibelline property, and Arnolfo himself laid the first stone on 3 May 1294.

The church underwent various stages of restoration and modification, with one of Vasari's infamous modernisations robbing it of some frescoes by Giotto's school in favour of heavy classical altars. Fortunately, he left the main chapels intact, though subsequent makeovers completely destroyed the decorations of the Cappella Tosinghi-Spinelli. Among the remaining gems are the fabulous stained-glass windows at the east end (behind the high altar) by Agnolo Gaddi, the marble tomb of Leonardo Bruni, and the Cavalcanti tabernacle (both flanking the side door on the south wall).

At the eastern end of the church, the **Bardi and Peruzzi chapels**, which were completely frescoed by Giotto, are masterpieces. That said, the condition of the frescoes is not brilliant – a result of Giotto painting on dry instead of wet plaster and daubing them with whitewash – and were only rediscovered in the mid 18th century. The most striking of the two chapels is the Bardi, with scenes from the life of St Francis in haunting, virtual monotone, the figures stylised just enough to make them otherworldly yet individual enough to keep them human. On the far side of the high altar is the Cappella Bardi di Vernio, frescoed by one of Giotto's most interesting followers, Maso di Banco, in vibrant colours.

Brunelleschi's geometric tour de force, the **Cappella dei Pazzi**, was planned in the 1430s and completed almost 40 years later, long after the architect's death. Its design is based on a central square, topped by an umbrella-like cupola flanked by a pair of barrel-vaulted bays. The pure lines of the interior alternate white plaster and grey sandstone and are decorated with Luca della Robbia's painted ceramic roundels of the 12 Apostles, while the four Evangelists are also considered Brunelleschi's. The chapel opens on to the cloisters resulting in a calm, detached atmosphere. The loggia was recently restored thanks to an international crowdfunding project whose outcome far exceeded the campaign's own

goal, bringing about new approaches to gathering restoration funds.

Across the courtyard is a small museum of church treasures; the collection includes Donatello's pious *St Louis of Toulouse* from Orsanmichele (*see p88*). The backbone of the collection is in the former refectory, with Taddeo Gaddi's imposing yet poetic *Tree of Life* above his *Last Supper* (unfortunately, in very bad condition). In November 2016, the momentous anniversary of the 1966 flood was celebrated with the return of Giorgio Vasari's monumental *Last Supper*, whose five wooden panels had been submerged for over 12 hours in water and muck and were finally restored and reassembled 50 years later, following an international conservation effort. In equally poor condition is Cimabue's *Crucifixion*, which hung in the basilica until it was damaged in the flood of 1966. There's also a small permanent exhibition of the woodcuts and engravings of the modern artist Pietro Parigi, while a bronze sculpture by Henry Moore – donated by his widow to the British Institute of Florence – is on display in the cloister.

❤ Don't miss

1 The Bardi and Peruzzi chapels
The genius of Giotto's ground-breaking frescoes defies their poor condition.

2 Cappella dei Pazzi
One of the city's most harmonious and elegant spaces.

3 Cimabue's Crucifixion *Sacristy*
A heartbreaking reminder of the devastating effects of the 1966 flood.

4 Donatello's Cavalcanti Annunciation *Right nave*
One of the few works by Donatello still in its original setting.

5 The lancet windows in the sanctuary
Agnolo Gaddi's original stained-glass windows behind the high altar.

6 Vasari's Last Supper *Refectory*
A monumental painting brought back to life 50 years after the 1966 flood.

Frescoes and stained glass windows (Agnolo Gaddi, c 1380), Cappella Maggiore, Santa Croce.

At the southwest corner of piazza Santa Croce, via de' Benci is dotted with craft shops and bohemian restaurants. The street runs down towards the Arno, past the **Museo Horne** (*see p152*), to the **ponte alle Grazie**. Like most of the bridges in central Florence, this one has a fascinating history: it was blown up just before the Germans' retreat at the end of World War II and only rebuilt in 1957. The

bridge gets its name from a chapel, devoted to Santa Maria delle Grazie, which was popular with distraught lovers seeking solace.

Continuing east you'll come across a square dominated by the **Biblioteca Nazionale**. Built to house the three million books and two million documents that were held in the Uffizi until 1935, the national library has two towers with statues of Dante and Galileo – nicknamed by Florentines, in mock disrespect, 'the asses' ears'.

West of the parish square are myriad winding streets, mostly given over to leather factories and tiny souvenir shops. Via del Proconsolo houses the **Bargello** (*see p146*) at its Piazza San Firenze end, while further north towards the Duomo is the **Museo di Antropologia e Etnologia** (*see opposite*) at the corner of borgo degli Albizi. Nearby are also the **Museo Fiorentino di Preistoria** (*see opposite*), accessed from via Sant'Egidio or through **Le Murate** library complex on via dell'Oriuolo, and **Casa Buonarroti** (*see opposite*) in via Ghibellina.

In the know
Once walled up, now freed up

A sizeable area between via Ghibellina and via dell'Agnolo is one of the city's most successfully reclaimed spaces. The building started as a nunnery and was later converted into a men's prison – hence the name Le Murate (walled up). It is now a hipster residential and commercial complex as well as a lively cultural space housing a literary café, a variety of festivals and a contemporary art project.

Street Shrines

This early Western street art encapsulates the city's once fervent religious nature

The Italian tradition of creating shrines to the Madonna, Jesus or patron saints on street corners is particularly strong in Florence. To prove their devotion to the Catholic Church (and avoid the nasty repercussions of being branded heretics), many individuals, trades, confraternities and guilds in the 14th century built tabernacles in conspicuous positions, often on the corner of their home. The tabernacle was usually a stone *edicola*, a frame for an icon, with a roof to protect the artwork and a mantle for offerings. The icon itself could be a fresco, painting, relief, tile or sculpture; sometimes famous artists were hired to create the venerable image and boost the cachet of the sponsor. The result is an art heritage of sometimes astonishing value. These shrines are among the most noteworthy:

Via Arte della Lana *corner with via di Orsanmichele, Duomo & Around.* **Map** *p63 L8.*

Via Ricasoli *corner with via de' Pucci, San Marco.* **Map** *p131 M5.*

Via de' Tornabuoni *corner with via della Vigna Nuova, Duomo & Around.* **Map** *p63 J8.*

In other parts of Florence, look out for:
Via degli Alfani *corner with borgo Pinti, Santa Croce.* **Map** *p145 P6.*

Piazza dell'Unità Italiana *corner with via Sant'Antonio, San Lorenzo.* **Map** *p119 J5.*

Via della Spada *near San Pancrazio, Santa Maria Novella.* **Map** *p101 H7.*

Sights & museums

💚 Casa Buonarroti
Via Ghibellina 70 (055 241752, www. casabuonarroti.it). **Open** *Mar Oct 10am-5pm Mon, Wed-Sun. Nov-Feb 10am-4pm Mon, Wed-Sun.* **Admission** *€6.50; €4.50 reductions. No cards.* **Map** *p145 P8.*

In 1612, Michelangelo Buonarroti the Younger took the decision to create a building in order to honour the memory of his rather more famous great-uncle. Although Michelangelo (1475-1564) never actually lived here, this 17th-century house, owned by his descendants until 1858, has a collection of memorabilia that gives an insight into Florence's most famous artistic son. On the walls are scenes from the painter's life, while the pieces collected by the artist's great-nephew Filippo include a magnificent wooden model for the façade of San Lorenzo (*see p122*) and two important original works: a bas-relief *Madonna of the Stairs* breastfeeding at the foot of a flight of stairs, and an unfinished *Battle of the Centaurs*.

Galleria Santo Ficara
Via Ghibellina 164r (055 2340239, www. santoficara.it). **Open** *9.30am-12.30pm, 3.30-7.30pm Mon-Sat. Closed Aug.* **Map** *p145 N8.*

The walls of this important city-centre gallery, with its tall vaulted ceilings, are hung with works by established modern and contemporary artists with an international market, such as 1950s Gruppo Forma member Carla Accardi.

Museo di Antropologia e Etnologia
Via del Proconsolo 12 (055 2756444, www. msn.unifi.it). **Open** *Oct-May 9.30am-4.30pm Mon, Tue, Thur, Fri; 10am-4.30pm Sat, Sun. June-Sept 10.30am-5.30pm daily.* **Admission** *€6 €3 (€10 combined for University Science museums). No cards.* **Map** *p145 N7.*

Among the mix of artefacts from all over the world on display here are a collection of Peruvian mummies, an Ostyak harp from Lapland, an engraved trumpet from the former Belgian Congo made out of an elephant tusk, Ecuadorian shrunken heads alongside a specially designed skull-beating club, and a Marini-meets-Picasso equestrian monument.

Museo Fiorentino di Preistoria
Via Sant'Egidio 21 (055 295159, www. museofiorentinopreistoria.it). **Open** *3.30-6.30pm Mon; 9.30am-12.30pm, 3.30-6.30pm Tue, Thur; 9.30am-12.30pm Wed, Fri, Sat; guided tours by appointment.* **Admission** *€3. No cards.* **Map** *p145 O6.*

Florence's Museum of Prehistory traces humanity's development from the Paleolithic to the Bronze Age. The first floor contains interesting displays of illustrations following hominid physical changes, and also examines Italy's prehistoric art. The second floor includes a fascinating collection of stone implements.

💗 Museo Horne

Via de' Benci 6 (055 244661, www.
museohorne. it). **Open** *9am-1pm Mon-Sat.*
Admission *€7; €5 reductions. No cards.*
Map *p145 N10.*

The 15th-century Palazzo Corsi-Alberti was
purchased in the 1800s by English architect
and art historian Herbert Percy Horne, who
restored it to its Renaissance splendour.
Formerly thought to be the work of Giuliano
da Sangallo, the building is now generally
attributed to Il Cronaca. When he died in 1916,
Horne left his *palazzo* and vast collection to
the state. Objects range from Renaissance
paintings and sculptures to furniture and
ceramics, but there are also everyday items
such as Florentine coins, a coffee grinder and
a pair of spectacles. Upstairs is a damaged
wooden panel from a triptych attributed to
Masaccio. Also, here is an *Exorcism* by the
Maestro di San Severino and, the pride of
the collection, a gold-back *Santo Stefano*
by Giotto.

Restaurants & wine bars

Acqua al 2 €€€

Via della Vigna Vecchia 40r (055 284170,
www.acquaal2.it). **Open** *12.30-3pm,*
7.00pm-1am daily. Closed Mon lunch. **Map**
p145 N8 ① *Traditional Italian*

The cosmopolitan feel of this Florence eatery
(which also has outposts in Washington
DC and San Diego) attracts big crowds. Its
barrel-vaulted ceiling and quirky interior
(the walls are lined with autographed plates
of the famous who have eaten there) make
it a favourite with students, travellers and
garrulous Florentines, who sit elbow-to-elbow
at tightly lined tables in a series of small
rooms. Since its opening forty-something
years ago, Acqua al 2 has made a name for
itself thanks to its delicious pasta, cheeses,
salads and desserts. Try the veal fillet cooked
with balsamic vinegar or with wild berries.
Packed most evenings, this place can get
noisy and chaotic, but the quality of the food
and ambience are worth it.

All'Antico Vinaio €

Via de' Neri 74r (055 2382723, www.
allanticovinaio.com). **Open** *10am-4pm,*
6-11pm Tue-Sat; noon-6pm Sun. Closed Mon.
Map *p145 M9* ② *Osteria*

There aren't many dishes to choose from at
this humble eatery, but everything served
is genuine and solidly good. The *polpette*
(meat balls) are popular, as are the traditional
Tuscan tasting boards lined with simple
cheeses, cold cuts and crostini. There's also
a modest selection of wines, but it's best
to stick with something simple and rustic.

Opposite is a popular sandwich shop of the
same name (*see p154*).

Arà è Sud €€

Via della Vigna Vecchia 4r (328 6117029,
www.caffeitaliano.it/ara-e-sud). **Open** *noon-*
11pm Wed-Mon. Closed Tue. **Map** *p145*
O8 ③ *Sicilian*

Tuscan fare is everywhere you turn in
Florence, but in recent years cuisine from
other regions has been creeping onto the local
scene. In a refined yet unintimidating setting,
Arà è Sud offers a refreshingly modern take
on Sicilian classics: *rigatoni alla norma* and
delicious *busiati* pasta with almond pesto
are two of the standouts, but don't miss
the desserts. The best part? Presentation
is impressive here, but not at the expense
of taste.

Baldovino €€€

Via San Giuseppe 22r (055 241773, www.
baldovinobistrot.com). **Open** *11am-11pm*
daily. **Map** *p145 P9* ④ *Traditional Italian*

One of the most popular eateries in the Santa
Croce area, Baldovino wins points for its
colourful decor, elegant bistro ambience and
flexible menus (you can have a full meal,
snack, a pizza or a salad; try the black squid
ink-infused spaghetti). The food is good and
so is the service. Prices are reasonable, there's
plenty of choice and the wine list is full
and varied.

Dal Fagioli

Beijing8 €€

Via dei Neri 46r (380 7968093, www.beijing8. com). Open 11am-10pm daily. Map p145 N9 ❺ *Asian fusion*

Opened in December 2016, Beijing8 is quite an anomaly: a Scandinavian 'slow fast food' Asian fusion chain just a short walk from the Uffizi. Dig into dumplings in ginger and chilli sauces and warm up with serve-yourself tea. The chic minimalist aesthetic, friendly service and tasty, well-priced bites (try the satisfying lunch-box offer) make this a worthy stop for when you need a break from *pappa al pomodoro*.

Boccadama €€

Piazza Santa Croce 25-26r (055 243640, www.boccadama.com). Open 11am-3pm, 6.30-10.30pm daily. Map p145 O9 ❻ *Traditional Italian*

This restaurant and wine bar offers light fare at lunchtime (salads, pastas, bruschetta and so on) and full dinners featuring traditional Tuscan dishes such as home-made *pappardelle al cinghiale* (pappardelle pasta with wild boar) and *salsiccia e fagioli all'uccelleto* (sausage and bean stew). Wine by the glass is rather limited for a place that stocks over 400 labels. Nevertheless, thanks to its location, Boccadama, which is under the same management as Finisterrae across the square, is swamped with tourists (particularly for lunch) during the summer, when the terrace comes into its own.

❤ Caffè Italiano €€

Via Isola delle Stinche 13r (055 289080, www. caffeitaliano.it). Open 12.30-3pm, 7-11pm Tue-Sun. Closed 3wks Aug. Map p145 O8 ❼ *Pizzeria*

This tiny venue with a wood-burning oven and just four bare tables has minimal choice – marinara, margherita or Napoli – but it's a good sign when a pizzeria sticks to the basics, despite growing attention and tourist traffic. The pizzas' light and puffy bases are topped with San Marzano tomatoes and proper *mozzarella di bufala* shipped fresh from Campania. After 10.30pm, the overflow is seated at the adjacent restaurant, Osteria del Caffè Italiano.

❤ Del Fagioli €€

Corso de' Tintori 47r (055 244285). Open 12.30-2.30pm, 7.30-10.30pm Mon-Sat. Map p145 O10 ❿ *Trattoria*

This is one of those unpretentious time-worn places where little has changed over the years. Opened by Luigi ('Gigi') Zucchini just after the flood in 1966, it offers traditional Florentine cooking and such standards as *ribollita, pappa al pomodoro* and *bollito misto con salsa verde* (mixed boiled meats served with a bright green parsley sauce). Del Fagioli is a family business: Gigi and his son-in-law Maurizio are in charge of the kitchen, while sons Antonio and Simone work in the restaurant. Gigi's *involtini* (thin rolls of beef stuffed with cheese, ham and artichokes) are delicious. There's warm apple cake to finish.

❤ Enoteca Pinchiorri €€€€

Via Ghibellina 87 (055 242757, www. enotecapinchiorri.com). Open 7.30-10pm Tue-Sat. Map p145 P8 ⓫ *High-end gastronomy*

One of the most expensive restaurants in Florence (and Italy), Enoteca Pinchiorri is considered one of Italy's great temples to gastronomic excellence. Although French co-owner Annie Féolde (along with Giorgio Pinchiorri) no longer does any cooking (the executive chef is creative Milanese Riccardo Monco), she oversees the kitchen and runs front-of-house, where the atmosphere is of the formal, luxuriously old-fashioned kind. You can opt for à la carte or choose from two tasting menus (which represent the best value), each featuring four (€150 per person) or seven (€225 per person) tiny but superbly executed courses (such as John Dory bites in squid ink, sprouts of spinach, Béarnaise sauce and lemon chamomile jelly). Then there's the stellar cellar: Pinchiorri has amassed a collection of wines that's second to none and offers one of the world's great wine lists. Wherever you eat – inside the *palazzo* or in the gorgeous, jasmine-scented courtyard – it all looks fabulous; service is elegant and prices are sky high. This place is so classy that men are required to wear jackets.

La Fettunta €

*Via dei Neri 72r (055 2741102, www. facebook.com/LaFettuntaFirenze). **Open** 9.30am-11.30pm daily. **Map** p145 M9* ⑫ *Rosticceria*

With its checked tablecloths and cheesy decor, La Fettunta could easily be mistaken for a tourist trap, but its hearty food and honest prices will convince you otherwise. You could pick up a sandwich or hot plate to go, but La Fettunta's best enjoyed as a spontaneous, conveniently located sit-in stop after a long day or tiring tour. Rather than getting bogged down with individual orders, opt for family-style here, feasting on baked chicken, potatoes, artichokes (when in season), spinach and other no-frills mains and sides, as well as Tuscan specialities such as *peposo* (peppery beef stew). The whole meal is likely to cost less than some of your museum tickets (but unlike the museums, you can't make a reservation).

Kome €€

*Via de' Benci 41r (055 2008009, www. komefirenze.it). **Open** Kaiten noon-3pm Mon, Tue; noon-3pm, 7-11pm Wed; noon-3pm, 7pm-midnight Thur-Sat; 7-11pm Sun. BBQ 7.30-11pm Mon-Sat. Izakaya 7.30pm-midnight Mon-Sat. **Map** p145 O9* ⑮ *Japanese*

Kome is the brainchild of architect Carlo Caldini, an epochal figure on Florence's nightlife scene, who has created such a warm ambience that this eatery is one of the best designed contemporary spaces in Florence. Downstairs in **Kaiten**, diners perch on avocado-green bar stools under a swooping gold ceiling to select good sushi, *sashimi*, *nigiri* and other Japanese classics from the belt, while excellent light *tempura*, *miso* soup and various 'fries' are made to order. On the more functional upper floor is **BBQ**, where a gas barbecue is set into each table. If you choose one of the set menus, a series of hors d'oeuvres and a soup arrive, followed by a plate of raw fish, chicken or beef fillet that you cook yourself and then eat, with sauces, folded into a lettuce leaf. In the basement is **Izakaya**, a wine and sake bar where smokers can light up.

Libreria Brac €€

*Via de' Vagellai 18r (055 0944877, www. libreriabrac.net). **Open** 10am-midnight Mon-Sat; noon-midnight Sun (brunch until 4pm). Closed 1wk Aug; Sun in June-Sept. **Map** p145 N10* ⑯ *Vegetarian*

This contemporary art bookshop has one important novelty: a kitchen. Its minimalist, stark white interior with exciting splashes of colour gives a nice ambience, while the charming outdoor courtyard makes it a great place to read the morning news over a soy cappuccino or to enjoy one of the rich pastas or salads on its vegetarian and vegan-friendly menu (there are also several gluten-free options). Try the Sicilian salad with fennel, olives, oranges, almonds and raisins, or opt for the potato *tortelloni* with rocket pesto, which has hints of ginger. Libreria Brac also serves as a contemporary art space featuring temporary art exhibitions and installations, book launches, film screenings and more (see the website for upcoming events). Sundays are dedicated to the Brac Brunch, which features pancakes, French toasts and fresh yoghurt with fruit and home-made sweets. Reservations recommended.

Osteria de' Benci €€

*Via de' Benci 13r (055 2344923, www. osteriadeibenci.it). **Open** 12.30-3.30pm, 7.30-11pm daily. **Map** p145 N9* ⑰ *Osteria*

Small and unpretentious, there's both great atmosphere and great value for your buck at this lively *trattoria*. You'll pay about €35 per kilo for a Florentine steak or €55 per kilo for the Chianina variety, a nice price for a big chunk of meat cooked over an open fire and served *al sangue* (rare). The bean and garlic soup is disappointingly bland, but if seasonal local specialities such as *ribollita* and *trippa alla fiorentina* are available, you won't be disappointed. Pasta dishes are interesting (spaghetti cooked in red wine with garlic and hot pepper – amusingly dubbed '*spaghetti all'ubriacone*', or 'drunkard's spaghetti') and side dishes are delicious – try the baked potatoes with onions and olives. A lunch menu is also available.

Cafés, bars & gelaterie

All'Antico Vinaio

*Via de' Neri 65r (055 2382723). **Open** 10am-10pm daily. **Map** p145 M9* ① *Sandwich bar*

The reliably long queue outside this Florentine sandwich institution has become something of a tourist attraction. Some days it's (slightly) shorter than others, and worth braving for the generously portioned panini stacked high with *sbriciolona*, a typically Florentine *salame*, or *mortadella*. Build your own sandwich or choose from the menu's recommended combos – just don't dare ask for two meats together or wonder where the pesto went (go to Genoa if that's what you're looking for, a delightfully unapologetic sign proclaims). Stake out a spot on the pavement (the few coveted stools and benches are rarely free) and wash down the salty sandwiches with a cup of self-service house wine. Across the street, the same owners have a more spacious *osteria* (*see p152*), but their sandwiches are far more famous.

❤ Caffetteria delle Oblate
Via dell'Oriuolo 26 (055 2639685, www. caffetteriadelleoblate.it). **Open** *2-7pm Mon; 9am-midnight Tue-Sat.* **Map** *p145 O7* ❹ *Café*

With a straight-on view of Brunelleschi's dome from its lovely outdoor terrace and indoor café – a delight that won't cost you a pretty penny – this hangout inside the Oblate Library is a real gem amid the tourist traps around the Duomo. On the second floor, the bright, light-filled space, popular with Italian students, offers gorgeous views over the rooftops of the *centro storico*, and serves everything from breakfasts to cocktails and late-night suppers, with occasional concerts, readings and performances.

Ditta Artigianale
Via de' Neri 32r (055 2741541, www. dittaartigianale it). **Open** *8am-midnight daily.* **Map** *p145 N9* ❼ *Café*

This neighbourhood hotspot quickly established itself as the city's go-to place for coffee connoisseurs and anyone who appreciates a stiff gin and tonic. It is as noted for its design quality and see-and-be-seen vibe as it is for its speciality coffees, selected from small producers around the world. The offerings go far beyond the local basics: filter brewing methods were practically unheard of in Florence before this pioneering place opened. Brunch bites and other menu items are more on the underwhelming end, but this is a must-stop for anyone interested in seeing Italy's coffee culture both celebrated and shaken up. Its local success has led to the opening of two other locations, in the heart of the Oltrarno (*see p173*) and inside La Compagnia cinema (*see p228*).

❤ Gelateria dei Neri
Via dei Neri 22r (055 210034). **Open** *10am-midnight daily.* **No cards.** **Map** *p145 N10* ❽ *Gelateria*

A gem for those who want to sample the Florentine frozen assets but have an intolerance to milk – it's one of the few parlours to serve soya ice-cream alongside the classic creamy gelati (go for the buttery salted caramel).

La Loggia degli Albizi
Borgo degli Albizi 39r (055 2479574, www.facebook.com/laloggiadeglialbizi produzionepropria). **Open** *7am-9pm daily. Closed Aug.* **Map** *p145 O7* ❾ *Café*

With some of the best pastries and cakes in town, La Loggia degli Albizi is the perfect stop-off after some hard shopping. Try the *torta della nonna* (crumbly pastry filled with baked pâtisserie cream) or the warm *bomboloni* (fried doughnuts), served after 5pm. They also have a reasonably priced lunch menu with tasty *primi* served by friendly staff.

Quelo
Borgo Santa Croce 15r (055 19991474, www.facebook.com/quelobar.firenze). **Open** *8.30am-1am daily.* **Map** *p145 O9* ❿ *Café*

Open all day, health food haven Quelo is an easy stop off for a quick snack, a morning cappuccino or an evening *aperitivo*. Cocktails are inexpensive and the accompanying buffet is veggie-friendly and fresh – you'll find cous cous salads, hummus, lentils and fresh veggies with crudités, all welcome alternatives to the *salame*-heavy spreads at similar happy hours around town. Decor is on the quirky side and the occasionally cramped seating means it's an easy place to strike up a chat with other patrons.

Le Vespe
Via Ghibellina 76r (055 3880062, www.levespecafe.com). **Open** *9am-3pm Mon-Fri, 10am-3pm Sat-Sun.* **Map** *p145 P8* ⓫ *Café*

With its cheerful decor, Canadian co-owner and savoury Sunday brunch menu, Le Vespe is particularly popular with international students – but you'll spot more than a few Florentines who know the merits of a hearty breakfast. Seasonal and ethically sourced ingredients are hallmarks of the menu, as are home fries, breakfast burritos and sizable smoothies.

Vestri
Borgo degli Albizi 11r (055 2340374, www.vestri.it). **Open** *10am-8pm daily. Closed Aug.* **Map** *p145 P7* ⓬ *Gelateria/shop*

Primarily a gourmet chocolate shop, in summer Vestri installs a few metal churns, from which are served up exquisite own-made ice-cream concoctions. The flavours are few but ingenious and adventurous – white chocolate with wild strawberries, chocolate and *peperoncino* (Italian chillies) and bitter chocolate with Cointreau.

❤ Vivoli
Via Isola delle Stinche 7r (055 292334, www.vivoli.it). **Open** *Summer 7.30am-midnight Tue-Sat, 9am-midnight Sun. Winter 7.30am-9pm Tue-Fri, 9am-9pm Sun. Closed mid Aug.* **No cards.** **Map** *p145 O8* ⓭ *Gelateria*

Local institution Vivoli has clung on jealously to its long-standing but increasingly threatened reputation as the best gelateria in Florence (they've even taken their Tuscan flair to Florida). The wickedly rich chocolate orange and divine *riso* (rice pudding) are still up there with the best of them. So too are its famous *semifreddi* – which are creamier and softer than ordinary gelato. Increasingly appreciated as the years wear on and the brand gets bigger is its ample seating area, where you can indulge leisurely at no extra charge – a rarity at joints this famous.

Shops

🖤 A Ritroso... A Rebours
Via Ghibellina 24r (055 243941, www. vintage-firenze.it). **Open** *10am-1pm, 4-7pm Tue-Fri.* **Map** *p145 R9* ❶ *Vintage fashion*

With a selection carefully curated by judicious owner and style muse Camilla, this tiny shop specialises in fashion from the 19th century up until the 1980s. Thanks to Camilla's local and international fashion contacts, you'll find incredible bargains on big-name brands from Yves Saint Laurent to Gucci, as well as labelless jumpers and boots for less than the price of lunch. Also, expect a variety of both famous and little-known Florentine labels, some of which have folded.

La Bottega dei Cristalli
Via de' Benci 51r (055 2344891, www. labottegadeicristalli.com). **Open** *10am-7.30pm daily. Closed mid Jan-mid Feb.* **Map** *p145 O9* ❷ *Gifts & souvenirs*

A lovely range of Murano- and Tuscan-made glass plates, picture frames, lamps and chandeliers, and tiny glass 'sweets' and bottles.

Casa della Cornice
Via Sant'Egidio 26r (055 2480222, www. casadellacornice.com). **Open** *9am-1pm, 3-7.30pm Mon-Fri; 9.30am-1pm Sat.* **No cards.** **Map** *p145 O7* ❸ *Homeware*

A huge catalogue of traditional and contemporary picture frames in silver and gold leaf.

🖤 Data Records 93
Via de' Neri 15r (055 287592, www. superecords.com). **Open** *10am-1pm, 3.30-7.30pm Mon-Sat. Closed 2wks Aug.* **Map** *p145 N9* ❺ *Vinyl*

Staff here are true music buffs with a local reputation for being able to find the unfindable. Home to thousands of titles on vinyl, CD and cassette tape, new and used, with an emphasis on psychedelia, blues, R&B, jazz and soundtracks.

🖤 Signum
Borgo de' Greci 40r (055 280621, www. signumfirenze.it). **Open** *9am-7.30pm Mon-Sat; 10am-7pm Sun.* **Map** *p145 N9* ⓬ *Gifts & souvenirs*

This delightful shop, housed in an ancient wine cellar, stocks an appealingly wide range of gifts, among them miniature models of shop windows and bookcases, and Murano glass inkwells and pens. **Other locations** Lungarno degli Archibusieri 14r, Duomo & Around (055 289393); via de' Benci 29r, Santa Croce (055 244590).

SANT'AMBROGIO

Until not so long ago, the area north of Santa Croce church stretching up to piazza de' Ciompi, was the rough-and-ready home to rival gangs of bored Florentine youths. Increasingly yuppified, it now yields trendy *trattorie* and wine bars.

Piazza de' Ciompi was named after the dyers' and wool workers' revolt of 1378 and is dominated by the **Loggia del Pesce**, built by Vasari in 1568 for the Mercato Vecchio, which previously occupied piazza della Repubblica. Taken apart in the 19th century as part of an urban renovation project, it was re-erected here in 1955. Further east is piazza Ghiberti, home of the authentic fruit and vegetable market, **Mercato di Sant'Ambrogio** (*see p159*), one of the highlights of the district. The church of Sant'Ambrogio is just to the north, from where **Borgo La Croce**, lined with shops, bars, *pizzerie* and restaurants, extends as far as piazza Beccaria and the eastern city gate, **Porta alla Croce** (erected 1284, modified 1530 and 1813. The gate sits in the middle of the *viali* (avenues) circling the historic centre of the city.

North-west of Sant'Ambrogio and just south of the piazza d'Azeglio is the **Sinagoga & Museo di Arte e Storia Ebraica** (*see below*), built in 1870, following the demolition of the Jewish ghetto. Further west, on borgo Pinti, watch out for the hard-to-find entrance to the church of Santa Maria Maddalena dei Pazzi at no.58.

In the know
Box Office

Via delle Vecchie Carceri 1, ex Murate complex, Sant'Ambrogio, (055 210804, www.boxofficetoscana.it information, www.boxol.it tickets). **Open** *10am-7pm Mon-Fri; 10am-2pm Sat.* **Map** *p145 S9.*

Central ticket agency for concerts, plays, sports events, festivals and exhibitions in Florence, across Italy and abroad.

Sights & museums

Sinagoga & Museo di Arte e Storia Ebraica

Via Farini 4 (055 2346654, www. jewishflorence.it). **Open** *June-Sept 10am-6.30pm Sun-Thur; 10am-5pm Fri. Oct-May 10am-5.30pm Sun-Thur; 10am-3pm Fri.* **Admission** *€6.50; €5 reductions. No cards.* **Map** *p145 R6.*

This 19th-century synagogue is an extraordinarily ornate mix of Moorish, Byzantine and Eastern influences, with its walls and ceilings covered in polychrome arabesques. The Museum of Jewish Art and History holds a collection tracing the history of Jews in Florence, from their supposed arrival as Roman slaves to their official introduction into the city as money-lenders in 1430. Exhibits include documented stories, jewellery, ceremonial objects and furniture, photos and drawings, many of which depict the ghetto that once occupied the area just north of piazza della Repubblica.

Restaurants & wine bars

Cibrèino €€€

Via de' Macci 122r (055 2341100, www. edizioniteatrodelsalecibreofirenze.it). **Open** *12.50-2.30pm, 7-11.15pm Tue-Sat. Closed Aug.* **Map** *p145 R7* ⑧ *Trattoria*

The reasonably priced sister of Cibrèo (*see below*), this *trattoria* doesn't take reservations (prepare to queue or arrive early). Typical of most home-grown *trattorie* in Florence, the atmosphere is rustic, the place is often overcrowded and the menu has little choice, but the food is excellent and much easier on the wallet than its more famous sibling. You'll get the added frisson of witnessing weak-stomached experience-hunters blanch when a chicken's head arrives on their plate.

Cibrèo €€€€

Via Andrea del Verrocchio 8r (055 2341100, www.edizioniteatrodelsalecibreofirenze.it). **Open** *1-2.30pm, 7-11.15pm Tue-Sat. Closed Aug.* **Map** *p145 R7* ⑨ *High-end gastronomy*

Cibrèo is a must-stop on any Florence foodie's hit list. Located in the heart of the Sant'Ambrogio market area, this is the flaghip of Fabio Picchi's little gastronomic empire (which also includes a bar, a *trattoria*, a theatre with buffet-style food, multiple cookbooks and a clothing and accessories line). It serves a modern interpretation of Florence's traditional *cucina povera* (peasant's food), with fresh prime ingredients and heavy use of fresh herbs and spices to create intense flavours (they're particularly

proud of the oregano). There's no menu, but a chummy waiter will sit at your table in the elegant, wood-panelled room to take you through the options. Dishes change daily, but you can count on a series of delicious *antipasti* arriving automatically, followed by *primi* with no pasta in sight. *Secondi* are divided between meat and particularly good fish. Desserts are fabulous (Bavarian cream and flourless chocolate cake are favourites), and the wine list is everything you might expect. Cibrèo provokes extreme opinions: some think it's the best restaurant in Florence, while others claim that it's overrated, overpriced and overcrowded with tourists. *See left* **Cibrèino**, *p158* **Teatro del Sale** *and p158* **Caffè Cibrèo**.

Ganzo €€

Via de' Macci 85r (055 241067, www. ganzoflorence.it). **Open** *noon-midnight Mon-Fri. Closed Sat & Sun.* **Map** *p145 Q8* ⑬ *Experimental Italian*

A cultural and culinary association established by the Florence University of Arts and the culinary school Apicius, Ganzo is not only a restaurant but also a social and events space for temporary art exhibitions, book presentations and artistic performances. Menus change according to the scholastic period, but you can always count on finding experimental and seasonal dishes inspired by the Tuscan culinary tradition; indulge in a bit of everything with their generously portioned tasting menu. Wednesday evenings (6-10pm) are reserved for the AperiGanzo, offering aperitifs and an abundant buffet (dinner not served), alternatively dubbed the 'AperiArt' when a new artist is exhibiting. Thursday is for themed dinner nights following the whims of the chef (from 8.30pm), while a wine club meets on Mondays at 6pm and sides take centre stage on Fridays with a strictly à la carte menu.

La Giostra €€€

Borgo Pinti 12r (055 241341, www. ristorantelagiostra.com). **Open** *12.30-2.30pm, 7pm-midnight Mon-Fri; 7pm-midnight Sat, Sun.* **Map** *p145 P7* ⑭ *Traditional Italian*

La Giostra's walls are covered with pictures of visiting celebs and its ceiling is draped

---

In the know
All played out

There aren't many playgrounds in Florence, but a lovely one can be found in piazza Massimo d'Azeglio (just north of the synagogue); this quiet recreational space is a haven for parents and kids alike.

with fairy lights. Founded by Prince Alberto Dimitri Kunz d'Asburgo Loreno, this eatery, now managed by his son Soldano, is always full of tourists, and prices are high. The food, however, is well worth it, complimentary prosecco is par for the course, and much of the menu draws from traditional recipes of the Hapsburg-Lorraine dynasty. The Austrian branch of the family is well represented with classics such as Wiener schnitzel, but the restaurant is often praised for its *pasta fresca* (think tagliatelle with porcini mushrooms), truffle-based dishes and tempting *antipasti* such as burrata and honey. If you have room for dessert, try the rich, gooey *sacher imperiale* (Sachertorte made from an old Hapsburg family recipe). The wine list features big names with big prices. Jacket and tie recommended.

❤ Il Pizzaiuolo €€
Via de' Macci 113r (055 241171, www. ilpizzaiuolo.it). **Open** *12.30-3pm, 5pm-midnight Mon-Sat. Closed Aug.* **Map** *p145 R8* ⑱ *Pizzeria*

If you're looking to sink your teeth into a delicious Neapolitan-style pizza, then Il Pizzaiuolo is the place to get it. Long considered the go-to place for the best pizza in Florence, it has the crowds to match, but the melt-in-your-mouth burrata cheese will make it all worthwhile. Il Piazzaiuolo also serves Neapolitan pasta dishes, which include spaghetti with tomato, olives and capers from Gaeta, or *trofie* (a kind of pasta) with pesto and cherry tomatoes. Finish the meal off with a *babà al rhum* (a rum-flavoured Neopolitan dessert). The small, white-tiled room is always packed (and often very noisy), so booking is a must here, and be prepared to find yourself sharing a table with strangers.

Ruth's €€
Via Farini 2a (055 2480888, www.kosheruth. com). **Open** *12.30-2.30pm, 7.30-10pm Mon-Thur; 12.30-2.30pm Fri.* **Map** *p145 Q6* ⑲ *Jewish*

Ruth's is located next to Florence's monumental synagogue, one of the biggest in Europe, and serves kosher vegetarian food as well as fish dishes, overseen by Rabbi Rav Joseph Levi. The dining area is a pleasant, modern and bright room with a full view of the open kitchen. The cooking has palpable Middle Eastern and North African influences, resulting in dishes such as falafel and other typical meze, fish or vegetable couscous, and cheese *brik* (deep-fried flaky pastry, a Tunisian speciality). You'll also find a range of salads and a soup of the day.

Teatro del Sale €€€
Via de' Macci 111r (055 2001492, www. edizioniteatrodelsalecibreofirenze.it). **Open** *times vary. Closed Sun evening, Mon all day & Aug.* **Map** *p145 Q8* ⑳ *Traditional Italian*

A sister of the Cibrèo restaurants (*see p157*), Teatro del Sale is the most innovative creation of the eccentric Florentine chef Fabio Picchi, and it continues to grow: plans are in the works for the venue to host a full academic programme on the 'theatre of cooking'. The Teatro sets itself apart on the Florentine culinary scene as a top-notch eatery that also has entertainment, giving its members a theatrical or musical bonus après dinner. At lunch and dinner the kitchen offers Tuscan-centred yet internationally inspired seasonal buffets that change daily (here you can go back for seconds and thirds, and the introduction of each dish is a mini-theatrical production – the first-time experience isn't complete without jumping in your seat when you first hear the kitchen staff yell what they're serving). Open all hours, from breakfast to dinner, the Teatro operates like a well-oiled machine thanks to its dedicated staff who make almost everything on the menu in-house. At the entrance, a big area sells quirky, prettily packaged homeware and food products, which would make great gifts (*see p160* Shops).

Cafés, bars & gelaterie

L'Arte del Sogno
Borgo La Croce 24/26r (055 0120293, www.facebook.com/larte.delsogno). **Open** *8am-7pm Mon-Sat, 3-7pm Sun.* **Map** *p145 S7* ❷ *Café*

With its whimsical decor, cosy ambience and extensive tea list, this colourful nook is the perfect find for escaping an unexpected rain shower or taking a leisurely Prosecco break. It's the kind of spot where you can linger with a book or tote along your laptop – a marked contrast from most standard city bars, where locals tend to knock back their *espressi* standing at the counter. The desserts are also worth sampling, and most of the *objet trouvé* furnishings are for sale.

Caffè Cibrèo
Via Andrea del Verrocchio 5r (055 2345853, www.edizioniteatrodelsalecibreofirenze.it). **Open** *8am-1am Tue-Sat. Closed 2wks Aug.* **No cards.** **Map** *p145 R8* ❸ *Café*

This delightful café, another of Fabio Picchi's Cibrèo (*see p157*) outposts, is worth visiting for ambience alone: it has exquisite carved wood ceilings, retro poster art that feels more refined than kitschy, antique furniture, a candlelit mosaic and outside tables, but also a

❤ Mercato di Sant'Ambrogio

Piazza Ghiberti 45 (www.mercato santambrogio.it). **Open** *7am-2pm Mon-Sat.* **Map** *p145 R8.*

Florence's oldest operating market was created as a replacement for the Mercato Vecchio near today's piazza della Repubblica, which was unceremoniously razed to the ground in 1885-95 in a typically Victorian bid to 'sanitise' the old city centre. Sant'Ambrogio was one of three proposed markets – the others being the grander Mercato Centrale (*see p127*) in the San Lorenzo district and an unexecuted third market in the Oltrarno.

The glass and cast iron structure was designed by Giuseppe Mengoni and began operating in 1873. While its San Lorenzo counterpart has all but surrendered to the 'touristification' of its neighbourhood, Sant'Ambrogio still retains the easygoing character and quaintness of an authentic local market. Meat and fish, fruit and vegetables, bread and fresh pasta, herbs and spices, olive oil and Chianti wine, pecorino cheese and cold cuts of *cinta senese* (an indigenous breed of pig): a heady mix of flavours fills the air, while the histrionic stallholders shout their sales pitches in the musical Florentine dialect.

With its 20 stalls, Sant'Ambrogio market is a foodie's heaven and the perfect spot to shop for a picnic or grab a quick lunch. Trattoria **Da Rocco** (*see p160*) is a food

kiosk where you can try local classics at steal prices, but the most adventurous should really sample the braised tripe or boiled *lampredotto* of **I'Trippaio di S. Ambrogio** (*see below* Follow the tripe trail). The market also supplies quality ingredients and locally sourced, organic, seasonal produce to the many restaurants and *osterie* of the neighbourhoods, so no wonder they rank among Florence's best.

The adjoining outdoor market features 60-plus stalls, including more food vendors and a miscellany of homeware, clothing, footwear, linen, fashion jewellery, toiletries and flower sellers. Pending an agreement about their future location, the antique and bric-a-brac dealers of the city's picturesque flea market (formerly housed in piazza dei Ciompi) can also be found across the square in neighbouring piazza Pietro Annigoni (*map p145 S8*).

SANTA CROCE

In the know
Follow the tripe trail

So popular is this traditional Florentine street food in the neighbourhood that two more *trippai* can be found in the vicinity: **Sergio Pollini** operating from a three-wheeler in via de' Macci and one of the locals' favourites, **I' Trippaio fiorentino** kiosk in Via Gioberti beyond piazza Beccaria (Outside the City Gates).

knack for making everything it presents look as beautiful as the bar itself (fresh flowers on each table here are standard). It's a relaxing stop where no one will give you the stink-eye for drinking a cappuccino mid-afternoon, and you'll feel perfectly in place scrawling in a notebook or partaking in any particularly literary activity.

Caffè Sant'Ambrogio
Piazza Sant'Ambrogio 7r (055 2477277). Open 10.30am–3am daily. Map p145 R7 ❺ *Bar/café*

Against the backdrop of the 11th-century Sant'Ambrogio church, spread over its own building and a sweet little *piazza* that gets crowded in the evening with locals and students, this bar, café, *enoteca* and restaurant isn't much to look at, but serves a great range of drinks, including reasonably priced classic cocktails and more than 50 wines by the glass. Modern Italian lunch specials draw punters from the nearby market, but it's the evening *apericena* (and generous, if not gourmet, buffet spread) that really pulls in the young and fashionable. The place is best in summer or warm weather when you can enjoy a Spritz alfresco (there's table service for the outdoor seating).

Da Rocco
Inside Sant'Ambrogio market, piazza Ghiberti (339 8384555, www. trattoriadarocco.it/). Open noon-2.30pm Mon-Sat. Map p145 R8 ❻ *Traditional Florentine*

At the centre of Sant'Ambrogio market, you'll find Rocco's food kiosk serving up Florentine specialities at very favourable prices, popular with students at the University of Florence. Choose from a selection of rustic local classics such as *pappa al pomodoro*, *spezzatino* (a kind of beef stew), *lampredotto* (a uniquely Florentine dish made from the fourth stomach of a cow), pasta with *ragù*, roasted potatoes and tripe salad. You'll have to queue up to order and you can take away or eat in at one of the tables. The wine is cheap too: order a flask of house wine and you only pay for what you drink.

Shops

Cup of Milk
Borgo Pinti 6r (055 3860576, www.cupofmilk. it). Open 10am-1pm, 3.30-7.30pm. Map p145 P7 ❹ *Kids' stuff*

A Scandinavian-inspired concept boutique, this tiny place is big on personality. You'll find colourful sleepwear in fun animal prints, adorable illustrations and decor ideas, party favours, paper bags that work well as hampers or no-fuss waste-paper baskets, shoes, accessories and more from a variety of leading international brands.

❤ Dolci e Dolcezze
Piazza Beccaria 8r (055 2345458, www. facebook.com/pasticceriadolciedolcezze). Open 8.30am-7.30pm Tue-Sat; 9am-1pm, 4.30-7.30pm Sun. Closed 2wks Aug. No cards. Map p145 T8 ❻ *Pâtisserie*

This pâtisserie is famous for its delectable, flourless chocolate cake, but you may also be tempted by the strawberry meringue, chocolate eclairs or sugar-dusted *cornetti* (croissants or sweet buns). Savouries are just as good. There's not really any seating but staff will let you indulge straight at the counter. Rather than an eat-in dessert stop, though, it's more popular as a go-to shop for cakes for parties or as gifts.

Lady Jane B Vintage Boutique
Via de' Pilastri 32b (055 242863, www. ladyjanebvintage.com). Open 3-8pm Mon, Wed-Sat. Map p145 Q7 ❼ *Vintage fashion*

Near piazza Sant'Ambrogio Lady Jane B is great for leather bags, but also stocks a range of clothing, jewellery and accessories. If you're after a specific item, staff will happily join in the hunt.

Libreria delle Donne
Via Fiesolana 2b (055 240384, www.facebook. com/libreriadonnefirenze). Open 10am-1pm Tue-Thur; 10am-7.30pm Fri, Sat. Closed Aug. Map p145 P7 ❽ *Books*

A good reference point for women in Florence, not just for its books (which span Virginia Woolf novels in translation to philosophical texts) but also for the useful noticeboard that has details on local activities, exhibitions and meet-ups. The bookshop frequently hosts its own events, though these are most often lectures held in Italian.

Lisa Corti Home Textiles Emporium
Piazza Ghiberti 33r (055 2345837, www. lisacorti.com). Open 9am-7pm Mon-Sat. Map p145 R8 ❾ *Homeware*

Brightly coloured cushions, bedspreads, quilts and curtains, in silks and cottons and with an oriental feel. Designer Lisa Corti has also created a small range of furniture and pottery.

La Raccolta
Via Giacomo Leopardi 2r (055 2479068, www. laraccolta.it). Open 8am-1pm, 7.30-9.30pm Tue-Fri. Closed Aug. Map p145 T6 ❿ *Food*

A mecca for the growing population of vegetarians in Florence, this seemingly out-of-place space is part bar, part restaurant and mostly health-food market. Enjoy daily 'bio lunch' specials or stock up on tasty beers, juices and jarred foods.

Sandra Dori

Via de' Macci 103r (348 3574726, www. sandradori.com). Open 10am-1pm Tue-Sat; afternoon by appt. Map p145 R7 ⓫ *Gifts & souvenirs*

Sandra Dori is mostly in the business of unusual lamps and candelabras, but her shop intersperses her unusual designs with sweet paintings, handmade chunky plastic and fabric jewellery, fans and all manner of oddities. It's a pleasure to browse.

♥ Société Anonyme

Via de' Niccolini 3f (corner of via della Mattonaia) (055 3860084, www. societeanonyme.it). Open Winter 3.30-7.30pm Mon; 10am-2pm, 3.30-7.30pm Tue-Sun Summer 4-8pm Mon; 10am-2pm, 4-8pm Tue-Sun. Map p145 S6 ⓭ *Boutique fashion*

With its list of avant-garde men's, women's, and androgynous brands chalked on to a blackboard at the entrance, Société Anonyme screams 'trendy', and it is. Inside, a deftly styled space filled with art and architectural oddities houses international brands (McQ by Alexander McQueen, Helmut Lang), but also fashion and accessories by up-and-coming Italian designers (local fashion institutes have frequently hosted events and shows inside the boutique). You could spend hours just poking around and trying things on, and prices are on the right side of reasonable for the design calibre offered. The formula is so successful that a second location has opened in the heart of the Oltrarno (via Maggio 60r).

Il Sole nel Borgo

Borgo la Croce 50r (333 2341453). Open 10am-7.30pm daily. Map p145 S7 ⓮ *Homeware*

Il Sole Nel Borgo offers a charming slice of the Amalfi Coast further north in Florence. Cheeky and colourful ceramic kitchenware makes up most of the inventory: mugs and teapots, salad bowls, containers of all types and party-perfect pitchers. Everything is handmade in the Salerno province and a cute café adds to the beachy ambience.

Teatro del Sale

See p158. Map p145 R8 ⓯ *Gifts & souvenirs*

Fabio Picchi's empire of Cibrèo eateries (*see p157*), clustered behind piazza Sant'Ambrogio, took a step in a retail direction with Teatro del Sale (*see p158*), which not only offers imaginative dinner-theatre evenings but also includes a huge foyer filled with lovely things for sale: lots of gorgeous Tuscan foodstuffs, as you'd expect, but also plenty of little personal gifts in the form of toiletries, candles and quirky homeware.

Société Anonyme

The Oltrarno

Without the Oltrarno (literally, the other side of the Arno), the first-time visitor could be forgiven for thinking Florence is nothing more than a large Renaissance theme park. Fortunately, the Oltrarno offers something else entirely. Its three complementary yet distinct districts – San Frediano and Santo Spirito in the west and San Niccolò in the east – encompass independent shops and artists' studios, contemporary jewellers' ateliers filled with work of extraordinary skill and originality, and bars, cafés and restaurants that are very hard to leave. But don't linger too long, or you'll miss the Oltrarno's big hitters: the gargantuan Palazzo Pitti, the lovely open spaces of Giardino di Boboli, and the antique charms of the Museo Bardini, to name but a few.

In the know
Getting around

In a neighbourhood where nearly every shop window commands attention and business owners wander in and out of each other's doors, the only way to have the 'full experience' is to move by foot. If you don't fancy the trek down the lengthy via dei Serragli, you can take buses 11, 36 or 37 from piazza Ottaviani (Santa Maria Novella) towards the street's southern tip facing Porta Romana.

❤ Don't miss

1 Galleria Palatina & Appartamenti Reali *p167*
Baroque and Renaissance masterpieces from the Medici collections, and the gateway to the sumptuous Appartamenti Reali.

2 Artisan studios *p179*
Watch local craftspeople carry on centuries-old techniques and reinvent and revive traditions.

3 Giardino di Boboli *p168*
Italian Renaissance garden created for the Medici; now Florence's most beloved green oasis.

4 Santa Maria del Carmine & Cappella Brancacci *p176*
Spend quality time with Masaccio, an early master of perspective.

5 Cenacolo di Santo Spirito *p168*
Fragments of a 14th-century Last Supper by Orcagna and an eclectic collection of sculptures.

6 Museo Bardini *p182*
The glorious collection of noted art dealer and antiquarian Stefano Bardini.

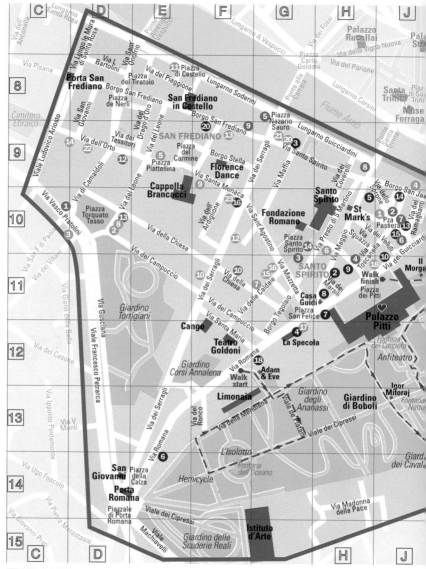

THE OLTRARNO

Restaurants &
wine bars

1 5 e Cinque
2 Al Tranvai
3 Alla Vecchia Bettola
4 Borgo San Jacopo
5 I Brindellone
6 La Casalinga
7 Il Chicco di Caffè
8 Culinaria Bistrot
9 Da Pescatore
10 Diladdarno
11 Essenziale
12 Fiaschetteria
    Fantappie
13 Gesto
14 Il Guscio
15 Gurdulu
16 Langolino
17 La Mangiatoia
18 Pitti Gola e Cantina
19 San Niccolò 39
20 Il Santino
21 Il Santo Bevitore
22 Trattoria dell'Orto
23 Vivanda
24 Le Volpi e l'Uva

Cafés, bars &
gelaterie

1 Café Circolo Aurora
2 Caffè degli Artigian
3 Caffè Ricchi
4 Carduccio
5 La Carraia
6 Ditta Artigianale
7 Gelateria della
  Passera

Gelateria Santa Trinita
Libreria Café La Cité
Mama's Bakery
Il Rifrullo
O'Scugnizzo
La Sorbetteria
Volume
Zeb

Shops

❶ Alessandro Dari
❷ And Company
❸ Angela Caputi
❹ Anita Russo Ceramic Studio
❺ BJØRK
❻ La Buca del Vino
❼ Celeste Vintage
❽ Dolcissima Firenze
❾ Giulia Materia
❿ Giulio Giannini e Figlio
⓫ KARASCIÒ Streetwear
⓬ Madova
⓭ Mirta Effe
⓮ Obsequium
⓯ Sara Amrhein & SelecArt
⓰ S. Forno
⓱ Le Sorelle
⓲ Tabesce
⓳ Il Torchio
⓴ Twisted

Giardino di Bobili
— — Walking Tour
See p169

SANTO SPIRITO

If the three primary Oltrarno districts were siblings, Santo Spirito would be the loudest and most attention-grabbing. At its heart is the **Basilica of Santo Spirito** and its surrounding square. **Piazza Santo Spirito** is the undisputed centre of community life, bustling with furniture restorers and restaurateurs – and, by night year-round, packed with people of all ages and nationalities sipping cocktails in plastic cups and chatting; in summer, the steps of the basilica are like the square's own living room. A morning market is held in the *piazza* from Monday to Saturday, with a flea market on the second Sunday of the month and an organic food market every third Sunday.

Running between the basilica and a maze of narrow streets to the east is the grand **via Maggio,** with its antiques shops and massive stone crests representing their original owners. But it's not all stuffy old nobles: it also holds a smattering of international contemporary art galleries, many with free admission. At its river end is a delightful triangular house with a fountain and tiny garden room where the street joins **borgo San Jacopo**. Backing directly on to the river, this San Jacopo mixes medieval towers, hip clothes shops and 1960s monstrosities built to replace houses bombed in the war. It leads to the southern end of **Ponte Vecchio**. Heading south-west down from the bridge is the well-beaten **via Guicciardini** with the littl Santa Felicita church (*see p182*). Lined wi expensive paper, crafts and jewellery shop (as well as plenty of street vendors selling bizarre toys), this is the main tourist route the Medicis' **Palazzo Pitti**. The palace wa built in 1457 for Luca Pitti, a Medici rival, supposedly to a design by Brunelleschi tha had been rejected by Cosimo il Vecchio as too grandiose. However, it also proved too grandiose for the Pitti family, who, galling were forced to sell the palace to the Medic Its ornate, opulent rooms now hold the va Medici collections, as well as later additio in various museums detailed below, of which the **Galleria Palatina** (*see right*) is the highlight. For general information on the palace, call 055 294883 or see www. polomuseale.firenze.it.

Beyond the Pitti Palace, the road ends in square dominated by Palazzo Guidi, housi **Casa Guidi** (*see below*), where poets Rober and Elizabeth Barrett Browning wrote some of their most famous works. Here via Maggio and via Guicciardini join to becom **via Romana**, a long, extremely straight thoroughfare leading to **Porta Romana**, lined with picture framers, antiques shops butchers, bakers and candlestick makers: you name it. Via Romana is also home to the gory **La Specola** museum (*see p170*) and an entrance to the extensive Giardino di Boboli (*see p168* and *p169* Stroll Around Boboli), across the street from the Giardin Annalena at via Romana 37A.

♥ Time to eat & drink

Breakfast bagels
Mama's Bakery *p174*

Lunch deals
Il Chicco di Caffe *p171*
I Brindellone *p177*

Gorgeous gelato
La Carraia *p180*
La Sorbettiera *p180*

Authentic pizza on-the-go
O'Scugnizzo *p180*

Seafood tasting menu
Da Pescatore *p177*

Discerning dinner
Il Santo Bevitore *p172*
Gurdulu *p171*

♥ Time to shop

Artisan jewellery
Alessandro Dari *p183*
Angela Caputi *p174*
Sara Amrhein & Scicc'Art *p176*

Beautiful gifts
And Company *p174*

Boutique bakery
S. Forno *p180*

Home flourishes
Le Sorelle *p176*

Wine by the glass
Vivanda *p178*
Le Volpi e L'uva *p183*

♥ Time well spent

Casa Guidi
Piazza San Felice 8
(055 354457, www.
browningsociety.org/
casa_guidi.html). **Open** Ap
Nov 3-6pm Mon, Wed, Fri.
Admission *by donation.*
Map *p164 H11.*
English poets Robert Browning and Elizabeth Barrett Browning came to Florence in April 1847 after a clandestine marriage, and for 14 years an apartment in this house was their home. Now owned by the Landma Trust and partly rented out as a holiday home, key roor of the apartment where the lived and wrote are open fo visits during certain month A few pieces in the flat are originals, including the pia used by their son, Pen.

🖤 Galleria Palatina

*Palazzo Pitti (055 2388614, www.
polomuseale.firenze.it).* **Open** *8.15am-
6.50pm Tue-Sun.* **Admission** *€8.50, €4.25
reductions, combined ticket with the Galleria
Palatina. Free on the first Sun of every month.
No cards.* **Map** *p164 J11.*

This opulent gallery has 28 rooms of
paintings, which are hung four- or five-
high on its damask walls. From its grand
staircase, the Scalone del Moro, to its final
exit, it's section after section of unabashed
overgilding and visual stimulation, so be
sure you're always looking upward. You'll
want to linger longest in the five planet
rooms, named after Venus, Mercury
(Apollo), Mars, Jupiter and Saturn. The **Sala
di Venere** (Venus), crowned by a gilded
stucco ceiling, is dominated by a statue
of Venus by Canova, but also contains
Titian's regal La Bella. The **Sala di Apollo**
houses the nine Muses and is crowded with
works by Rosso Fiorentino and Andrea del
Sarto. The restored **Sala di Marte** (Mars)
glimmers with the Baroque splendour of
Pietro da Cortona's vault and is home to
Anthony van Dyck's celebrated Portrait
of Cardinal Bentivoglio; Rubens's Four
Philosophers and the other works from
this room are on show in the **Sala della
Nicchi**. In the **Sala di Giove** (Jupiter) look

up to admire the lofty depiction of Jupiter
with his eagle and lightning. Look too
for Raphael's lover, so-called 'baker girl'
Margherita Luti, in his La Velata. Finally, the
Sala di Saturno (Saturn) contains some of
Raphael's best-known works: among them
the Madonna of the Grand Duke, which
shows a distinct Leonardo influence, and
his last painting, Holy Family, seemingly
inspired by Michelangelo.

As if the gallery weren't already
extravagant enough, a three-year
collaboration between the Pitti museums
and the Uffizi by the fashion tastemakers at
Pitti Immagine Discovery means
temporary style-themed exhibitions have
been infiltrating this and other spaces; so
far, the results have been riveting, if not
without controversy. Why not gild the
lily, right?

Also occupying the piano nobile (noble
floor) of the Palazzo Pitti are the glorious
Appartamenti Reali. The sumptuous
Royal Apartments were the private
residence of several ruling families in
Florence, including the Medici and, briefly
from 1866-1870, King Vittorio Emanuele II
of Savoy, when Florence ruled as capital of
Italy. Within the 14 rooms you can find
period furniture and accessories from the
16th to the 19th century.

THE OLTRARNO

Sala di Giove (Jupiter Room), Galleria Palatina

Sights & museums

Basilica di Santo Spirito

Piazza Santo Spirito (055 210030, www.basilicasantospirito.it). **Open** *9.30am-12.30pm, 4-5.30pm Mon, Tue, Thur, Fri.* **Admission** *free.* **Map** *p164 H10.*

Behind the exquisitely simple 18th-century cream façade is one of Brunelleschi's most extraordinary works. In 1397, the resident Augustinian monks decided to replace the church that had been on this site from 1250, eventually commissioning Brunelleschi to design it. Work started in 1444, two years before the great master died, and the façade and exterior walls were never finished. Vasari wrote that if the church had been completed as planned, it would have been 'the most perfect temple of Christianity' and it's easy to see why. Santo Spirito's structure is a beautifully proportioned Latin-cross church, lined with a colonnade of dove-grey *pietra serena* pilasters that shelter 38 chapels. The church is open at weekends to worshippers, but it's worth calling ahead to make sure the official opening hours are being kept to.

Interior of Santo Spirito

♥ Cenacolo di Santo Spirito

Piazza Santo Spirito 29 (055 287043, www.museicivicifiorentini.comune.fi.it). **Open** *10am-4pm Mon, Sat, Sun.* **Admission** *€4.* **No cards.** **Map** *p164 H10.*

Orcagna's 14th-century fresco *The Last Supper*, housed in a former Augustinian refectory, was butchered by an 18th-century architect commissioned to build some doors into it. Only the fringes of the fresco remain, though there's a more complete (albeit heavily restored) *Crucifixion* above it. The small **Museo della Fondazione Romano** here houses an eclectic collection of sculptures given to the state in 1946 on the death of sailor Salvatore Romano.

Galleria d'Arte Moderna

Palazzo Pitti (055 2388616, www.polomuseale.firenze.it). **Open** *8.15am-6.50pm Tue-Sun.* **Admission** *€8.50; €4.25 reductions (combined ticket with the Galleria Palatina). Free on the first Sun of every mth.* **No cards.** **Map** *p164 J11.*

The 30 second-floor rooms of the Pitti Palace were royal apartments until 1920; today they're given over to Florence's modern art museum. The collection covers neoclassical to early 20th-century art, with highlights including Giovanni Dupré's bronze sculptures of Cain and Abel and Ottone Rosai's simple *Piazza del Carmine*. Also showcased here is the work of the Macchiaioli school, the early Italian Impressionist group who were ridiculed for painting-by-dots (*macchie*), and works by Giovanni Fattori and Telemaco Signorini.

♥ Giardino di Boboli

Entrances via Romana, the central door of Pitti Palace, Porta Romana and Forte Belvedere (055 2388786/2651838). **Open** *Nov-Feb 8.15am-4.30pm daily. Mar 8.15am-5.30pm daily. June-Aug 8.15am-7.30pm daily. Apr, May, Sept, Oct 8.15am-6.30pm daily. Closed 1st and last Mon in mth.* **Admission** *€7; €3.30 reductions (incl Tesoro dei Granduchi, Museo della Moda e Del Costume, Museo delle Porcellane & Giardino Bardini). Free on the first Sun of every mth. No cards.* **Map** *p164 J12 (main entrance).*

Boboli is the best loved of the few green spaces and parks in the city centre, and is a popular oasis, particularly on hot summer days. Far to the left of the main entrance is a fountain showing Cosimo I's obese dwarf as a nude *Bacchus*, heralding the walkway that leads to Buontalenti's grotto with Bandinelli's statues of *Ceres* and *Apollo*, casts of Michelangelo's *Slaves*, and a second grotto adorned with frescoes of classical Greek and Roman myths and encrusted with shells. The

Stroll around Giardino di Boboli

This cool green space is worth its entrance fee

Start at the via Romana ('Annalena') entrance to the Boboli Gardens. Ahead of you is a small grotto sheltering statues of Adam and Eve. At the top of the hill, turn left and then right on to the viale de' Platani and continue uphill. About halfway along this covered path is the entrance to the **botanical gardens**, also called the **Giardino degli Ananassi** after the pineapples once grown here. Continue on the same path to the **viale de' Cipressi** ('il Viottolone'), an avenue lined with statues. Turn right here.

At the bottom of the viale de' Cipressi lies the gorgeous **Isolotto**, a small island sitting in a circular moat laid out in 1612. In the middle is the *Fountain of Oceanus*, designed by Il Tribolo for Cosimo II. Beyond the Isolotto is the English-style lawn known as the **Hemicycle**. Turn right to rejoin viale della Meridiana, passing the lovely **Limonaia** (orangery/ winter gardens). You emerge with the Meridiana wing of Palazzo Pitti on your left and a huge Roman *vasca* (basin) on your right.

Take one of the steep paths that climb the hill to get splendid views of Florence. Follow the path on the left side of the tree-lined lawn, past a bronze sculpture by Igor Mitoraj. To the right is the viale de' Cipressi. Walk straight on past the row of old houses on your right to an elegant stairway that sweeps up to the walled **Giardino del Cavaliere**. From here the views are purely rural: villas, the odd tower, olive groves and cypress trees.

Back at the bottom of the steps, the path to the right brings you to *Abundance*, an enormous statue clutching a sheaf of golden corn. Instead of going down the steps, take the path that hugs the walls of Forte di Belvedere until you come to the back gate of the fort. From here, follow the path opposite past the pale peppermint green **Kaffeehaus**, a Rococo gem built in 1775 for Pietro Leopoldo (it occasionally opens for visits, usually during the summer; check local press for up to date information). Continue straight on down a steep path, which brings you out above the huge **amphitheatre**. This faces the rear façade and entrance of the Pitti Palace, where you'll find the **Fontana del Carciofo**, a superb Baroque fountain, named after the bronze artichoke that once topped it.

Head around to the right, and a wide gravel path leads to a small rose garden dominated by Baccio Bandinelli's *Jupiter*. The little path to the right ends at the small **Grotticina di Madama**, dominated by bizarre statues of goats and the first of the several grottoes for which the garden is known.

Back at *Jupiter*, follow the railings to the end and descend the steps to the wonderful **Grotta Grande** or the **Grotta di Buontalenti**. It's not always possible to walk into the chambers, but you can see through the railings. The Grotta di Buontalenti was built between 1557 and 1593 by heavyweights Vasari, Ammannati and Buontalenti. The last curiosity before leaving through the Palazzo Pitti exit is a statue of Pietro Barbino, Cosimo I's pot-bellied dwarf, known as Il Morgante.

▶ *The route of this walk is shown on the map on p164.*

▶ *The route of this walk is shown on the map on p164.*

Giardino di Boboli with Fontana di Nettuno

THE OLTRARNO

ramps take you to the amphitheatre, where Jacopo Peri and Giulio Caccini's *Euridice* was staged for the Medici in 1600. At the top of the hill is the **Museo delle Porcellane** *(see below)*, entered through the Giardino dei Cavalieri. For a peaceful stroll in the gardens follow our guided walk *(see p169* Stroll around Giardino di Boboli).

Museo delle Porcellane

Casino del Cavaliere, Giardino di Boboli, Palazzo Pitti (055 2388709, www. polomuseale.firenze.it). **Open** *Nov-Feb 8.15am-4.30pm daily. Mar 8.15am-5.30pm daily. June-Aug 8.15am-7.30pm daily. Apr, May, Sept, Oct 8.15am-6.30pm daily. Closed 1st & last Mon of mth.* **Admission** *€7; reductions €3.50 (incl Tesoro dei Granduchi, Museo dell Moda e Del Costume, Giardino di Boboli & Giardino Bardini). Free on the first Sun of every mth. No cards.* **Map** *p164 K13.*

Built by Leopoldo de' Medici, this outhouse at the top of the Giardino di Boboli was once a reception room for artists. The museum has ceramics used by the various occupants of Palazzo Pitti and includes the largest selection of Viennese china outside Vienna. Most visitors are more interested in the views.

Adamo ed Eva (Adam and Eve)
(Michelangelo Naccherino, 1590-1610)
Giardino di Boboli

Museo della Moda e del Costume

(Galleria del Costume)
Palazzo Pitti (055 2388713, www.polomuseale. firenze.it). **Open** *Nov-Feb 8.15am-4.30pm daily. Mar 8.15am-5.30pm daily. June-Aug 8.15am-7.30pm daily. Apr, May, Sept, Oct 8.15am-6.30pm daily. Closed 1st and last Mon in mth.* **Admission** *€7 (incl Tesoro dei Granduchi, Museo delle Porcellane, Giardino di Boboli and Giardino Bardini). Free on the first Sun of every mth. No cards.* **Map** *p164 H12.*

The sumptuous Costume Museum is in the Pitti's Palazzina della Meridiana, which periodically served as residence to the Lorraine family and the House of Savoy. Formal, theatrical and everyday outfits from the museum's collection of 6,000 pieces spanning five centuries are shown in rotation, changing every two years. Some more important get-ups are permanently on display, among them Cosimo I's and Eleonora di Toledo's clothes, including her grand velvet creation from Bronzino's portrait.

La Specola

Via Romana 17 (055 2756444, www.msn.unifi. it). **Open** *Tue-Sun 10.30am-5.30pm, closed Mon.* **Admission** *€6; €3 reductions. No cards.* **Map** *p164 G12.*

A dream day out for older kids with horror fixations, La Specola is the zoology department of the Natural History Museum. The first 23 rooms are crammed with stuffed and pickled animals, including many famously extinct species, and up to here the museum can also be fun for younger children. From Room 24 onwards, however, exhibits are more gruesome. A *Frankenstein*-esque laboratory is filled with wax corpses on satin beds, each a little more dissected than the last, and walls are covered with realistic body parts crafted as teaching aids in the 18th and 19th centuries.

Tesoro dei Granduchi (Museo degli Argenti)

Palazzo Pitti (055 2388709, www. polomuseale.firenze.it). **Open** *Nov-Feb 8.15am-4.30pm daily. Mar 8.15am-5.30pm daily. June-Aug 8.15am-7.30pm daily. Apr, May, Sept, Oct 8.15am-6.30pm daily. Closed 1st & last Mon of mth.* **Admission** *€7; reductions €3.50 (incl Museo delle Porcellane, Museo della Moda e Del Costume , Giardino di Boboli & Giardino Bardini). Free on the first Sun of every mth. No cards.* **Map** *p164 J11.*

This extravagant two-tier museum section of the Pitti Palace houses an astonishing hoard of treasures amassed by the Medici: not just silver, but everything from tapestries and rock crystal vases to breathtakingly banal miniature animals.

Restaurants & wine bars

5 e Cinque €€

Piazza della Passera 1 (055 2741583). **Open**
noon-3pm, 7.30-10pm Tue-Sun. **No cards.**
Map *p164 J10* ❶ *Vegetarian/organic*

Named after a traditional, economical
chickpea sandwich from Livorno, 5 e Cinque
serves vegetarian-oriented dishes and organic
foods and wines, and gets points for quality
as well as ambience. Choose from cheese-
filled *focaccie, frittate* and vegetable quiche,
and the strictly seasonal soups and salads.
Try the *cecina* (chickpea *focaccia*), a speciality
that you won't easily find on other restaurant
menus in the city. Although the selection
is not vast, you'll be lured by the prices and
friendly service. The menu changes daily,
but try to go when they're serving the chicory
linguine with olives, garlic, chilli pepper and
salted ricotta cheese.

Borgo San Jacopo €€€€

Borgo San Jacopo 62r (055 281661, www.
lungarnocollection.com/borgo-san-jacopo).
Open *12.30-2.30pm, 7-10pm daily.* **Map**
p164 J9 ❹ *Gastronomy*

This posh eatery on the Arno wins the
Oscar for the finest seats in Florence: the
mini-terrace facing the Ponte Vecchio is as
dramatic as an opera stage. Indoors, too,
is a 'room with a view' to rival all others.
Serving creative takes on Italian cuisine,
Trentino-born chef Peter Brunel earned the
restaurant's first Michelin star in December
2015. The à la carte menu features heavenly
main dishes, such as veal prepared with
cheek stew, chicory, Jerusalem artichoke,
plum, chestnuts and Vin Santo; there are also
two themed tasting menus priced at €105
and €115 each. The staggeringly long wine
list includes about 800 varieties; by-the-
glass options average around €20. Through
the restaurant's popular 'Spoon' series, a
rotating rota of Michelin-starred chefs make
monthly appearances at Borgo San Jacopo,
each teaming up with Brunel to create a one-
night-only menu.

La Casalinga €

Via de' Michelozzi 9r (055 218624, www.
trattorialacasalinga.it). **Open** *noon-2.30pm,*
7-10pm Mon-Sat. Closed 3wks Aug. **Map**
p164 H10 ❻ *Traditional Italian*

Expect to queue at this Oltrarno favourite.
After five decades of serving wholesome
Florentine home cooking at affordable prices,
family-run La Casalinga today boasts an
impressive following of tourists, locals and a
smattering of VIP clients. Still, some dishes
are better than others: avoid anything made
with table cream (panna) in favour of such
local specialities as *minestrone di riso e cavolo*

or *pasta e ceci* (warming soups with rice and
black cabbage or pasta and chickpeas), roast
guinea fowl and apple cake.

❤ Il Chicco di Caffé €

Via della Chiesa 16r (055 2654354). **Open**
noon-3pm, 7-10.30pm daily. **Map** *p164*
G11 ❼ *Traditional Italian*

This cute corner spot is a must for a
modestly priced lunch after perusing the
morning's market finds in piazza Santo
Spirito. Simple, seasonal fare is served at
lunch, with multiple parties seated at each
table; service is friendly and extra efficient.
Come dinnertime, there are indulgent dishes
on offer (try the artichoke and pork jowl *pici*
pasta when available).

Diladdarno €€

Via dei Serragli 108r (055 224917, www.
trattoriadiladdarno.it). **Open** *noon-3pm,*
7pm-12.30am Tue-Sun. **Map** *p164 F11* ❿
Traditional Italian

Ask to be seated outside (the back porch
makes the appropriate seasonal heating or
cooling adjustments) at this relaxed trattoria
and you'll feel as if you're dining in a friend's
backyard. And, as it happens, you are: the
waiting staff are some of the kindest you'll
find in Florence and are genuinely curious
about their customers. Their warmth is
complemented perfectly by the comfort
food: gnocchi with creamy goat's cheese and
porcini mushrooms, *pici* with *cavolo nero*
(black cabbage), sausage and pecorino. Don't
skip dessert: if you're put off by the €18 price
tag for the oddly titled 'Coffee Time' treat,
know that it's not an espresso shot but an
artfully designed dessert, a Moka pot-shaped
sweet to be shared with the table.

Fiaschetteria Fantappie

Via dei Serragli 47r (055 287420, www.
fiaschetteriafantappie.com). **Open**
9am-1.30pm, 4.30-10pm Mon-Sat. **Map**
p164 F10 ⓬ *Wine bar*

Fantappie is a no-frills neighbourhood wine
bar run by personable staff and crawling with
charismatic regulars all day long, especially
since it jazzed up its outdoor seating and
introduced plentiful tasting platters to its
repertoire. Wines by the glass are a steal at
€2.50 to €4.

❤ Gurdulu €€€

Via delle Caldaie 12 (055 282223, www.
gurdulu.com). **Open** *7.30-11pm Tue-Sat;*
12.30-2.30pm, 7.30-11pm Sun. **Map** *p164*
G11 ⓯ *Fusion*

Gurdulu's kitchen is run by Albania-born,
Piedmont-raised chef Entiana Osmenzeza,
whose elegant, worldly seasonal cuisine is

marked by her Balkan influences, as well as by the tenets of cooking traditions in Italy and throughout Europe – seasonality chief among them. These are tastes that linger in your memory: the crisp octopus with red wine, shallots, braised garlic, lovage and celery sorbet is unforgettable. Before dining, have a cocktail, crafted expertly by local punch priestess Sabrina Galloni, as colourful and spirited as the bold lounge-y decor. In summer, opt to sit in the charming little garden at the back, and make it a casual evening by switching out traditional Tuscan *aperitivo* for Osmenzeza's top-notch tapas plates.

Langolino
Via delle Caldaie 8r (055 294690, www.facebook.com/langolinofirenze). Open 11am-2am Tue-Sat; 11am-midnight Sun. Map p164 G11 16 *Wine bar*

This intimate corner haunt serves high-quality cold cuts (try the *soprassata*, an Italian dry salami) and heavenly cheeses in varying combinations, paired with a range of excellent wines. It's clear from the furnishings that this place could be nowhere but the Oltrarno: beautifully hand-crafted chairs shaped like the façade of Santo Spirito line the bar. Perfect for *aperitivo* and a lovely late-night (for Florence) drink locale.

La Mangiatoia €
Piazza San Felice 8-10r (055 224060, www.trattorialamangiatoia.com). Open noon-3pm, 7-10pm Tue-Sun. Map p164 G12 17 *Traditional Italian/Pizzeria*

A combination of a *rosticceria* and *pizzeria*, La Mangiatoia is a popular stop among local Santo Spirito residents, students and tourists filtering through from Palazzo Pitti, thanks to its rock-bottom prices and good, honest home-cooking. Order takeaway veggies, roast meats or fried snacks from the counter in the front or go through to one of a series of rooms behind the shop, where, aside from standard *rosticceria* fare (lasagne, spit-roast chicken, roast meats), there's a long menu of Italian classics and good pizzas.

Pitti Gola e Cantina
Piazza Pitti 16 (055 212704, www.pittigolaecantina.com). Open 1pm-midnight Wed-Mon. Closed on occasions in winter. Map p164 J11 18 *Wine bar*

Wine and dine in the shadow of Palazzo Pitti at this small, charming *enoteca*. Its popularity means it's often packed with a heavy tourist flow (prompting staff to post a tongue-in-cheek sign declaring 'No water, only wine'). Prices are on the high side, but many locals still swear by this place. The atmosphere is very pleasant, and the staff, though knowledgeable, aren't plagued by the preciousness often seen among wine enthusiasts. Wines are heavily weighted towards Tuscany, and Sangiovese reigns supreme, since the owner is a self-described single-grape purist. Snacks include cured meats and cheeses.

Il Santino
Via Santo Spirito 60r (055 2302820, www.ilsantobevitore.com). Open 12.30-11.30pm daily. Map p164 G9 20 *Wine bar*

Formerly a wine cellar, this local favourite is an offshoot of nearby Il Santo Bevitore (*see below*), serving decadent *crostini* and fine cuts of high-quality Tuscan meats carefully chosen to complement their selection of wines (by-the-glass options abound). Space is precious and seating coveted: there's just a peppering of bar stools and four tables, so expect a wait (well worth it) if you come at the height of happy hour, especially at weekends.

♥ Il Santo Bevitore €€
Via Santo Spirito 64-66r (055 211264, www.ilsantobevitore.com). Open 12.30-3pm, 7.30-11.30pm Mon-Sat; 7.30-11.30pm Sun. Closed 3wks Aug. Map p164 G9 21 *Gastronomy*

Attracting a diverse clientele of young and trendy locals, off-duty food journalists and discerning travellers, this restaurant is one of the best in the Oltrarno. Occupying a large, vaulted room and adjacent tower just south of the river, it's busy at lunch and especially crowded in the evenings. Menus change every month to stay in line with the seasons and the prime ingredients are all top quality. The prices are honest as is the varied and nicely priced wine list. As well as the ever-present wooden platters laden with selections of cheeses and cold meats, try the fresh *garagnelli* pasta with Calabrian hot sauce Ndujia, and the tartar of *chianina*. The owners also run tiny but top-notch wine bar Il Santino a few steps away (*see above*) and bakery shop S. Forno (*see p180*).

Cafés, bars & gelaterie

Caffè degli Artigiani
Via dello Sprone 16r (055 291882 caffedegliartigiani.wordpress.com). Open 8am-1am daily. Map p164 J10 2 *Bar*

Caffè degli Artigiani is easily one of the Oltrarno's most charming neighbourhood bars: it's the kind of local go-to where friends' paths cross unplanned, but no one is ever surprised to see each other. In winter, the upstairs room, complete with a piano, board games and twinkly lights, is the Oltrarno's sweetest spot for winding down with a glass of wine; warmer weather brings coveted green tables set up outdoors on the adjacent side street. There's light local fare, including *crostini*, salads, *panini* and *carpacci*, plus a modest *aperitivo* buffet, but this place is better suited for a coffee and snack or after-dinner drinks. The memorably medieval-esque toilet is the café's only 'pitfall', pun intended.

Caffè Ricchi
Piazza Santo Spirito 8/9r (055 215864, www. ristorantericchi.com/caffericchi). **Open** *7am-11pm Mon-Sat; 8am-11pm Sun. Closed last 2wks Aug.* **Map** *p164 G11* ❸ *Café*

Ricchi's glory days are far behind it, but the café remains a great place for a coffee, cake and a catch-up. You can sip alfresco facing the Basilica of Santo Spirito (at a steeper cost). Alternatively, taking a seat in the back room of the café doesn't cost extra and it's big on charm, with quirky Santa Spirito façade-themed artwork. It's an ideal rain refuge when you're caught browsing through the square's market wares sans umbrella.

Carduccio
Sdrucciolo de Pitti 10r (055 2382070, www. carduccio.com). **Open** *8am-8pm Mon-Sat; 10am-5pm Sun.* **Map** *p164 H11* ❹ *Café-bistro*

This earthy-chic eatery calls itself an 'organic living room', winning over visitors with its greenhouse-y vibe and vitamin-rich menu. Fresh new biodynamic fruits and veggies are brought to Carduccio each morning, setting the stage for the day. The creative duo in charge then build a menu around the ingredients to hand, lending the dishes an element of spontaneity to go with the seasonality. Cold-pressed farm-to-table juices are Carduccio's bread and butter, and there's also Fairtrade and frozen coffee, plus a rotating selection of natural, organic and biodynamic wines.

Ditta Artigianale Oltrarno
Via dello Sprone 5r (055 0457163, www. dittaartigianale.it). **Open** *8am-midnight Mon-Fri; 9am-midnight Sat, Sun.* **Map** *p164 J10* ❻ *Coffee bar/fusion food*

Francesco Sanapo's oft-cited coffee revolution began at the original Ditta Artigianale (*see p155*), and a year later the brand opened this bold Oltrarno offshoot, stylish and surpassing its predecessor in popularity. Ditta Artigianale – particularly at this location – is a place that generates strong opinions: some say it's the best thing to ever happen to Florentine coffee culture, while naysayers cry that it's a pretentious sham built for Instagram likes and bearded hipsters. Truthfully? It's a touch of both. Structurally, it's striking, housed in a revamped building originally designed by the late Giovanni

Michelucci, the architect behind Santa Maria Novella station. Coffee-wise, it's of the same calibre and has the same variety you'd find in the via dei Neri location – from flat whites to drip coffee to the 'Big Cappuccio,' a colossal-sized cappuccino that manages to not be overwhelmed by milk. The main difference is that this location offers a full restaurant menu designed by Arturo Dori, who takes the same eclectic, international approach to food as Sanapo does to coffee.

Gelateria della Passera
Via Toscanella 15r (piazza della Passera) (055 291882, gelaterialapassera.wordpress.com). **Open** *Winter noon-8.30pm daily. Summer noon-midnight daily.* **Map** *p164 J10* ❼ *Gelateria*

This whimsical hole in the wall is set on the corner of one of Florence's most postcard-perfect squares. All *gelati* are made using super-fresh ingredients, usually from Tuscany and always traceable. With the €1 per scoop price tag it's easy to keep both your budget and portion size in check. The fruity flavours are the highlights here: try citrusy favourites, grapefruit or lemon.

Gelateria Santa Trinita
Piazza Frescobaldi 11-12r (Ponte Santa Trinita) (055 2381130, www. gelateriasantatrinita.it). **Open** *11am-11pm daily.* **Map** *p164 H9* ❽ *Gelateria*

This conveniently central gelateria is housed in the beautiful Palazzo Frescobaldi at the foot of the shop's namesake bridge. It tends to overflow with tourists, but it's not a trap: prices are fair for the quality, particularly if you prefer a thicker consistency. Gelato junkies on a mission to sample the city's most strangely delicious flavours should queue for

In the know
The most famous Florentine face?

You won't find Leonardo's legendary Mona Lisa in Florence, of course, but her roots are here – in unsuspecting side street via Sguazza. Monnalisa Gherardini, the model for the beguiling painting, was born in a modest, rented Florentine apartment on 15 June 1479. At the western edge of via Sguazza, look up to spot a plaque (in Italian) commemorating her birth in the neighbourhood. It's juxtaposed with a 21st-century tabernacle by Franco Bini, dedicated in 2013 and coinciding with the first Monalisa Day. Now an annual event it includes a parade through the piazza della Passera area, temporary exhibitions of Mona Lisa-themed art, installations, celebratory DJ sets and more fun.

Black Sesame; it's smooth and mildly savoury, almost reminiscent of creamy peanut butter. There are seats inside, but most customers perch on the bridge to enjoy the view of Ponte Vecchio and streams of passersby.

❤ Mama's Bakery
*Via della Chiesa 34r (055 219214, www. mamasbakery.it). **Open** 8am-5pm Mon-Fri; 9am-3pm Sat, Sun. **Map** p164 F11* **❿** *American café*

American Matt and his Pratese partner Cristina provide good service and taste-of-home comforts for the city's many US residents, and particularly students, who often camp out here for the free Wi-Fi and cute, study-friendly space. Matt and Cristina have also earned a loyal Italian following through the years, and not just for the novelty factor: quality of ingredients and consistency have helped them along. Club sandwiches are particularly good; salads err on the side of overpriced. It's best to go for the breakfast food and baked desserts, washed down with a cup of American Joe (with one free refill for dine-in customers).

Volume
*Piazza Santo Spirito 5r (055 2381460, www. volume.fi.it). **Open** 8.30am-1.30am daily. **Map** p164 G10* **⓮** *Café*

Volume's space was once occupied by a woodworking studio belonging to the Bini brothers, who made hat forms. Many of their sculptures and forms are still on display, and the original woodworking table now serves as seating. Tools of the trade add to the aesthetic, as do the stuffed leather chairs and photogenic bookshelves. A Wurlitzer plays Creedence Clearwater Revival, Al Green

and the kind of classics that will perk your ears up track after track. In the evening, the perfectly portioned pre-dinner spreads (olives, crudites, crisps and seasoned crackers in spicy dips) pair well with bitter *aperitifs*. Come back for breakfast: the huge savoury crêpes and *centrifughe* (fresh fruit-and-veggie juices) are a healthier alternative to greasy hangover food, should you unwittingly overindulge on the crisp cocktails.

Shops
❤ And Company
*Via Maggio 51r (055 219973, www. andcompanyshop.com). **Map** p164 H11* **❷** *Gifts & souvenirs*

Walking by Anglo-Italian Betty Soldi's eclectic shop and studio, you might recognise the playful squiggly writing on the windows: the creative calligrapher's work has appeared in prestigious publications and collaborations with brands the world over. And Company is packed with cosmopolitan Betty's charming bric-a-brac, from Florentine monument-themed mugs and espresso cups to tote bags, notebooks, decorative marble slabs, holiday ornaments and much more. The magic happens in her hidden workspace in the back of the shop. Hours can be erratic: pop by if you're in the area, but call ahead if you're heading across town specifically for the visit.

❤ Angela Caputi
*Via Santo Spirito 58r (055 212 972, www. angelacaputi.com). **Open** 10am-1pm, 3.30-7.30pm Tue-Sat. **Map** p164 G9* **❸** *Jewellery*

Colourful costume jewellery in plastics, resin and crystal from this legendary Florentine designer. Styles are exuberant, with ethnic, art deco and psychedelic patterns. Much of Caputi's inspiration comes from the golden age of Hollywood. **Other locations** Borgo SS Apostoli, Duomo & Around (055 292993).

Anita Russo Ceramic Studio
*Via Romana 11r (055 9063823, www. facebook.com/pg/Anita-Russo-Ceramic-Studio-Firenze-479169925458813). Variable hours. **Map** p164 G12* **❹** *Ceramics*

Anita Russo's inviting space at the foot of via Romana is framed by a cheery blue-green door that sets the tone for the colourful space you'll find inside. The stock is heavy on beautifully made kitchenware and accessories for bed and bath: think serving platters, salt and pepper shakers, salad bowls, toothbrush holders, little trays for keys or jewellery. Jewellery isn't as much of a speciality but you'll still find a few well-priced statement rings. Everything is made in Russo's workspace just behind the counter,

In the know
Meet Clet

Spotted any strange characters, faces or symbols on more than a few street signs? That's the work of adoptive Florentine Clet Abraham, a French artist and local legend known for his playful touches spread throughout the city. One of his most memorable installations in recent years was when he gave the tower of San Niccolò (piazza Giuseppe Poggi) a nose. His studio and showroom is in the heart of San Niccolò (via dell'Olmo 8); original works and reproductions in postcards, magnets and prints are available for purchase. Occasionally you might even see him at work, but more often than not, he's out and about. Hours can be iffy, so plan to go when you're on your way to area museums or Piazzale Michelangelo.

where she often teaches courses to the cerami-curious.

BJØRK
Via dello Sprone 25r (333 979 5939 , www. bjorkflorence.com). Open 10.30am-1.30pm, 2.30-7pmMon-Sat. Map p164 H10 ❺ *Contemporary clothing*

BJØRK is a concept boutique with some Scandinavian tendencies, all minimalist decor and sleek clothes with a mostly androgynous aesthetic. Brands are largely non-Italian but you'll find a few trailblazing Tuscan players such as the footwear label New Kid. Another big draw, particularly for local fashion students, is the stacks of avant-garde style and contemporary art and culture magazines (POP, Kinfolk, Monocle and so on), the likes of which are tough to find in Florence.

La Buca del Vino
Via Romana 129r (055 2335021, www.facebook.com/La-Buca-del-Vino-56075521225/). Open 4.30-8pm Mon; 10am-1.30pm, 4.30-8pm Tue-Sat. Map p164 E14 ❻ *Wine*

Literally translated as 'the wine hole,' this miniscule neighbourhood business big on friendliness and humility is a true hole in the wall. Shelves are lined floor-to-ceiling with *sott'oli* (pickled vegetables), Modena balsamic vinegar, Tuscan olive oil and a wide selection of wine labels considering the shop's size. Most of the products are Tuscan but you'll find a few Piedmontese items lurking. Chat with the kind owners, who'll walk you through the *vino sfuso* (think 'wine on tap' or 'bulk wine') experience: bring in a clean glass bottle or get one from the shop for a nominal fee, then watch them fill up your bottle with a well-researched table wine for around €2 to €4.

Celeste Vintage
Piazza San Felice 1r (055 0500731, www.facebook.com/Celeste-Vintage-310571722300695). Open noon-6.30pm Mon; 10am-1.30pm, 3-7.30pm Tue-Fri; 10am 7.30pm Sat. Map p164 H11 ❼ *Vintage*

Celeste has very enticing window displays: Chanel, Yves Saint Laurent and Salvatore Ferragamo finds are standard, and price tags can range from rock-bottom to bordering on inflated, depending on the day and the item. There's also a solid selection of less prestigious brands or label-less items that are easier on the wallet, and plenty of bargain accessories, particularly costume jewellery, bags and wallets.

Dolcissima Firenze
Via Maggio 61r (055 2396268, www. dolcissimafirenze.it). Open 7.30am-8pm Tue-Sat; 8.30am-2pm Sun. Map p164 H11 ❽ *Sweets*

A delightful shop from another age, featuring the sweet-tooth-satisfying creations of acclaimed patissier Alessio Lai. Exquisite chocolates are displayed in gilded cabinets, and glass cake stands hold delicious-looking concoctions, including an unmissable chocolate and pear cake.

Giulia Materia
Sdrucciolo de' Pitti 13r (055 9753975, www. giuliamateria.com). Open 10am-7pm Tue-Sat; 12am-7pm Sun. Map p164 H11 ❾ *Gifts & artisan objects*

As you stroll down Sdrucciolo de' Pitti, this colourful shop and *atelier* is sure to catch your eye with its ornate doorway, usually framed by some of its coolest items. Music may also reel you in: man of the house Enzo moonlights as a DJ and hosts occasional sets inside. Tuscan artisan Giulia is the other creative half and the mastermind behind the project. For their cheery brand, they craft notebooks, pocketbooks and more miscellany using punchy recycled fabrics, as well as silkscreen products, instantly identifiable clothing and duffels to die for.

Giulio Giannini e Figlio
Piazza Pitti 37r (055 212621, www. giuliogiannini.it). Open 10am 7pm Mon-Sat; 11am-6.30pm Sun. Map p164 J11 ❿ *Gifts & souvenirs*

Family-run firm stocking marbled paper, leather desk accessories and greetings cards.

Madova
Via de' Guicciardini 1r (055 2396526, www. madova.com). Open 10.30am-7pm Mon-Sat. Map p164 K10 ⓬ *Leather gloves*

Madova makes gloves in every imaginable style and colour in its factory, just behind this tiny shop. The generations-deep, family-run business proudly purports to be the only shop in Europe both selling and producing exclusively leather gloves.

Mirta Effe
Via dello Sprone 14 (055 285667, www. facebook.com/Mirta-Effe-989560047749767) Open 12.30-7.30pm Mon-Sat. Map p164 J10 ⓭ *Womenswear*

This dainty, wood-panelled women's boutique is big on patterns, ruffles and other feminine flourishes. The warmth and playfulness of it all feels pulled straight from a children's book.

Obsequium

Borgo San Jacopo 17 (055 216849, www. obsequium.it). **Open** *11am-9pm Mon-Thur; 11am-midnight Fri, Sat; 12-9pm Sun.* **Map** *p164 J10* ⓴ *Wine*

A treasure trove for wine-lovers, in a 12th-century tower. As well as an incredible cellar of fine and everyday wines, spirits and liqueurs, the place stocks all manner of drink-themed gadgets.

❤ Sara Amrhein & SciccArt

Via dello Sprone 9 (392 9613197, www.sara-amrhein.com). **Open** *11am-7.30pm Mon-Fri.* **Map** *p164 J10* ⓵⑤ *Statement jewellery & Tuscan crafts*

This delightful space is shared between American jewellery designer Sara Amrhein, who makes bold polymer clay pieces (necklaces, earrings and bracelets in cheery colours), and crafty curator Tiziana Salvi, who hand-selects a hotchpotch of Tuscan artisanal goods (Montelupo Fiorentino ceramics, tiles, teacups, soaps and so forth). A tip: Sara is also the co-founder of local cultural association Creative People in Florence, a broad network of designers, artists and artisans making their mark on 21st-century Florence.

❤ Le Sorelle

Borgo San Jacopo 30 (055 216223, uashmama.com). **Open** *10.30am-7.30pm daily.* **Map** *p164 K10* ⓵⑦ *Homewares & cosmetics*

This family-run Tuscan company began with a little shop in Lucca and now has multiple outposts around the region, all united in their pure, unadulterated prettiness. The items, which range from scented soaps to dishtowels, are all handmade at the Lucca workshop. Bestsellers are the famous washable paper bags by the house brand Uashmama – these beauties can be used as plant holders or paper flower pots, storage for household items, laundry hampers, you name it.

Tabesce

Via Romana 39r (346 6476720, www.facebook.com/tabesce). **Open** *10.30am-6.30pm Tue-Fri; 10am-7pm Sat.* **Map** *p164 G12* ⓵⑧ *Glass*

Chiara Camagni's shop gives new meaning to *The Glass Menagerie*. Her artful creations are carried out through a diligent glass-fusing process, a craft she also teaches. You'll find animal-shaped knick-knacks and paperweights, flowerpots and mobiles, mood-lifting mini-objects for hearth and home, plus jewellery, vases, clocks, light fixtures and women's accessories. Browsing is a treat – just handle with care.

SAN FREDIANO

The beating blue collar heart of the Oltrarno is the San Frediano area, roughly beginning with the western side of the lengthy via dei Serragli and extending out to the Porta San Frediano, one of the city's medieval gates. It's dominated by **piazza del Carmine**, a square that's been gradually regaining its social-hub status since it was pedestrianised in 2014; it has flaunted a dedicated open-air events venue and a concert stage for several summers now. The arrival of trendy new bars and restaurants has sparked debate over whether the district is undergoing a welcome revival or soul-stripping gentrification. Local flavour is best found at lunchtime, when many of its most characteristic *trattorie* teem with construction employees chowing down on hearty fare. The action happens in the shadow of **Santa Maria del Carmine** church with its wonderfully frescoed Cappella **Brancacci**. Piazza Tasso, meanwhile, with its park benches and outdoor bars, brings together multiple generations in a spot that feels less 'prettified' than its sister squares in Santo Spirito.

Sights & museums

❤ Santa Maria del Carmine & Cappella Brancacci

Piazza del Carmine (055 2768224, www. museicivicifiorentini.comune.fi.it). **Open** *Chapel 10am-5pm Mon, Wed-Sat; 1-5pm Sun. Phone ahead to book.* **Admission** *€4. No cards.* **Map** *p164 E9.*

This blowsy Baroque church is dominated by a huge single nave, with pilasters and pious sculptures overlooked by a ceiling fresco of the Ascension. This isn't what visitors queue for, however: they're here for the Cappella Brancacci (Brancacci Chapel). Frescoed in the 15th century by Masaccio and Masolino, it is one of the city's greatest art treasures. Masaccio, who died aged 27, reached his peak with this cycle of paintings, especially the tangibly grief-stricken Adam and Eve in the *Expulsion from Paradise*, a work that entranced Michelangelo.

Restaurants & wine bars

Al Tranvai €€

Piazza Tasso 14r (055 225197, www. altranvai.it). **Open** *12.30-2.30pm, 7.30-10.30pm Tue-Sat; 7-10.30pm Mon.* **Map** *p164 D10* ❷ *Traditional Italian*

A favourite among local artisans, Al Tranvai is especially busy at lunch, attracting crowds for the wholesome, down-to-earth cooking

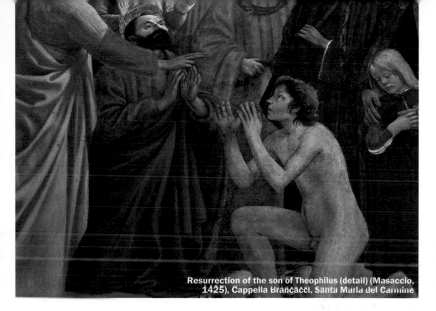

Resurrection of the son of Theophilus (detail) (Masaccio, 1425), Cappella Brancacci, Santa Maria del Carmine

THE OLTRARNO

and great prices. Dishes hail from the *cucina popolare* tradition: *ribollita*, a hearty Tuscan bread and vegetable soup (or summery bread salad *panzanella* when in season), *lesso rifatto con le cipolle* (a tasty beef and onion stew) and simple tagliatelle with leeks. Top off your feasting with a slice of homemade fig and nut cake. The house plonk is just fine.

Alla Vecchia Bettola €€
Viale Ariosto 32-34r (055 224158). **Open** *noon-2.30pm, 7.30-10.30pm Tue-Sat. Closed 3wks Aug.* **Map** *p164 C10* ③ *Italian*

Still very popular among area residents, this lively *trattoria*, situated on a busy ring road behind piazza Tasso, serves up some of the city's best traditional Florentine fare. The menu of hearty, rustic dishes includes daily specials alongside such regulars as *penne alla Bettola* (with tomato, chilli pepper, vodka and a dash of cream) and a superb beef carpaccio topped with artichoke hearts and shaved parmesan, while offal fans can enjoy tripe and *lampredotto*. The Chianina steak is truly succulent.

❤ I Brindellone €€
Piazza Piattellina 10 (055 217879). **Open** *noon-2pm, 7.30-10pm Tue-Sun.* **Map** *p164 E9* ⑤ *Traditional Italian*

Tuscan comfort food in all its simple glory. This inexpensive, rough-and-tumble *trattoria* between piazzas Carmine and Tasso still has the blue-collar soul of old San Frediano, serving up simple *primi*, hearty steak and house wine to boisterous crowds of Florentines. It's named after the fancy cart

paraded through town during the annual Scoppio del Carro tradition *(see p222)*, and old photos of that ritual and other events line the walls in the front room. A particularly good stop for Florentine steak and the lunchtime deals, perhaps after visiting the nearby Brancacci Chapel (Cappella Brancacci) *(see p176)*.

Culinaria Bistrot €
Piazza Tasso 13r (055 229494, www.facebook. com/culinaria.degustibus.bistro). **Open** *noon-3pm, 6.45-11pm daily.* **Map** *p164 D10* ⑧ *Organic bistro*

Prices are on point at this cosy 'indoor garden' of sorts, where everything on the menu is made using ingredients sourced from the De Gustibus network of farmers. There are scrumptious soups of the day, starting at just €6; inventive starters such as sweet corn pancakes with duck breast; house-made houmous, not easy to find elsewhere in Florence; and, of course, the satisfaction of knowing you're directly supporting a grassroots group of producers.

❤ Da Pescatore €€€
Piazza del Carmine 7r (055 219978, www. dapescatore.it). **Open** *7.30-11.30pm Mon-Sat. Lunch by reservation only. Closed 1mth in winter.* **Map** *p164 F9* ⑨ *Seafood*

A contemporary, fresh take on seafood dining in Tuscany. You can order à la carte here (a sample dish: spider crab with gnocchi, green apple and mango), but taking the safe, and substantially more expensive, route is not particularly interesting: better to partake in the fun tasting 'itinerary' experience this restaurant was set up to offer. The three- to 10-course tasting trips feature a range of artfully prepared yet accessible seafood, from octopus to monkfish. The details are often not spelled out in advance (you'll need to advise the kitchen of any allergies or concerns ahead of time). A sense of adventure and some trust in Daniele's tastes is required (hint: trust him).

Essenziale €€
Piazza di Cestello 3r (055 2476956, www. essenziale.me). Open 7-10pm Tues-Sat; 11am-4pm Sun. Closed Dec, Jan. Map p164 E8 ⑪ *Experimental Italian*

Spearheaded by the talented Simone Cipriani, this concept restaurant makes its principles clear: here, it's about the essentials, stripping away everything that's extraneous and focusing on crafting creative dishes that taste good. The design is chic but the vibe is laid-back, with surprisingly fair prices, nothing marked up for meaningless exclusivity. The tasting menus deliver excellent value: the 'Conoscersi' option offers three courses for €35, including Cipriani's succulent Comfort Spaghetti, while a Salvator Dali-inspired set costs €55 for five dishes. For lighter, but no less flavour-packing options, look to the 'Fast and Casual' section of the menu, which features a Tuscan club sandwich made with guinea fowl and pork cheek and a taco lasagna made with Sriracha sauce, Bechamel, meat ragu, Parmesan cheese and lettuce. A prizeworthy three-course Sunday brunch is served for a modest cost of €28, unlimited coffee and water included.

Gesto
Borgo San Frediano 27r (055 241288, www. gestofailtuo.it). Open 6pm-2am daily. Map p164 F9 ⑬ *Bar-restaurant*

The brainchild of an enterprising Italian twentysomething, this popular, sustainability-focused local is the perfect place to sample a variety of bites with friends in a casual, relaxed atmosphere. Don't be stressed out by the ordering system and overall concept, which can throw some visitors off after dining in mostly traditional *trattorie* – at Gesto, everything is done in the greenest way possible, starting with the non-waiter who'll bring you a chalkboard on which you jot down your order, which'll later become your plate (just go with it). The menu's snack-size portions are divided into meat, vegetables, fish and sweets. Mix it up: options include a mini-kebab or fish burger, creative cauliflower, octopus salad and even chicken nuggets, surprisingly one of the highlights.

Il Guscio €€
Via dell'Orto 49a (055 224421, www.il-guscio. it). Open 12.30-2pm, 7.30-11pm Mon-Fri; 7.30-11pm Sat. Closed Aug. Map p164 D9 ⑭ *Traditional Italian*

This new-generation *trattoria* in the heart of the San Frediano area offers carefully prepared versions of dishes that hail from Tuscany's traditional rural cuisine, with the odd variation. The strictly seasonal menu (on a cheeseboard) features a sizeable antipasto section (fried artichokes with melt-in-your-mouth Burrata cheese are a standout), and numerous *primi* and *secondi*, including the fillet of beef cooked in *vin santo* and topped with a slab of liver pâté, a long-time favourite. The notable wine selection includes a high number of labels from Alto Adige, Sicily and Piedmont in addition to Tuscan standards and surprises, with bottles starting at €15.

Trattoria dell'Orto €€
Via dell'Orto 35a (055 224148, www. trattoriadellorto.com). Open noon-3pm, 7.30-11.30pm Sun, Mon, Wed-Sat. Map p164 D9 ㉒ *Traditional Italian*

Skip the relatively lacklustre first courses and head straight for the meaty specialities at this solid San Frediano haunt. Also yummy are the mixed fried veggies and generous appetiser platter named after kitchen king Arturo Caminati. Dotted with house plants, the softly lit terrace at the back is covered in cold weather and makes for an atmospheric evening.

❤ Vivanda
Via Santa Monaca 7r (055 2381208, www. vivandafirenze.it). Open 11am-3pm, 6pm-midnight daily. Map p164 F10 ㉓ *Wine bar*

Florence's first *enoteca* dedicated to organic wines, Vivanda opened in 2010 and still has a big local fan base. Located between piazza Santo Spirito and piazza del Carmine, Vivanda boasts an extensive wine list of around 100 organic and biodynamic labels from across Italy and the world. They also produce their own label, Dalle Nostre Mani, which has a food and wine shop of the same name around the corner. The kitchen offers a good assortment of antipasti, *primi* and *secondi* including fresh pasta and a variety of vegetable choices. All prime ingredients are locally sourced and seasonal. You can eat here and not worry about your carbon footprint: plates and cutlery are all biodegradable.

💙 Explore the Oltrarno's artisan studios

*Start **Map** p164 D8.*

Florence is rightly proud of its Renaissance treasures, but few visitors are aware of the artisan community that has existed in the city for some 500 years.

Until the Medici moved into the Pitti Palace in the mid 16th century, the Oltrarno was a solidly working-class area with a reputation for low life. However, with the arrival of the royal family, Florentine bigwigs began to move in, building magnificent palaces in streets such as via Maggio and via Santo Spirito. With them came the attendant cabinet-makers and restorers, wood-carvers, dressmakers and cobblers, metal workers and gilders that, added to the *botteghe* (workshops) already established in the area, made for a rich and varied pool of artisan talent that thrived for centuries.

Begin your explorations by crossing over into the Oltrarno via Ponte Amerigo Vespucci. First up is a wondrous operation to witness: **Antico Setificio Fiorentino** (via Lorenzo Bartolini 4, 055 213861, www. anticosetificiofiorentino.com). The only artisan silk workshop left in Florence, open by appointment only, it's a must for anyone interested in fabric and interior design – just be sure to book before you go.

Move through the small piazza di Verzaia to reach the nearby via San Giovanni, where you'll find experienced *corniciaio* (framer) Pierluigi Franceschi (no.11, 055 220642, www.franceschicornici. com). Born in the Oltrarno, he learned his elaborate picture-framing craft from his uncle. Nowadays, his most profitable work is for foreign customers; one of his frames even graces a Mondrian piece in the Guggenheim Museum in New York.

Take a detour through via dell'Orto to piazza Piattellina, where you can stop off for a traditional lunch at I Brindellone (*see p177*); or, if you're feeling bold or just want to stay more on-route, pass through piazza dei Nerli instead, stopping off at the tiny *trippaio* stand for the ultimate workers' lunch, a *lampredotto panino*, made from the fourth stomach of a cow.

Once sufficiently fueled, find your way to the quintessential workshops concentrated in the rough-hewn side streets running off borgo San Frediano. You'll pass pubs and *pizzerie* before veering onto the splendidly named 'Street of the Golden Dragon'. Follow this side street until you reach the **Ugolini brothers'** bronze workshop (via del Drago d'Oro 25r, 055 215 343, www. bronzistugolini.com). Founded in 1800, this family firm still uses traditional methods of casting, engraving and polishing bronze to produce exquisite lamps and lighting fixtures and home accessories.

Inch your way back inward and upward toward piazza Santo Spirito, where you'll find metalworkers **Giuliano Ricchi** and **Gianni Bricci** – but not if you didn't know where to look. Their workspace is hidden within the walls of a residential *palazzo* (piazza Santo Spirito 12), but they're very receptive – happy to show guests the finer points of their metal magic, and how they produce everything from photo frames to candelabras.

If talk of the Oltrarno's 'glory days' has you wondering who will keep this district alive, swing south of the *piazza* toward borgo Tegolaio and then turn down via dei Preti, where an innovative workspace of new-generation artisans will give you faith in the future. Margherita de Martino Norante steers the ship at **Officine Nora** (via dei Preti 4, 055 975 8930, www.officinenora. it), a collective workspace of Italian and international jewellery designers. It's traditional in the important ways (witness their dedication to techniques), but completely revolutionary in others. The 'sharing economy' generation has transformed this former mechanic's space into a co-working studio where several designers set up shop long-term and others come in for one-off workdays or courses with the chief artisans.

Finally, turn back down borgo Tegolaio, take a right on via Sant'Agostino and pass through piazza San Felice, perhaps stopping off for a snack in the square first. Right at the beginning of via Romana you'll find **Anita Russo** (*see p174*), another young, inspiring artisan honing her ceramic craft in the heart of the city. The bold colours and bizarre shapes she uses in creating her home, kitchen and bath accessories, jewellery and knick-knacks set her apart from the typical Italian ceramicists, and she regularly holds night courses in her workspace in the back of her shop.

Cafés, bars & gelaterie

Café Circolo Aurora
Viale Vasco Pratolini 2, corner of piazza Tasso (055 224059, www. circoloaurorafirenze.it). Open 6.30pm-midnight daily. Map p164 C10 ① *Bar*

Located in a little tower on the city walls, this sweet spot is filled with delights – second-hand furniture and architectural salvage sit next to mad modern seats (the bum ones are particularly arresting) in a space that feels more like an overstuffed antiques shop than a café. The interior charms in the colder months, but the expansive terrace – with its twinkling lights and local feel – always wins out in the summer. The crowd here transcends many typical social boundaries – mixed ages, couples with the occasional kid in tow, Italian uni students, international residents and so forth.

❤ La Carraia
Piazza N. Sauro 25r (055 280965, www. lacarraiagroup.eu). Open Winter 11am-10pm daily; Summer 11am–midnight daily. Closed Jan. Map p164 G8 ⑤ *Gelateria*

Head honcho Signora Eleanora's modest gelato business has grown into an international franchise with a Florida location opening in 2017. Carraia's queues are crazy in the summer, but it shouldn't be skipped if you're doing the gelato grand tour. You can't really go wrong with a €1 tasting cone, which is a pretty sizeable serving for the price. The crème caramel is lush.

Libreria Café La Cité
Borgo San Frediano 20r (055 210387, www. lacitelibreria.info). Open 9am-2am Mon-Sat; 3pm-2am Sun. No cards. Map p164 F9 ⑨ *Literary café*

La Cité has given this part of the Oltrarno a true Left Bank feel. The mezzanine café area of this bookshop-café, ideal for both study and socialising, is in rustic reclaimed woods with metal bolts, and the bookshelves downstairs lined with countercultural gospel and punk rock biographies. Home-baked cakes, freshly made fruit and veggie juices and coffees are all served. Evening concerts and literary events are organised fairly regularly. By night, the hip yet unintimidating mixed-age crowd spills out into the streets, house wine in hand.

❤ O'Scugnizzo
Via dell'Orto 25r (055 2286471, www. oscugnizzo.net). Open 7-11.30pm daily. Closed Aug. Map p164 D9 ⑫ *Pizzeria*

If you're looking for atmosphere and pampering, the bare-bones, fluorescent-lit O'Scugnizzo is the last place you need to be. But if you're on the hunt for a local pizza joint where thrifty Italians grab takeaway in droves, this is it. Tuck in to fresh Neapolitan-style pies prepared by a native bunch (who, true to southern stereotypes, tend to operate rather sporadically in summer – best to call ahead to make sure someone's cooking, although the idea of making a reservation seems laughable). One of the menu's tastiest options is a *pizza bianca* made with mozzarella, sausage and *friarelli* (a broccoli-esque topping). If the venue's measly two tables are occupied, grab your pizza and a Peroni and head for the steps of the nearby Santa Maria del Carmine.

❤ La Sorbettiera
Piazza Tasso 11 (055 5120336, www. lasorbettiera.com. Open 12.30-11.30pm Mon-Sat; 11am-1pm, 3-11.30pm Sun. Map p164 D10 ⑬ *Gelateria*

This humble hut in the heart of piazza Tasso is where you'll find arguably the neighbourhood's tastiest, freshest gelato, often served by its friendly southern owner, Antonio. The salted caramel option is divine, and when you order in a cup, always say 'yes' to the thin biscuit topper they offer, which somehow tastes better here than anywhere else, and makes a great edible utensil. Who needs spoons?

Shops

❤ S. Forno
Via Santa Monaca 3 (055 2398580, www. ilsantobevitore.com). Open 7.30am-7.30pm daily. Map p164 F10 ⑯ *Bakery*

A boutique bakery if there ever was one, this stylish shop completes the 'Santo' holy trinity – Il Santo Bevitore restaurant (*see p172*) and its spinoffs. There is a plethora of jams, craft beers, juices and pastas up for sale, as well as fresh bread, sweet treats and traditional bakery favourites. *Panini* are served up fresh for a high-quality quick bite at lunchtime.

Twisted
Borgo San Frediano 21r (055 282011). Open 9am-1pm, 3.30-7.30pm Mon-Sat. Map p164 F9 ⑳ *Vinyl*

A specialist jazz centre with rare recordings and more mainstream sounds. The stocked artists span 1950s trad jazz right through to acid and nu jazz.

Forte di Belvedere

SAN NICCOLÒ

Beyond the Pitti complex moving east, crowds are smaller and streets are quieter in the whimsical **San Niccolò** district, whose colourful shopfronts and seesawing streets make it feel a bit like a village *fuori Firenze* (outside Florence) at times. South-east of the Ponte Vecchio are the *coste* ('ribs'). These pretty, narrow lanes snake steeply uphill towards the **Forte di Belvedere** *(see below)*. Halfway up costa di San Giorgio is one of the two entrances to the spectacular green space of **Giardino Bardini** *(see p182)*; the other is in via de' Bardi, a quiet street, running uphill behind the riverbank, that turns into via di San Niccolò and leads to the **Casa Museo Rodolfo Siviero** *(see right)*. Behind lies the **lively western side** of the Oltrarno, leading as far as Porta San Niccolò in **piazza Poggi**. This is a quiet area until the evening, when the wine bars and *osterie* along via de' Renai open up, overlooking the riverside piazza Demidoff. Here too you'll find the quiet **Museo Bardini** and its glorious collection of antiques *(see p182)*. Before you leave the district, bear in mind that San Niccolò is also the gateway to **piazzale Michelangelo** *(see p191)* and unmissable **San Miniato al Monte** *(see p190)*.

Sights & museums

Casa Museo Rodolfo Siviero
Lungarno Serristori 1-3 (055 2345219, www. museocasasiviero.it). **Open** *Sept-June 10am-1pm Mon, Sun; 10am-6pm Sat. July, Aug 10am-1pm Mon, Sun; 10am-2pm, 3-7pm Sat.* **Admission** *free.* **Map** *p164 P12.*

This was previously the house of government minister Rodolfo Siviero, dubbed the 'James Bond of art' for his efforts to prevent the Nazis plundering Italian masters. The pieces he saved were returned to their owners, but Siviero left his own private collection to the Regione Toscana on condition it would be open to the public. Among the 500 pieces on display are paintings and sculptures by friends of Siviero, including de Chirico, Annigoni and da Messina.

Forte di Belvedere
Via San Leonardo (055 27681). **Open** *phone for details.* **Admission** *free.* **Map** *p164 L13.*

Giardino Bardini

Named after its creator, antiquarian Stefano Bardini (1854-1922), this 2,000-strong collection includes sculpture, paintings and applied art from the Middle Ages and Renaissance. Brought together over decades, it was housed here by Bardini, who renovated the former church and convent of San Gregorio della Pace in 1881 into the elegant Renaissance-style structure it is today. Stand-out pieces include the *Madonna della Mela*, the *Madonna dei Cordai* by Donatello and *Atlas* by Guercino, as well as a gorgeous collection of oriental rugs and 15th-century chests. But the museum is as much about the collector as his collection, with the work still exhibited in a layout designed by Bardini.

Santa Felicita

Piazza Santa Felicita 3 (055 213018, www. santafelicitafirenze.it). **Open** *9.30am-12.30, 3.30-5pm Mon-Sat.* **Admission** *free.* **Map** *p164 K10.*

This church occupies the site of the first church in Florence, founded in the second century AD by Syrian Greek tradesmen. The oldest surviving part is the portico, built in 1564; the interior mainly dates to the 18th century. Most who come here do so to see Pontormo's striking Mannerist *Deposition* altarpiece in the Cappella Barbadori-Capponi.

Villa Bardini

Costa di San Giorgio 2 (055 2638599, www. bardinipeyron.it). **Open** *10am-7pm Tue-Sun.* **Admission** *€8. No cards.* **Map** *p164 M12.*

The restored Villa Bardini is home to a permanent exhibition of the fabulously extravagant creations of couturier Roberto Capucci. The villa also contains a newer museum dedicated to the works of Italian artist Pietro Annigoni, and regularly hosts high calibre exhibitions that are rarely, if ever, crowded.

This star-shaped fortress was built in 1590 by Bernardo Buontalenti to protect the city from insurgents. It was then used as a strong room for the Medici Grand Dukes' treasures. After a painfully drawn-out restoration, the fort is open once again for temporary art exhibitions, shows and events. (When nothing is running, the fortress is closed to the public.)

Giardino Bardini

Via de' Bardi 1r, costa di San Giorgio 2 (055 290112, www.bardinipeyron.it). **Open** *Nov-Feb 8.15am-4.30pm daily. Mar 8.15am-5.30pm daily. Apr, May, Sept, Oct 8.15am-6.30pm daily. June-Aug 8.15am-7.30pm daily. Closed first & last Mon of mth.* **Admission** *€7 (incl Tesoro dei Granduchi, Museo dell Moda e Del Costume, Museo delle Porcellane & Giardino di Boboli). No cards.* **Map** *p164 M12.*

First created in the 1200s by the Mozzi family, this intriguing garden underwent five years of painstaking restoration recently, and is a delight. The garden is divided into three distinct areas: the Baroque steps, leading to a terrace with amazing views; the English wood, a shady haven of evergreens; and the farm park, with a dwarf orchard, rhododendrons and a 'tunnel' of wisteria and hydrangea.

❤ Museo Bardini

Via de' Renai 37 (055 2342427, www. museicivicifiorentini.comune.fi.it/en/ bardini/). **Open** *11am-5pm Fri-Mon.* **Admission** *€6.* **Map** *p164 N11.*

In the know
Beach life

Map *p164 Q11.* On a raised stretch of the river at lungarno Serristori, city beach Easy Living and its wood-decked restaurant just above 'sea level' are open day and night to sun seekers between June and September. (Just don't attempt to swim in the Arno river.) Chill on a lounger under a parasol by day, drink a toast to summer on the restaurant terrace by night. The Association Piazzart and various local groups host activities and event programming at the beach, from literary readings and yoga sessions to DJ sets, plus a now-famous sandcastle building competition held annually mid August on *Ferragosto.*

Restaurants & wine bars

San Niccolò 39 €€
Via San Niccolò 39r (055 2001397, www. sanniccolo39.com). **Open** *7.30-10.30pm Tue-Sat.* **Map** *p164 P12* ⑲ *Seafood*

An evolution of the former fish eatery Filipepe, this restaurant is now steered by smooth operator Paul Feakes, a British man-about-town whose discerning taste defines the place. The kitschy-cool decor remains and sumptuous fish dishes still make up the bulk of the menu, all prepared creatively by young chef Vanni (try the *baccalà* burger). The wine list focuses primarily on highlighting a few small producers at a time, so you won't be overwhelmed by choice, just satisfied by quality.

❤ Le Volpi e l'Uva
Piazza de' Rossi 1r (055 2398132, www. levolpieluva.com). **Open** *11am-9pm Mon-Sat.* **Map** *p164 K10* ㉔ *Wine bar*

Attracting a diverse range of local wine lovers, this wine bar is a great place for a glass of plonk and a snack. It can get cramped in winter with seats only at the bar, but there's more room in summer thanks to the terrace (reservations are still recommended for outdoor seating). Much of what's on offer will be unfamiliar to all but the most clued-up oenophiles: owners Riccardo and Emilio seek out small, little-known producers from all over Italy, with an eye on value for money. A delicious selection of snacks includes tasting plates of Italian and French cheeses, cured meats, a range of *crostoni*, *crudités*, fish carpaccios and rich duck foie gras.

Cafés, bars & gelaterie

Il Rifrullo
Via San Niccolò 55r (055 2342621, www. ilrifrullo.com). **Open** *7.30am-1am Mon-Sat; 8am-1am Sun. Closed 2wks Aug.* **Map** *p164 O12* ⑪ *Café-lounge*

This long-time favourite of Florentines in peaceful San Niccolò is decked out in pale stained woods and cool greens. The atmosphere is usually sleepy and laid-back during the day, but the mood mutates for the evening *aperitivo*, when the music comes on, and the back rooms open to accommodate the crowds and plates of snacks and cocktails are served on the charming summer roof garden in warmer weather (you'll definitely need a reservation if you want to be seated on the terrace). The fixed price €20 Sunday brunch (water and coffee included) is another crowd-puller, with its roasted meats, pancakes, scrambled eggs, smoked salmon and fruit salad.

Zeb
Via San Miniato 2r (055 2342864, www. zebgastronomia.com). **Open** *Apr-Oct 7.30-10.30pm Mon, Tue; noon-3.30pm, 7.30-10.30pm Thur-Sat. Nov-Mar noon-3.30pm, 7.30-10.30pm Thur-Sat.* **Map** *p164 O12* ⑮ *Bistro-deli*

There's no outdoor seating at Zeb, but don't let that put you off; grab a stool at the central bar or in the window of the bright and pretty interior and enjoy an excellent selection of home-style small plates, always served with seasonal ingredients. As is evident from the freshly handwritten menu hanging outside each day, the options are always shifting, but you can generally count on finding outrageously good pastas and salads with creatively tossed fresh ingredients. It's all carried out under the watchful eye of owner Alberto Navari who serves dishes designed by his mother, Giuseppina, in a space that formerly housed their family grocery store.

Shops

❤ Alessandro Dari
Via di San Niccolò 115r, (055 244747, www. alessandrodari.com). **Open** *10am-7.30pm Mon-Sat; 11am-7.30pm Sun.* **Map** *p164 N12* ❶ *Jewellery*

Physically close to the Ponte Vecchio, Alessandro Dari's stunning creations couldn't be further away from so much of the tat you find on the bridge, with the craftsman's pieces inspired by everything from Renaissance art to more obscure and arcane art from earlier periods, and ancient mythology.

KARASCIÒ Streetwear
Via San Niccolò 67r (055 243943, www. karasciostreetwear.com). **Open** *10am-1pm, 3-7.30pm daily.* **Map** *p164 O12* ⑪ *Contemporary fashion*

A small but well-stocked boutique catering to aesthetically assertive women and men who like their platforms stacked high and their jewellery to resemble weaponry. Signature brands include Windsor Smith, Dr. Martens and Jeffrey Campbell.

Il Torchio
Via de' Bardi 17 (055 2342862, www. legatoriailtorchio.com). **Open** *10am-1.30pm, 2.30-7pm Mon-Fri; 10am-1pm Sat.* **Map** *p164 L11* ⑲ *Gifts & souvenirs*

Young Canadian transplant Erin Ciulla took over this spot to carry on the bookbinding tradition passed down to her by Anna Anichini, with whom she apprenticed. Watch her work in action, and stock up on handmade notebooks, paper boxes, stationery and albums.

Outside the City Gates

Follow the ring roads of central Florence and you'll realise how small the city centre really is – and how easy it is to escape the throngs of tourists.

South of the river, large sections of the 13th-century city walls still survive, and the tree-lined avenues that form an umbrella round this side of the city are picturesque. Here you'll find the best walks, views and sights; as the hills rise – practically from the banks of the Arno – gently meandering lanes take you within minutes into gorgeous countryside.

North of the Arno, the old city walls were pulled down in the 1870s to make way for *viali* (avenues) – now traffic-clogged multi-lane arteries circling the city – and only the main city gates are still standing. The winding roads to historic Fiesole and charming Settignano are dotted with elegant country houses and offer a taste of what the rest of Tuscany has in store for you: fabulous views, sublime countryside and fascinating cultural sights.

❤ Don't miss

1 San Miniato al Monte *p190*
The finest Florentine Romanesque church.

2 Badiani's Buontalenti gelato *p194*
Hard-to-beat ice-cream worth the bus ride out of the city centre.

3 Piazzale Michelangelo *p191*
Picture-perfect views from the city's balcony.

4 Area Archeologica & Museo Civico in Fiesole *p198*
Roman and Etruscan remains, and a scenic theatre still in use after two millennia.

5 Museo Stibbert *p196*
A fascinating collection of arms, armour, textiles, furniture and whatnots.

In the know
Getting around

Exploring the area immediately beyond the eight surviving city gates is easy by foot. For any sights lying further afield, the ATAF bus network has regular services to the suburbs and to nearby Fiesole.

Piazzale di Porta Romana

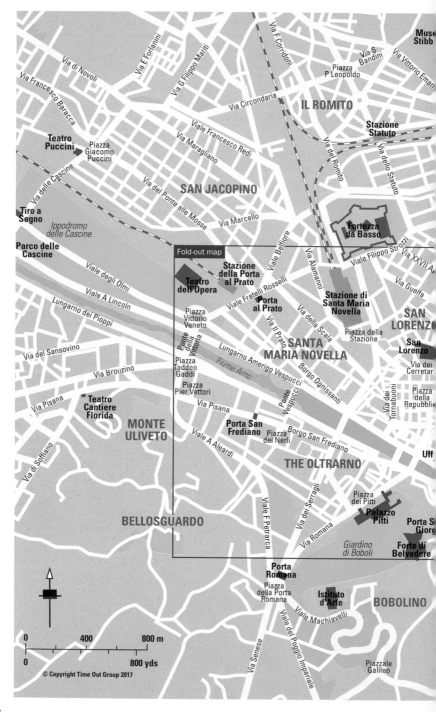

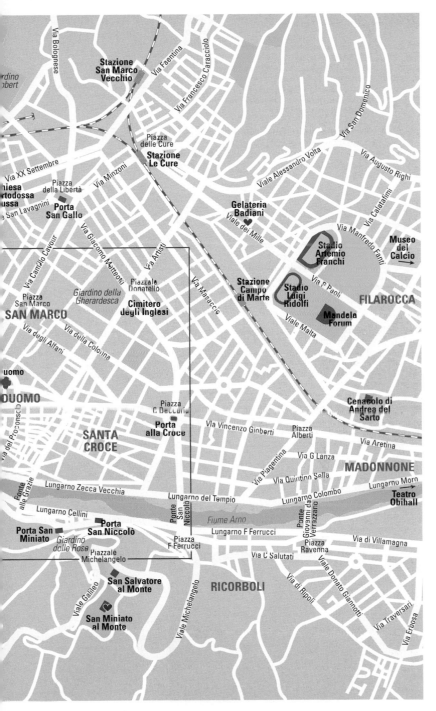

Via Bolognese

rdino
obert

Stazione
San Marco
Vecchio

Via Faentina

Via Francesco Caracciolo

Via San Domenico

Via XX Settembre

Via Minzoni

Piazza
delle Cure

Stazione
Le Cure

Via Augusto Righi

Viale Alessandro Volta

hiesa
rtodossa
ussa

Piazza
della Libertà

Porta
San Gallo

e San Lavagnini

Gelateria
Badiani

Via Manfredo Fanti

Via Calatafimi

Museo
del
Calcio

Viale dei Mille

Via Giacomo Matteotti

Via Artisti

Piazzale
Donatello

Via Masaccio

Stadio
Artemio
Franchi

Via Camillo Cavour

Piazza
San Marco

Giardino della
Gherardesca

Cimitero
degli Inglesi

Stazione
Campo
di Marte

Stadio
Luigi
Ridolfi

Via P Paoli

FILAROCCA

SAN MARCO

Via degli Alfani

Via della Colonna

Mandela
Forum

Viale Malta

uomo

DUOMO

Piazza
C. Beccaria

Porta
alla Croce

Via Vincenzo Ginberti

Piazza
Alberti

Cenacolo di
Andrea del
Sarto

Via del Proconsolo

SANTA
CROCE

Via Aretina

Via Piagentina

Via G Lanza

MADONNONE

Via Quintino Sella

Lungarno Zecca Vecchia

Lungarno del Tempio

Lungarno Colombo

Lungarno Moro

Ponte
alle Grazie

Lungarno Cellini

Porta
San Niccolò

Ponte
San
Niccolò

Fiume Arno

Ponte
Giovanni da
Verrazzano

Teatro
Obihall

Porta San
Miniato

Giardino
delle Rose

Lungarno F Ferrucci

Via di Villamagna

Piazza
F Ferrucci

Piazzale
Michelangelo

Piazza
Ravenna

Via C Salutati

RICORBOLI

Viale Galileo

San Salvatore
al Monte

Viale Michelangelo

Via di Ripoli

Viale Donato Giannotti

Via Traversari

Via Erbosa

San Miniato
al Monte

SOUTH OF THE RIVER

South of the Arno, steep lanes lined with high walls and impenetrable gates that protect beautiful villas rise sharply from the riverbank. From the city centre, the *coste* (steep, uphill streets) and long flights of mossy steps make short but testing walks up to fine vantage points on the hills.

The most famous viewpoint in Florence is probably from **piazzale Michelangelo**, a large, open square providing vistas over the entire city. From here it's a short walk to the exquisite **San Miniato al Monte**, one of Florence's oldest churches.

Bellosguardo & Certosa del Galluzzo

A 20-minute walk west of Porta Romana, meanwhile, leads to a less visited but just as gorgeous hamlet of **Bellosguardo** ('beautiful sight'), a higgledy-piggledy group of old houses and grand villas around a shady square; the only sign of modern life, apart from the cars, is a post box on a wall. The most impressive of the buildings is **Villa Bellosguardo**, down a little turning to the left. It was built in 1780 for the Marchese Orazio Pucci (ancestor of fashion designer Emilio Pucci) and bought, more than a century later, by the great tenor Enrico

Caruso, who lived here for three years before his death in 1921. Just before reaching the piazza di Bellosguardo, another vantage point affords a glimpse of every important church façade in central Florence.

About five kilometres (three miles) south-west of Porta Romana, the **Certosa del Galluzzo** monastery looms like a fortress above the busy Siena road.

Sights & museums

Certosa del Galluzzo
*Via della Certosa 1, Galluzzo (055 2049226, www.cistercensi.info/certosadifirenze). Bus 36, 37. Closed Mon & Sun morning. Tours summer 9am, 10am, 11am, 3pm, 4pm, 5pm; winter 10am, 11am, 3pm, 4pm. **Admission** by donation. **Map** p186.*

The imposing complex was founded in 1342 as a Carthusian monastery by Renaissance bigwig Niccolò Acciaiuoli and is the third of six built in Tuscany in the 14th century. It's been inhabited since 1958 by Cistercian monks, but a recent announcement stated that the monks will be replaced by a different religious community in the near future; visiting arrangements may change as a consequence, so please check. Twelve cells surround the main cloister, each with a well, vegetable garden and study. The main entrance leads into a courtyard and San Lorenzo church, said to be designed by Brunelleschi.

❤ Time to eat & drink

Lip-smacking coffee
Caffè Pasticceria Serafini *p197*

Relaxed lunch and great wine
Fuori Porta *p192*

Authentic Neapolitan pizza and vibe
Vico del Carmine *p192*

❤ Time to shop

Hand-cut coins
Moneta Traforata *p199*

Top quality handmade glass
Moleria Locchi *p192*

Wine-lovers' heaven
Enoteca Bonatti *p197*

❤ Time well spent

Giardino delle Rose
*Viale Giuseppe Poggi 2 (055 2625323). Bus 12, 13. **Open** May-Sept 9am-8pm. Mar, Apr & Oct 9am-6pm. Nov-Feb 9am-5pm. **Admission** free. **Map** See right P13.* Created in 1865 by architect Giuseppe Poggi, today the garden contains around 1,000 varieties of plants and over 350 species of roses. Sandwiched between viale Poggi, via di San Salvatore and via dei Bastioni, it covers about one hectare of land with panoramic views of the city. The garden is also home to nine bronzes and two plaster sculptures bequeathed by the widow of Belgian artist Jean-Michel Folon (1934-2005) to the city after a 2005 exhibition at nearby Forte di Belvedere (*see p181*).

A Walk with a View

Leave the crowds behind and enjoy a new perspective on the city

Our suggested walk to San Miniato al Monte (see *p190*) is best timed to coincide with the mystical Gregorian chants (see *p191*). Beginning in the Oltrarno from the southern end of the **Ponte Vecchio** (see *p89*), with your back to the river, turn left along via de' Bardi. At piazza Santa Maria Soprarno, bear right and walk under the arch up costa de' Magnoli, which, after a short distance, merges into costa San Giorgio just opposite the Romanian Orthodox church of **San Giorgio**. This is an enchanting little street, but the ascent is quite steep. A little further on to the left, a fabulous view of the Florence skyline suddenly appears in a gap between buildings. Press on, admiring the tall shuttered buildings and their rooftops as you go. Galileo's house is on the right at no.19.

Five minutes from the city centre, you'll hear the first twitters of bird song. At the top of costa San Giorgio, pass through the **Porta San Giorgio** city gate and walk a short distance along via San Leonardo, leading straight ahead past the main entrance to **Forte di Belvedere** (see *p181*). After five minutes, on your left, is the church of **San Leonardo in Arcetri**. This medieval *pieve* (parish church) is guarded by cypress trees and contains canvases by Francesco Conti.

Retrace your steps back to the Porta and bear right, down via di Belvedere, to begin your descent. Hugging the city walls, you'll soon come to the bottom of the hill opposite **Porta San Miniato**. Head up via del Monte alle Croci, perhaps stopping for a slurp at the charming **Fuori Porta** wine bar (see *p192*). After a short walk, you'll reach the pretty, tree-lined steps of San Salvatore al Monte. Either take this – the express route to the top – or follow the road on its tortuous journey past olive groves, finally arriving at the busy main road of viale Galileo Galilei. Directly opposite is splendid **San Miniato al Monte** (see *p190*). Now all that's left to do is admire the view.

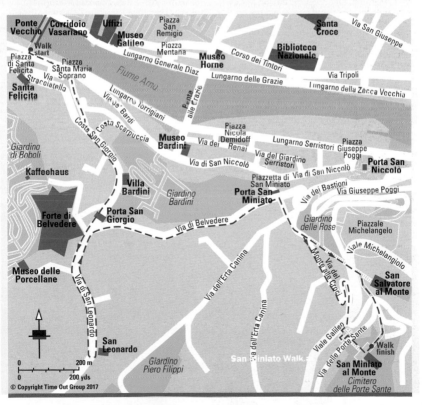

💜 San Miniato al Monte

*Via delle Porte Sante 34 (055 2342731, www.
sanminiatoalmonte.it). Bus 12, 13.* **Open**
*Summer 9.30am-1pm, 3-8pm Mon-Sat;
8.15am-8pm Sun. Winter 9.30am-1pm, 3-7pm
Mon-Sat; 8.15am-7pm Sun.* **Admission** *free.*
Map *p186.*

On a fine day, the view over Florence from
San Miniato is nothing short of breathtaking.
Whether you strolled here from nearby
Piazzale Michelangelo (*see p191*) or you
took the more taxing climb from the Oltrarno
(*see p189* A Walk with a View), take your
time and soak up the beauty before you.

Miniato (Minias) was an Armenian
deacon and a member of the early Christian
community in Florence. Martyred around
AD 250, according to legend he picked up
his own decapitated head and walked uphill
from the banks of the Arno to here, where he
finally expired and was later buried by his
companions. There has been a chapel on this
site since at least the fourth century, later
replaced with a Benedictine monastery built
in the early 11th century on the orders of
reforming Bishop Hildebrand.

The Romanesque church façade is
delicately inlaid with geometric figures
in white Carrara and green Verde di Prato
marble, and its 13th-century mosaic of *Christ
Enthroned between the Madonna and St.
Minias* echoes the larger, more detailed one
in the apse. The copper eagle surmounting
the façade is the symbol of the Calimala (wool
merchants) Guild which administered the
convent from 1288. The original bell tower
collapsed in 1499, and Baccio d'Agnolo's 1518
replacement was never quite completed.

The split-level interior is one of
Tuscany's loveliest; its walls a patchwork
of faded frescoes and its marble pavement
beautifully inlaid with the signs of the
zodiac and stylised lions and lambs. The
serene 11th-century crypt is divided into
seven small aisles by 38 slender columns.
By the staircase to the right you can see red
sinopia drawings on the wall. These were
preparatory guidelines for a *fresco* painting.
On the right-hand side of the presbytery is a
square pulpit whose lectern is supported by
a lion, a man and an eagle with outstretched
wings one on top of the other.

In the middle of the main nave, what
looks like an altar between the stairs
leading up to the raised chancel and down
to the crypt is really a chapel tabernacle. It
was commissioned by Piero di Cosimo de'
Medici and attributed either to Bernardo
Rossellino or Michelozzo, and was built to
hold the Crucifix of St. John Gualberto (now
in Santa Trinita, *see p108*). The elaborate
barrel vault is by Luca della Robbia, and the
altarpiece by Agnolo Gaddi.

In the sacristy, a cycle of frescoes by
Spinello Aretino (1387-88, but heavily
restored in 1840) on the life of St Benedict
was the first undertaking of the Olivetan
monks after they took over the abbey in 1373.

You may also want to stroll through
the adjoining monumental Cimitero delle
Porte Sante. Buried here are many notable
characters such as artists Pietro Annigoni
and Ottone Rosai, writers Vasco Pratolini
and Carlo 'Collodi' Lorenzini (the creator of
Pinocchio), actor Paolo Poli and cookbook
author Pellegrino Artusi.

Cappella del Cardinale del Portogallo, San Miniato al Monte

♥ Piazzale Michelangelo

Between viale Galileo and viale Michelangelo.
***Open** always.* ***Admission** free.* ***Map** p186.*

Perched on the hill directly above piazza
Poggi (*see p181*), Piazzale Michelangelo is
considered the city's balcony. Despite the
view being slightly inferior to that from the
Forte di Belvedere (*see p181*) further west, the
piazzale has the added value of being readily
accessible at all times. As a consequence, its
stone balustrade is perennially crowded with
tourists. The spacious *piazza* is also slowly
but steadily being reclaimed from its former
disgraceful status as a parking area for events
ranging from summer festivals to New Year's
Eve concerts.

Laid out in 1869 by Giuseppe Poggi,
Piazzale Michelangelo is dominated by a
bronze replica of Michelangelo's *David*. Now
at the V&A in London, the plaster cast of the
original *David* (*see p134* Accademia) that
was used to make it was gifted in 1857 by the
Grand Duke of Tuscany to Queen Victoria,
who reportedly found the nude outrageous
and had his private parts promptly covered
with a fig leaf.

You can reach the *piazzale* with a pleasant
but taxing hike from the Ponte Vecchio,
along via San Niccolò to Porta San Miniato,
up via del Monte alle Croci and left up the
flight of stone steps winding between villas
– or alternatively, up the rococo staircase
Poggi designed to link Piazzale Michelangelo
with the *piazza* in his name below. The lazy
alternative is buses 12 and 13, which take the
scenic route in opposite directions round
Poggi's *viali*. In any case, wait for the sunset
for picture-perfect photos.

Restaurants & wine bars

Bibe €€€

*Via delle Bagnese 1r, Galluzzo (055 2049085,
www.trattoriabibe.com).* ***Open** 6-10.30pm
Mon, Tue, Thur, Fri; 12.30-2pm, 6-10.30pm
Sat, Sun. Closed 2 wks Jan-Feb & 2wks Nov.*
***Map** p186.* *Trattoria*

Family-run Bibe is located in an old
farmhouse about 3km (2 miles) south of
Porta Romana and the best way to get to
this rustic country *trattoria* is by car, but it's
worth the effort. From the menu, try deep-
fried courgette flowers stuffed with ricotta,
or sublime herb-infused *zuppa di porcini e
ceci* (porcini soup with chickpeas). *Secondi*
are classic Tuscan dishes: frog and deep-fried
chicken, rabbit and brains are specialities. In
summer, eat on the flower-filled terrace.

In the know
Celestial harmony

Try to time your San Miniato visit to coincide
with the atmospheric vesper service held
in Latin and accompanied by mystical
Gregorian chants, sung daily by the white-
robed Benedictine monks at 5.30pm and
lasting about 30 minutes. It's the perfect
complement to the harmonious interior of
this medieval wonder.

Da Ruggero €€

Via Senese 89r (055 220542). Bus 11, 36, 37. **Open** *noon-2.30pm, 7.30-10.30pm Mon, Thur-Sun. Closed Aug.* **Map** *p186. Trattoria*

This rustic *trattoria*, a short walk south of Porta Romana, is one of Florence's best-kept secrets. Family-run by the Corsis for over 30 years, it serves a menu of traditional dishes that changes with the seasons, but always includes a hearty soup or two and an excellent spicy *spaghetti alla carrettiera* (literally, cart-driver's spaghetti). Among the roast meats, try the tasty pigeon or go for the exemplary *bollito misto* (classic beef and veal stew) served with tangy, parsley-fresh *salsa verde*.

♥ Fuori Porta €€

Via Monte alle Croci 10r, San Niccolò (055 2342483, www.fuoriporta.it). Bus D. **Open** *12.30pm-12.30am daily. Closed 2wks Aug.* **Map** *p186. Wine bar*

One of Florence's best-stocked wine bars, Fuori Porta is situated in the lovely San Niccolò neighbourhood at Porta San Miniato and has a charming terrace overlooking the old city gate. It's a relaxed spot for a glass and a snack at lunch; evenings are buzzier. At any time, there are between 500 and 650 labels on the list, with about 50 available by the glass and 250cl carafe, which rotate roughly every week. Tuscan and Piedmontese reds dominate, but other Italian regions are also well represented; there are formidable lists of *grappa* and Scotch too. The wine bar is also known for its excellent pastas, *carpaccio* and salads; the classic snack here is delicious *crostini*. Make reservations before 9pm for dinner or expect to queue.

Omero €€€

Via Pian de' Giullari 47, Pian de' Giullari (055 220053, www.ristoranteomero.it). Bus 38. **Open** *12.15-2.30pm, 7.30-10.30pm daily. Closed Aug.* **Map** *p186. Trattoria*

In the Florentine hillside, Omero is located in the quiet, exclusive hamlet of Pian de' Giullari. The menu features traditional Florentine food; though reliable, the prices are high. The wine list has over 300 labels, favouring Tuscan wines, and the kitchen uses only the best-quality local extra virgin olive oil. Come for the old-fashioned atmosphere, respectful service and fine location.

♥ Vico del Carmine €€

Via Pisana 40r (055 2336862). **Open** *7.30pm-12.30am Mon-Sat; 12.30-2pm, 7.30pm-12.30am Sun.* **Map** *p186. Pizzeria*

Just a stone's throw from Porta San Frediano, this restaurant and *pizzeria* is done out as a typical street in old Naples (complete with washing lines strung across a balcony). Almost always full and noisy, it often loses points for brusque service and higher than average prices. Yet the quality of the food keeps pizza-lovers piling in. Baked in an authentic wood-burning oven and with ingredients that are strictly sourced from the Campania region (as are most of the wines), the pizzas have light, puffy crusts and miraculously un-soggy bases. Highly recommended is the remarkable 'a chiummenzana: the folded-over crust is stuffed with ricotta while the base is topped with smoked scamorza cheese and cherry tomatoes. Less remarkable (but perfectly decent) are the pasta and fish choices.

Shops

♥ Moleria Locchi

Via Burchiello 10 (055 2298371, www.locchi.com). **Open** *9am-1pm, 3-6.30pm Mon-Fri.* **Map** *p186. Glass*

Not your usual walk-in shop, Moleria Locchi is worth a visit for its unique old-fashioned glass and lead crystal workshop. It offers a restoration service and creates bespoke replacements for glass items and heirloom objects such as chandeliers, with tag prices to match. A classy choice for a wedding gift, but look elsewhere for holiday souvenirs.

NORTH OF THE RIVER

To the west, **Porta al Prato** and the hellish traffic of the *viali* mark the edge of the centre. Just south of the old gate, skirting the northern bank of the Arno for three kilometres (two miles) is the green oasis of the **Parco delle Cascine** (*see p196*), a public park backed by woods. The empty shell of the old **Stazione Leopolda**, Florence's earliest train station (1848-60) is now a meeting and exhibition centre. Behind it, in an area formerly occupied by the train maintenance depot, a modern **Teatro dell'Opera** (*see p250*) was officially opened in December 2011, but has been fully operational only since May 2014. The complex aims to become a large Parco della Musica e della Cultura (Park of Music and Culture).

Coming back towards the centre of town, five minutes' walk from Santa Maria Novella train station along viale Fratelli Rosselli, is the massive pentagonal stone **Fortezza da Basso** (*see right*). Just north of the fortress lies Florence's decorative **Chiesa Russa Ortodossa** (Russian Orthodox church) (*see right*).

From here, head across the Mugnone stream to via dello Statuto and catch a bus north-west to visit the eccentric **Museo Stibbert** (*see p196*) or two fine Medici country mansions, **Villa della Petraia** (*see p196*) and **Villa di Castello** (*see p196*). Back along the *viali*, **piazza la Libertà** is the key northern access point to the city. It has constant traffic jams and a rather graceless triumphal arch built in 1744 to mark the arrival in Florence of the eighth Grand Duke of Tuscany.

Heading south-east towards **piazza Beccaria** is the atmospheric **Cimitero degli Inglesi** (*see below*). East are the **Stadio Artemio Franchi** (*see p196*) at Campo di Marte, the **Museo del Calcio** (*see below*) in Coverciano and the **Museo del Cenacolo di Andrea del Sarto** (*see below*) near San Salvi.

Sights & museums

Cenacolo di Andrea del Sarto

Via San Salvi 16, San Salvi (055 238 8603, www.polomusealetoscana.beniculturali.it). Open 8.15am-1.50pm Tue-Sun. Closed Mon. Admission free. Map p186.

A refectory cum museum, it was part of the Vallombrosan monastery of San Salvi, and is notable for Mannerist Andrea del Sarto's lunette-shaped *Last Supper*. Commissioned in 1511, it was carried out largely in 1520-25.

Chiesa Russa Ortodossa

Via Leone X 12, Fortezza (055 490148, www. chiesarussafirenze.org) Visits and guided tours by appt. Map p186.

With its five polychrome onion domes completed in 1904, this church is a reminder that the city was once popular with wealthy Russians (Dostoyevsky, Tchaikovsky and Gorky among them) as a retreat from the harsh winters back home.

Cimitero degli Inglesi

Piazzale Donatello 38 (055 582608). Open Summer 9am-noon Mon; 3-6pm Tue-Fri. Winter 9am-noon Mon; 2-5pm Tue-Fri. Closed Sat, Sun & hols. Map p186.

Florence's little Swiss Protestant cemetery, better known as the English Cemetery, or to locals as *l'isola dei morti* (the island of the dead), makes a wonderful stroll. The cemetery dates back to 1827, when the Swiss Evangelical Reformed Church purchased land outside the medieval wall and gate of Porta a' Pinti for an international and ecumenical cemetery. By the 19th century the city's swelling English community resulted in a surge of English occupants and a fascinating range of elegant headstones, graves and statuary, marking the tombs of writers such as Elizabeth Barrett Browning, Walter Savage Landor, Frances Trollope, Arthur Hugh Clough and Theodore Parker, who campaigned (with Barrett Browning) against slavery.

Fortezza da Basso

Viale Filippo Strozzi 1 (055 49721, www. firenzefiera.it). Open for events and trade fairs only. Admission prices vary. Map p186.

Designed by Antonio da Sangallo, it was commissioned in 1534 by Alessandro de' Medici and is a prototype of 16th-century military architecture. Restored in the 1990s, it's now Florence's main exhibition centre. The name 'da Basso' (lower) distinguishes it from the city's other fortress, the 'upper' Forte di Belvedere (*see p181*).

Giardino dell'Orticultura

Access from Via Bolognese 17 or from Via Vittorio Emanuele II 4 (055 483698). Bus 25. Open daily Apr-May & Sept 8.30am-7pm. June-Aug 8.30am-8pm. Oct-Mar 8.30am-6pm. Admission free. Map p186.

Created in the 1850s for the Società Toscana di Orticultura in the wake of the late 19th-century craze for art of gardening, this charming park is a peaceful haven just a little walk or bus ride away from the centre. The spring Mostra Mercato di Piante e Fiori (*see p222* Events) is still held here every year. Giacomo Roster's beautiful tepidarium, made of cast iron and glass and built in 1880 in the style of London's Crystal Palace, was restored after decades of neglect from damage suffered during World War II. It now occasionally serves as an events venue. A further terraced section of the park known as Orti del Parnaso climbs north of the railway tracks to via Trento.

Museo del Calcio

Viale Palazzeschi 20, Coverciano (055 600526, www.museodelcalcio.it). Bus 17 to the Viale Volta Terminus. Open 9am-1pm, 3-7pm Mon-Fri. 9am-1pm Sat. Closed Aug. Admission (incl audio guide) €5; €3 6-14s; free under-6s. Map p186.

Soccer fans will be enthralled by Florence's football museum, housed in a converted barn adjoining Casa Italia in Coverciano. '*Casa Italia*' is the nickname for the central training grounds of the Italian national football team and technical headquarters of the Italian Football Association. Exhibits in the museum range from the actual World Cups won by Italy to a vast collection of football-related postage stamps, as well as the shirts of Italian and international footballers. The huge multimedia databank provides entertaining photos and video footage from 1898 to the present day.

❤ Gelato

A visit to Florence would not be complete without a taste of the cold stuff. Florentines have long claimed to have created the first gelato. In the 16th century, Medici court architect Bernardo Buontalenti (1531-1608) was also in charge of staging theatrical performances and fireworks. A creative cook and amateur chemist to boot, he treated his patron's guests to a special frozen dessert made from fruit, honey and *zabaglione* (dessert made with egg yolks, sugar and sweet wine), with snow and ice from his specially-built ice houses in Giardino di Boboli and Cascine park. Around the same time, Caterina de' Medici is believed to have introduced 'cream ice' to the French courts.

With such lofty antecedents, it's no wonder that rivalry among the city's gelaterie has always been fierce. Recently the competition has shifted from the amount and outlandishness of flavours offered, to whose cold stuff is most genuine – home-made, natural and using the highest-quality ingredients. In fact, the most on-the-pulse places tend to be paring down their selection these days in favour of focusing on perfecting a few flavours.

Produzione propria (home-made) and *gelato artigianale* (artisan gelato) are the buzzwords, and parlours are going to ever-greater lengths to make the authenticity grade. Ploys include making the ice-cream in full view of shoppers, shipping in fresh ingredients daily and using gourmet chocolate, organic milk, seasonal fruits and exotic spices sourced from far-flung locations.

The latest trend comes from the popular **Seven Brothers** (*see p92*) where the

Italian gelato tradition meets New York-style dispensary in a self-service gelateria: you build your own ice-cream and decorate it with toppings ranging from fresh fruit to syrup and from cereals to nuts. Since the 'seven' concept is partially based on the same number of deadly sins, it's safe to say the owners welcome a little decadence.

While gelato parlours with neon signs and industrially produced fluffy stuff in dubious hues spring up like mushrooms along the San Lorenzo–Duomo–Ponte Vecchio–Pitti tourist route, you usually have to venture a little off the beaten path to find the real gems.

If you have enough of a sweet tooth to take a trek, head where the locals go: the award-winning **Gelateria Badiani** (*see p197*), near the stadium in the Campo di Marte area, is well known for its unique secret gelato flavour called Buontalenti – you won't taste it anywhere else in Florence. Plus, it

---

In the know
Not-so-icy cream

Too chilly for ice-cream? Try indulging your sweet tooth with the less familiar *semifreddo* (literally, half-cold) instead! Creamier and softer than gelato, halfway between ice-cream and mousse, *semifreddo* is lightly whipped cream and a choice of flavourings worked into an egg base. It is a popular cream ingredient for desserts, but can also be scooped just like gelato. All the best gelaterie carry a variety of *semifreddo* flavours in the colder months.

stays open late. If you're in town stop by two of the most historically popular gelato hotspots: **Vivoli** (*see p155*) if you're in need of a breather and **Perché No!** (*see p92*) if you're craving something sweet as you stroll. Why the distinction? Vivoli is one of the few famous spots in town with a spacious seating area and no additional charge for kicking back for a few minutes. Perché No! has minimal space but is right in the thick of some of Florence's most scenic streets – perfect for ambling through, cone in hand. Nearby **Vestri** (*see p155*) is primarily a chocolatier, so, unsurprisingly, its chocolate flavours are hard to beat.

Located in The Oltrarno opposite the bridge of the same name, **La Carraia** (*see p180*) has a constant queue of locals and tourists snaking outside its door in the summer months. This no-frills gelateria – the classic pistachio and hazelnut are their best sellers – is easily one of the best-loved ice-cream shops in town and probably the best value for money you can get, with the bonus of charming riverside views. While you're in the area, stop by at **La Sorbettiera** (*see p180*); this tiny kiosk serves up creamy, delicious gelato in a range of flavours.

However, let's not forget the franchise **Grom** (*see p74*), right by the Duomo. Though its arrival in Florence made a splash, some say it's overhyped, but most agree that its signature flavour Crema di Grom – a simple combination of organic egg, soft cookies and Valrhona Ecuadorian chocolate – is sensational.

If you are lactose intolerant, milk-free alternatives are the Sicilian-style sorbets from **Carabè** (*see p140*) in the San Marco neighbourhood, while in Santa Croce the traditional **Gelateria dei Neri** (*see p155*) offers soy-based gelato in heavenly flavours such as salted caramel.

❤ Museo Stibbert

Via Stibbert 26, Rifredi (055 486049, www. museostibbert.it). Bus 4. **Open** *10am-2pm Mon-Wed; 10am-6pm Fri-Sun (last entry 1hr before closing). Closed Thur.* **Admission** *€8; €6 reductions.* **Map** *p186.*

A fascinating but bizarre collection that belonged to Frederick Stibbert (1838-1906), a brother-in-arms to Garibaldi, is housed here. Stibbert was born to an English father and Italian mother, who left him her 14th-century house. He bought the neighbouring mansion and joined the two to house his 50,000 artefacts. Crammed into the 64 rooms are Napoleon's coronation robes (Stibbert was a fan), a hand-painted harpsichord, arms and armour, shoe buckles, snuff boxes, chalices, crucifixes and even an attributed Botticelli. The rambling garden has a lily pond, stables, a neoclassical folly by Poggi, and ancient Greek and Egyptian-inspired temples.

Parco delle Cascine

Entrance nr ponte della Vittoria (055 2768806, parcodellecascine.comune.fi.it). Bus 17C, Tram T1. **Map** *p186.*

Stretching west of the city on the right river bank with its 160 hectares (395 acres) of woods, lawns and sports facilities, the Cascine is the city's lung. It's at its busiest on Tuesday mornings when a large market is held, and on Sundays with parties playing football and families picnicking. Playgrounds dot the park; in-line skates can be hired, and a tourist information point and visitor centre is open at weekends in the former stables.

The first major changes to the park for decades have been made with the building of the T1 Tramvia (tramway). Trees were cut down, avenues converted to tracks and traffic diverted to make way for it. A dedicated bridge over the Arno was also built. There was a fierce debate over whether this complied with the terms of the Medici bequest of the park to the city.

In summer, the Cascine is used as a venue for events and gigs. It's safe enough when summer events are held, but be aware that the area is seamy at night, with prostitutes touting for business along the park's main roads and adjoining *viali*.

Stadio Artemio Franchi

Viale Manfredo Fanti 14, Campo di Marte (For football: 055 503011, www.acffiorentina. it. For concerts: 055 667566, www.bitconcerti. it). Bus 7, 11, 17. Ticket prices vary. **Map** *p186.*

Pier Luigi Nervi's football stadium near Campo di Marte station was built in 1930-32 and enlarged for the 1990 World Cup. It has an average capacity of around 45,000. Besides hosting the ACF Fiorentina home matches,

the stadium moonlights as a music venue for Italian and international big-name gigs.

Villa di Castello

Via di Castello 47, Castello (055 452691, www.polomusealetoscana.beniculturali.it). Closed 2nd & 3rd Mon of mth. **Admission** *free.* **Map** *p186.*

Although the villa itself is closed to the public, its gardens designed by Il Tribolo are well worth a visit. Don't miss Ammanati's sculpture *Allegory of Winter* and Il Tribolo's extravagant *Grotta degli Animali*, full of animal and bird statues and stone water features, finished by Vasari. This is one of the Medici villas recently included in the list of World Heritage Sites by UNESCO (*see p271*).

Villa La Petraia

Via della Petraia 40, Castello (055 452691, www.polomusealetoscana.beniculturali.it). Closed 2nd & 3rd Mon of mth. **Admission** *free.* **Map** *p186.*

Sitting on a little hill, the villa and grounds, which were acquired by the Medici family in 1530, stand apart from the surrounding industrial mess. Originally a tower belonging to Brunelleschi's family, the villa and its fabulous formal terraced gardens by Il Tribolo are among those immortalised by Giusto Utens in his famous 14 lunettes, which since 2014 are attractively displayed here following a thorough restoration. It is another one of the Medici villas included in the UNESCO list of World Heritage Sites (*see p271*).

Restaurants & wine bars

Il Povero Pesce €€€

Via Pier Fortunato Calvi 8r, Campo di Marte (055 671218). **Open** *noon-3pm, 7-11pm daily.* **Map** *p186. Fish*

Simple, unpretentious and good-value fish and seafood dishes make up the backbone of the menu at this fish-only *trattoria* located near the football stadium in the Campo di Marte area. With its modern, vaguely nautical-themed interior and keen prices, it's popular among locals and is often full in the evenings. The menu changes daily, as it is based on market availability, but a typical meal might feature a starter of the house *antipasto misto* (you'll get five or six little tasters), *spaghetti alle vongole* (clams) or *all' astice* (lobster) and grilled swordfish. A tart *sorbetto al limone* is a good way to finish.

Salaam Bombay €€

Viale Fratelli Rosselli 45r (055 357900, www. salaambombay.it). Bus 23. **Open** *11.30am-2.45pm, 6-11.30pm daily.* **Map** *p186. Indian*

One of Florence's first Indian restaurants, Salaam Bombay is still popular among locals and foreigners looking for a change from the classic *ribollita* or *tagliatelle ai funghi*. Tapestries adorn the walls of the single, galleried room; sit upstairs if you want to look down on the buzzy action below. The menu offers the sort of safe but decently cooked standards found on the menus of most Indian restaurants in Italy: tandooris and Mughlai dishes, vegetarian options, great naans and own-made mango chutney. It's good value, and you can take out or eat in.

Santa Lucia €
Via Ponte alle Mosse 102r (055 353255). Bus 30, 35. **Open** *noon-2.30pm, 7-11.30pm Mon, Tues, Thur, Sun; 12.30-2.30pm, 7-11.30pm Fri; 7pm-midnight Sun. Closed Aug.* **Map** *p186. Pizzeria*

Many Florentines make the ten-minute walk north-west of Porta al Prato for the Neapolitan-style pizza, considered one of the best in town. These pizzas are just as you'd get them in Naples: they have a light and puffy base, sweet tomatoes and the milkiest mozzarella. If you don't want pizza, terrific fish dishes include *spaghetti alle vongole veraci* and octopus in spicy tomato sauce; the bill will be hiked up accordingly. Book in advance or be prepared to queue.

Cafés, bars & gelaterie
♥ Caffè Pasticceria Serafini
Via Gioberti 168r (055 2476214, www. pasticceriaserafini.it). **Open** *7am-8.45pm Mon-Sat.* **Map** *p186. Café*

This bakery, café and bar close to piazza Beccaria is a local favourite, and what most of the locals drink here is the *fornacino*, a creamy, delicious coffee with chocolate that defies description, or belief. Equally unbelievable are the *aperitivi*, which include not just superior quality olives, *crostini*, pizzas and nibbles, but more substantial dishes such as gnocchi with prawns and various side dishes – all yours for the taking with a €6 glass of wine. It gets crowded, so get here early.

♥ Gelateria Badiani
Viale dei Mille 20, Campo di Marte (055 578682, www.gelateriabadiani.it). Bus 17. **Open** *summer 7am-1am daily. Winter 7am-1am Fri, Sat; 7am-midnight Sun-Thur. Closed Mon, winter only.* **Map** *p186. Gelateria*

This hugely popular *gelateria*, located near the Stadio Artemio Franchi (*see p196*), offers a terrific selection of flavours including monthly specials based on seasonal fruit –

think figs or fresh strawberries – or novelty flavours such as salted caramel, pistachio pesto or black sesame. However, its pride and joy is Buontalenti, a well-guarded secret mix of just cream, milk, sugar and egg yolks. At €2 for a *piccolo* (small cup), it's also a bargain compared to city-centre gelaterie. Gorgeous cakes, coffee and, at lunchtime, a small selection of savouries complete the picture.

Shops
♥ Enoteca Bonatti
Via de' Gioberti 66/68r (055 660050, www. enotecabonatti.it). Bus C2, 14. **Open** *3.30-7.30pm Mon; 9.30am-1pm, 3.30-7.30pm Tue-Sat.* **Map** *p186. Wine*

Arguably the best selection of wines in town, with good prices, helpful service from a family who set up the wine and olive store in 1934, and weekly wine tasting events. French wines complement the huge Italian selection, along with a nice range of artisan beers.

Sorelle Orlandi Cardini Kids
Viale Don Minzoni 60r (055 5002176, www. sorelleorlandicardinikids.com). **Open** *9.30am-7.30pm Mon-Sat, 9am-7.30pm Sun.* **Map** *p186. Children's toys and clothing*

Run by charismatic Tuscan sisters, this cute children's shop is chock full of traditional handmade toys, lovingly crafted, customisable clothing, stuffed animals, socks and a treasure trove of other kids' items. Everything is made in Italy, and the sisters offer tons of options for shoppers on the hunt for something unique and artisanal.

Villa La Petraia

FIESOLE & AROUND

From Via La Pira (around the corner from San Marco, see p138), ATAF operates regular transport to Fiesole (bus 7) and Settignano (bus 10). There's no direct public transport to link them, but the long walk between the two neighbouring hilltop towns is picturesque.

Founded centuries before Florence, Fiesole could be credited with the city's very existence: this stubborn Etruscan hill town was so difficult for the Romans to subdue, they were forced to set up camp in the river valley below. The road leading up to the town winds by beautiful villas and gardens – still highly desirable addresses. Today, around 14,000 people live in Fiesole.

Piazza Mino is named after the 15th-century local sculptor Mino da Fiesole. Dominated by the 11th-century **Duomo**, the square is lined with cafés and restaurants, some with views over Florence. Fiesole has a few fine museums which can be accessed either separately, or with a joint ticket: the **Museo Bandini** (see p199) displays Florentine art from the 13th to 15th centuries; down the hill, the relics of Roman Fiesole can be seen in the **Area Archeologica & Museo Civico** (see right). Further down via Dupré, the **Fondazione Primo Conti** (see right) focuses on Futurism and the avant-garde cultural movements of the early 20th century.

There are some lovely walks around Fiesole, the best down steep via Vecchia Fiesolana. To the left on the way down is the **Villa Medici** (see p199), while at the bottom of the hill the 15th-century church and convent of **San Domenico** (see right) are where painter Fra Angelico was a monk. From here, via delle Fontanelle snakes to Villa La Torraccia, home to the **Scuola Musica di Fiesole** (see p250) and the Orchestra Giovanile Italiana (Italian Youth Orchestra), while opposite the church of San Domenico itself, a lane leads down to the **Badia Fiesolana**, Fiesole's cathedral until 1028.

The village of **Settignano** lies on the hill to the east of Fiesole and has stunning views. Lacking major landmarks, Settignano is an almost tourist-free trip out of town, and its history is littered with eminent names: sculptors Desiderio da Settignano

and the Rossellino brothers were born here, and Michelangelo spent part of his childhood at the **Villa Michelangelo** (via della Capponcina 65), known locally as Villa Buonarroti.

Sights & museums

♥ Area Archeologica & Museo Civico
Via Portigiani 1, Fiesole (055 5961293, www. museidifiesole.it). Bus 7. Closed Tue in winter. **Admission** *€7 Area Archeologica only; €10 with Museo Civico; €12 incl Museo Civico & Museo Bandini; free under-6s.*

The Teatro Romano, built at the end of the first century BC, still hosts concerts and plays in summer; the archaeological complex houses the remains of two temples, partially restored Roman baths and Etruscan walls. The museum has Bronze Age, Etruscan and Roman finds, and Greek vases.

Badia Fiesolana
Via Roccettini 9, Fiesole (468 5399). Bus 7. **Open** *Summer 9am-6pm Mon-Fri. Winter 9am-5pm Mon-Fri.* **Admission** *free.*

This was Fiesole's cathedral until 1028. The façade incorporates the front of the older church, with its elegant green and white marble inlay. Enter via the cloister if the church doors are closed. The church and adjoining monastery are now the seat of the European University Institute.

Duomo (San Romolo)
Piazzetta della Cattedrale 1, Fiesole (055 59242, www.diocesifiesole.it). Bus 7. **Open** *8am-noon, 3-5.30pm.* **Admission** *free.*

Built by Bishop Jacopo il Bavaro in 1028 and extended in the 13th century, the cathedral is dedicated to martyred bishop St Romulus. The interior of the church is markedly Romanesque, with three naves separated by stone columns, each different from the next, but all with splendid capitals. The church and its chapels house works by Cosimo Rosselli, Mino da Fiesole and the Ghirlandaio school. The high altar polyptych is by Bicci di Lorenzo. Major renovation works began in 1878 on the inner and outer walls which gave the façade the Neo-Gothic look it has today.

Fondazione Primo Conti
Via Duprè 18, Fiesole (055 597095, www. fondazioneprimoconti.org). Bus 7. **Open** *9am-2pm Mon-Fri; by appt Sat, Sun.* **Admission** *€3.*

The 15th-century Villa Le Coste – where Futurist painter Primo Conti (1900-88) lived for many years – was set up in 1980 by the artist himself to house a foundation with

---

In the know
For further information about Fiesole

Contact the Tourist Office (Via Portigiani 3, 055 5961311, www.fiesoleforyou.it. Open 10am-6.30pm Apr-Sept; 10am-5.30pm Mar & Oct; 10am-1.30pm Nov-Feb).

Badia Fiesolana

the aim of studying the avant-garde cultural movements of the early 20th century. The museum displays over 60 paintings and 160 drawings by Primo Conti himself.

Museo Bandini
Via Dupré 1, Fiesole (055 5961293, www. museidifiesole.it). Bus 7. **Open** *Apr-Sept 9am-7pm Fri-Sun. March & Oct 10am-6pm Fri-Sun. Nov-Feb 10am-3pm Fri-Sun. Closed Mon-Thur all year.* **Admission** *€5; €3 reductions; €12 incl Area Archeologica & Museo Civico.*

The museum originates from a collection of paintings and pottery assembled in the 18th century by cleric Angelo Maria Bandini. When he died in 1803, he left his artworks to the Bishop and Chapter of Fiesole. The museum opened in 1913 and has since been enriched with several more works from the vast territory of the diocese. It houses an array of Florentine paintings dating from the 13th to 15th centuries; two newer rooms display previously unshown works, including some Della Robbia terracottas.

San Domenico
Piazza San Domenico 11, Fiesole (055 59230). Bus 7. **Open** *8.30am-noon, 4-6pm daily.* **Admission** *free.*

The 15th-century church and convent where painter Fra Angelico was a friar still houses his delicate *Madonna and Angels* (1420), while in the chapter house of the adjacent monastery is one of his frescoes (ring the bell at no.4 for entry).

Villa Medici
Via Beato Angelico 2, Fiesole (www. villamedicifiesole.it).

Built by Michelozzo for Cosimo il Vecchio, this was the childhood home of Anglo-American writer Iris Origo. Only the gardens can be visited, strictly by appointment only.

Shops

♥ Moneta Traforata
Via Dupré 10r, Fiesole (055 59478, www.monetatraforata.it). Bus 7. **Open** *9.30am-1pm, 3.30-7.30pm Tue-Sun. Closed Mon. Jewellery*

Argentinian craftsman Nestor Hugo Alvarez turns painstakingly hand-cut coins into beautiful accessories such as earrings, bracelets, rings, pendants, cufflinks and keyrings. Find his workshop just opposite the archaeological area.

> **In the know**
> **India upon the Arno**
>
> In 1870 His Highness Rajaram II, Maharaja of Kolhapur, aged 21, died suddenly while visiting Florence. His body was burned on a funeral pyre at the downriver end of the Cascine park, despite cremation being banned in the city. The spot is marked by a monument called *L'Indiano*, financed by the British government, which also gives its name to the nearby bridge over the Arno, Ponte all'Indiano, built in 1972-78.

Day Trips

Heading out in any direction from Florence you'll find a multitude of delightful towns and villages perfect for a day trip. Away from the tourist hordes, the pace of life slows as the countryside opens out into panoramic vistas of vineyards, olive groves, valleys and hills. Nor does culture start and end in Tuscany's capital: Pisa, Siena, Lucca, Pistoia, Prato and Arezzo all have fascinating buildings, art and monuments that deserve at least a whole day of your time. Visit the ornate churches and galleries, but try not to spend hours driving around the countryside to fit in all the sights – find time to sit down once each day to a Tuscan meal, and, if you need to recuperate from sightseeing, go walking, visit a winery or spend a few hours at one of the region's thermal spas.

❤ Best viewpoints

Torre del Mangia, Siena *p211*
A bird's-eye view of the shell-shaped Campo below.

Torre Guinigi, Lucca *p207*
Spectacular views over Lucca from an oak-topped tower.

Torre Pendente, Pisa *p211*
An aerial perspective of the Duomo complex, but it's the climb that's memorable.

Torre Grossa, San Gimignano *p215*
One of San Gimignano's 14 remaining medieval towers.

Campanile, Pistoia *p205*
On a fine day, the view reaches as far as Florence.

In the know
Transport in Tuscany

Driving is the best way of getting around Tuscany. While the larger cities are all conveniently served by train and bus lines, trying to reach the smaller towns by public transport will be a time-consuming option. If you don't have a car, it's possible to reach many parts of Tuscany by bus, although, in most villages, buses are timed to coincide with the school day. Plan your journey online at muoversintoscana.regione.toscana.it/navigator.aspx.

If you're interested in Tuscan crafts, **Arttour** (www.artour.toscana.it; also available as an iPhone app) takes you on a journey through Tuscany's artisan workshops and galleries, and offers over 90 itineraries.

▶ *For more information on transport, see p294 Getting Around.*

When to visit

In summer, many places get busy. The gorgeous hill town of San Gimignano, for instance, is like honey to the tourist bees: visit in months either side of the rush when temperatures are also more pleasant. There are fewer crowds in winter, but many attractions, restaurants and rural hotels may be shut or only open for limited hours, and the weather won't be so good. Tourist information offices will provide advice on accommodation options, but in most cases, will not be licensed to make bookings on your behalf.

PRATO, PISTOIA & AROUND

Prato

Immediately to the west of Florence is Prato. The city has been a thriving trading centre since the Middle Ages, and its reputation as little more than an industrial suburb of Florence is undeserved. In a bid to raise its profile, the council has spent squillions to upgrade Prato's attractions, and the improvements have led to a number of new restaurant, bar and club openings.

The city's cloth-making heritage is celebrated at the **Museo del Tessuto** (Via Santa Chiara 24, 0574 611503, www.museodeltessuto.it), housed in a 19th-century factory building. The exciting **Lottozero centre** for textile design (Via Arno 10, 340 2787854, www.lottozero.org)

projects this industrial past into the future by combining manufacturing with design, art, experimentation and research.

The Romanesque **Duomo** (Piazza del Duomo, 0574 26234, www.diocesiprato.it) is dedicated to Santo Stefano. Inside is a 15th-century pulpit by Michelozzo, carved with reliefs by Donatello, and frescoes by Agnolo Gaddi, Paolo Uccello and Filippo Lippi. Many important works from the cathedral, including the original pulpit reliefs, are displayed at the **Museo dell'Opera del Duomo** (Piazza del Duomo 49, 0574 29339, www.diocesiprato.it) in the Bishop's Palace.

The renovated **Museo di Palazzo Pretorio** (Piazza del Comune, 0574 1934996 Mon-Fri, 0574 1837860 Sat, Sun, www.palazzopretorio.prato.it) is a delightful, uncrowded museum that provides a chronological journey into Pratese art from the Middle Ages to the 1900s. Also on

In the know
Prato Musei card

The three-day, €16 Prato Musei card (www.pratomusei.it) covers the Museo di Palazzo Pretorio, Museo del Tessuto, Centro per l'Arte Contemporanea Luigi Pecci, Museo dell'Opera del Duomo and Lippi's frescoes in the cathedral. Unlimited bus rides within the city are also included. A family Prato Musei card for two adults and up to two children is also available for €28.

❤ Best frescoes

Piero della Francesca's Legend of the True Cross *p217*
A masterpiece of volumes and perspective. San Francesco, Arezzo.

Ambrogio Lorenzetti 's The Allegory of Good and Bad Government *p214*
Fascinating details of medieval daily life. Museo Civico, Palazzo Pubblico, Siena.

Buffalmacco's Triumph of Death *p210*
Restored after the damage caused by World War II. Camposanto, Pisa.

Domenico Ghirlandaio's Stories of p215
The artist's first known major commission. Collegiata, San Gimignano.

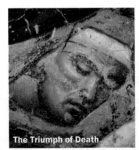
The Triumph of Death

❤ Best filming locations

Arezzo *p216*
Roberto Benigni's *Life is Beautiful* (1997).

Montepulciano *p215*
Chris Weitz's *The Twilight Saga: New Moon* (2009).

San Gimignano *p215*
Franco Zeffirelli's *Tea with Mussolini* (1998).

Lucca *p206*
Jane Campion's *Portrait of a Lady* (1996).

Siena *p211*
Marc Forster's *Quantum of Solace* (2008).

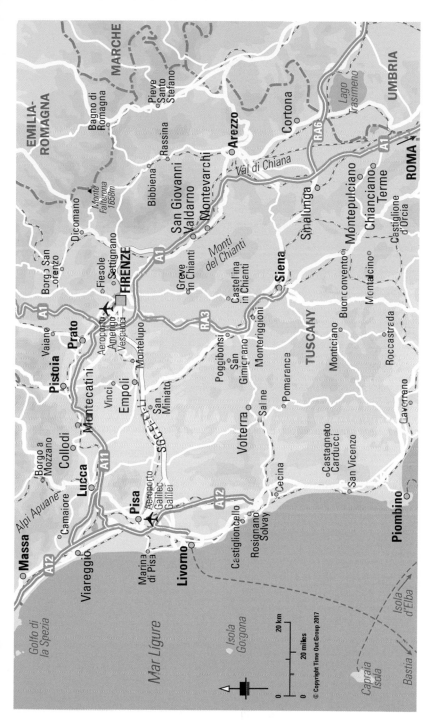

Palazzo Pretorio, Prato *p202*

display are some of the works by Lithuanian Cubist Jacques Lipchitz (1891-1973).

The Renaissance church of **Santa Maria delle Carceri** (0574 440501, www.diocesiprato.it) and the 13th-century **Castello dell'Imperatore** (0574 38207) both grace Piazza Santa Maria delle Carceri. The castle ramparts, accessed through a staircase in the eastern tower, afford an impressive view over Prato, and, in the summer, the courtyard hosts open-air events. Follow the castle ramparts to Piazza San Marco to find Henry Moore's white marble *Square Form with Cut* (1974), irreverently dubbed 'The Hole' or 'The Molar' by locals.

Prato's progressive taste blooms outside the city walls, where the recently revamped **Centro per l'Arte Contemporanea Luigi Pecci** (Viale della Repubblica 277, 0574 5317, www.centropecci.it) houses one of Italy's most important collections of contemporary art. Reopened in October 2016 after a €14.4-million overhaul, it now boasts an spaceship-like extension by Maurice Nio.

Wine is produced in the hills south of Prato, around the town of **Carmignano**. The Carmignano Wine Road consortium sells wine, olive oil, cold cuts, biscuits, honey and preserves from its local producers in town at **aTipico** (Via Ricasoli 13, 388 5884804, www.stradavinicarmignano.it). Nearby, **Biscottificio Antonio Mattei** (Via Ricasoli 20, 0574 25756, www.antoniomattei.it) invented the almond-studded Biscotti di Prato and has been baking it on the premises since 1858. **Osteria Cibbè** (Piazza Mercatale 49, 0574 607509, www.cibbe.it, €€) is your best bet to sample authentic Tuscan and Pratese dishes including the *bozza di Prato*, *mortadella di Prato*, s*edani ripieni* (stuffed celery) and *castagnaccio* (chestnut-meal cake).

Pistoia

Despite being Italian Capital of Culture for 2017, Pistoia is little known outside Tuscany. The quiet old town itself is enchanting, with an almost perfectly intact historic centre encircled by medieval walls and few fellow tourists to spoil your enjoyment. The countryside for miles around is characterised by the neat rows of dwarf trees and small shrubs in the area's plant nurseries.

Pistoia's history is a bloody one: it was where the Catiline conspirators were rounded up after they failed to destroy the

---

In the know
Vinci

To enjoy a leisurely driving tour from Florence, take the SS66 road to Poggio a Caiano in order to visit **Villa Ambra** (*see p271* Medici Villas & Gardens), then head south-west through the **Carmignano** wine country to the quaint hill town of Vinci, in search of Leonardo da Vinci's origins. Leonardo was born near Vinci on 15 April 1452 and lived in the town with his uncle and grandparents before being apprenticed to Verrocchio's studio in Florence. A joint €11 ticket (www.museoleonardiano.it) covers four Leonardo sites, including his birthplace.

Roman Republic in 62 BC; it fought bitter wars with Renaissance rivals Florence and Lucca; it was the birthplace of the brutal feud between the Black and White Guelphs (referred to by Dante in his *Divine Comedy*); and it's even rumored to have given its name to the pistol.

Many of Pistoia's monuments combine Florentine and Pisan elements. The heart of the old city centre is Piazza del Duomo with the octagonal 14th-century **Baptistery**, whose green-and-white striped exterior was built to a design by Andrea Pisano, and the **Cathedral**. The cathedral has an arcaded Pisan façade, a simple Romanesque interior and houses the famous gold and silver *Altar of St James* in the Cappella del Crocifisso. To climb the **Campanile**, you need to book a visit at the tourist office, which is also on the square (*see p206*); on a perfect day, the view is said to stretch as far as Florence.

The piazza isn't just the civil and religious heart of the city the city, it's also home to a busy twice-weekly market (Wed, Sat) whose earliest records date back to the 10th century. Nearby **La Sala** hosts a colourful produce market and is lined with shops that retain their medieval appearance with wooden shutters, awnings and stone benches. As the day progresses, La Sala becomes a prime spot for an *aperitivo*.

One of the city's most impressive sights is the frieze decorating the *portico* of the **Ospedale del Ceppo** (Piazza Giovanni XXIII, 0573 368023, www.irsapt.it). The Ceppo was founded in 1277 and gives access to a fascinating underground network of vaulted passageways with Roman and

In the know
Vintage trains

Pistoia has been Italy's train-manufacturing capital for over a century. The local collection of steam and diesel trains is due to become a permanent museum (visit www.fondazionefs.it for updates), but in the meantime rail enthusiasts can ask at the train station – or better still at the Dopolavoro Ferroviario Railworkers' Club on the opposite side of piazza Dante Alighieri – for an informal visit.

medieval remains including a bridge, washtubs and two mills. The nearby church of **Sant'Andrea** (Via Sant'Andrea, 0573 21912) boasts a magnificent pulpit by Giovanni Pisano.

There's also a contemporary side to Pistoia, as the art at **Palazzo Fabroni** (Via di Sant'Andrea 18, 0573 371214, www. palazzofabroni.it) and the **Fondazione Museo Marino Marini** (Corso Fedi 30, 0573 30285, www.fondazionemarinomarini.it) attests. Well-established cultural festivals include the **Giostra dell'Orso** (Joust of the Bear) and the **Pistoia Blues** music festival, both in July. For a taste of Pistoian cuisine, try the two branches of **La BotteGaia**: the first (Via del Lastrone 17, 0573 365602, www. labottegaia.it, €€) is a delightful tavern – hence *botte gaia* (merry barrel), while the other is a food shop (Via di Stracceria 4, 0573 358450) – as in *bottegaia* (shopkeeper).

Montecatini Terme *p206*

Montecatini Terme

Some of Tuscany's best known thermal springs are west of Pistoia around **Montecatini Terme**, an upmarket spa town whose warm saline waters are supposed to be particularly beneficial for digestive complaints. In the late 19th and early 20th century, Montecatini was one of the most fashionable destinations in Europe, which explains the wealth of 'Liberty' (art nouveau) architecture and decor. A scenic red cable car or *funicolare* (Viale Diaz 22, 0572 766862, www.funicolare-montecatini.it) joins Montecatini Terme and Montecatini Alto.

Thousands still come each year to be pampered at the town's *stabilimenti termali* (spa resorts), such as the **Terme di Montecatini** (Viale Verdi 61, www.termemontecatini.it) and the **Terme Leopoldine** (Viale Giuseppe Verdi, 61, 0572 778551), which is housed in a luxury 18th-century villa remodelled by Ugo Giovannozzi. At **Monsummano Terme**, you can take your health kick even further by experiencing an underground thermal cave where temperatures hover around 34°C (90°F).

Essential Information

Tourist information

Prato *Piazza Buonamici 7, 0574 24112, www.pratoturismo.it.* **Open** *9am-1pm, 3-6pm Mon-Sat; 10am-1pm Sun.*
Pistoia *Piazza del Duomo 4, 0573 21622, www.pistoia.turismo.toscana.it)* **Open** *9am-1pm, 3-6pm daily.*
Montecatini Terme *Viale Verdi 66, 0572 772244, www.montecatiniturismo.it.* **Open** *9am-1pm, 3-6pm Mon-Fri; 9am-1pm Sat.*

Getting there

To reach Prato and Pistoia by **car**, head west on the A11 motorway from Florence. A more leisurely route to Pistoia is via the SS66 road. **Cap** (055 214637, www.capautolinee.it) runs **buses** between Florence and Prato, while **Blubus** (055 214637, www.blubus.it) operates services to Pistoia. Connecting lines from Pistoia then go to Montecatini. There are also buses to Montecatini from Lucca. Frequent **trains** from Florence to Bologna stop at Prato Centrale (about 20mins), while those from Florence to Lucca use the more central Porta al Serraglio (about 30mins), before continuing to Pistoia and Montecatini Terme.

LUCCA

Lucca stands slightly aloof behind its perfectly preserved 16th-century walls. Unlike Florence and Siena, Lucca has few must-see sights, though in many ways it's a more attractive proposition for the curious traveller, thanks to its handsome *piazze*, tree-shaded fortifications and a cultured but welcoming atmosphere. Most of the *centro storico* is pedestrianised and the best way to discover it is on foot.

The city centre is defined by its tree-lined Renaissance **ramparts** (0583 583086, www.lemuradilucca.it), where you'll see Lucchesi of all ages strolling, picnicking and enjoying the views from *le nostre mura* ('our walls'). Built in the 16th and 17th centuries, the fortifications are 12 metres (39 feet)

Tettuccio Terme

Torre Guinigi, Lucca

high and 30 metres (98 feet) wide, with a circumference of just over four kilometres. They are punctuated by 11 sturdy bastions, topped with trees designed to reinforce the earthworks and provide fuel in case of siege. Climb 44 metres (144 feet) to the summit of **Torre Guinigi**, with its distinctive cluster of oak trees, for spectacular views over Lucca's rooftops to the countryside beyond.

Focal points of the city centre are the distinctively oval-shaped **Piazza dell'Anfiteatro**, the huge **Piazza Napoleone**, which hosts a pop/rock **Summer Festival** in July (www.summer-festival.com), and, directly to its north, **Piazza San Michele** – the old town's social hub. Near here is the birthplace of operatic composer Giacomo Puccini, on Corte San Lorenzo. The city's main shopping artery, **Via Fillungo**, is the place to find well-known designer and high-street names. **Piazza San Giusto** has permanent book stalls selling second-hand books, comics and prints, and also hosts a crafts market on the last weekend of the month.

In the south of the historic centre, Lucca's **Cattedrale di San Martino** or **Duomo** (Piazza San Martino, 0583 490530, www.museocattedralelucca.it) has an asymmetrical façade that was designed by Guidetto da Como to squeeze next to the existing **Campanile**. Highlights of the dimly lit interior include Tintoretto's *Last Supper* and Matteo Civitali's octagonal marble Tempietto (1484), home to a dolorous wooden crucifix known as the *Volto Santo* (Holy Face); the relic is still venerated during highly dramatic night-time processions on 13 September. The Duomo's Sacristy contains the other top attraction: the tomb of Ilaria del Carretto (1408), sculpted by Sienese master Jacopo della Quercia. Other objects from the cathedral are on display at the **Museo della Cattedrale** (Piazza Antelminelli, 0583 490530, www.museocattedralelucca.it.)

Lucca is aptly nicknamed 'the city of a hundred churches'; as well as the **Duomo**, visit nearby **San Giovanni e Reparata** (Via del Duomo), which originally served as Lucca's cathedral and lies on the site of a pagan temple. Excavations in the 1970s discovered architectural remains ranging from a second-century Roman bath to a Paleo-Christian church. **San Michele in Foro** (Piazza San Michele, 0583 48459) has a Pisan-Romanesque façade that contrasts sharply with its sombre interior, where you'll find a *Madonna and Child* by Andrea della Robbia and Filippino Lippi's simple and serene *Saints Jerome, Sebastian, Rocco and Helena.* Also worth a look is **San Frediano** (Piazza San Frediano, 0583 493627), with a Byzantine-like mosaic façade. Nearby are the gardens of **Palazzo Pfanner** (Via degli Asili 33, 0583 954029, wwwpalazzopfanner.it) – a lovely place to while away an afternoon. (Film buffs might recognise the gardens as a backdrop from *The Portrait of a Lady*.)

In contrast to its churches, Lucca's museums – **Museo Nazionale di Palazzo Mansi** (Via Galli Tassi 43, 0583 55570, www.luccamuseinazionali.it) and **Museo Nazionale di Villa Guinigi** (Via della Quarquonia, 0583 496033, www. luccamuseinazionali.it) are really only worth bothering with if the weather is lousy, although the Baroque extravagance of the former is worth an ogle. Otherwise, your time is much better spent strolling around. There are excellent food shops at each turn, stocked with regional wines and local delicacies. Two of the best are **La Grotta** (Via dell'Anfiteatro 2, 0583 467595, www. pizzicherialagrotta.it) and **Delicatezze** (Via San Giorgio 5, 0583 492633). The *trattoria* **Da Giulio in Pelleria** (Via delle Conce 45, 0583 55948, €€) is credited with serving the heartiest *zuppa di farro* (spelt soup) in town, while a local *cecina* (chickpea-flour pancake) is available for a quick lunch from **Pizzeria Itaco** (Via San Paolino 58, 0583 581037, €). The local pudding is *buccellato*, a doughnut-shaped sweet bread flavoured with aniseed and raisins and topped with sugar syrup.

Essential information

Tourist information
Vecchia Porta San Donato *Piazzale Giiuseppe Verdi (0583 583150, www. turismo.lucca.it). Open Apr-Oct 9am-7pm daily. Nov-Mar 9qm -5pm daily.*
Information points are found at several locations across the city, including at the train station. If you're visiting in the autumn, ask about the many cultural events of **Settembre Lucchese** (Sept-Oct) and the hugely popular **Lucca Comics & Games festival** (late Oct/early Nov, www. luccacomicsandgames.com).

Getting there
The A11 *autostrada* connects Florence and Lucca. **Vaibus** (0583 587897, www.lucca. cttnord.it) runs at least one **bus** an hour from Florence to Lucca's piazzale Verdi, and frequent **trains** from Florence Santa Maria Novella to Viareggio also stop at Lucca (1hr 20 mins).

PISA

Tourists flock to see the elegant **Campo dei Miracoli** (Field of Miracles; *see opposite*) encompassing the iconic **Leaning Tower**, the **Duomo**, **Baptistery**, **Camposanto** and the **Museo delle Sinopie**. Venture beyond it, however, and you'll find that there's much more to Pisa than the sum of its most famous parts. Highlights from the

Lucca

Campo dei Miracoli

list of worthy sights include the churches of **San Nicola** (Via Santa Maria 2) and **Santa Maria della Spina** (lungarno Gambacorti); the **Museo Nazionale di Palazzo Reale** (lungarno Pacinotti 46, 050 926573), housing many Medici-related works, and the **Museo Nazionale di San Matteo** (Piazza San Matteo in Soarta, 050 541865), which has Pisan and Islamic medieval ceramics, plus works by Masaccio, Fra Angelico and Ghirlandaio and Donatello. The **Museo delle Navi Romane** (Arsenal Medice, lungarno Simonelli 14, 055 5520407, by appt only) displays 18 2,000-year-old ships, discovered in 1998 beneath layers of protective silt, that bear witness to Pisa's early maritime power and wealth. Also check out the retrospectives and themed shows at **Palazzo Blu** (Lungarno Gamborcorti 9, 050 2204650, www.palazzoblu.it), an exhibition space housed within a vibrantly blue 16th-century *palazzo* on the Arno.

Pisa is home to numerous research institutes, an eminent university and the prestigious Scuola Normale Superiore, whose main building is the beautiful Palazzo della Carovana in **Piazza dei Cavalieri**. The **Orto Botanico** (Via Luca Ghini 5, 050 2211310) is the oldest university garden in Europe. The academic population lends the streets a youthful pulse: there are a number of bars and nightclubs here, as well as some good eateries. The best area in which to sample Tuscan *aperitivi* and sharing plates is around the borgo Stretto. **Il Colonnino** (Via Sant'Andrea 37, 050 544954, www.ristorantecolonnino.it, €€)

offers an interesting variety of set menus, while the unassuming **Gelateria De' Coltelli** (lungarno Antonio Pacinotti 23, 345 4811903, www.decoltelli.it) is consistently voted among Italy's best. Pisa's main shopping drag is corso Italia, but across from the ponte di Mezzo is a funkier zone, starting at the loggia of borgo Stretto. The antiques market takes place where the two meet, on the second weekend of every month, offering modern arts and crafts as well as antiques.

Campo dei Miracoli

The scale and elegance of Pisa's cathedral complex is undeniable. The 13th-century court astrologer Guido Bonatti argued that the spatial design of this holy space was symbolic of the cosmos, and of the zodiac of Aries in particular. The **Museo delle Sinopie** (050 835011, www.opapisa.it) on the south side of the piazza serves as the information and ticket office for the whole complex; tickets are also available online in advance. The former Museo dell'Opera del Duomo is due to reopen in 2018 as a museum of Pisan sculpture; the project is entrusted to Adolfo Natalini, the architect behind the Museo dell'Opera del Duomo in Florence.

Baptistery
Open Nov-Mar 9am-6pm daily. Apr-Sept 8am-8pm daily. Oct 9am-7pm daily. *Admission* €5, €7 with Camposanto or Sinopie Museum, €8 for all 3.

The marble Baptistery was designed by Diotisalvi (literally 'God-save-you') in 1152, with later decorative input by Nicola and Giovanni Pisano. The magnificent pulpit by Nicola Pisano (1260) is still there to be admired in situ (compare it to his son's 1310 pulpit in the Duomo). The harmonious, onion-shaped dome was a later addition, from the mid 14th century. Every half-hour, singing attendants demonstrate the building's extraordinary acoustics.

Camposanto

Open *Nov-Mar 9am-6pm daily. Apr-July, Sept 8am-8pm daily. Aug 8am-10pm daily. Oct 9am-7pm daily.* **Admission** *€5, €7 with Baptistery or Sinopie Museum, €8 for all 3.*

The Camposanto (cemetery; literally, 'Holy Field'), begun in 1277 by Giovanni de Simone, is a felicitous stylistic misfit, with elements of Gothic and Romanesque, plus more than 100 Roman sarcophagi. Pisan legend has it that the soil in the middle of the Camposanto was imported from the Holy Land. In 1944, the roof collapsed as a result of Allied bombardment, destroying frescoes and sculptures, including a fabulous cycle by Benozzo Gozzolli. However, a few survived, including, appropriately enough, *Triumph of Death*, *Last Judgement* and *Hell*.

Duomo

Open *Nov-Mar 10am-6pm daily. Apr-Sept 10am-8pm daily. Oct 10am-7pm daily.* **Admission** *free but ticket or token required.*

Begun in 1063 by Buscheto (who's buried in the wall on the left side of the façade), Pisa's cathedral is one of the finest examples of Pisan Romanesque architecture. The delicate, blindingly white marble incorporates Moorish mosaics and glass within the arcades. The brass doors (touch the lizard for good luck) by the Giambologna school were added in 1602 to replace the originals, which were destroyed in a fire in 1595. Another door facing the Leaning Tower is called the Portale di San Ranieri and features the original bronze panels by Bonanno Pisano (1180).

After the fire, the Medici family immediately began restoration work; the ornate ceiling features their coat of arms for this reason. Sadly, at the time, nothing could be done to save Giovanni Pisano's superb Gothic pulpit (1302-11), which was incinerated. Legend has it the censer suspended near the pulpit triggered Galileo's discovery of the principles of pendular motion, but it was actually cast several years later. Crane your neck to admire the Moorish dome decorated by a vibrant fresco of the Assumption by Orazio

Historic pageant for the Giugno Pisano, Pisa

and Girolamo Riminaldi (1631). Behind the altar is a mosaic by Cimabue of St John (1302). Giuliano Vangi's 2001 pulpit and altar are noticeably more modern in style, and kicked up something of a fuss locally.

Museo delle Sinopie

Open Nov-Mar 9am-6pm daily. Apr-July, Sept 8am-8pm daily. Aug 8am-10pm daily. Oct 9am-7pm daily. Admission €5, €7 with Baptistery or Camposanto, €8 for all 3.

The 1944 bombings and subsequent restoration work uncovered the *sinopie* (preliminary sketches, made with a reddish-brown pigment) from beneath the frescoes in the Camposanto. They were supposed to be hidden forever, after the artist covered the original *arriccio* (dry plaster) with a lime-rich plaster called *grassello*. The *sinopie* show what brilliant draftsmen the painters were, and also give the observer an intriguing sense of scale.

Torre Pendente (Leaning Tower)

Open Nov-Mar 9am-6pm daily. Apr-mid June 8am-8pm daily. Mid June-Aug 8.30am-10pm daily. Sept 9am-10pm daily. Oct 9am-7pm daily. Admission €18. No under-8s; under-18s must be accompanied by an adult.

The south-east corner of the Campo holds Pisa's most popular attraction, and one of the most famous curiosities on earth. When construction began on Pisa's emblematic campanile in 1173, it rapidly became clear that local architect Bonnano Pisano had neglected to do his groundwork: the sand and clay beneath the new structure simply could not support it. By the time the third storey was completed, the tower was tilting northwards, and in 1178 work was suspended. It was nearly 100 years before construction resumed, during which time the tower had begun veering to the south, its present direction. It was not until the second half of the 14th century that the world's most famous leaning tower was finally completed.

In the know
Palio di San Ranieri

Each year Pisa celebrates its patron saint's day on 17 June with a boat race between the four quarters of the town. The winner is the team whose *montatore* (climber) is the first to climb a rope and grab the correct flag at the top of a 10 metre pole on a boat anchored at the finish line. The evening before, about 100,000 candles and torches line the route for the **Luminara**. Both events are part of the month-long festival **Giugno Pisano** (see *p226* Events).

However, over the centuries, as millions of visitors made the unnerving climb of the tower's 293 steps, so the campanile continued to tilt, until in 1989, close to its maximum discrepancy from the vertical of 4.47 metres (15 feet), it was deemed in danger of collapse. A complex rescue operation, involving enormous counterweights and suspenders and a reduction in the depth of the soil between the north and south sides of the tower, swung slowly into action. The aim was never to straighten the tower entirely (who'd visit it then?) but to correct its tilt by 40cm (18in). Work was not completed until 2001. Despite the tower's popularity, a timed-ticketing system means there are few queues and plenty of time to get to the top of the campanile and back. It's well worth it to experience the lean as you climb and to enjoy the views from the top. Visits are strictly timed so don't miss your slot!

Essential information

Tourist information

Piazza del Duomo *(050 550100, www.turismo.pisa.it). Open 9.30am-5.30pm daily (earlier closing time may apply in winter).* Services include guided tours, bike rentals and luggage deposit. Another tourist office is near the train station in Piazza Vittorio Emanuele II 16 (050 42291, www.pisaunicaterra.it).

Getting there

The best way of getting to Pisa from Florence is by **train**, with frequent services between Santa Maria Novella and Pisa Centrale (journey time 1hr). Please note, the closest train stop to Piazza dei Miracoli is Pisa San Rossore, not Pisa Centrale. To get here by **car**, take the Firenze–Pisa–Livorno road.

▶ *For details of Pisa's airport, see p294 Getting Around.*

SIENA

The Sienese are fond of saying that theirs is the most perfect medieval city in the world, and it's easy to agree. Not only has Siena preserved its exquisite monuments, it has also maintained its traditions and passion for local cuisine. Head for the 13th-century **Piazza del Campo** – often described as one of Italy's most beautiful squares. The Campo is uniquely shell-shaped, fanning out in nine segments of herringbone paving. It houses the red-brick **Palazzo Pubblico**, itself home to the superb **Museo Civico** and crowned by the **Torre del Mangia** (0577 292615/292342), one of

Siena's Palio

Don't call it a pageant: it's a lifestyle

Piazza del Campo, (0577 292210, www. paliodellecontrade.com, www.comune.siena. it/La-Citta/Palio). **Date** *2 Jul and 16 Aug.*

Siena's Palio is the explosive culmination of centuries-long neighbourhood rivalries, and the event that defines the social, cultural and political fabric of the city each year. There's a single objective: to win at all costs. Cheating, biting and dosing opponents' horses with laxatives have all been tried. No one seems to care very much when the hired bareback jockeys – often dismissed as mere mercenaries – fall off their horses. The horse, on the other hand, is adored, receiving special rites and banquets.

The *contrade* that contest the Palio are districts of Siena that trace their roots back to the 12th century and vaguely represent the military groups that once protected it. Originally, the city was divided into 42 *contrade*, but the numbers shrank to the current 17 in 1729; of these, ten are selected to participate each year.

The Palio takes place in the piazza del Campo twice a year, commemorating the feast of the Virgin Mary on 2 July and the Assumption on 16 August. On the perimeter, there are balconies and stands for spectators (usually wealthy tourists) willing to shell out several hundred euros to watch the race in comfort. Most Sienese – up to 30,000 of them – stand under the blazing sun in the centre of the square.

The Palio starts in the late afternoon with a parade of costumed drummers and flag carriers. The horses charge three times round the square; the first one over the line (regardless of whether its jockey was thrown off during the race) wins and earns a banner (the Palio) of the Virgin Mary as a trophy – not to mention adulation from fans. The event is normally over in a startlingly brief 70 seconds, as riders spur on their bareback steeds (and attack enemy riders) with their *nerbo*, a whip made of dried ox penis.

The reactions of the Sienese, depending on their allegiance, range from weeping and hair-tearing to rapturous embracing; second place is considered a far worse way to lose than last place, and next best to winning is seeing your sworn-enemy *contrada* lose. The actual event is preceded by three days of trials, every day at around 9am and 7.30pm in the Campo, plus dress rehearsals, banquets and horse blessing. Banquets and festivities sponsored by the winning *contrada* then last into September.

medieval Italy's tallest towers. The *torre's* size is not coincidental – it reaches the same height as the cathedral's bell tower, to mark the equal status of the city's civic and religious powers.

On a summer's night, Piazza del Campo turns into a great eating bowl. There are a dozen establishments from *birrerie* to *pizzeria*; most are mediocre, but what you'll remember is the location, not the food. Best bets are **Al Mangia** (no.43, 0577 281121, www.almangia.it, €€) and **L'Osteria del Bigelli** (no.60, 0577 42772, www.osteriabigelli.it, €€). Wine bar **Liberamente Osteria** (no.27, 0577 274733, www.liberamenteosteria.it) has a short, tasty menu, and decor by artist Sandro Chia. The third Sunday of the month sees an **antiques market** at Piazza del Mercato, behind the Campo, while the Campo itself hosts a fascinating medieval market before Christmas.

When you visit the **Duomo**, remember to have a look at the aborted **Duomo Nuovo** to the east, near the **Museo dell'Opera Metropolitana**. In the 1340s, the city leaders planned to build a huge new cathedral, of which the present Duomo would be the transept. But the Black Death that decimated the population in 1348 dealt a deadly blow to the project, and it was finally abandoned in 1357. Today, only the *facciatone* (big façade) remains.

The main shopping street, Via di Città, curves its way between the Campo and Piazza del Duomo. While this tourist corridor has lots to offer, ambling through Siena's quiet alleys is the best recommendation for the idle traveller. Head north-west of the Campo for beautiful **Piazza Salimbeni**, flanked by three glorious *palazzi*, **Tantucci**, **Spannocchi** and **Salimbeni**. North-east of here is **Piazza San Francesco** with its eponymous Gothic church, built in 1326 by the Franciscans, as well as the 15th-century **Oratorio di San Bernardino**, with its magnificent fresco cycle (1496-1518) by Sodoma, Beccafumi and Girolamo del Pacchia.

The historic centre is divided into three sections. **Terzo di Città** was the original residential nucleus and includes the Duomo; **Terzo di San Martino** grew around the Via Francigena, the pilgrim route south to Rome, and **Terzo di Camollia** contains churches and basilicas to the north. These three sections encompass the 17 *contrade* (city districts), whose rivalry erupts with unreserved fervour at the Palio, the world-famous horse race, in summer (*see opposite* Siena's Palio). Each *contrada* is a tightly knit community grouped around a church and a piazza. Children in Siena are baptised twice: once as Christians, and once as *contradaioli* from the neighbourhood's official fountain, and outsiders can only be accepted as members if sponsored by a senior *contradaiolo*. *Contradaioli* who wed outside their *contrada* maintain their original allegiance, and many a marriage has been known to fail for Palio-related differences.

Sights & museums

Battistero

Piazza San Giovanni (0577 286300, www. operaduomo.siena.it). **Open** *Mar-Oct 10.30am-7pm daily. Nov-Feb 10.30am-5.30pm daily. Christmas holidays 10.30am-6pm daily.* **Admission** *€4.*

Built in 1317-25 to support an extension of the apsidal part of the Duomo, the Baptistery is, unusually, rectangular, rather than octagonal. The unfinished Gothic façade includes three arches adorned with human and animal busts, while inside, colourful frescoes by various artists (mainly by Il Vecchietta) fill the room. The focal point is the central font (1417-34), designed by Jacopo della Quercia and featuring gilded bronze bas-reliefs by Jacopo della Quercia, Donatello and Lorenzo Ghiberti. In the same complex is the restored Crypt.

Complesso Museale di Santa Maria della Scala

Piazza del Duomo 1 (0577 534511, www. santamariadellascala.com). **Open** *10am-5pm Mon, Wed, Thur; 10am-8pm Fri; 10am-7pm Sat, Sun.* **Admission** *€9, €7 reductions.*

This is the site of Siena's brilliant **Museo Archeologico** and often hosts important temporary exhibitions. Founded in the ninth century, it was one of Europe's oldest hospitals and a hospice for pilgrims walking the Francigena way to Rome. Entry to the museum is at the Pellegrinaio (Pilgrim's Hall), decorated by, among others, Domenico di Bartolo (1440-43), with elaborate frescoes depicting the history of the hospital. The archaeological museum lies underground, in a labyrinth of chambers.

Duomo

Piazza del Duomo (0577 286300, www. operaduomo.siena.it). **Open** *Mar-Oct 10.30am-7pm Mon-Fri; 10.30am-6pm Sat; 1.30-6pm Sun. Nov-Feb 10.30am-5.30pm Mon-Sat; 1.30-5.30pm Sun. Christmas holidays 10.30am-6pm Mon-Fri; 10.30am-5.30pm Sat; 1.30-5.30pm Sun.* **Admission** *€4 Duomo; €7 Duomo & floor Aug-Oct; €2 Piccolomini Library; other ticket options available.*

Piazza del Campo, Siena

Construction on Siena's Duomo started in 1150 on the site of an earlier church. The resulting structure is Gothic in style but Romanesque in spirit. The black-and-white marble façade was started in 1226; 30 years later work began on the dome, one of the oldest in Italy. The lower portion of the façade and the statues in the centre of the three arches were designed by Giovanni Pisano.

Inside, the cathedral's polychrome floors are its most immediate attraction but they are usually only revealed in all their glory between late August and late October. In the apse is a carved wooden choir, built between the 14th and 16th centuries. Above it is a stained-glass window made by Duccio di Buoninsegna in 1288 (this is a copy; the recently restored original is in the Museo dell'Opera Metropolitana). The tabernacle has Bernini's *Maddalena* and *San Girolamo* statues. Another highlight is the marble pulpit by Nicola Pisano. The Piccolomini altar includes four statues by a young Michelangelo (1501-04).

Museo Civico
Palazzo Pubblico, Piazza del Campo (0577 292615/0577 292232, www.comune.siena.it). **Open** *Mid Mar-Oct 10am-7pm daily. Nov-mid Mar 10am-6pm daily.* **Admission** *€9, €8 reductions, free under-11s.*

In the Anticappella of the Museo Civico you can admire a number of frescoes by Taddeo di Bartolo (1362-1422), which reflect his fascination with Greek and Roman antiquity and mythological heroes, plus a *Madonna and Child with Saints* by Sodoma at the altar of the Cappella del Consiglio. The Sala del Mappamondo was decorated by Ambrogio Lorenzetti around 1320-30 with cosmological frescoes depicting the universe and celestial spheres. This room also houses the *Maestà* (Enthroned Virgin) fresco painted by Simone Martini in 1315. It is thought to be one of his earliest works and is said to represent devotion to the Republic's princes. Finally, in the Sala della Pace, is *The Allegory of Good and Bad Government* by Lorenzetti (1338-40). The largest secular fresco since Roman times, its details of medieval daily life are of exceptional interest.

Museo dell'Opera Metropolitana
Piazza del Duomo 8 (0577 286300, www. operaduomo.siena.it). **Open** *Mar-Oct 10.30am-7pm daily. Nov-Feb 10.30am-5.30pm daily. Christmas holidays 10.30am-6pm daily.* **Admission** *€7.*

The museum is worth visiting if only for Duccio di Boninsegna's *Maestà*, including its richly decorated underside, and for a close-up look at his stained-glass window from the Duomo. The museum also provides access to the so-called *facciatone* of the Duomo Nuovo; the view from the summit is worth the uncomfortable climb.

Strade del Vino

Chianti country, San Gimignano, Montalcino and Montepulciano

When people think of rural Italy, they conjure up images of rolling hills dotted with cypresses, tiny hamlets unchanged for centuries and al fresco tables groaning with delicious local food. A good way to experience these clichés for real is to make a tour of provincial Siena, which is dominated by its excellent wines: Chianti Classico, Vernaccia di San Gimignano, Brunello di Montalcino and Vino Nobile di Montepulciano. You will need a rental car for two to four days to follow this itinerary. Factor in an extra day for an optional detour to Volterra from San Gimignano.

For the first leg, take the SRT 222 south of Florence through the **Chianti** region (tourist information 055 82285, www. stradachianticlassico.it). You will pass through **Greve in Chianti**, **Panzano** and **Castellina in Chianti**, all worth stopping at. The surrounding slopes are clad with vines, olive groves and woodland, much of it inhabited by wild boar; in fact, the area has become so desirable that there's hardly a barn here that hasn't been renovated.

From Castellina, head west to Poggibonsi and take the S68 via **Colle di Val d'Elsa** to Castel San Gimignano, then head north to **San Gimignano** (tourist information 0577 940008, www.sangimignano.com), with its 14 towers (there were once as many as 72) rising high above the terracotta roofs. The best way to appreciate the heritage is to climb the 218 steps of Torre Grossa, the 'big tower' of the Palazzo Comunale. The town's main sights are conveniently covered by one €6 ticket (0577 286300, www.sangimignanomusei.it) and

include the displays of Florentine and Sienese art at the Pinacoteca, and the 11th-century Collegiata that features the beautiful Santa Fina chapel by Ghirlandaio.

From San Gimignano, you can make a detour to the Etruscan town of **Volterra** (tourist information 0588 87257, www. volterratur.it), which stands proudly on a peak between the Cecina and Era valleys in Pisa province. Alternatively, retrace your steps to Poggibonsi and take the S2 Cassia south to Monteriggioni, Siena and beyond. The next destination is **Montalcino** (tourist information 0577 849331, www.prolocomontalcino.com), a proud hill town with a gentle Tuscan quality. Brunello de Montalcino is one of Italy's most celebrated red wines; for a vast selection of local labels, stop at **Enoteca La Fortezza** (0577 849211, www.enotecalafortezza. com) inside the keep.

From Montalcino, reach its historic rival **Montepulciano** (tourist information 0578 757341, www.prolocomontepulciano.it) via **San Quirico d'Orcia** and **Pienza**, both worth visiting. Montepulciano's Piazza Grande is one of Tuscany's favourite filming locations, with its 16th-century Duomo and imposing town hall remodelled by Michelozzo to resemble Florence's Palazzo Vecchio. An unmissable sight for wine lovers is the majestic **Cantina del Redi** under Palazzo Ricci (0578 757166, www.cantinadericci.it), which has lofty arches and vaulted ceilings resembling a medieval cathedral. From Montepulciano, the easiest route back to Florence is via the nearby A1 motorway.

Vineyards, Chianti

Piazza Grande, Arezzo

Pinacoteca Nazionale

*Palazzo Buonsignori, Via San Pietro 29
(0577 281161, www.pinacotecanazionale.
siena.it).* **Open** *9am-1pm Mon, Sun;
8.15am-7.15pm Tue-Sat.* **Admission** *€4, €2
reductions. No cards.*

One of Italy's foremost art collections, this
lovely 15th-century *palazzo* holds more
than 1,500 works of art and is particularly
renowned for its Sienese *fondi oro* (paintings
with gilded backgrounds). The second floor
is devoted to Sienese masters from the 12th
to the 15th centuries; the first floor houses
works by the Sienese Mannerist school of the
early 1500s, while the third floor holds the
Spannocchi Collection, containing works by
northern Italian and European artists of the
16th and 17th centuries.

Essential Information

Tourist information
**Ufficio Informazioni e Accoglienza
Turistica** *Palazzo Squarcialupi, Piazza
Duomo 1 (0577 280551, www.terresiena.
it).* **Open** *Apr-Oct 9am-7pm daily.
Nov-Mar 10.30am-4.30pm Mon-Fri,
10.30am-6.30pm Sat, Sun. A smaller tourist
information point is operated by the Comune
di Siena inside the City Hall.*

Getting there
The RA3 dual carriageway links Florence
and Siena (45 mins), or there's the more
rural SS2. **Tiemme Spa - Toscana Mobilità**
(800 373760, www.tiemmespa.it) runs the
majority of the **bus** services between the
two cities (75 mins). There are few direct
trains between Florence's SMN station and
Siena; you usually have to change at Empoli
(journey time up to 2hrs).

AREZZO

Famed as a centre of the gold and textile
industries, Arezzo's main pleasures are to
be found in its retail opportunities and its
artistic heritage. The city is an essential stop
on any Piero della Francesca trail, housing
his in the church of **San Francesco** and a
Mary Magdalene (c1465) in the **Duomo**.

Construction on Arezzo's Gothic
cathedral (Piazza del Duomo, 0575 23991)
began in 1277, but the finishing touches
weren't made until the early 1500s, and it
was a further 300 years before its campanile
was erected. As well as Piero della
Francesca's *Mary Magdalene*, don't miss the
Cappella della Madonna del Conforto and
the exquisite stained-glass windows (c1515-
20) by Guillaume di Marcillat.

Most of the city's sights lie in the quiet,
hilly streets of the old town, the heart of
which is **Piazza Grande**, a bonanza of
architectural irregularity which you may
remember from Roberto Benigni's Oscar-
winning *La vita è bella* (Life is Beautiful).

The jumble of styles includes Baroque **Palazzo del Tribunale**, the Romanesque **Pieve di Santa Maria** and the **Palazzo della Fraternità dei Laici**, designed mostly by Bernardo Rossellino. Giorgio Vasari designed the arcaded **Palazzo delle Logge**, presiding over the medieval homes around the rest of the square. The restaurants and cafés overlooking Piazza Grande are priceless for people-watching, but the location comes at a price.

West of Piazza Grande is the church of **San Francesco** (0575 352727, www. pierodellafrancesca-ticketoffice.it), whose interior, begun by Franciscan friars in the 13th century, was adorned with frescoes, chapels and shrines during the 1500s, thanks to Arezzo's merchant class. The church was used as a military barracks in the 19th century, but happily, the *Legend of the True Cross*, Piero della Francesca's magnum opus, survives in the Bacci Chapel. Some of the frescoes are too high to be appreciated by the naked eye, so take a pair of binoculars, and be prepared for some neck-craning.

Outside, on Piazza San Francesco, **Le Chiavi d'Oro** (0575 403313, www. ristorantelechiavidoro.it, €€) serves Tuscan fare in pleasing modern surroundings. Nearby is the **Badia delle Sante Flora e Lucilla** (Piazza di Badia, 0575 356612), which has a giant *Crucifixion* by Segna di Bonaventura, a marble-effect altar by Vasari, and an ingenious trompe l'oeil dome by

Andrea Pozzo (1703). North of the cathedral is the church of **San Domenico** (Piazza San Domenico 7, 0575 23255), which was started by Dominicans in 1275. Inside you'll find a magnificent crucifix by Cimabue. Arezzo's only park – **Il Prato** – is located between the Duomo and the **Fortezza Medicea** in the east.

Anyone interested in Vasari should visit **Casa Vasari** (Via XX Settembre 55, 0575 409040, www.museistataliarezzo.it), which the artist decorated in extravagant style before moving to Florence in 1564. Today, the museum proudly exhibits a number of Vasari frescoes and other late Mannerist paintings. Nearby is **Santa Maria delle Grazie** (Via Santa Maria), housing the Renaissance's first porticoed courtyard, by Antonio da Maiano.

In the lower part of town is the Roman amphitheatre and the **Museo Archeologico Mecenate** (Via Margaritone 10, 0575 20882, www.museistataliarezzo.it), which houses a fine collection of Etruscan and Roman artefacts.

When you've had your fill of art, get some retail therapy on Arezzo's well-stocked shopping streets. Italy's top fashion buyer, Beppe Sugar' Angiolini, runs **Sugar** (0575 354631, www.sugar.it), a string of luxury boutiques along the top end of corso Italia; you'll be well catered for if you're after the latest from designer fashion labels. Mainstream shops give way to a proliferation of antiques vendors around Piazza Grande. On the first weekend of the month the city centre is taken over by a huge **antiques fair** (www.fieraantiquaria. org) at which almost 400 vendors – and up to 30,000 customers – arrive from all over the country to deal in everything from ornate candlesticks to collectable junk.

Essential information

Tourist information *Piazza della Libertà 2 (0575 401945, www.arezzointuscany.it). Open June-Aug 11am-1.30pm, 2-5.30pm daily. Sept-May 2-4pm daily. Also by the train station in Piazza della Repubblica 22-23 (0575 26850).*

Getting there

Arezzo is about on hour from Florence off the A1 (Florence-Rome) autostrada. There's a convenient car park just outside the walls on the north side, behind the church of San Domenico. Regional **trains** (892021, www. trenitalia.it) link Arezzo with Florence in 50-60mins. The train station is located at Piazza della Repubblica. The bus terminal is opposite the train station, but services from Florence are slow and irregular.

Experience

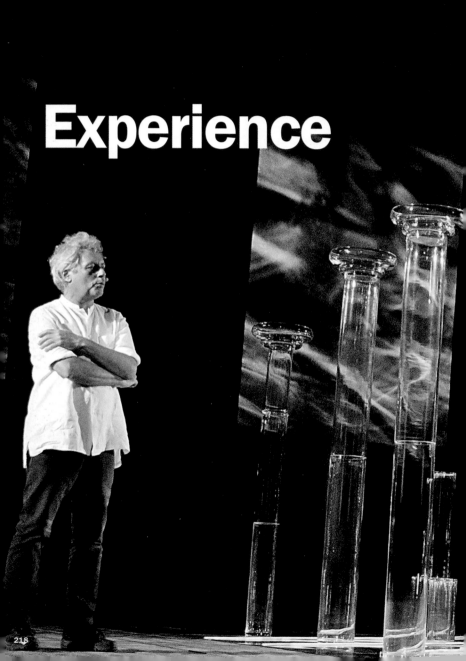

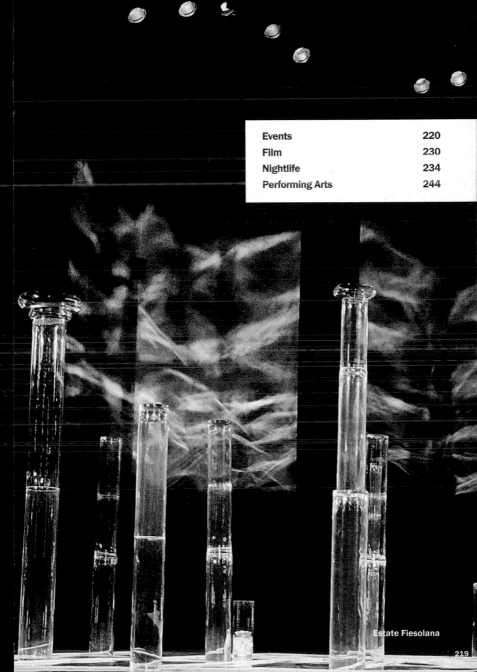

Estate Fiesolana

Events

A rundown of Florence's packed calendar

Nothing impresses in Florence quite like its artistic heritage... except perhaps the pageantry of its many annual traditions. Spring brings the bizarre pyrotechnics of the Scoppio del Carro, when an antique cart festooned with fireworks is escorted through the streets. *Sbandieratori* (flag-throwers) are spotted year-round, but you'll know summer is near when you see the procession heading toward Santa Croce to perform ahead of the first *calcio storico* match. Crowds stand along the Arno to marvel at the sky during the San Giovanni fireworks display, and say goodbye to summer with La Rificolona lantern parade through the city. And Christmas festivities culminate with an elaborate Magi procession to celebrate the Epiphany. These and other traditional festivities are supplemented by a summer-long cultural festival, plus one-off film, food and family events.

Scoppio del Carro *p222*

Spring

Festa della Donna
Date 8 Mar.

For International Women's Day, women are traditionally presented with yellow mimosa flowers. Civic museums typically offer free or reduced admission for women and in the evening, restaurants and clubs such as **Otel Variete** (viale Generale della Chiesa 13, Firenze Sud, 055 650791, www.otelvariete. com) get packed with girlie gangs set on having a wild night out.

Taste
Stazione Leopolda, viale Fratelli Rosselli 5, Outside the City Gates. (www.pittimmagine. com/corporate/fairs/taste.htm). Date Sat, Sun in March.

Held each March in Stazione Leopolda, this food festival, put on by Pitti Immagine, brings together 250 Italian artisanal producers of everything from truffle pâtés, salami, cured lard and chocolate to olive oil, wine, beer and silver-leaf spumante. For a reasonable admission and wine glass fee, you can sample the best that Italy has to offer. What's not to like? Hmmm, perhaps that cured lard…

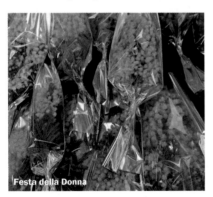
Festa della Donna

Holy Week and Pasquetta
Throughout Tuscany. Date Mar/Apr.

Many Tuscan towns celebrate Holy Week with religious processions, often in period costume. The most impressive of them involves almost 600 performers and takes place in the evening of Good Friday in the small town of Grassina in Bagno a Ripoli (055 646051, www.catgrassina.org), just outside Florence. Bakeries around Florence sell traditional Easter rosemary buns called *pan di ramerino*. Pasquetta, on the Monday following Easter, is a holiday in its own right, with many civic and state museums opening their doors for the occasion.

❤ Scoppio del Carro
Piazzale della Porta al Prato to piazza del Duomo. Date Easter Sun.

At 9.30am on Easter morning, a parade of costumed musicians, flag-throwers and dignitaries escort a wooden cart, the *Brindellone*, laden with fireworks and pulled by four white oxen, from via il Prato (watch for the three-storey wooden doors on the left of the Hotel Villa Medici) to a jam-packed piazza del Duomo. Meanwhile, another parade departs from the church of Santissimi Apostoli (*see p96*) with a holy fire kindled with the flints from the Holy Sepulchre. At 11am, during mass, a dove-shaped rocket shoots along a wire from the high altar to the *carro* (wagon) outside, starting the fireworks. If all goes smoothly, it's said that the year's harvest will be good.

Mostra Mercato di Piante e Fiori
Giardino dell'Orticoltura, via Vittorio Emanuele 4, Outside the City Gates. Date late Apr/early May, and early Oct.

Growers from all over Tuscany proudly exhibit and sell their plants and blooms at these spectacular horticultural shows, which are laid out around a grand 19th-century glasshouse.

❤ Best seasonal events

Scoppio del Carro *see above*
An explosive Easter ritual full of Florentine pageantry.

Estate Fiorentina *p224*
Embrace summer with this multifaceted arts festival.

La Rificolona *p225*
A September lights spectacle with a paper lantern parade.

Epifania *p229*
Festivities led by a witch and three kings.

❤ Best music festivals

Pistoia Blues *p205*
Born for the blues, now genre-defying.

LuccaSummerFestival *p207*
From rock gods to Italian teenyboppers.

Tempo Reale *p229*
Experimental trailblazers.

EVENTS

Drummers parade for Scoppio del Carro

Maggio Musicale Fiorentino
Opera di Firenze, piazzale Vittorio Gui 1, Porta al Prato, Outside the City Gates (055 2779309, www.maggiofiorentino.com). **Date** *late Apr-early July.*

Founded in 1933, Florence's 'Musical May' is universally acclaimed as one of the best festivals in Italy for opera, concerts and dance performances.

Artigianato e Palazzo
Corsini Gardens, via della Scala 115, Santa Maria Novella (055 2654589, www. artigianatoepalazzo.it). **Date** *Sat, Sun in mid May.*

Master artisans from Italy and beyond demonstrate their skills and sell their wares at this upmarket craft show in one of Tuscany's finest Italianate gardens.

Festa del Grillo
Parco delle Cascine, entrance nr ponte della Vittoria, Porta al Prato, Outside the City Gates. **Date** *6th Sun after Easter.*

On the feast of Ascension, Florentine families traditionally came to the Cascine park for a picnic, and part of the fun was chasing (or buying) crickets and taking them home in brightly painted little cages. Live crickets have been replaced by chirping mechanical devices, and this traditional event now has the feel of a general market.

Amico Museo
Throughout Tuscany (www.regione.toscana. it/amicomuseo). **Date** *3wks in May.*

This event means special and late openings, events, concerts and guided visits to familiarise the crowds with the region's lesser-known local museums. Family-friendly activities abound; the initiative typically takes place in the weeks surrounding the Europe-wide Night at the Museum. Pick up a brochure from any tourist office.

Fabbrica Europa
Stazione Leopolda, viale Fratelli Rosselli 5, Porta al Prato, Outside the City Gates (055 2480515, www.fabbricaeuropa.net). **Date** *6 wks in May/June.*

This interdisciplinary, innovative performing arts showcase is anchored at this former railway station by Porta al Prato, but spin-off events and shows take place throughout Florence and Tuscany. The festival has taken on a more international vibe in recent years, highlighting established and emerging performers in theatre, music, dance and multimedia arts.

Mille Miglia

Across Tuscany (030 2318211, www. millemiglia.it). **Date** *Sat in late May.*

Vintage car lovers get an eyeful in Florence with a grand spectacle: almost 400 vintage cars take part in this 1,600km (1,000-mile) race, winding their way back from Rome to Brescia, moving through Siena and entering Florence for a jaunt through much of the city, passing Porta Romana on the way to piazza della Signoria and exiting the city via piazzale Michelangelo. Then it's onwards to Bologna via the Mugello.

Cantine Aperte

Throughout Italy (0577 847047, www. movimentoturismovino.it). **Date** *last Sat, Sun in May.*

Wine-producing estates, many of which would not normally be open to the public, show their cellars to visitors and hold tastings. Winery openings are of course concentrated in the countryside, but some producers come in to Florence proper to offer tastings or related events in host bars.

Summer

Florence Dance Festival

Borgo Stella 23r, the Oltrarno (055 289276, www.florencedancefestival.org). **Date** *June-July.*

Staged mostly in the courtyard of the Bargello Museum (*see p146*), this festival fuses some of the greatest names in contemporary, traditional and classical dance. Past editions have included quite a variety, spanning Japanese *butoh* to Shakespeare-inspired ballet.

♥ Estate Fiorentina

Throughout Florence (www.estatefiorentina. it). **Date** *June-Sept.*

This festival is an ever-expanding and loosely connected series of arts and cultural events, and smaller-scale festivals, that run throughout the summer. However, sporadic events under the Estate Fiorentina umbrella have been known to pop up as early as April and as late as December. Headlining

Calcio storico played in piazza Santa Croce

Florence Queer Festival p228

events usually include big-name concerts at the Visarno Arena and Amphitheatre at Le Cascine, while more artsy initiatives run at contemporary hubs such as Le Murate, Palazzo Strozzi and the Museo Novecento. Outdoor cinema, circus shows, electronic music festivals, and elegant outdoor dinners: the programme is as varied as they come.

Calcio Storico
*Piazza Santa Croce, Santa Croce (055 290832). **Date** June.*

When an upsurge in violence prompted authorities to crack down on game regulations, the future for Florence's rugby-football-boxing hybrid known as the *calcio storico* seemed uncertain. But it's still going strong and pretty much as it has been since the 16th century. Two preliminary matches are normally played in early June, while the final is held on 24 June, a city holiday. Teams representing the city's ancient quarters (Santa Croce, Santa Maria Novella, Santo Spirito and San Giovanni) parade through the streets before settling old rivalries in a no-holds-barred 27-a-side match played by bare-chested lads in bright medieval breeches. Yes, really.

Festa di San Giovanni
*Throughout the city. **Date** 24 June.*

A public holiday in Florence. A huge fireworks display takes place at 10 pm near piazzale Michelangelo to honour the city's patron saint, John the Baptist. It's best enjoyed from the *lungarni* (just follow the crowds) or on the Arno 'beach' (*see p182*).

Festa di San Lorenzo
Piazza San Lorenzo, San Lorenzo. **Date** 10 Aug.

August is usually a quiet month in Florence, but things pick up with this annual morning parade and evening party honouring San Lorenzo's martyrdom. Coinciding with the peak of the Perseid meteor shower (San Lorenzo is said to be shedding tears in the sky), and the wine event Calici di Stelle, the feast day begins with a court procession through the centre. The main fun comes at sundown when the saint's namesake piazza hosts music, dancing and even dinner – free watermelon and lasagne are distributed.

❤ La Rificolona
Throughout the city. **Date** 7 Sept.

In the past, country folk used to walk to Florence on the eve of the Nativity of the Virgin Mary, as a pilgrimage as well as for the fair that's still held in piazza SS Annunziata. They carried paper lanterns, or *rificolone*, to light their way. Today, children still parade through the city proudly swaying their colourful candlelit paper lanterns. Smaller neighbourhood versions run across town, and many craft shops and children's venues host lantern-decorating competitions and runway-esque *rificolona* shows.

Unmissable Events In Tuscany

If Florence starts feeling too picture-perfect, it's time to venture further afield

Innumerable folklore festivals, food and wine events and historical re-enactments all give visitors a deeper insight into what Tuscany is really about. The *lungarni* (river embankments) of Pisa are lit up on 16 June, the feast of the local patron saint: 70,000 candles illuminate the façades of palaces along the Arno during the charming **Luminara di San Ranieri**. But this is just one in a series of **Giugno Pisano** ('Pisan June') events: including **Il Gioco del Ponte** – a 16th-century 'push-of-war' – fought on the last Sunday of June on the ponte di Mezzo between teams from the two sides of the Arno.

Closer to Florence and containing more modern flair from mid-June to early September is **Estate Fiesolana** (*see p247*). Take bus no.7 up the hill past San Marco and enjoy an assorted mix of performing arts shows and cinema screenings in scenic settings like the Roman theatre and the Maiano stone quarries.

Moving back in time once again is the glorious **Giostra del Saracino** in Arezzo's piazza Grande (0575 377462, www. giostradelsaracinoarezzo.it), held on the penultimate Saturday of June and the first Sunday in September. This ancient jousting tournament was first recorded in 1535. Five centuries later, it's still plenty of fun.

But perhaps no Tuscan faceoff is more famous than the **Palio delle Contrade** in Siena, a bareback, breakneck horse race staged in piazza del Campo on 2 July and 16 August (*see p212*). At 5pm the procession of horses and jockeys, each representing one of the *contrade* (historic neighbourhoods), enters the piazza del Campo, and the race – three laps of the square – gets going around 7pm and is all over in 90 seconds. Tickets are tough to come by and expensive, but it's quite the spectacle.

The Palio isn't the only example of how Tuscans value neighbourhood ties. Montepulciano's **Bravio delle Botti** (www. braviodellebotti.com) takes place on the last Sunday in August and brings together champions from the city's eight historic districts. The brawny athletes compete in an exhausting wine barrel-rolling contest up the steep and winding route to piazza Grande, in the height of summer heat.

As the season starts to cool, so does Prato: the city hosts its annual **Settembre Prato** series (www.settembreprato.it), a festival with concerts (Interpol and Air have performed in the past), sport, children's activities and quirky rituals such as the celebration of the Holy Girdle of the Virgin. Allegedly, the belt that Mary handed to Saint Thomas on ascending into Heaven was brought to Prato from the Holy Land around 1141. On 8 September, it's paraded through piazza del Duomo and around town.

If food sounds more appealing than relics of dubious origin, head to the charming medieval setting of Certaldo during the first two weekends of October for **Boccacesca** (339 1720019, www.boccaccesca.it). Both the upper and lower parts of the town host a much-acclaimed celebration of the finest Tuscan produce, with wine, olive oil and the unique local onions – all in the name of the town's most famous export, poet Giovanni Boccaccio.

Just after the dawn of the new year, head to beach town Viareggio for a party to end all others, running from late January to early March. Viareggio's **Carnevale** (0584 58071, www.ilcarnevale.com) dates back to 1873 and is held on the three Sundays before Shrove Tuesday (at 3pm), on Shrove Tuesday (again at 3pm) and on the following Sunday (from 5pm, followed by the award ceremony for the best floats and a firework display). The parades consist of floats with over-the-top satirical papier-mâché figures that take 100 people the best part of a year to assemble. You can buy seats in one of the stands flanking the Lungomare, but, as long as you watch out for your valuables, it's more fun among the revelling crowds.

Viareggio's Carnevale

Autumn

50 Days of International Cinema

Cinema la Compagnia, via Cavour 50r, San Marco (055 268451, www.50giornidicinema. it). **Date** *late Oct-early Dec.*

Founded in 2007 as a way of centralising Florence's internationally orientated film festivals, this movie marathon is now an established favourite for film buffs, though the venues have shifted through the years. Now screenings take place at the recently restored La Compagnia, converted into a cinema in late 2016. The season traditionally kicks off with France Odeon, spotlighting French cinema, and wraps up with the NICE City of Florence Award, honouring an Italian film selected by American audiences. Films are shown in their original language and subtitles in English are now standard for most.

Biennale Enogastronomica

Throughout Florence (www. biennaleenogastronomica.it). **Date** *2 wks in Nov every other year.*

Much of the programming at this mega biennial event is geared toward industry insiders. But you can always count on finding temporary food and wine markets set up downtown for the occasion, as well as local restaurants, shops and bars offering themed menus, discounts or special events related to the foodie festivities.

Florence Queer Festival

Throughout Florence (www. florencequeerfestival.it). **Date** *mid Nov.*

A landmark LGBTQ event in Italy, Florence Queer Festival technically forms part of 50

Days of International Cinema (*see left*), but the focus extends beyond film into theatrical performances, exhibitions, parties and conferences. Past editions have included exhibitions of nightclub photography, drag shows and talks on the many shades of identity, sexual and otherwise. Many events are headquartered at or spearheaded by the LGBTQ community organisation **Ireos** (via dei Serragli 3, the Oltrarno, 039 055 216907, www.ireos.org) and past editions of the festival have extended their reach to Prato's **Teatro Metastasio** (via B Cairoli 59, Prato, 039 0574 6084, www.metastasio.it).

Florence Tattoo Convention

Fortezza da Basso, viale Filippo Strozzi 1, Outside the City Gates (www. florencetattooconvention.com). **Date** *Oct or Nov.*

Florence embraces art in all its forms, and autumn visitors needing a break from Botticelli and Brunelleschi can explore ink artistry at this fascinating event. There are opportunities to get tattooed, of course, but also to watch burlesque shows, catch ink masters demonstrating their craft and, for adventurous parents, to take part in creative workshops with the kids.

Musica dei Popoli

FLOG see p239 (www.musicadeipopoli. com). **Date** *late Oct-late Nov.*

Starting the first weekend in October and running for about a month, this is one of the area's most vibrant and varied world music festivals, bringing together musicians from Senegal to Spain. Genres run the gamut from folk to funk. Not to be missed.

Cavalcata dei Magi

❤ Tempo Reale Festival
Villa Strozzi, via Pisana 77, and various venues throughout the city (055 717270, www.temporeale.it). **Date** *late Sept–early Oct.*

Cult Florentine music organisation Tempo Reale puts together a variety of concerts, events and exhibitions throughout the year, but it is most active during this two week showcase of experimental sounds. Branded more as sensory based experiences than strictly musical performances, the shows bring together individual musicians, sound artists and unusual orchestras from around Italy and abroad. Tempo Reale is an acquired taste, but even pop music devotees will find the free concerts worthwhile, particulary the opportunity to see the Villa Strozzi, the festival's headquarters, as well as other extraordinary venues where events are held.

Winter

Christmas Market
Piazza Santa Croce, Santa Croce. **Open** *10am–10 pm daily.* **Date** *early Dec.*

This picturesque German-style Weihnachtsmarkt has become an irresistible destination for Christmas cheer. The shopping isn't usually anything special, but the festive atmosphere is tough to resist, with friends and couples cosying up for mulled wine and holiday treats.

Natale
Christmas in Florence is marked by the usual suspects of shopping, decorations, eating and drinking, and special events throughout December. An ice-skating rink is set up at the Parterre in piazza della Libertà, while piazza del Duomo hosts a huge Christmas tree, which gets a ceremonial lighting every year on 8 December, the Feast of the Immaculate Conception. Meanwhile, the Uffizi hosts an annual series, I Mai Visti (never-before-seen) displaying major artworks from the museum's collections. Concerts take place throughout the season, many put on by local and regional orchestras. Some restaurants are open on Christmas Day, but you'll find more choice on 26 December.

Christmas Concert
Teatro Verdi, via Ghibellina 99, Santa Croce (055 2340710, tickets 055 212320). **Date** *24 Dec.*

This annual concert by the Orchestra Regionale Toscana doesn't necessarily include Christmas music, but there is usually something worth checking out.

San Silvestro
Throughout Tuscany. **Date** *31 Dec.*

Restaurants and clubs charge preposterous amounts for dinner and dancing parties, so an increasing number of Italians spend the long festive night of San Silvestro among friends and family at home, with a gigantic meal (including the mandatory stuffed pigs' trotters and lentils) and a fair supply of firecrackers and sparklers to 'burn' the past year and welcome in the new. If you can brave the cold, the city now puts on a major concert in piazzale Michelangelo and hosts pop-up parties and entertainment in select squares both within and beyond the gates. Similar initiatives take place in several Tuscan towns.

❤ Epifania
Central Florence. **Date** *6 Jan.*

Epiphany is on par with 25 December for children in Italy. *La Befana*, a ragged old kindly witch riding a broomstick, rewards well-behaved children with stockings full of toys and sweets, while naughty kids receive a sockful of coal. Many small towns around the region hold street parties in celebration, while in Florence, events centre on the Arno river when the Canottieri Comunali rowing group hosts a morning with *La Befana*, who passes out delights afterward. In the afternoon, the **Cavalcata dei Magi**, or Procession of the Three Kings, runs from piazza Pitti to piazza Duomo. It's a costumed affair with hundreds of participants, and the whole scene is modelled after Benozzo Gozzoli's elaborate procession fresco at Palazzo Medici Riccardi.

▶ *For more on seasonal Florence, see p24 When to Visit.*

Film

Film sets that are pure romance and a fine alfresco cinema scene

Romanticised, picture-perfect scenes from *A Room with a View* have burned an image of Florence into the collective psyche of the English-speaking world and beyond. Although Merchant-Ivory's adaptation of the Edwardian classic is now three decades old, it still strikes a chord with visitors who, like Lucy Honeychurch, come to Florence to be transfigured by Giotto's frescoes in Santa Croce. Ridley Scott's *Hannibal* represents the polar-opposite, capturing the psychopathic, dark, medieval heart of Florentine history through its allusion to the Pazzi conspiracy.

Florence has also seen a surge of 'bestseller-based' tourism since the release of *Inferno,* a Dante-themed Dan Brown novel adapted into a race-against-the-clock on the big screen by Ron Howard in 2016. The apocalyptic plot is forgettable, but the breathtaking aerial shots of Florence have likely inspired many flight bookings since the film's release. And, for all its historical inaccuracies and hiccups, the Rai 1 programme *Medici: Masters of Florence* screened on Netflix in 2016-17 has also reignited interest in the Renaissance city.

The Portrait of a Lady (Jane Campion, 1996)

English-language and international screenings

Most of Florence's cinema offerings are in Italian (either Italian films or dubbed), but original language screenings of films from Anglophone countries and far beyond do pop up year-round, especially as cinemas catch on to Florence's increasingly international tastes. The very central **Odeon Cinema**, with its Original Sound programme, continues to show international films exclusively in their original languages (*versione originale*). Venues such as **Spazio Alfieri** and **La Compagnia**, while screening fewer English-language films than the Odeon, also have an international slant – the latter hosts the annual film series 50 Giorni di Cinema Internazionale (50 Days of International Cinema; *see below*) and Primavera di Cinema Orientale (an Eastern film festival held in spring; *see opposite*). English-language news magazine *The Florentine* (*see p302*) has cinema listings for Anglophones.

Getting a seat

Italians have an aversion to booking, especially for the cinema, so expect chaos on Friday and Saturday nights for new releases. You may also find yourself invaded by people looking for the best seats for the next show before your show has finished. When the *posto in piedi* light is lit, the tickets sold are standing-room only. Note that tickets to the matinées offered at many main cinemas are often cheaper than nighttime showings. For festivals and other special events, check listings in The Florentine, *Firenze Spettacolo* or in the local supplement of the national daily *La Repubblica*.

Cinemas

The multiplex **UCI Cinemas** (via del Cavallacio, 39 055 892 960, www.ucicinemas. it, tram line 1), slightly out of town in the Scandicci area, has been drawing cinemagoers away from the city centre. The consequence has been predictable, if unfortunate: many of the old central cinemas can no longer maintain their customer base, so some are turning into bingo halls while others just lie idle and abandoned.

British Institute of Florence

Harold Acton Library, Lungarno Guicciardini 9, Oltrarno (39 055 267781, www.britishinstitute.it). **Open** *Wed Lectures from 6pm; screenings from 8pm. Tickets €6. No cards.* **Map** *p164 H9.*

The British Institute runs a Talking Pictures programme on Wednesday evenings, always preceded by a 6pm lecture – sometimes related to the film, other times as a separate event. Films, which are always either in English or subtitled in English, are

Seasonal Cinema

Grab a seat at one of the region's best film festivals

50 Giorni di Cinema Internazionale (50 Days of International Cinema) (various locations, www.50giornidicinema.it), which runs from late September or early October to December, is the umbrella title for Florence's longstanding major international film festivals in the autumn/winter. Screenings are in the original language, usually with Italian and English subtitles. The highlights include **France Odeon** (055 214053, www.franceodeon. it), a celebration of French film in October/ November and the opener for 50 Days that includes events and screenings at the French Institute (piazza Ognissanti 2, 055 2398902, institutfrancais-firenze.com), as well as at La Compagnia. In November, **Il Cinema Ritrovato** (festival.ilcinemaritrovato.it/en) brings restored classics back to the big screen, featuring legendary faces from Charlie Chaplin to Marcello Mastroianni. The same month, films form a mini festival with the **Florence Queer Festival** (*see p228*) and **Lo Schermo dell'Arte** (www.schermodellarte.org) screens a range of art-related movies. Numerous related events, talks and readings take place, and there is typically a linked art exhibition held at the CCC Strozzina (*see p95*). In November/December, the **Festival dei Popoli** (055 244778, www.festivaldeipopoli.org) screens dramas and smart, often award-winning documentaries in clubs and cinemas throughout Florence, usually accompanied by a smattering of related culinary events and concerts. The **River to River** Indian film festival (055 286929, www.rivertoriver.it) is held in December; films are mostly in English, or in the original language with English subtitles. Also part of the festivities is the **Premio Fiesole ai Maestri del Cinema**, which pays homage to the works of one director – past editions have focused on Ken Loach, Bernardo Bertolucci, Stefania Sandrelli and Spike Lee. Finally, in summer, stand-alone multifaceted festival **Estate Fiesolana** (www.estatefiesolana.it) features cinema and concerts held in Fiesole's open-air Roman theatre.

sandwiched between an introduction and a discussion. The institute also runs courses in Italian language, complemented by cinema screenings and events.

La Compagnia
*Via Camillo Cavour, 50/R, 50121, San Marco (39 055 268451, www.cinemalacompagnia. it). **Open** Box office 1hr before start of film. Tickets €5-€8; cinema & aperitivo €10; cinema & dinner €15. **Map** p131 M4.*

A historic theatre recently converted into a cinema, La Compagnia has given the Odeon some local competition, hosting an impressive range of events, including lectures and meet-and-greets. In addition to its regular line-up of Italian and international films, the theatre is also the headquarters for Florence's annual 50 Days of International Cinema showcase and Primavera di Cinema Orientale, a springtime series of Eastern film festivals (regulars include Middle East Now, Florence Korea Film Fest, Dragon Film Festival and Wa! Japan Film Festival).

Odeon Original Sound
*Piazza Strozzi 2, Duomo & Around (39 055 295051/295331, www.odconfirenze.com). **Open** Box office times vary. Closed Aug. Tickets €6-8. No cards. **Map** p63 K7.*

Mondays, Tuesdays and Thursdays are big draws for English-speakers at this stunning art nouveau cinema as films on current release in English are screened, usually with Italian subtitles. There's a discount of up to 40% with a club card for eight films from a programme of 13 (€36). Before or after your screening, you can socialise with other English-speakers in the bar and bistro; a discount is offered on the *aperitivo* buffet when you show your ticket.

Spazio Alfieri
*Via dell'Ulivo, 6, 50122, Santa Croce (39 055 532 0840, www.spazioalfieri.it). **Open** Box office 30mins before screening. Tickets €5-7; cinema & aperitivo €12. **Map** p145 P8.*

This converted arthouse cinema hosts children's events, DJ sets and concerts in addition to its well-rounded programme of film screenings. Every autumn and spring it hosts Italian Identities as Told through Cinema, a free-entry festival put on in collaboration with two American universities, screening Italian films (subtitled in English) and followed by a discussion with a film scholar or someone in the film's cast or crew.

Stensen Cineforum
*Viale Don Minzoni 25c, Outside the City Gates (39 055 576551/5535858, www.stensen.org). Bus 1, 7, 17, 20. **Open** Film times vary. Tickets €4.50-8. No cards. **Map** p186.*

The cinema is just one facet of this broadly focused cultural organisation, inspired by the worldview of Danish doctor and geologist Niels Stensen. Films shown are Italian and international (dubbed) and include new releases as well as classics and one-off events.

Open-air screens
For Italian-speakers (though international films are sometimes shown in their original language) or those wanting to sample local life, there are the open-air cinemas, which show recent releases from June to September. Shows start as darkness falls – around 9pm or 9.30pm – and some cinemas run double bills, with the second film finishing around 1.30am.

Cinema Arena di Marte
*Mandela Forum, Piazza Enrico Berlinguer, Outside the City Gates (39 055 678841, www. mandelaforum.it). Bus 10, 17, 20. **Open** late June-late Aug from 8pm daily (show time 9.15pm). Tickets €5. **Map** p186.*

One of the two screens at this major outdoor venue shows cult and non-mainstream films; the larger screen runs the previous year's major blockbuster movies. There's a good outdoor restaurant too.

Cinema Chiardiluna Arena
*Via Monte Oliveto 1, Outside the City Gates (055 233 7042, www.facebook.com/ CinemaChiardiluna). Bus 12, 13. **Open** June-Sept 8.30pm daily (show time 9.30 pm). Tickets €5.50-€7.50. No cards. **Map** p186.*

Surrounded by woodland, Chiardiluna is cooler than the other outdoor cinemas. The movies are generally recent commercial releases, with some double bills. To take advantage of promotional prices, those in Florence for longer periods can purchase Firenze al Cinema membership for €20 (see www.firenzealcinema.info for information).

❤ Best film festivals

Il Cinema Ritrovato *see opposite*
Classics revisited on the big screen.

Festival dei Popoli *see opposite*
Smart documentaries from Italian and foreign shores.

Queer Film Festival *p228*
LGBT films from all over the world, part of Florence Queer Festival.

Lo Schermo dell'Arte *see opposite*
Connecting art and cinema.

Nightlife

As night falls, indulge in a different kind of culture

The popularity of the *aperitivo* has led to a seismic shift in Florentine nightlife patterns. Although it's still standard practice to go home for dinner directly after work before hitting the town after 10pm, it's now equally commonplace to go straight from the office to one of the many bars serving complimentary, if sometimes underwhelming, buffets with drinks – and then move on to another nightlife spot.

The late-night club is the loser in this new evening timetable: several historic city-centre clubs have closed, while other nightlife venues tend to close down or change hands as quickly as they crop up. Some spaces have morphed into bar/clubs serving early-evening *aperitivi* in the hope of roping punters in for the night. That's not to say clubbing has died a death; it's just treated less as a nightly entertainment and more as a one-off occasion.

Meanwhile, many of the nightlife venues in the suburbs, and some in town, survive on the euros of music junkies. Considering its size, the city has a rich indie music scene, with a smattering of local labels and international musicians of all genres performing in even the smallest venues. Note that the opening times of bars and clubs are notoriously vague and erratic, and phones are rarely answered.

DRINKING

Drinking establishments have gained ground over dance clubs in recent years. A much wider choice is available in summer, when al fresco venues pop up all over the city (*see p240* Summer Bars & Clubs).

Bars & pubs

Art Bar

Via del Moro 4r, Santa Maria Novella (055 287661, www.facebook.com/pg/ AnticoCaffeDelMoroArtBarFirenze). **Open** *6.30pm-1am daily. Closed 3wks Aug.* **Map** *p101 H7.*

Battered French horns hanging from the ceiling and sepia photos of blues and jazz musicians lend a beatnik air to this tiny but popular bar, best known for its beautiful cocktails adorned with kiwi, strawberry and other eye-catching accents. The ambience is cosy but animated, with student types holed up in the brick cellar sipping their potent piña coladas.

Caffe' Notte

Via delle Caldaie 18, Oltrarno (055 223067, www.facebook.com/caffenotte). **Open** *7.30am-midnight Mon-Wed; 7.30am-2.30am Thu-Sun.* **Map** *p164 G11.*

A cute hole-in-the-wall on an unsuspecting corner of the Oltrarno, not five minutes' walk from piazza Santo Spirito, this charming spot keeps Christmas lights up year-round and attracts a mixed-age crowd of local residents, international students and resident neighbourhood 'characters'. It's open all day for coffee and food but the nighttime is the right time to go here, hence its name.

Dolce Vita

Piazza del Carmine 6r, Oltrarno (055 284595, www.dolcevitafirenze.it). **Open** *6pm-2am daily.* **Map** *p164 F9.*

Dolce Vita closed and then reopened; it generally attracts an older crowd who

remembers its glory days, but it's still going strong after years of dominance in the summer nights-out stakes. Inside, the cold metal and glass bar leads to a smaller salon, with sofas and soft lighting from beautiful crystal lamps, usually inhabited by those too weary to move on to the clubbing scene.

James Joyce

Lungarno Benvenuto Cellini 1r, Oltrarno (055 6580856, www.facebook.com/ jamesjoycefirenze). **Open** *4pm-2.30am daily. No cards.* **Map** *p164 Q12.*

The large enclosed garden with long wooden tables makes this one of the best of Florence's pubs in spring and summer. Inside, it's equally sprawling, and makes a comfortable hangout during the colder months.

Mad Souls & Spirits

Borgo S. Frediano 36-38r, Oltrarno (055 627 1621, www.facebook.com/ madsoulsandspirits). **Open** *6pm-2am daily.* **Map** *p164 F9.*

Craft cocktails are the bread and butter of this Borgo San Frediano haunt. Here it's more about the art of a stiff drink than socialising with strangers: expect expert descriptions from the bar staff, who will guide you to a choice of cocktail based on the classics you tell them you like. Although you're welcome to order an old-fashioned standard, you should never ask for a Vodka Red Bull. As the detailed cocktail menu states: 'Drink like a serious person'.

Mayday Lounge Café

Via Dante Alighieri 16r, Duomo & Around (055 2381290, www.maydayclub.it). **Open** *7pm-2am Tue-Sat. Closed 2wks Aug.* **Admission** *free, membership required (free).* **Map** *p63 M8.*

This wacky joint with odd art installations and hundreds of old Marconi radios hanging from the ceilings is dark and edgy and has something of a cult following. There's a diverse programme of events to sample.

❤ Best for live music

Glue Alternative Concept Space *p239*
Homegrown acts and international names.

NOF *p239*
Casual locale with upbeat cover bands.

Jazz Club *p239*
For late-night live sets.

❤ Best for dancing

Rex Café *p237*
Easygoing crowd; punchy music.

Babylon *p241*
Downtown disco.

Tenax *p241*
Serious beats.

Negroni

Moyo

*Via de' Benci 23r, Santa Croce (055 2479738, www.moyo.it). **Open** 8am-2 am daily. **Admission** free. **Map** p145 N10.*

The cool wood decor and outdoor seating make for a welcoming year-round environment at this buzzy bar. Come *aperitivo* time, it's packed out with Florentines and students.

❤ Rex Café

*Via Fiesolana 25r, Santa Croce (055 2480331, www.rexfirenze.com). **Open** 6pm-2.30am daily. Closed June-Aug. **Map** p145 P6.*

Clubby Rex is more than a quarter century old and still king of the east of the city, filling up with loyal subjects who sashay to the sounds of the session DJs playing bassy beats and jungle rhythms. Gaudí-esque mosaics decorate the central bar, wrought-iron lamps shed a soft light, while a luscious red antechamber creates welcome seclusion for more intimate gatherings. Tapas are served during the *aperitivo* happy hour (5-9.30 pm), and there are blues, funk and jazz nights, as well as the famed 'Venus' evenings spotlighting local women DJs.

Slowly

*Via Porta Rossa 63r, Duomo & Around (055 0351335, www.slowlycafe.com). **Open** 12pm -2am Mon-Sat. **Map** p63 K8.*

The ultimate chill-out bohemian-chic bar, Slowly is softly lit by candles in mosaic lanterns, with big soft sofas in alcoves, laid-back staff and mellow Buddha Bar sounds when the DJ gets stuck in. Even the inevitable crowds of pretty young things can't break the nice and easy spell. The restaurant overlooking the bar serves imaginative global cuisine.

Soul Kitchen

*Via de' Benci, 34R, Santa Croce (055 263 9772, www.soulkitchenfirenze.it). **Open** 11am-2am Mon-Fri; 6pm-2am Sat & Sun. **Map** p145 O9.*

This is one of the few via de' Benci venues not overflowing with early-20s students and teenagers posing as such. The *aperitivo* spread is one of the tastier ones downtown, and the seating tucked downstairs is a fun mingling area for singles, but can also accommodate groups.

La Terrazza Lounge Bar

*Vicolo dell'Oro 6r, Duomo & Around (055 27265987, www.lungarnocollection.com/ la-terrazza-lounge-bar). **Open** Apr-Oct 2.30-11.30pm daily. **Map** p63 K9.*

In-the-know Florentines mix with hotel guests at sundown for aperitifs at the Hotel Continentale's swanky rooftop bar. The sides of the bar are lined with smart biscuit-coloured upholstered benches, and cocktails are served with crudités and mini-brioches. Occasional yoga classes are even held here. The main attraction, though, is the 360-degree bird's-eye view of the city. The bar is open in the warmer months, or as the Florentines term it, '*la bella stagione*'; although it's officially closed in winter, the season may be extended for a few weeks if the weather is good.

Aperol spritz

In the know
All white on the night

Hard-working, hard-drinking Florentines don't need an excuse for a party, but perhaps you do? If so, make sure you're here for Prima Notte d'Estate (First Night of Summer), colloquially known as Notte Bianca (White Night) on 30 April. Seemingly every street, piazza, park and public space puts out stages, decks, chairs and pop-up bars, and many shops and restaurants keep their doors open all night long. The authorities have tried to reframe Notte Bianca as more of a cultural initiative than a city-wide party, emphasising late-night museum openings, readings and guided tours, but the night's reputation precedes it. A programme of events is posted online a few days before (www.estatefiorentina. it), but if you don't catch it don't worry, you'll probably find yourself meandering through the streets with the rest of the city.

Piazzale Michelangelo at dawn

Zoe

Via de' Renai 13r, Oltrarno (055 243111,
www.zoebar.it). **Open** *9am-2am Sun-Wed,*
9am-3am Thu-Sat. **Map** *p164 N10.*

Zoe's red neon sign lures punters in with
one of the sexier atmospheres among the
Oltrarno's many drinking holes. The long thin
bar area is a proxy catwalk and bassy beats
pump out from the DJ room at the back. Zoe
also has the best red cocktails in town (rule of
thumb: if it's red, drink it).

LIVE MUSIC

One of the best ways to find out about
gigs is to pick up **Firenze Spettacolo**.
This monthly Italian-language magazine
showcases what's hot on the music scene in
Florence. Don't fret if your language skills
aren't up to scratch, there's a sizeable event
calendar in English for live music, from
international musicians and rock bands
to local home-grown jazz musicians. Also
worth a look is the free English-language
news magazine *The Florentine*, which
contains information on upcoming live
events and concerts. Jazz junkies could
also try contacting gig-promoter **Musicus
Concentus** (piazza del Carmine 14, 055
287347, www.musicusconcentus.com) for
more on forthcoming events.
    To book tickets for concerts (regardless of
genre), call the venue directly or contact the
Box Office ticket agency (*see p157*).

Major venues

Nelson Mandela Forum

Piazza Enrico Berlinguer, Viale Paoli 3,
Outside the City Gates (055 678841, www.
mandelaforum.it). Bus 10, 17, 20. **Tickets**
prices vary. No cards. **Map** *p186.*

This 7,000-capacity hall is where Florence
houses major touring artists – Italian stars
like singer Emma Marone and international
acts such as Cirque du Soleil and Mika. *See p254*
Performing Arts.

Sala Vanni

Piazza del Carmine 14, Oltrarno (055
287347, www.musicusconcentus.
com). **Tickets** *prices vary. No cards.*
Map *p164 E9.*

Sadly underused, this warehouse-like
auditorium is a great place to hear progressive
jazz and contemporary classical groups. The
venue hosts an excellent series of concerts
organised by Musicus Concentus in autumn
and winter.

Teatro Obihall

Via Fabrizio de André, nr lungarno A Moro
3, Outside the City Gates (055 6504112,
www.obihall.it). Bus 14. **Tickets** *prices*
vary. **Map** *p186.*

This 4,000-capacity venue hosts mainstream
acts from Italy and abroad – PJ Harvey and
Macy Gray have played here. There are
upper balcony seats, but the main standing
hall downstairs has better sound. *See p254*
Performing Arts.

Teatro dell'Opera

Piazzale Vittorio Gui 1, Outside the City Gates (055 2779309, www.operadifirenze.it). Bus C1, C2, D. Tram T1. Box Office 10am-6pm Tue-Fri, 10am-1pm Sat, 2hrs prior to shows. Season year-round. **Map p186.**

The spectacular open-air venue on the roof of this new, modernistic theatre hosts class acts such as Kraftwerk. *See p250* Performing Arts.

Visarno Arena

Viale Manfredo Fanti 4, Campo di Marte, Outside the City Gates (055 503011). Bus 7, 17, 20. **Tickets** *prices vary. No cards.* **Map p186.**

This converted former racetrack in the Parco delle Cascine has become a major hub for open-air summer concerts and music festivals, hosting everyone from Massive Attack and Sting to Radiohead and Aerosmith.

Smaller venues

Auditorium FLOG

Via M Mercati 24b, Outside the City Gates (055 487145, www.flog.it). Bus 4, 14, 20. **Open** *times vary Tue-Sat. Closed June-Aug.* **Tickets** *€7-€20. No cards.* **Map p186.**

At FLOG, music runs from rock to Tex-Mex rockabilly, reggae and ska, and there's usually a DJ after the bands. Dance parties and theatrical shows take place early in the week, and the venue hosts the world music festival Musica del Popoli and Azione Gay e Lesbica parties (*see p243*).

Combo Social Club

Via Mannelli, 2, Campo Di Marte, Outside the City Gates (340 5385830, www.combosocialclub.com). **Open** *times vary.* **Tickets** *prices vary.* **Map p186.**

Inside, COMBO is pretty bare-bones, a favourite low-ceilinged hangout for hip local music aficionados and record label managers. It doubles as a recording studio during the daytime.

Girasol

Via del Romito 1, Outside the City Gates (055 474948, www.girasol.it). Bus 2, 14. **Open** *7pm-2.30am Tue-Sun. Closed June-Aug.* **Admission** *free.* **Map p186.**

One of the most colourful bars in Florence, Girasol tops the list when it comes to Latin sounds, playing live music pretty well nightly. Instructors from local dance schools occasionally give free lessons in tango and samba to get you in the mood. Drinks are on the pricey side, but the exotic mixes blend in perfectly with the colourful decor.

♥ Glue Alternative Concept Space

Viale Manfredo Fanti 20, Campo Di Marte, Outside the City Gates (www.gluefirenze.com). Bus 10, 17. **Open** *8pm-12.30am Fri, 10pm-2am Sat. €10 membership.* **Admission** *free.* **Map p186.**

Glue is a members-only music haven, but pay for an annual membership card and you'll have access to all concerts and special events, including cinema nights and exhibitions. It's a prime space to see young, budding Florentine bands as well as more established, primarily Italian acts.

Golden View

Via de' Bardi 58r, Oltrarno (055 214502, www.goldenviewopenbar.com). **Open** *noon-2am daily.* **Admission** *free.* **Map p164 K10.**

The uninspiring decor of this restaurant and bar is more than made up for by the direct views afforded of the Ponte Vecchio and the Uffizi. The jazz comes from a resident pianist, in duos and trios on a Monday, Friday and Saturday.

♥ Jazz Club

Via Nuova de' Caccini 3, Santa Croce (055 2479700, www.facebook.com/jazzclubfirenze.it). **Open** *11pm-3am Tue-Thu, Sun; 11pm 4am Fri-Sat. Closed July, Aug.* **Admission** *€6. No cards.* **Map p145 P6.**

One of the few places in Florence where you can hear live jazz almost nightly, this hard-to-find club is worth searching out. It hosts an array of popular local jazz bands, and it has also welcomed notable international acts.

♥ NOF

Borgo S. Frediano, 17/19r, Oltrarno (333 6145376, www.nofclub.it). **Open** *6.30pm-2.30am Mon-Sat.* **Tickets** *prices vary.* **Map p164 F9.**

This Oltrarno hideaway makes an easy watering hole for anyone passing through the area, but it's more famous for its gigs, which always attract a sweaty, dancing, mixed-age crowd. Its music schedule is very sporadic but worth checking out.

Pinocchio Jazz at Circolo Vie Nuove

Viale Giannotti 13, Outside the City Gates (055683388, www.pinocchiojazz.it). Bus 8, 23, 31, 32, 80. **Open** *Nov-Jan 9pm-2am Sat. Closed Feb-Oct.* **Tickets** *€10 €13; €7-€10 reductions; ARCI or UISP membership required.* **Map p186.**

Pinocchio Jazz is a winter music series held at Circolo Vie Nuove, hosting internationally recognised jazz stars such as Roots Magic and Ivan Mazuze Quartet, as well as Italian

Summer Bars & Clubs

How to enjoy those warm evenings with music alfresco

From the end of May to the beginning of September most Florentine nightlife shifts to outdoor venues – or informal gatherings – in *piazze*, gardens and villas. Most venues have free admission and stay open until the small hours. Each summer brings new openings to replace previous closures, as well as the return after absence of established venues.

Popular spots in recent years have included **OFF Bar**, set up in the gardens at the Fortezza da Basso (viale Filippo Strozzi 6, www.facebook.com/off.bar); **Tamburello Benci Bar**, a collective of via de' Benci venues that combine to form a hub at the Parco delle Cascine; and more culture-focused spaces such as outdoor bar **FLOWER** in piazzale Michelangelo (www.facebook.com/flowêralpiazzale), a literary alternative to the glamorous nearby club **Flo** (viale Michelangiolo 82, 055650791, www.flofirenze.com), well known for turning away anyone whose summer outfit isn't up to standard.

Piazza del Carmine also plays host to nightly gigs and events through its **Di Cultura in Piazza** initiative (www.diculturainpiazza. eu), which boasts a seasonal pizzeria to boot. The neighbouring piazza Santo Spirito occasionally hosts special events, too, but the square's church steps, central fountain and cheap bars have a makeshift vibe that's more melting pot-meeting point than true gig venue. Other one-off events are organised in piazza Pitti, the Boboli Gardens and Forte di Belvedere, as well as at the Stazione Leopolda, particularly during the **Fabbrica Europa** performing arts festival in June. Through the music stronghold Visarno Arena, which hosts international giants in the summertime, the **Parco delle Cascine** is experiencing a revival, although most of the park is still considered dodgy after dark. For riverside fun, head to **Fiorino sull'Arno** (lungarno Pecori Giraldi, 328 2013217, www. facebook.com/fiorino.sullarno), a sprawling bar-pizzeria-concert venue and the summer counterpart of **Combo Social Club** (*see p239*), or the can't-go-wrong seasonal favourite **Easy Living** (*see p182*).

Bear in mind that the local council grants permission to these summer-only venues on a year-by-year basis, so the situation can change at any time. Check the local press for details.

artists. Later in the evening, the atmosphere becomes more mellow, with soft jazz filling the air.

Porto di Mare

Via Pisana 128, Outside the City Gates (055712034, www.palcodautore.org). **Open** *7pm-2am Sun; 11am-3pm Mon; 11am-3pm, 7pm-2am Tue-Sat. Closed Aug.* **Admission** *free.* **Map** *p186.*

This club is perfect for a simple night out. Starting at the top floor of the three-tiered club is a rustic pizzeria. On the second floor is a quaint pub with a large TV screen and comfy chairs. Head down to the basement to catch a live show from a local rock or folk musician.

Stazione Leopolda

Via Fratelli Rosselli 5, Outside the City Gates (055 212622, www.stazione-leopolda. com). Bus 1, 9, 12, 16, 17, 26, 27, 80 or tram T1. **Open** *hours vary according to events.* **Tickets** *prices vary.* **Map** *p186.*

This huge disused station is only open for specific events, but you'll find quite a variety, from wine showcases, food fairs and vintage fashion markets to major music events and explosive parties. The Fabbrica Europa performing arts festival is held here (*see p247*).

Tender Club

Via Alemanni 4, Santa Maria Novella (www.facebook.com/tenderclub). **Open** *9.30pm-3.30am Fri & Sat.* **Tickets** *prices vary.* **Map** *p101 F2.*

While the venue itself isn't particularly memorable, Tender is a great place to hear live music – mainly Italian bands and rock – and people-watch Florentine hipsters.

Viper Club

Via Pistoiese, 50145, Outside the City Gates. (055 019 5912, www.viperclub.eu). **Open** *hours vary according to events. Bus 35, 56.* **Tickets** *prices vary.* **Map** *p186.*

Viper is increasingly known for its themed parties put on by branded outfits, such as Hot Shot – '90 in da House! (you read that

---

In the know
ID

The age of consent in Italy is 18; clubs and bars check ID. For some venues, especially cruise clubs and saunas, you will need an ANDDOS or ArciGay/Lesbica membership card, which is available at any of the venues that require it (noted below) – photo ID is required.

---

correctly), a frequent throwback evening paying tribute to the gadgets, trends, tunes and television shows of the 1990s – mostly from across the Atlantic. These events are usually expertly marketed but often involve lengthy queues outside – and since getting to Viper is a bit of a haul, your time is better spent on a more musically oriented night. Viper is one of Florence's best places to catch the latest sounds, whether live – the likes of Black Mountain, Marracash and Italian pop sensation Levante – or in storming DJ sets from international names.

The William

Via Antonio Magliabechi 7r, Santa Croce, (055 2440870, www.thewilliamfirenze.it). **Open** *11am-3am daily.* **Admission** *free.* **Map** *p145 O10.*

This popular, spacious drinking den does a fine line in live music on a tiny stage, where you're just as likely to see an Irish folk musician as a noisy Italian thrash metal band.

CLUBBING

Nightclubs usually charge an admission fee that includes a drink, although some still use the unpopular card system. At these venues, you're given a card that's stamped whenever you buy drinks or use the cloakroom. You then hand the card in at the till and pay before leaving (be warned: don't lose it). Some smaller clubs are members-only, but becoming a member usually just means paying a nominal one-time fee for an annual card.

Nightclubs

❤ Babylon

Via dei Pandolfini, 26/r, Santa Croce. (340 791 3985, www.facebook.com/ BabylonClubOfficialPage). **Open** *11.30pm-4am Sun, Tue & Thur, 11.30pm-4.30am Fri & Sat.* **Admission** *€10.* **Map** *p145 N8.*

Babylon doesn't have many fancy tricks up its sleeve – it's just a fun disco on a couple of different (small) levels that can start to feel a little like a maze once you've had a couple of (modestly priced) drinks. Themed nights are frequent, from Black & White dress code parties to bass-heavy evenings or international student soirees.

❤ Tenax

Via Pratese 46, Peretola, Outside the City Gates (055 308160, www.tenax.org). Bus 29, 30. **Open** *10pm-4am Sat. Closed mid May-Sept. Ticket prices vary.* **Map** *p186.*

The most influential and international of the Florentine clubs is the warehouse-style Tenax in Peretola. Far enough outside the centre to make a night out an adventure, but not too far to be impractical without a car, it's best known as a live venue for hip international bands and for its DJ exchanges. When it's closed in the summer, Tenax also organises one-off events, often in the Stazione Leopolda. Big-name DJ Alex Neri's Nobody's Perfect on Saturday is the hottest night in the city by a long shot, heaving with house, big beat, progressive and drum 'n' bass.

YAB

Via de' Sassetti 5r, Duomo & Around (055 215160, www.yab.it). Open 7pm-4am Mon, Wed, Thur-Sat. Closed June-Sept. Admission free (€15 drinks minimum-spend Fri, Sat). Map p63 K8.

Some refer to this large city-centre locale as a disco; others, a 'glamour club'. You Are Beautiful – popularly known as YAB – has existed since the late 1970s, and plays up to any narcissist tendencies, not only by its name but also its liberal use of mirrors, flattering lighting and on-tap female-focused compliments from the stalwarts. The powerful sound system has the mammoth dancefloor shimmying with dancers (and more than a few handsy-teenager types), while the wall-to-wall bar areas cater to those with tired feet. Downstairs there's a private room that draws the pretty people.

LGBT FLORENCE

Though Florence has been popular with gay writers, artists and travellers for centuries, it was only in 1970 that the city got its first proper gay disco, **Tabasco**, which sadly closed in 2017. Around the same time, the **Fronte Unitario Omosessuale Rivoluzionario Italiano** (FUORI – Italian for 'out'), Tuscany's first gay and lesbian organisation, was set up. Other landmarks include the opening of the gay cultural space **Banana Moon** in borgo degli Albizi in 1977 and the founding of the regional chapter of **ArciGay/Lesbica**, the leading organisation for gay political initiatives in 1980s Italy. In the 1990s, it split into two groups: **IREOS** (www.ireos.org), a social, cultural and information centre (its via dei Serragli 3 location hosts exhibitions, events and gives free HIV testing), and more political **Azione Gay e Lesbica** (www.gayelesbica.it).

The scene

Holding hands in the street in Florence and Tuscany is common among same-sex couples; despite Italy's traditional Roman Catholic culture and Florence's sometimes provincial tendencies, Tuscans tend to be more understanding and progressive towards the LGBT community. In 2004 Tuscany was the first Italian region to ban

Tenax

discrimination against homosexuals in public life. Florence hosted its first Pride parade in 2016, drawing thousands to the streets, including the mayor and regional president, but for the rest of the year, the city's LGBT scene can seem limited and many people prefer to head for Bologna or Rome. However, while the fixed, definitively LGBT spaces are few, many venues host one-off events throughout the year, particularly during the **Florence Queer Festival** in November (*see p228*) or **Pride** season in the spring. In 2016, Pride parties ran at venues such as FLOG (*see p239*) and the Limonaia di Villa Strozzi (via Pisana 77, Oltrarno, www.limonaiastrozzi.it). Limonaia also hosted the first **Toscana Pride Park** in 2016, which featured a week-long series of LGBT-themed DJ sets and parties, performances, lectures and conferences and concerts. Check local press for what's on while you're in town – magazines such as *Firenze Spettacolo* and *Firenze Urban Lifestyle* have dedicated LGBT sections.

▶ *For other LGBT resources in Florence see p302.*

Florence Queer Festival p228

Bars

Crisco Club
Via Sant'Egidio 43r, Santa Croce (055 244080, www.facebook.com/crisco.club). **Open** *10pm-5am daily.* **Admission** *€10-15, incl 1 drink.* **Map** *p145 O7.*

Found in the centre of the city with a cruising area in the cellar, Crisco club's clientele is mainly men, but on the weekend and outside cruising hours, it's a straight-friendly techno/house/electro dance club.

Piccolo Caffè
Borgo Santa Croce 23r, Santa Croce (055 2001057, www.facebook.com/piccolocafefirenze). **Open** *7 pm-2.30am daily.* **Admission** *free.* **Map** *p145 O9.*

Attracting a very mixed crowd of mostly men, the Piccolo Caffè gets especially packed on Friday and Saturday nights. Check out the frequent art exhibitions and live shows.

Queer
Borgo Allegri, 9, Santa Croce (366 275 9210, www.bargayfirenze.it). **Open** *8.30pm-3am daily.* **Admission** *free.* **Map** *p145 Q9.*

A small space with billiard hall games and friendly bartenders, Queer is newish on the LGBT scene and brings together a range of ages and gender identities. Staff are sociable, seating is comfy, cocktails are inexpensive and the mood is light and cheery.

Clubs

Azione Gay e Lesbica at Auditorium FLOG
For listing, see p239 Auditorium FLOG. Once a month on a Friday, a megafest of DJs, cabaret acts and bands draws a huge and diverse crowd out to this Poggetto venue for the 'Necessariamente' evening in support of Azione Gay e Lesbica (*see p301*). It's also a great place to stock up on literature and information.

Fabrik
Viale del Lavoro, 19, Calenzano (349 8906645 mobile, www.fabrikfirenze.it) Bus 2, regional train to Calenzano. **Open** *10pm-3am Wed-Thu & Sun; 10pm-4am Fri-Sat.* **Admission** *with ANDDOS membership €8-€15. No cards.* **Map** *p186.*

About 15km (nine miles) from Florence, Fabrik constitutes two storeys of post-industrial decor, featuring a video-bar and an open-air garden. There's a cruising area with roomy cabins and a darkroom. Entry is reserved to of-age men only.

FAIRY at Full Up
Via della Vigna Vecchia 25r, Santa Croce (www.facebook.com/FairyGold). **Open** *11.30pm-4am Sat.* **Admission** *€12-15 incl. 1 drink.* **Map** *p145 N8.*

This Saturday evening LGBT night isn't exactly known for stellar service, but the crowd is a fun mix of ages and genders and the pop music and occasional drag performances put everyone in a dancing mood. The vibe is less overtly 'cruiser' than some other locales, making it nice for a light night out.

Performing Arts

Despite financial woes, the performing arts scene is thriving

Florence is home to around 15 professionally run theatres and a fluid number of music venues, with more opening each year as historic spaces are restored and fitted with modern equipment, state-of-the-art facilities and the required safety standards. Most theatres host regular programmes and audience numbers are on the rise. Despite this, budget restraints have resulted in short seasons, lower production values and an increasing number of monologues. Most theatre productions are in Italian, but you can find English-language shows and a fair amount of non-verbal theatre, while dance and music performances are, of course, universally enjoyable without language barriers.

Estate Fiesolana

Public funding for the arts has plummeted to an all-time low in recent years, especially for smaller, less established companies. Theatres have learnt the hard way that their only means of escape from the long-term crisis is networking. In Florence and half a dozen neighbouring towns, 20 venues have joined forces to form **Firenze dei Teatri**, an association whose most successful scheme is **Passteatri**, a voucher booklet that allows the holder to pick six performances out of a choice of more than 50. This has finally made theatre-going truly affordable, while encouraging audiences to step out of their comfort zone and try different venues.

Similarly, the regional network **Fondazione Toscana Spettacolo** (www.toscanaspettacolo.it) manages or co-manages theatre, dance and children's seasons for around 50 theatre venues, plus a handful of festivals across Tuscany.

One success story brought about by the shift in public funding policies is the birth (and prompt rise to National Theatre status) of the **della Toscana** *(see p253)*, a joint project of Teatro della Pergola and Pontedera Teatro.

Despite financial worries and gargantuan overheads (it sustains a full orchestra, chorus and armies of staff) Florence's classical music life focuses around the new **Teatro dell'Opera** *(see p250)*, one of Italy's foremost opera houses.

The city's other orchestra, **Orchestra della Toscana** *(see p249)*, is based at the **Teatro Verdi**, while the excellent **Amici della Musica** *(see p248)* chamber music programme takes place at the **Teatro della Pergola**. In the tourist season, Florence is also awash with concerts and small opera stagings, often held in churches or museums, whose standard can sometimes be surprisingly good.

Tickets & timings

You can buy tickets for most venues and events several months in advance from the Box Office ticket agency in Santa Croce (*see p157*) or from its website www.boxol.it. A **Passteatri** booklet costs €48. Unsold seats can be bought from the theatre's ticket office from one hour prior to the performance, but note that smaller or occasional venues may not accept card payments. Many hotels and travel agents also book tickets for major events.

As a rule, Monday is the day off. With the exception of the Teatro dell'Opera where evening shows start at 8pm, the standard time for evening shows (Tue-Sat) is 9pm, while Sunday matinees start around 4pm. In fact, expect the curtains to open around 15 minutes after the stated time. Most of the largest music and theatre seasons run roughly from October to April, while in the summer months the scene transfers to open-air venues and festival performances, including a number of street arts festivals scattered throughout Tuscany.

Festivals

Careggi in Musica

Aula Magna Ospedale di Careggi, Largo Brambilla 3, Outside the City Gates (055 580996, www.agimusfirenze.it). **Date** Oct-May 10.30am Sun.

♥ Best for theatre for kids

Teatro Cantiere Florida *p254*
This theatre hosts Florence's best, and certainly most diverse, junior theatre season.

Pupi di Stac *p254*
Handmade wooden puppets tell traditional fairy tales in miniature theatres.

Il Paracadute di Icaro *p253*
Great entertainment for kids in museums across town.

FESTA *p253*
Shows and workshops for children by Florence's English-language theatre company.

♥ Best immersive experience

Teatro della Pergola *p250*
Behind-the-scenes visits at Florence's top theatre.

Estate Fiesolana *p247*
The hard-to-beat feeling of watching a show as an ancient Roman would have done.

Teatro del Sale *p255*
Performing and culinary arts mingle in informal surroundings.

Zauberteatro *p254*
Hear a captivating story while gliding down the Arno in a boat.

♥ Best international scene

Fabbrica Europa *p247*
Since 1994, the festival showcases performers from across Europe and beyond.

Intercity Festival *p247*
Emerging playwrights from a new city each year.

Teatro Verdi *p255*
Momix, Cirque Éloize and all the big acts stop here.

Teatro di Rifredi *p255*
Check out their International Visual Theatre programme.

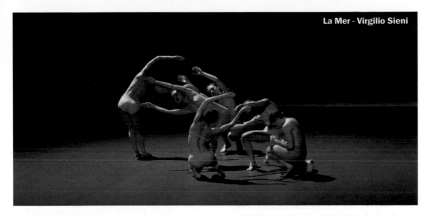
La Mer - Virgilio Sieni

The lecture hall of a working hospital is an unusual backdrop for chamber music, but with more than 550 concerts so far, this must be one of Florence's most active music seasons. **Agimus Firenze** (*see p248*) founded it to provide entertainment to the hospital's patients and their families, but it's free for everyone.

DanzainFiera
Fortezza da Basso, viale Filippo Strozzi 1, Outside the City Gates (0574 575618, www. danzainfiera.it). **Date** *Feb.*

Professionals, amateurs, schools, dance companies and specialist suppliers meet in Florence for a weekend-long international trade show dedicated to ballet, dance and ballroom dancing.

La Democrazia del Corpo
Cango, via Santa Maria 25, Oltrarno (055 2280525, www.virgiliosieni.it). **Date** *Oct-Dec.*

Virgilio Sieni and Teatro della Pergola present a joint project that links the two sides of the city with site-specific performances, shows, productions, residences, meetings and workshops.

Estate al Bargello
National Museum of Bargello, Santa Croce (055 2388606, www.estatealbargello.it). **Date** *May-Sept.*

Staged in the intimate courtyard of the Bargello, the festival offers a pleasant mix of plays and readings selected by the **Teatro della Toscana** (*see p253*), classical concerts by the **Orchestra da Camera Fiorentina** (*see p249*) and a good chunk of the Florence Dance Festival programme (*see p247*).

♥ Estate Fiesolana
Teatro Romano, via Portigiani 1, Fiesole, Outside the City Gates (055 5961293, www. estatefiesolana.it). **Date** *Summer.*

Although in recent years the focus has increasingly shifted onto music, the programme of Italy's oldest open-air festival always includes at least a few theatre and dance shows, usually in July. The fascinating setting and excellent acoustics make up for the extremely uncomfortable seating arrangements on the Roman stone steps, that wafer-thin cushions hardly mitigate (*see p226* Events).

♥ Fabbrica Europa
Stazione Leopolda, viale Fratelli Rosselli 5, Outside the City Gates (055 2480515, www. fabbricaeuropa.net). Bus C1, C2, D. Tram T1. **Date** *May.*

The large space of this former railway station by Porta al Prato is well suited to an international festival of contemporary theatre, music, dance and multimedia arts, which in recent years has also started to expand to other locations across the city and beyond (*see p223* Events).

Florence Dance Festival
Borgo della Stella 23r, Oltrarno (055 289276, www.florencedancefestival.org). **Date** *June-July.*

The festival brings to Florence some of the greatest international names in contemporary, traditional and classical dance (*see p224* Events). It's staged mostly in the courtyard of the Bargello within the **Estate al Bargello** (*see p247*) and at the Teatro Romano in Fiesole within the **Estate Fiesolana** (*see p247*). Other venues include **Teatro Verdi** (*see p255*) and piazza del Carmine in the Oltrarno.

♥ Intercity Festival
Teatro della Limonaia, via Gramsci 426, Sesto Fiorentino, Outside the City Gates (055 440852, www.teatrodellalimonaia.it). Bus 2. **Date** *Sept-Oct.*

Every year the festival presents emerging playwrights from a different city. From New York (1988) to Bucharest (2016) and many more, over three decades Intercity has built a 12,000-strong library of plays and introduced a huge number of authors previously unknown in Italy, notably Sarah Kane.

Magic Florence
Obihall, via Fabrizio de André, Outside the City Gates (055 213496, www.magicflorence. com). Date Feb.

This three-day festival showcases the best Italian magicians and illusionists and is growing bigger by the year.

The Medici Dynasty Show
Il Fuligno, via Faenza 48, San Lorenzo (349 1310441, www.medicidynasty.com). Date year-round with more shows in summer.

This entertaining and original play is performed in English. A concise introduction to Medici history, the show centres on the family's final two heirs; the flamboyant Gian Gastone and future-oriented Anna Maria Luisa, who ensured that the family's art collections would remain in Florence.

O Flos Colende
Cattedrale di Santa Maria del Fiore, piazza Duomo, Duomo & Around (055 2302885 www. operaduomo.firenze.it). Date Apr-Sept. Tickets free.

Translating roughly from the Latin as 'O Venerable Flower', this sacred music festival first took place in 1997 to celebrate the 700th anniversary of the Duomo cornerstone laying. Ranging from organ concerts to Gregorian chants, and from Gospel to Baroque music,

---

In the know
Opera in the making

Conservative Florentines – like most Italians – don't take kindly to directors messing with their favourite operas, and any experimenting is likely to be met with slating critiques and boos from the audience. It wasn't always this way. Back in the 15th century, Florence was on the cutting-edge of musical culture when the Florentine Camerata intellectuals began setting words to music. Pieri and Caccini's *Euridice*, widely considered to be the world's oldest surviving opera, was first performed in the Giardino di Boboli in 1600. Florence's musical importance continued into the early 17th century; after this time, the country's musical focus shifted northwards, with the Venetian school of composition becoming the country's most progressive.

---

the festival offers various free events that are unmissable if they happen to coincide with your visit in Florence. Email ofloscolende@operaduomo.firenze.it to reserve seats or show up early.

CLASSICAL MUSIC & OPERA

Opera has a special place in the heart of many Italians, and if you get the chance to catch an Opera di Firenze production, go for it: a performance of a Puccini or Verdi by a good Italian orchestra and chorus is almost always a worthwhile experience, even though the performances here are rarely innovative. Also keep an eye open for their summer performances at **Palazzo Pitti** (*see p166*); while the acoustics aren't always perfect, the setting is superb.

There's lots on offer in the way of symphonic and chamber concerts, with two resident symphony orchestras, a clutch of smaller groups and a world-class chamber music series. Smaller events are promoted on fly posters and in local media. From June to October there are concerts in churches, plus outdoor concerts at villas, gardens and museums, some of them free.

Performers & promoters
AgiMus Firenze
055 580996, www.agimusfirenze.it.

The Florence branch of the nationwide Associazione Giovanile Musicale organises **Careggi in Musica** (*see p246*) and the yearly international contest Premio Crescendo for musicians between 11 and 30 years old. The AgimusArte orchestra features 25 young performers aged 10-20.

Amici della Musica
055 608420/607440, www.amicimusica.fi.it.

This organisation, founded in 1906, promotes world-class chamber music concerts, mostly at the gorgeous **Teatro della Pergola** (*see p250*), from September through to late April/early May. The annual series always features some of the world's great string quartets and recitalists. Early music groups of the calibre of Fabio Biondi's Europa Galante and Jordi Savall also appear regularly. Afternoon and evening concerts are usually on Saturdays and Sundays.

Coro Viri Galilei
328 0427031, www.gregoriano-virigalilaei.it

A mixed Gregorian choir of about 20 elements. Catch their vesper performances in Santa Croce on the first Saturday of each month between November and May.

L'Homme Armé
055 695000, www.hommearme.it.

Until recently, the repertoire of this small, semi-professional chamber choir ranged from medieval to Baroque, but they have introduced an interesting contemporary element. It gives about ten concerts a year in Florence and runs excellent courses on aspects of early music.

Italian Opera Florence
329 7843935. Tickets www.classictic.com

Young professional musicians and singers perform an almost daily programme of concerts featuring Baroque and classical opera arias, duets and trios in the ex church of Santa Monaca in the Oltrarno.

Opera di Firenze / Maggio Musicale Fiorentino
055 2340710, www.orchestradellatoscana.it.

The **Maggio Fiorentino Orchestra** (named after Florence's historic festival, *see p223* Events) accompanies the symphonic and operatic productions of the Opera di Firenze. Since 1985, its principal conductor is Zubin Mehta. Just as widely appreciated for its versatility is the Maggio Fiorentino Chorus, whose young master Lorenzo Fratini is also in charge of the 66-element Children's Choir.

When on form, the Opera di Firenze orchestra and chorus are considered on a level with La Scala in Milan, but lack of funds means that big-name conductors and soloists are sometimes padded out with unknowns who just don't get the same results.

Orchestra da Camera Fiorentina
055 783374, www.orchestrafiorentina.it.

This young chamber orchestra, under its principal conductor Giuseppe Lanzetta, plays a series of concerts mostly in the museum of **Orsanmichele** (*see p88*) and the **Auditorium di Santo Stefano al Ponte** (*see p77*). It also performs for the **Estate al Bargello** festival in the summer. The venues mean it attracts a good tourist-based audience, but standards vary. Concerts are usually held on Sunday and Monday evenings.

Orchestra della Toscana
055 2340710, www.orchestradellatoscana.it.

The Orchestra della Toscana was founded in 1980 with the brief of taking classical music into Tuscany. It has a dynamic management team and artistic director, who are responsible for a wider repertoire than that of the Maggio Orchestra. Emphasis is placed on rarely heard 19th-century music, early 20th-century composers and contemporary works, but there's plenty more. International names frequently appear as soloists and conductors, and during the season (Oct-May) the orchestra (or smaller ensembles of

Orchestra della Toscana

its members) gives two or three concerts a month at the **Teatro Verdi** (*see p255*), and up to 40 in other Tuscan towns.

Scuola di Musica di Fiesole
055 597851, www.scuolamusicafiesole.it.

One of Italy's most famous music schools occupies a 16th-century villa in beautiful grounds (*see p198*). Founded in 1974 by the charismatic viola player of the Quartetto Italiano, Piero Farulli, it's the home of the Orchestra Giovanile Italiana, the country's number one youth orchestra. The annual Festa della Musica, a musical open day with concerts and workshops by pupils, is held on 24 June, while concerts take place in the **Auditorium Sinopoli** (*see p250*).

Venues

Accademia Bartolomeo Cristofori
*Via di Camaldoli 7r, Oltrarno (055 221646, www.accademiacristofori.it). **Open** by appointment. **Map** p164 D9.*

Named after the piano's inventor, the academy houses a fine private collection of early keyboard instruments. Chamber concerts and seminars are held in a beautiful little hall next door, usually at 9 pm on Tue once a month (Jan-May; tickets €10, €5 reductions).

Auditorium Sinopoli
*Villa La Torraccia, via delle Fontanelle 24, San Domenico, Fiesole, Outside the City Gates (055 597851, www.scuolamusicafiesole.it). Bus 7, then 10 min walk. **Map** p186.*

The 200-seat auditorium of Villa La Torraccia serves as the concert hall of the **Scuola di Musica di Fiesole** (*see p250*) and from January to May hosts free Sunday morning musical performances twice a month.

St Mark's English Church
*Via Maggio 16, Santa Spirito, Oltrarno (340 811 9192, www.concertoclassico.info). **Tickets** €15-€45 opera, €10-€30 concerts. **Map** p164 H10.*

Apart from one or two slight adaptations to suit the intimate setting, the performances for Opera at St Marks are complete operas with professional singers in full costume accompanied on the piano. There are also concerts of opera arias and Neapolitan songs at other times of the year.

Teatro Goldoni
*Via Santa Maria 15, Oltrarno (call Teatro dell'Opera; see below). **Box office** contact relevant organising body. **Season** varies. **Map** p164 F12.*

This divine little theatre in the Oltrarno dates from the early 19th century and seats only 400 people. A long, drawn-out restoration was finally finished in the late 1990s and the theatre is now partially under the direction of the **Opera di Firenze** (*see p249*) on behalf of the city council. It's used – though not regularly enough – for chamber music, small-scale opera and ballet.

Teatro Niccolini
For listings, see Theatre & Comedy

Teatro dell'Opera
*Piazzale Vittorio Gui 1, Outside the City Gates (055 2779309, www.operadifirenze.it). Bus C1, C2, D. Tram T1. **Box office** 10am-6pm Tue-Fri, 10am-1pm Sat, 2hrs prior to shows. **Season** year-round. **Map** p186.*

The brand new, contemporary music hall designed by Paolo Desideri at the mouth of the Cascine Park was inaugurated in December 2011 and is in use only since May 2014. At 1,800 seats, it has roughly the same capacity as the old Teatro del Maggio, but the stage area is twice as big as most opera theatres, proving exciting possibilities for elaborate sets.

The theatre's performing year is divided roughly into three parts: October to April is the main concert and opera season; the **Maggio Musicale Fiorentino** (*see p223 Events*) festival then runs for two months from late April to late June with a mix of opera, ballet, concerts and recital programmes; finally, the summer season is held outdoors between June and July in the Ammannati courtyard of **Palazzo Pitti** (*see p166*). At the same time, the Teatro dell'Opera 2,000-seat open-air auditorium on the theatre's roof hosts quality pop and rock events (*see p239*).

Since MaggioDanza was cut to meet budget constraints, ballet only features occasionally in the programmes. Many seats are taken by holders of season tickets so advance booking is a good idea; otherwise, turn up on the night for the chance of returns. Tickets go on sale at face value through the official website several months in advance, although phone or ticket office purchases are charged 10% extra.

♥ Teatro della Pergola
*Via della Pergola 18-32, San Marco (055 22641 information, 055 0763333 tickets, www.teatrodellapergola.com). **Box office** 9.30am-6.30pm Mon-Sat. **Season** Oct-Apr. **Map** p131 O6.*

Inaugurated in 1661, the exquisite Pergola is one of Italy's oldest theatres. Shakespeare, Pirandello and Goldoni feature regularly in the programme of old and modern classics presented by this historic theatre, which is now part of the **Teatro della Toscana National Theatre** (*see p253*). Watch out for behind-the-scene guided visits on Sunday mornings (advance booking necessary). Richly decorated in red and gold and with three layers of boxes, La Pergola is ideal for chamber music and small-scale operas. The excellent series of chamber music concerts promoted by the **Amici della Musica** (*see p248*) is held here, usually on Saturday afternoons and on Monday evenings when there are no theatre shows.

Teatro Verdi
For listings, see Theatre & Comedy

DANCE

The contemporary dance scene is still lively and Tuscan dance companies have a far more solid international reputation than their theatrical counterparts. Virgilio Sieni's **Cango** was picked by Mibact as one of just three national Centri di Produzione Danza (centres for dance productions). Ballet, however, suffered a big blow when MaggioDanza (the dance ensemble of the Teatro dell'Opera) was axed in 2015.

Dance companies
Compagnia Simona Bucci
055 697823, www.compagniasimonabucci.it.

Choreographer Simona Bucci's company focuses on creating dance shows based on legends and fairy tales, aimed at children aged three to eight.

Compagnia Virgilio Sieni Danza
055 2280525, www.virgiliosieni.it.

Dancer/choreographer Virgilio Sieni directs one of the few local avant-garde dance companies to have achieved global recognition, appointed a Centre for Dance Productions by the Ministry of Culture in 2015. Projects often involve musicians, visual artists and even fashion designers. The company is based at the **Cango** (*see p252*).

Junior Balletto di Toscana
055 351530, www.danzatoscana.it.

Founded and directed by Cristina Bozzolini, this ballet company provides a professional training opportunity for 16 to 21-year-old dancers.

Kaos Balletto di Firenze
392 6849536, www.ballettodifirenze.it,

Roberto Sartori and Katiuscia Bozza's contemporary dance ensemble has a unique, unconventional style that mixes different art forms.

Opus Ballet
055 2335138, www.opusballet.it.

Rosanna Brocanello's dancers combine fine technique and a great versatility, thanks to constant contact with the diverse influences of resident performers, visiting artists and guest choreographers.

Momix, Teatro Verdi

Versiliadanza
055 350986, www.versiliadanza.it.

Dancer/choreographer Angela Torriani Evangelisti founded this small company in 1993. Versiliadanza concentrates on contemporary pieces, but also has experience with Baroque and Renaissance dance. Since 2012, Versiliadanza is the resident dance company at the **Teatro Cantiere Florida** (*see p254*).

Venues

Cango Cantieri Goldonetta Firenze
Via Santa Maria 23-25, Oltrarno (055 2280525, www.virgiliosieni.it). **Box office** *10am-5pm Mon-Fri.* **Seasons** *Sept-Dec, May-June.* **No cards.** **Map** *p164 F12.*

Cantiere (building site) refers to this venue's status as a project-in-progress. As well as performances by the resident **Virgilio Sieni** (*see p251*), there are workshops and festivals.

Florence Dance Cultural Centre
Borgo Stella 23r, Oltrarno (055 289276, www. florencedance.org). **Box office** *varies. Closed Aug.* **Map** *p164 F9.*

Directed by former *étoile* Marga Nativo and American choreographer Keith Ferrone, this eclectic centre hosts a range of dance classes as well as a programme of visual art events called Etoile Toy. It is also the driving force behind the **Florence Dance Festival** (*see p247*).

Teatro Cantiere Florida
For listings, see Theatre & Comedy

Teatro Goldoni
For listings, see Classical music & Opera

Teatro dell'Opera
For listings, see Classical music & Opera

Teatro Verdi
For listings, see Theatre & Comedy

THEATRE & COMEDY

Tuscany has fostered a huge number of talented comedians – think Oscar winner Roberto Benigni – who honed their skills in workers' clubs, village *sagre* (food festivals) and local TV channels. This generation has now risen to national television or cinema blockbuster status, and in Florence they perform before huge audiences in halls like **Obihall** and **Mandela Forum**.

Meanwhile Stefano Massini, one of Italy's best young playwrights – who grew professionally at the **Teatro di Rifredi** (*see p255*) in Florence and the Teatro Manzoni in nearby Calenzano – has been appointed artistic advisor of Milan's prestigious Piccolo Teatro, and his plays (notably the *Lehman Trilogy*, a five-hour saga about the failed bankers), are being staged across the world.

Theatre shows usually run for one week (Tue-Sun or Fri-Sun depending on venues) and hardly ever longer than two, although some successful productions can have re-runs year after year – famously, Pupi & Fresedde's L'ultimo Harem (The Last Harem) was reprised at the Teatro di Rifredi for 11 years running. Details of events can be found in the local press or on the Firenze dei Teatri website (www.firenzedeiteatri.it).

Theatre companies

Compagnia Lombardi Tiezzi
055 600218, www.lombarditiezzi.it.

Director Federico Tiezzi and actor Sandro Lombardi have worked together since 1972. Catch their elegant renderings of classical plays in the seasons of the **Teatro della Toscana** (*see p253*) and during the **Estate al Bargello** (*see p247*) summer festival.

FESTA

Teatro della Toscana

Four venues, one National Theatre: a success story

When the Ente Teatrale Italiano (Italian Theatre Authority) was axed in 2010, the future looked bleak for Florence's public **Teatro della Pergola** (see *p250*). But director Marco Giorgetti had a solid artistic and managerial plan, and the Comune di Firenze came to the rescue together with banking foundation Ente Cassa di Risparmio. The resulting Fondazione Teatro della Pergola has had three successful seasons, with increasingly healthier budgets and growing audiences.

Up to this point, La Pergola had been mostly a presenting venue, and a new reform by the Ministry of Culture threatened it anew by setting in-house production as one of the mandatory requirements for public funding. Thankfully, Giorgetti's ever-resourceful team came up with another brilliant plan: enter the Fondazione Pontedera Teatro from Pontedera, near Pisa, who joined forces with La Pergola and created the **Fondazione Teatro della Toscana**. The bid for funding was successful, and in February 2015 it was picked as one of just seven National Theatres in Italy for the 2015-2017 term.

The change has been momentous: while La Pergola's main season still showcases the finest classical plays by touring companies from across Italy, in its new capacity as **Teatro della Toscana** it now also produces (or co-produces) several plays each year, both enlisting leading directors and encouraging new talent. It also hosts shows, talks and readings in the delightful Saloncino (ballroom); runs workshops, classes and tours; maintains a specialist library and a museum; organises events for children and stages exhibitions. In short, its doors are now open virtually every day of the year, all day and into the late hours.

This bustle of new activity has spread beyond the theatre's historic premises overlooking via della Pergola, with the Fondazione Teatro della Toscana now also managing the **Teatro Niccolini** (see *p254*) and **Teatro Studio Mila Pieralli** (see *p255*) in nearby Scandicci. With their varying sizes and vocations, each of the four venues of the Teatro della Toscana play a different role in the project: La Pergola hosts large-scale, classical productions; the intimate Teatro Niccolini is perfect for monologues and narrative theatre; the modern Teatro Studio in Scandicci serves as a permanent workshop for experimental theatre; while Pontedera's **Teatro Era** combines theatrical research and tradition.

Compagnia delle Seggiole
338 7259209,
www.lacompagniadelleseggiole.it.

Fabio Baronti and his company specialise in site-specific theatre journeys and dramatised guided visits, including the hugely successful ones offered at the **Teatro della Pergola** (see *p253*). Other locations include the **Certosa del Galluzzo** (see *p188*), **Palazzo Davanzati** (see *p95*) and **Museo Casa Martelli** (see *p120*). Its signature show however is Niccolò Macchiavelli's Mandragola.

❤ FESTA
www.facebook.com/festatheatre.

The Florence English Speaking Theatrical Artists (FESTA) is a group of theatre professionals dedicated to providing English-language theatrical activities and shows for English-speakers, including children.

Magma
055 5535626, www.magmafirenze.it.

Magma (short for Magnoprog Music & Arts) specialises in musical shows and performs in different venues across Florence and Tuscany. Its *Rocky Horror*

Nights are a Hallowe'en, New Year's Eve and Carnival staple.

Murmuris
329 9160071, www.murmuris.it.

Murmuris is the resident company at the **Teatro Cantiere Florida** (see *p254*), where it is in charge of the *Materia Prima* (raw matter) season devoted to experimental theatre and young companies.

❤ Il Paracadute di Icaro
333 9562624, www.ilparacadutediicaro.it.

Il Paracadute di Icaro offers children's shows inspired by Italo Calvino's *Novelle Italiane* (Italian fairy tales). Besides the family shows at the **Teatro di Rifredi** (see *p255*), catch them in several museums including the **Museo Marino Marini** (see *p106*).

Pupi e Fresedde
055 4220361, www.toscanateatro.it.

Founded in 1976, the managing company of the **Teatro di Rifredi** (see *p255*) is named after Peter Schumann's politically radical Bread & Puppet theatre. It has an eclectic repertoire of original titles about literature, science, current social issues and the Tuscan dialect.

♥ Pupi di Stac
055 3245099, www.pupidistac.it.

Stac is short for Carlo Staccioli, the company's founder in 1946. His peculiar style of telling traditional fairy tales with old-school wooden pupi (puppets) continues a few generations down the line and still bewitches Florentine children... of all ages!

♥ Zauberteatro
055 5000640, www.zauberteatro.com.

Since 1985, Zauberteatro produces and stages site-specific shows in unusual settings. For several years now, it has been offering evening shows onboard the boats of the old renaioli (sand diggers) on the river Arno, in collaboration with the **Estate Fiorentina** (*see p224*).

Venues

Obihall Teatro di Firenze
Via Fabrizio de André, nr lungarno Aldo Moro 3, Outside the City Gates (055 6504112, www.obihall.it). Bus 14. **Tickets** *prices vary.* **Map** *p186.*

Crowd-pullers such as big-hitting musicals, TV stars and large-scale gigs usually transfer to this 4,000-seater, which also hosts ballroom dancing festivals. *See p238* Nightlife.

Mandela Forum
Viale Paoli 3, Outside the City Gates (055 678841, www.mandelaforum.it). Bus 10,17,20. **Tickets** *prices vary.* **Map** *p186.*

Stand-up comedians such as Giorgio Panariello, Maurizio Crozza or Beppe Grillo need this 7,000-capacity hall (and often multiple performances) to accommodate their fans, as do family pleasers such as *Disney on Ice* or modern operas such as *Notre-Dame de Paris. See p238* Nightlife.

♥ Teatro Cantiere Florida
Via Pisana 111r, Outside the City Gates (055 7135357, www.teatroflorida.it). Bus 6, 26, 27. **Box office** *10am-6pm Mon-Fri, 1hr prior to show time.* **Season** *Oct-Apr.* **No cards.** **Map** *p186.*

This bare-walled 288-seat theatre aims to promote young performers, directors and authors of both theatre and dance, and to appeal to young audiences. Productions range from reworks of Shakespearean classics to experimental pieces. Family shows are on Sunday afternoons.

Teatro Niccolini
Via Ricasoli 3, Duomo & Around. Information and tickets Teatro della Pergola (see p250). **Season** *Oct-Apr.* **Map** *p63 M6.*

Dating from 1648, Teatro Niccolini is the oldest theatre in Florence. It finally reopened in 2016 after 20 years of neglect thanks to publishing entrepreneur Mauro Pagliai, who restored it to its former glory. Its theatre season is part of the **Teatro della Toscana** (*see p253*).

Pupi di Stac

La Bastarda di Istanbul, Teatro di Rifredi

Teatro della Pergola
For listings, see Classical Music & Opera

Teatro Puccini
Via delle Cascine 41 (piazza Puccini), Outside the City Gates (055 362067, www. teatropuccini.it). Bus 17, 30, 35. **Box office** *4-7pm Thur-Sat.* **Season** *Oct-Apr.* **No cards.** **Map** *p186.*

Housed in a 1940s listed building, the Puccini focuses on comedy and satirical shows but also hosts a well-loved programme for young audiences.

♥ Teatro di Rifredi
Via Vittorio Emanuele 303, Outside the City Gates (055 4220361, www.teatrodirifredi.it). Bus 8, 14, 20, 28. **Box office** *4-7pm Mon-Sat.* **Season** *Oct-May.* **No cards.** **Map** *p186.*

A programme devoted mainly to contemporary and fringe shows with an emphasis on emerging playwrights and directors. There's also the odd classic production, plus appearances by guest companies. Non-Italian speakers will appreciate their unique offer of international visual theatre artists. Kids are also well catered for in collaboration with **Il Paracadute di Icaro** (*see p253*).

♥ Teatro del Sale
Via de' Macci 111r, Santa Croce (055 2001492, www.teatrodelsale.com). Closed Sun-Mon all year, Aug. Membership required. **Map** *p145 R7.*

It's hard to tell whether this is a stage with restaurant, or the reverse. The shows are free but club membership is required, and you will find all the seats taken unless you come early and join the buffet dinner (*see p158* **Teatro del Sale**). There are around 240 events (usually stand-up comedy or music gigs) every year, Tuesday to Saturday. See website for details.

Teatro Studio Mila Pieralli
Via Donizetti 58, Scandicci, Outside the City Gates (055 7351023, www. teatrostudioscandicci.it). Tram T1. **Tickets** *Teatro della Pergola (see p250) prior to show time only.* **Season** *Oct-May. Special projects Oct-Dec.* **Map** *p186.*

This unusual space (formerly a school gym) is the latest addition in the **Teatro della Toscana** (*see p253*) network, and one of the best spots to see alternative theatre.

♥ Teatro Verdi
Via Ghibellina 99, Santa Croce (055 212320, www.teatroverdionline.it). **Box office** *10am-1pm, 4-7pm Mon-Fri.* **Season** *Oct-Mar.* **Map** *p145 O8.*

The city's largest theatre at just over 1,500 seats, Teatro Verdi hosts all the top-notch light comedies, musicals and dance shows whose lavish sets and elaborate choreography would not fit in any of the smaller venues in town. The theatre is also home to the 45-element **Orchestra della Toscana** (*see p249*), with midweek concerts between October and May.

Understand

256

The Last Judgement (Giorgio Vasari and Federico Zuccari, 1579), Duomo

History

Past glories and gory stories: how a tiny outpost became the birthplace of the modern world

Practically the whole of Florence's reputation rests on its history – a tale that stretches back to an almost forgotten European civilisation and takes in some of the most monumental cultural shifts of the last 500 years. Thirteen centuries of war, creativity, innovation, natural disaster, astonishing minds, crafty hands and business cunning have shaped the city from a tiny Roman settlement to the cradle of the Renaissance; and beyond that, to its present cumbersome role of as one of the most treasured shrines of western art.

►*About the author*

Nicky Swallow is a freelance writer who has been based in Florence for over 30 years. She is the author of several travel books on Italy.

Detail of Pianta della Catena (Francesco di Lorenzo Rosselli, c1471-1482)

The early years

From around the eighth century BC, much of central Italy was controlled by the Etruscans, who may have drifted in from Asia Minor. Etruscan city states in what is now Tuscany were Volterra, Populonia, Arezzo, Chiusi and Cortona. The Etruscan civilisation reached its peak in the seventh and sixth centuries BC, when their loose federation of cities dominated much of what is now southern Tuscany and northern Lazio. At the end of the seventh century BC, the Etruscans even captured the small town of Rome and ruled it for a century before being expelled. The next few hundred years witnessed city fighting city and tribe battling tribe, until the emerging Roman republic overwhelmed all by the third century BC.

The Etruscans had entirely overlooked the site that we now know as Florence, making hilltop Fiesole (*see p198*) their northernmost stronghold. But in 59 BC, Julius Caesar established a colony for army veterans along the narrowest stretch of the Arno, and Florentia was born. Strategically located at the heart of the Italian territory, it grew into a flourishing commercial centre, becoming the capital of a Roman province in the third century AD.

In typical Roman style, Florentia's street plan was characterised by a grid of straight roads crossing at right angles, still identifiable around today's piazza della Repubblica (where the Roman Forum once stood). Archaeological digs have located Florentia's Roman baths, the sewage system, some temples and the theatre, whose ruins can be visited underneath Palazzo Vecchio (*see p78*). Just west of piazza Santa Croce, via Torta, via Bentaccordi and piazza Peruzzi mark the curved perimeter of the amphitheatre.

The shaping of Tuscany

In the fifth century, the Western Roman Empire finally crumbled. After three centuries of Barbarian rampages that left the area badly battle-scarred, in the eighth century much of the country finally came under the (at least nominal) control of emperor Charlemagne. In practice though, local warlords carved out feudal fiefs for themselves and threw their weight around.

The imperial margravate of Tuscany began to emerge as a region of some promise during the tenth and 11th centuries. On her death in 1115, Matilde di Canossa had established Florence, Siena and Lucca as independent city-states, or *comuni*. As a prosperous merchant class developed in cities all over Tuscany, the region sought to throw off the constraints and demands of its feudal overlords and became a patchwork of tiny, but increasingly self-confident and ambitious, independent entities. The potential for conflict was huge, and by the 13th century it had crystallised into the intractable, seemingly interminable, struggle of Guelphs and Ghibellines.

Guelphs versus Ghibellines

The names Guelph and Ghibelline were the distorted Italian forms of Welf (the family name of the German emperor Otto IV) and Waiblingen (a castle belonging to the Welfs' rivals for the role of Holy Roman Emperor, the Hohenstaufen), but by the time the appellations crossed the Alps into Italy (probably in the 12th century), their significance had changed.

'Guelph' was attached primarily to the increasingly influential merchant classes. In their continuing desire to be free from imperial control, they looked around for a powerful backer and found one in the emperor's enemy, the pope. Anyone keen to uphold imperial power and opposed to papal designs and rising commercial interests – mainly the old nobility – became known as a 'Ghibelline'.

Although bad feeling had been simmering for decades, it was a family feud that sparked the open conflict in 1215. Into and throughout the 14th century, power ebbed and flowed between the two (loosely knit) parties across Tuscany and from city to city, but antagonism flourished within the parties too. In around 1300, open conflict broke out within the Guelphs between the virulently anti-imperial 'Blacks' and the more conciliatory 'Whites', with the former eventually booting out the latter for good. Among those sent into exile was the poet and philosopher Dante Alighieri.

Eventually, the Guelph/Ghibelline conflict ran out of steam. It says much for the energy, innovation, graft and skill of the Tuscans that throughout this stormy period, the region was booming economically.

Medieval might

By the beginning of the 14th century, Florence was one of the five biggest cities in Europe, with a population of almost 100,000. Despite the 1348 plague epidemic that carried off an estimated half of the population, the city prospered, due in no small part to its woollen cloth industry, whose *ciompi* (wool carders) formed guilds and gained representation in city government. By the mid 1380s, the three guilds formed in the wake of the uprising began to lose ground to the *popolo grasso* (wealthy ruling class; literally, plump citizens), a small group of the wealthiest merchant families, who had united with the Guelphs to form an oligarchy in 1382. The *popolo grasso* held sway in the *signoria* (governing authority) for 40 years, during which time intellectuals and artists were becoming increasingly involved in political life.

Not all of Florence's business community backed the *popolo grasso*. Banker Cosimo de' Medici's stance against the extremes of the *signoria* gained him the support both of other dissenting merchants and of the *popolo minuto* (poor workers) of the less-influential guilds. Cosimo's mounting popularity alarmed the *signoria*, and the dominant Albizi family had him exiled on trumped-up charges in 1433. A year later he returned to Florence by popular consent and – with handy military backing from his allies in Milan – was immediately made first citizen, becoming 'king in all but name'. For most of the next 300 years, the dynasty remained more or less firmly in Florence's driving seat (see p263 A Medici Who's Who).

A family affair

Cosimo's habit of giving large sums to charity and endowing religious institutions with art helped make Florence a centre of artistic production. And by persuading representatives of the Eastern and Western churches to try to mend their schism at a conference in Florence in 1439, he hosted Greek scholars who could sate his hunger for classical literature. This artistic and intellectual fervour gathered steam through the long 'reign' of his grandson Lorenzo il Magnifico, which saw Florence become, for a while, the intellectual and artistic centre of the Renaissance that was about to transform Christendom. Under his de facto leadership, Florence enjoyed a long period of relative peace, aided to some extent by Lorenzo's diplomatic skills in minimising squabbles between Italian states.

By the end of the 15th century, Lorenzo's son Piero had handed Florence to the French king Charles VIII as he passed through on his way to Naples. Florence turned for inspiration and guidance to Girolamo Savonarola (1452-98), a fire-and-brimstone-preaching monk who perfectly captured the end-of-century spirit, winning a fanatical devotion: not only of the poor and uneducated, but also of artists and art patrons who willingly threw their works and finest possessions onto the monk's 'Bonfire of the Vanities' in piazza della Signoria in 1497 (see p76).

Savonarola set up a semi-democratic government, firmly allied to Charles VIII, then allowed his extremist tendencies to get the better of him, alienating the Borgia pope Alexander VI and getting excommunicated. Florence's desperate economic state saw

Execution of Girolamo Savonarola in Piazza della Signoria (Francesco di Lorenzo Rosselli)

the region devastated by pestilence and starvation, and resentment turned on Savonarola, who was summarily tried and burned at the stake in piazza della Signoria in May 1498.

The republic created after his death was surprisingly democratic but increasingly ineffective, making stronger leadership look enticing to disaffected Florentines. In 1502, Piero Soderini, from an old noble family, was elected *gonfalonier* (banner bearer) for life, along the model of the Venetian doges. His pro-French policies brought him into conflict with the pro-Spanish pope Julius II, who had Cardinal Giovanni de' Medici whispering policy suggestions in his ear. In 1512, Soderini went into exile. Giuliano de' Medici, Duke of Nemours, was installed as Florence's most prominent citizen, succeeded by his nephew Lorenzo, Duke of Urbino. The family's already considerable clout was reinforced in 1513 when Giovanni became Pope Leo X. The Medici clan got a second crack at the papacy in 1524, when Giulio, Lorenzo's illegitimate nephew, became Clement VII, only to enrage the Habsburg emperor Charles V, who humiliated him in Rome. Back in Florence, the local populace exploited the Medici ignominy in Rome to reinstall a short-lived republic, but the city was back in Medici hands by 1530 when Clement brought Alessandro to power and Charles V made him hereditary Duke of Florence. Buoyed by support from Charles, whose daughter he had married, the authoritarian Alessandro trampled on Florentines' traditional rights and privileges, and the city entered one of its most desperate periods.

His successor, Cosimo I, had different, though no less unpleasant, defects; nor was he much cop at reversing Tuscany's gentle slide into the economic doldrums. Still, this dark horse – whom the pope made the first Grand Duke of Tuscany in 1569 – at least gave the city a patina of action, extending the writ of the *granducato* to all of Tuscany except Lucca, and adorning the city with vast new *palazzi*, including the Uffizi and Palazzo Pitti.

A squalid end

Cosimo's descendants continued to rule for 150 years: they were fittingly poor rulers for what was by now a very minor statelet in the chessboard of Europe. The *granducato*'s farming methods were backward and the European fulcrum of wool-making and banking had shifted to Northern Europe, leaving Florence to descend inexorably into depression. Its glory – and a very dusty glory it was – hung on its walls and adorned its palaces, with only the occasional spark

of intellectual fervour (such as Cosimo II's spirited defence of Galileo Galilei when the astronomer was accused of heresy) to recall what the city had once represented.

Florence's dusty glory hung on its walls and adorned its palaces with only the occasional spark of intellectual fervour to recall what the city once represented

The male Medici line came to a squalid end in the shape of Gian Gastone, who died in 1737. His pious sister Anna Maria handed over the *granducato* to the House of Lorraine, cousins of the Austrian Habsburgs. Grand Duke Francis I and his successors spruced up the city, knocked its administration into shape, introduced new farming methods and generally shook the place out of its torpor. Tuscany even made history again when the Grand Duchy formally abolished capital punishment on 30 November 1786.

Napoleon's triumphant romp down the peninsula at the end of the 18th century brought him into possession of Tuscany in 1799, to the joy of liberals and the horror of local peasantry, who drove the French out in the Viva Maria uprising, during which they also wreaked their revenge on unlucky Jews and anyone suspected of Jacobin leanings.

It wasn't long before the French returned, installing Louis de Bourbon of Parma as head of the Kingdom of Etruria in 1801. Napoleon's sister, Elisa Baciocchi, was made Princess of Piombino and Lucca in 1805, and Grand Duchess of Tuscany from 1809 to 1814.

Unification across the nation

By the 1820s and 1830s, under the laid-back if not overly bright Grand Duke Leopold II, Tuscany enjoyed a climate of tolerance that attracted intellectuals, dissidents, artists and writers from all over Italy and Europe.

For a time, Leopold and his ministers kept the influence of the Grand Duke's uncle, Emperor Francis II of Austria, at arm's length, while also playing down the growing populist cry for Italian unification. But by the 1840s, even relaxed Florence was swept up in nationalist enthusiasm, causing Leopold to clamp down on reformers and

A Medici Who's Who
The good, the bad and the ugly of a legendary dynasty ▶

The name Medici (pronounced with the stress on the 'e') is all but synonymous with Florence, where the family's largely well-judged patronage funded some of the world's greatest artworks. The name's etymology suggests that the family's origins probably lie in the medical profession, though their later wealth was built on banking. Many of their bodies are interred in the Cappelle Medicee (*see p121*).

Giovanni di Bicci (1360-1429)
The fortune Giovanni di Bicci quietly built up through his banking business – boosted immensely by handling the papal account – provided the basis for the Medici's later clout. He sat on the committee that appointed Ghiberti to make the Baptistery doors.

Cosimo 'il Vecchio' (1389-1464)
Cosimo 'the Elder', Giovanni di Bicci's son, ran Florence informally from 1434, presiding over one of the city's most prosperous and prestigious eras. An even more astute banker than his father, he spent lavishly on charities and public building projects, introducing a progressive income tax system and balancing the interests of the volatile Florentine classes relatively successfully. Cosimo was also an intellectual who encouraged new Humanist learning and developments in art, built up a wonderful public library (see *p124* Biblioteca Medicea Laurenziana) and financed scholars and artists. He also had a magnificent town mansion built by Michelozzo (see *p120* Palazzo Medici Riccardi), where the family would reside for the next century.

Piero 'il Gottoso' (1416-69)
All the Medici suffered from gout, but poor Piero the Gouty's joints gave him such gyp that he had to be carried around for half his life. During his short spell at the helm he proved a surprisingly able ruler: he crushed an anti-Medici conspiracy, maintained the success of the Medici bank and patronised the city's best artists and architects.

Lorenzo 'il Magnifico' (1449-92)
Cosimo's grandson Lorenzo was the major Medici, famous in his own time and legendary in later centuries. Lorenzo was a gifted poet, and he gathered around him a supremely talented group of scholars and artists. The climate of intellectual freedom he fostered was a major factor in some of the Renaissance's greatest achievements.

Lorenzo maintained a façade of being no more than primus inter pares ('first among equals'), and he was a tactful leader who significantly contributed to bringing peace to Italy, but he could be ruthless with his enemies. As a businessman, though, he wasn't a patch on his predecessors and the Medici bank suffered a severe decline.

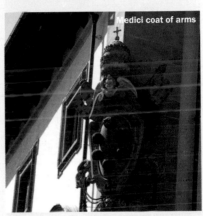
Medici coat of arms

Piero di Lorenzo (1471-1503)
Lorenzo's eldest son Piero, 'the Unfortunate', couldn't live up to his father: ruthless, charmless and tactless, he had a violent temper, no sense of loyalty and a haughty wife. His father described him as foolish, and he did nothing to help his cause when he surrendered the city to the French in 1494. He spent the rest of his days skulking around Italy, trying to persuade unenthusiastic states to help him regain power in a Florence that had no wish to see his mug again.

Giovanni, Pope Leo X (1475-1521)
Il Magnifico's second son wasn't as inept as his brothers, and Lorenzo decided early on that Giovanni would be destined for a glittering ecclesiastical career. Serious papal ear-bending ensured he became a monk at eight, a cardinal at 16 and pope by 1513. Pope Leo was a likeable, open character and, though lazy, he was a generous host and politically conciliatory. He was also a collector and patron of the arts – his favourite artists being Michelangelo and Raphael – but his exploitation of the sale of indulgences to pay for his lavish lifestyle prompted Martin Luther's momentous schism.

Castello di Montegufoni

impose some censorship. Yet in 1848 – a tumultuous year of revolutions throughout Italy – insurrections in Livorno and Pisa forced Leopold to grant concessions to the reformers, including a Tuscan constitution.

When news reached Florence that the Milanese had driven the Austrians out of their city, and that Carlo Alberto, King of Sardinia-Piedmont, was determined to push them out of Italy altogether, thousands of Tuscans joined the cause. A turbulent decade followed until, in April 1859, the French and Piedmontese swept the Austrian armies before them. In Florence, nationalist demonstrations forced the government to resign and on 27 April, Leopold left Tuscany for the last time. The following year, the Tuscan people voted in favour of unification with the Kingdom of Piedmont.

Capital of Italy

Five years later, with Rome holding out against the forces of unification, Florence was declared temporary capital of Italy. The Florentines greeted their new king with enthusiasm when he arrived in February 1865 to take up residence in Palazzo Pitti *(see* p166), but the influx of northerners was met with mixed feelings: business boomed, but the Florentines didn't take to Piedmontese flashiness.

Huge changes were wrought to the city. Ring roads encircled the old centre, avenues, squares (such as piazza della Repubblica) and suburbs were built, and parks were laid out. Intellectuals and socialites crowded the salons and cafés.

Florence's brief reign as capital ended when Rome finally fell to Vittorio Emanuele's troops in 1870 and Italy was united for the first time since the fall of the Roman Empire.

Fascism and war

Florence began the 20th century pretty much as it ended it – as a thriving tourist centre. In the early 1900s, it drew an exclusive coterie of writers, artists, aesthetes and the upper-middle classes. An English-speaking industry sprang up to cater for the needs of these wealthy foreigners.

The city was neither occupied nor attacked in World War I, though it suffered. Post-war hardship inspired a fierce middle-class rage for order that found expression in the black shirt of Fascism. Groups of *squadristi* (the paramilitary wing of the National Fascist Party) were already forming in 1919, organising parades and demonstrations in the streets of Florence.

When Mussolini was elected in 1923, there began in Florence a campaign to expunge the city of foreign elements and influences. Hotels and shops with English names were put under pressure to sever their Anglo-Saxon affiliations. The Florence that had been described as a *ville toute anglaise* by the French social-historian Goncourt brothers was under threat.

Italy entered the war on Germany's side on 10 June 1940. The Florentines were confident that their city would never be attacked from the air: Florence was a museum, a testament to artistic evolution, and its monuments were surely its best protection. Nevertheless, the Fascist regime, perhaps for propaganda reasons, began protecting the city's art. Photos of the period show statuary disappearing inside comically inefficient wooden sheds, while the Baptistery doors were bricked up and many treasures from the Uffizi and Palazzo Pitti were taken for safe-keeping to the Castello di Montegufoni – owned by the British Sitwell family – away in the Tuscan countryside.

The Germans occupied Florence on 11 September 1943, just weeks after Mussolini was arrested and the armistice signed. Only when it became necessary to

A Medici Who's Who
The good, the bad and the ugly of a legendary dynasty ▶

Giuliano, Duke of Nemours (1478-1516)
The third son of Lorenzo was an improvement on his brother Piero only in the sense that he was more nonentity than swine. Giuliano was ruler of Florence in name only, being little more than a puppet of his brother, Cardinal Giovanni, who went on to become Pope Leo X.

Giulio, Pope Clement VII (1478-1534)
Lorenzo's illegitimate nephew, Giulio had honours heaped on him by his cousin, Pope Leo, until he swung the papacy in 1524. Pope Clement was notorious for his indecision, disagreeable personality and disloyalty. He abandoned his alliance with Charles V only to regret it when the emperor's troops sacked Rome in 1527.

Lorenzo II, Duke of Urbino (1492-1519)
The son of Piero di Lorenzo was puny, arrogant, high-handed and corrupt. Few wept when he died of tuberculosis and syphilis. His only significant legacy was his daughter, Catherine, who, as wife and then widow of Henri II, wielded considerable power in France.

Alessandro (1510-37)
Officially the son of the Duke of Urbino, but thought by many to be in fact Pope Clement's illegitimate son, Alessandro abandoned all pretence of respect for the Florentines' treasured institutions and freedoms: he tortured and executed his opponents and managed to outrage the good Florentine burghers by his appalling rudeness and sexual antics. A deputation of senior figures complained to Charles V to no avail. He was assassinated by order of Lorenzino, his distant relative and supposed bosom buddy.

Cosimo I (1519-74)
With no heir in the direct Medici line, the Florentines chose the 18-year-old grandson of Lorenzo il Magnifico's daughter Lucrezia, thinking they could manipulate him. But they could not have been more wrong: cold, secretive and cunning, Cosimo set about ruling with merciless efficiency. His general unpleasantness, however, did not stop him from restoring stability in Florence and boosting the city's international image. He was granted the title of Grand Duke of Tuscany by Pope Paul V in 1569, and he was the first Medici to move out of Palazzo Medici and settle with his family first in the Palazzo della Signoria (see p78 Palazzo Vecchio), then in

Palazzo Pitti (see p166). Vasari and Bronzino were his favourite court artists.

Francesco I (1541-87)
Short, skinny, graceless and sulky, Francesco had little in common with his father Cosimo. He retreated into his own little world at any opportunity, to play with his pet reindeer, dabble in alchemy and invent a new process for porcelain production.

Ferdinando I (1549-1609)
Ferdinando was an improvement on his brother Francesco. He reduced corruption, promoted trade and farming, encouraged learning and developed both the navy and the port of Livorno. By staging lavish popular entertainments and giving dowries to poor girls, he became the most loved Medici since Lorenzo il Magnifico.

Cosimo I

Florence floods in November 1966

hinder the Nazis' communication lines to Rome were aesthetic scruples set aside: in September 1943, a formation of American bombers swooped in to destroy Florence's Campo di Marte station. The operation was bungled, leaving 218 civilians dead, while the station remained in perfect working order. Further air raids were banned by orders from the highest levels.

At the beginning of the war, Florence had a Jewish population of more than 2,000. The chief rabbi saved the lives of many Jews in the city by advising them to hide in convents or little villages under false names. Still, three raids were carried out by Nazis and Fascists on the night of 27 November 1943. The largest of them was on the Franciscan Sisters of Mary in piazza del Carmine, where dozens of Jews were concealed. The second train to leave Italy bound for the gas chambers set out from Florence, carrying at least 400 Jews from Florence, Siena and Bologna; not one of them is known to have returned.

By 1944, allied commanding officers had extracted permission from their leaders to attack Florence using only the most experienced squadrons, in ideal weather conditions. On 11 March, the Americans began unleashing their bombs on the city, causing casualties but leaving the *centro storico* and its art intact. On 1 August, fighting broke out in various parts of the city, but poorly armed Florentine patriots couldn't prevent the Germans from destroying all the Arno bridges except the Ponte Vecchio. Along with the bridges, the old quarter around the Ponte Vecchio was razed to the ground.

British and US infantry reinforced their lines on the Arno on 1 September 1944. The German army abandoned Fiesole a week later. When the Allies eventually reached Florence, they discovered a functioning government formed by the partisan Comitati di Liberazione Nazionale (CLN). Within hours of the Germans' departure, work started to put the bridges back into place. The ponte Santa Trinita was rebuilt, stone by stone, in exactly the same location.

Ordeal by fire and water

Two decades later, the Florentine skill at restoration was required again, this time for a calamity of an altogether different nature: in the early hours of the morning of 4 November 1966, citizens awoke to find their homes flooded by the Arno, which had broken its banks; soon all the main *piazze* were under water. An estimated 15,000 cars were destroyed, 6,000 shops put out of business and almost 14,000 families left homeless. Many artworks, books and archives were damaged, treasures in the refectory of Santa Croce were blackened by mud, and in the church's nave Donatello's *Cavalcanti Annunciation* was soaked with oil up to the Virgin's knees. As word of the disaster spread around the world, public and private funds were pumped into restoration, and young volunteers from across the globe came to the rescue, earning the name of *angeli del fango* ('mud angels').

The city's cultural heritage took yet another direct hit in May 1993, when a bomb planted by the Mafia exploded in the city centre, killing five people. It caused

A Medici Who's Who

The good, the bad and the ugly of a legendary dynasty

Cosimo II (1590-1621)
The son of Ferdinando I, Cosimo protected Galileo from a hostile Catholic Church – the only worthwhile thing he would ever do.

Ferdinando II (1610-70)
Porky, laid-back, moustachioed Ferdinando did little to pull Florence from the backwater into which it had sunk. He loved to hunt, eye up boys and collect bric-a-brac.

Cosimo III (1642-1723)
Though trade was drying up and plague and famine stalked the land, Cosimo, a joyless, gluttonous, anti-Semitic loner, did nothing to improve Tuscany's lot during his 53 years at the helm. Instead, intellectual freedom took a nosedive, taxes soared and public executions were a more or less daily occurrence.

Gian Gastone (1671-1737)
Cosimo's disaster of a son was forcibly married to Anna Maria Francesca of Saxe-Lauenberg, who dragged him off to her gloomy castle near Prague, where he drowned his sorrows in taverns before escaping back to Florence in 1708. He was shocked to find himself heir to the Grand Duchy after his elder brother's early death in 1723. In the early years of his rule, he tried to relieve the tax burden and reinstate citizens' rights, but quickly lapsed into chronic apathy and dissolution.

Anna Maria Luisa, Electress Palatine (1667-1743)
Every visitor to Florence since the mid-18th century has reason to be grateful to the straight-laced, pious Anna Maria, who was Gian Gastone's sister and the very last surviving Medici. In her will, she bequeathed all Medici property and treasures to the Grand Duchy in perpetuity, on the sole condition that they never leave Florence.

Anna Maria Luisa

structural damage to the Uffizi, destroying the Georgofili library and damaging the Corridoio Vasariano. Not that you'd know it now: in a restoration job carried out in record time, one of the world's most-visited art repositories was returned to its pristine state and tourists began queuing outside again, confirming the modern city's vocation for living off its past.

In recent years, however, the Florentines have faced several long-needed structural changes to their city. While most of the action is going on outside the city gates, a lot is also happening behind the façades of the old centre (*see p26* Florence Today). At the same time – after a few decades in the backwaters of Italian politics – Florence has risen to the limelight again, after its former mayor, Matteo Renzi, took Rome by storm and became Italy's youngest-ever prime minister, installing his Tuscan inner circle in key institutional positions.

Architecture

Plain and simple: building the Renaissance city

Across a millennium of architectural history from the High Middle Ages through Arnolfo's Gothic, Vasari's Mannerism and all the way to the 20th-century rationalism of Giovanni Michelucci, Florence has maintained a remarkably consistent taste in architecture, characterised by a simple, balanced, sharp-edged design, harmonious proportions and solid materials such as marble and stone. Whenever imported styles were embraced, they were promptly transformed into a local variant by this distinctive imprint. Not surprisingly, for instance, Baroque never really took hold here. This may well be due to the fact that the vast majority of prominent architects who worked in Florence were local, or locally trained.

▶*About the author*

Sophia Cottier is an interiors and design PR and freelance journalist. She has travelled extensively in Italy and studied at the British Institute in Florence. She also has an MA in Art History from the University of St Andrews.

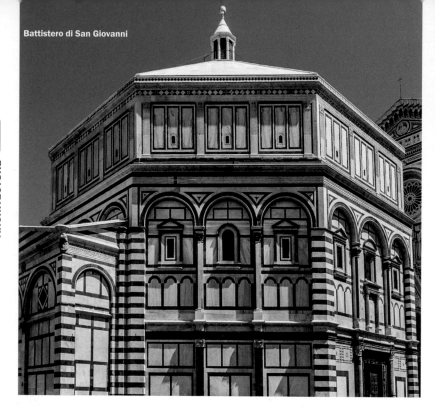

Battistero di San Giovanni

A Florentine style emerges

Founded by the **Romans** (see *p260* History), Florence flourished in the tenth and 11th centuries, when a large amount of money was spent on constructing religious buildings, generating an indigenous architectural style. Piazza del Duomo's **Battistero di San Giovanni**, also known as Baptistery of Saint John, believed to be the oldest building in the city, was completed around the middle of the 11th century, although its foundations are thought to date back to the fourth or fifth century. Famous for Ghiberti's bronze door on the

east side, the Baptistery exemplifies what can only be termed the 'Florentine style'. A number of prominent Florentine and Tuscan architects worked and developed this style over the centuries. The most important were, chronologically: **Arnolfo di Cambio** (c1245-1302), **Giotto** (1266/7-1337), **Filippo Brunelleschi** (1377-1446), **Michelozzo di Bartolomeo Michelozzi** (1396-1472), **Leon Battista Alberti** (1404-72), **Giuliano da Sangallo** (c1445-1535), **Il Cronaca** (1454-1508), **Michelangelo Buonarroti** (1475-1564), **Giorgio Vasari** (1511-74), **Bartolomeo Ammannati** (1511-92), **Bernardo Buontalenti** (1531-1608), and later **Giuseppe Poggi** (1811-1901) and **Giovanni Michelucci** (1891-1991).

Renaissance ideals of architectural beauty raised the status of the profession – no longer just skilled labourers, the architects became artists

Romanesque and Gothic

San Miniato al Monte (*see p190*), constructed in 1018 on the site of a fourth-century chapel, is one of the most beautiful Romanesque structures in Florence. With its wonderful green and white façade, the church is actually rather simple in design, and its 15th-century campanile remains unfinished. During the Siege of Florence (1529-30), this important religious site was

Medici Villas and Gardens

A UNESCO-worthy collection of country mansions and pleasure parks

Italy has a world-record 51 UNESCO Heritage Sites and seven of these are in Tuscany, including the historic centres of Florence (inscribed 1982), San Gimignano (1990), Siena (1995; see p211) and Pienza (1996), as well as the Campo dei Miracoli in Pisa (1987; see p209). The latest addition to this elite club of the region's jewels is a so-called 'serial property' comprising 12 villas and two pleasure gardens built by the Medici around Florence and across northern Tuscany between the 15th and the 17th centuries. According to UNESCO, they 'form the first example of the connection between architecture, gardens, and the environment and became an enduring reference for princely residences throughout Italy and Europe.' Although these 14 sites are well under half the total number of country mansions built or owned by the Medici, they offer a good overview of the stylistic development throughout the three centuries of their rule.

The earliest villas on the list are the **Trebbio** and **Cafaggio** castles in the Mugello valley north of Florence, where the Medici dynasty originated and owned agricultural property; the last is the neoclassical **Villa del Poggio Imperiale** on the Arcetri hill south of town.

But perhaps the most iconic of the lot is **Villa Ambra** at Poggio a Caiano, south of Prato along the main road to Pistoia. Built by Giuliano da Sangallo for Lorenzo il Magnifico from around 1485, this fine building is a simple rectangular block with a temple portico, plain walls and sharp eaves (the curved staircases are a later addition). The villa now houses two museums: the monumental apartments on the ground floor, and an intriguing gallery of still-life paintings on the second floor.

Ferdinando I (see p265 A Medici Who's Who) was so proud of the family villas that in 1599–1602 he had them painted in 17 lunettes by Giusto Utens. The 14 surviving vistas are now on display at **Villa La Petraia**, itself a UNESCO-listed Medici mansion together with nearby **Villa di Castello** (for both, see p196).

The two listed gardens are **Boboli** (p168) in the Oltrarno, Florence, and the park of the since demolished **Villa Demidoff** at Pratolino, a dozen kilometers north of the city by the old via Bolognese. Designed by Bernardo Buontalenti and laid out in 1569-81, this splendid Mannerist park is famous for its Appennine Colossus by Giambologna.

Appennine Colossus (Giambologna, 1579-1580)

surrounded with fortified walls, hastily constructed by Michelangelo.

Michelozzo is credited with developing the form of the Florentine palazzo, considered one of the most important architectural products of the Renaissance

The 11th-century church of **Santissimi Apostoli** (*see p96*), in piazza del Limbo, is considered one of the most elegant examples of Romanesque architecture in the city, and is believed to have heavily influenced Brunelleschi in his designs for the church of San Lorenzo. Santissimi Apostoli was reworked during the 15th century and only restored to its original Romanesque appearance in the 1930s.

Gothic style dominated new architectural works from the 13th century, with builders using pointed arches to make higher and wider structures. **Santa Maria Novella** (*see p104*) was constructed between

1278 and 1360, and is perhaps the most beautiful structure commissioned by the Dominican monks.

The **Duomo** (*see p65*) – or Santa Maria del Fiore, to give it its proper name – was designed by Arnolfo di Cambio in 1297. However, its design was altered several times, and after Arnolfo's death in 1302 the project was overseen by a number of other architects, including Francesco Talenti and Giovanni di Lapo Ghini.

Santa Croce (*see p148*) another major Gothic church in the city; begun in 1298, it has also been attributed to Arnolfo. A timbered roof combines with seven bays with pointed arches to give the illusion of loftiness, at the same time drawing the eye down to the altar.

The **Campanile** of Santa Maria del Fiore in piazza del Duomo (*see p68*), designed by Giotto (1334) and built with white and green marble, was only completed after his death. As the storeys rise, the windows multiply – a traditional feature of medieval Florentine architecture.

Early Renaissance

Florence is a shrine to Renaissance architecture – its centre is filled with palaces, monuments and churches constructed with an artistic and cultural

Giotto's Campanile p68

Ospedale degli Innocenti

intelligence that was unsurpassed at the time. A pilgrimage to Rome to study the ancient structures was seen as a vital part of an architect's training (see p279 The Renaissance), and as the architects absorbed the styles of these classical structures, a new architectural vocabulary developed encompassing columns, pilasters, entablatures, arches and pediments.

The treatise of the first-century BC Roman architect Vitruvius also formed an important part of Renaissance education, helping to define Renaissance ideals concerning architectural beauty. These ideals subsequently raised the status of the profession – no longer just skilled labourers, the architects became artists. Renaissance architecture is defined by strict mathematical proportions, measurements based on the human body and balanced form. In Florence, the period was dominated by three great architects: Brunelleschi, Michelozzo and Alberti.

Brunelleschi, who gave the Duomo its cupola (the largest such construction since ancient Roman times), went on to design two of the city's finest churches: **San Lorenzo** (1422-69; see p122), with its independent Old Sacristy (1422-29), and **Santo Spirito** (1444-81; see p168). Less heralded, but equally notable, is his **Cappella dei Pazzi** (begun 1422; see p149), a small private family building in the garden of Santa Croce, based on perfect proportions. The Duomo's cupola, a symbol of the Renaissance, influenced many High Renaissance and Baroque architects: even

Michelangelo's cupola for St Peter's in Rome, designed more than 100 years later, has roughly the same interior diameter at 42 metres (138 feet).

Brunelleschi's signature style can clearly be seen in piazza della SS Annunziata's **Ospedale degli Innocent** (see p136), begun in 1419. Through a series of arcades with Corinthian columns, friezes, pedimented windows and matching loggias, Brunelleschi created the most unified square in Florence.

It's the architect Michelozzo, however, who is widely credited with developing the form of the Florentine *palazzo* (or mansion), considered one of the most important architectural products of the Renaissance. Michelozzo often worked for Cosimo il Vecchio, the founder of the Medici family's fortunes (see p263 A Medici Who's Who). His most notable construction was Cosimo's town residence, Palazzo Medici, now called **Palazzo Medici Riccardi** (1444; see p120). The regularity of the building, its two façades and its strongly rusticated orders heralded a new era in *palazzo* construction.

Michelangelo took Alberti's bold, classicising style and gave it a sense of uncertainty, but also great energy and rhythm

Palazzo Rucellai

Completing the trio is Leon Battista Alberti, who completed the façade of **Santa Maria Novella** (1470; *see p104*) and designed the highly original **Palazzo Rucellai** (c1446-51; *see p102*) in via della Vigna Nuova, on which he first introduced to Florence his innovative system of pilasters and capitals of the three classical orders, which ascend in importance on each storey, and are separated by ornate friezes. In 1450, Alberti published his *Ten Books on Architecture* – the text became an indispensable guide for all those designing buildings during the Renaissance and beyond.

Giuliano da Sangallo, the preferred architect of Lorenzo il Magnifico, was greatly concerned with instilling in his designs a refined classicism that he'd learnt in Rome. The best example of his work is the beautiful **Villa Ambra** at Poggio a Caiano (*see p271* Medici Villas and Gardens).

Later Renaissance

Michelangelo was one of the most important High Renaissance architects, although he came to architecture rather late in his career, at the age of 40. He took Alberti's bold, classicising style and gave it a sense of uncertainty, but also great energy and rhythm. Rather than making the exteriors of his buildings imitate those of ancient Rome, Michelangelo gave his creations a pagan grounding orientated towards man's emotional state.

Michelangelo undertook two key projects in Florence for Pope Leo X (formerly Giovanni de' Medici): the **New Sacristy** (*see p121*) and the **Biblioteca Mediceo-Laurenziana** (Laurentian Library; *see p124*), both in the church of San Lorenzo, which had become an important symbol of dynastic power for the Medici. A third important project designed by Michelangelo is the **Cappelle Medicee** (1519-34; *see p121*), adjacent to San Lorenzo. Although it was never entirely completed, it's arguably the best example in existence of Michelangelo's architectural sculptural designs, where the boundaries between the walls, floors and artwork become blurred.

Both the **Fortezza da Basso** (1534; *see p193*), the strongest side of which faces the city, and the **Forte di Belvedere** (1590; *see p181*), which dominates from just above the Ponte Vecchio, were commissioned by the Medici family and are symbolic of the great control that the family exercised over the city and its inhabitants. The vast **Palazzo Pitti** (1457; *see p166*), where the Medici lived in the mid 16th century, pays further tribute to the family's strength: designed by Brunelleschi and Fancelli, it was built with massive blocks of stone, some of which measure six metres in length.

The main court architects at this time were Vasari, Ammannati and Buontalenti. However, all ended up following Michelangelo to Rome. While in Florence, Vasari, assisted by Buontalenti, designed the **Uffizi** (1560; *see p82*), which was filled with offices and workshops, leaving the top floor for the gallery. He also constructed the corridor that bears his name, running from the Uffizi, across the Ponte Vecchio to Palazzo Pitti; it was used by the Medici family to avoid the throngs on the street.

In 1557, Ammannati designed the **ponte Santa Trinita** (*see p108*) over the Arno to replace a bridge that had collapsed in 1557. He also began the 300-year expansion of Palazzo Pitti. Meanwhile, Buontalenti extended Palazzo Vecchio to its present eastern limits and built the palaces for the Medici at Petraia (1587) and Pratolino (1568, later demolished).

The fall and rise of modern Florence

From 1600 to the death of the last Medici ruler in 1737, hardly any new building work was commissioned in Florence and, although many of the Renaissance palaces were enlarged and gardens added, the city fell into a state of decline. Garden design, however, did come to be seen as another form of art: at Palazzo Pitti, an extra 45,000 square metres (484,000 square feet) were added to the **Giardino di Boboli** (*see p168*). Two of the city's historic theatres, **Teatro Niccolini** and **Teatro della Pergola** (*see p250*), also date from the mid 17th century.

Between 1865 and 1870, large parts of the city underwent significant redevelopment as Florence became the capital of the unified Kingdom of Italy. Giuseppe Poggi (1811-1901) had been named the principal town planner and architect by the Florentine authorities in 1864, and his ambitious redevelopment project included constructing wide boulevards to accommodate carriages, as well as several elegant *piazze*: **piazza Beccaria** and **piazza della Libertà** are superb examples of these new city-centre squares, both designed in the neoclassical and neo-Renaissance styles – and both unfortunately now submerged in daily traffic.

One of Poggi's most impressive projects was constructing **Piazzale Michelangelo** (1869; *see p191*) on the south side of the river. This large open space offers an excellent view over Florence. He also enlarged a number of boulevards around the *piazzale*, which continued along the side of the hills facing Florence and the Forte di Belvedere, and then came back down again to the Porta Romana. The existence of this wonderful drive of roughly six kilometres, one of Italy's prettiest, is also due in great part to Poggi's vision.

As Poggi was busy creating beauty, town planners were busy changing the architectural face of Florence through wholesale destruction of its medieval centre around piazza della Repubblica; the central government in Rome demolished further stretches of the city, in Santa Maria Novella and Santa Croce, in the early 20th century. In 1944, only 50 years after the centre of Florence had been gutted, scores more irreplaceable ancient buildings were destroyed by the Germans, who blew up almost all the bridges over the Arno (only the Ponte Vecchio was spared), along with all the buildings to the immediate north and south of the Ponte Vecchio.

As Poggi was busy creating beauty, town planners were busy changing the architectural face of Florence through wholesale destruction of its medieval centre

Today, as a result of these periods of destruction, you can walk all the way from the Duomo, down via Roma, across piazza Repubblica, through via Calimala and via Santa Maria, and all the way down the ponte Vecchio without passing more than two or three buildings that are more than a century old. And the newer buildings are, on the whole, banal at best and ugly at worst.

There are a few notable 20th-century buildings in the city, however, including the 1930s **Santa Maria Novella station** (*see p107*) with the adjoining **Palazzina Reale**, both designed by Giovanni Michelucci and his Gruppo Toscano partners. A reception building intended for the Italian royal family, the Palazzina has recently found new life thanks to the patronage of the local guild of architects, which has a taken a 12-year lease over it. Parts of the complex also house a tapas bar. Other interesting buildings include the 1932 **Stadio Artemio Franchi** (*see p196*) designed by Pier Luigi Nervi (1891-1979) and widely considered to be one of the most impressive contemporary structures in Florence; the **Instituto Aeronautica Militare** academy in the Cascine Park; and the **Cinema Teatro Puccini** in piazza Puccini near the Cascine park. Also designed by Michelucci is the 1960s church of **San Giovanni Battista** at the crossing of the Autostrada del Sole (A1) and Autostrada del Mare (A11) west of town. For ongoing architectural changes in the city, *see p26* Florence Today.

Art

The cradle of the Renaissance is a treasure house of art

UNESCO estimates that Italy contains up to 60 per cent of the world's most important works of art, over half of which are located in Florence. Considered the spiritual home of the Renaissance, Florence and its environs spawned a huge number of great artists: Michelangelo, Botticelli, Leonardo and Fra Angelico among them. Wealthy Florentine families entrusted these artists to decorate their palaces, chapels and city with sumptuous images that would never be forgotten. This kept Florence at the forefront of the artistic and intellectual world during the 15th and 16th centuries, as poets, artists and philosophers mingled in the city, vying for patronage and fame.

Detail of Primavera (Allegory of Spring) (Sandro Botticelli, c1482)

The Death of St Francis (Giotto, 1325)

Medieval money

Prior to the 14th century, the Catholic Church had been the primary commissioner of works of art, but this was set to change: bankers, merchants and princes were becoming richer, so the demand for privately commissioned art grew.

In the 1320s, the Bardi, a powerful banking family, commissioned **Giotto** (1267-1337) to decorate their chapel in the church of Santa Croce (*see p148*). Here, Giotto demonstrates the stylistic shift between medieval and early Renaissance painting. Although obscured by tombs and damaged by the 1966 flood, the figures in the *Death of St Francis* are set in a believable environment with an outpouring of human emotion. As seen in his design for the Duomo's Campanile, Giotto's style is characterised by clarity and simplicity, rendering his works legible and accessible.

Also in the church of Santa Croce is a painted *Crucifix* by Giotto's predecessor, **Cimabue** (1240-1302). With its ties to the previous Byzantine tradition, this work brings Giotto's naturalism into focus. The Uffizi (*see p82*) provides direct comparisons between the two artists, with Cimabue's *Maestà* (1285-6) beside Giotto's *Ognissanti Madonna* (1300-10).

Ignoring the new naturalism of Giotto, **Andrea Orcagna** (1308-68) fashioned his tabernacle in the church of Orsanmichele (1359; *see p88*) in the more popular Gothic style. This highly decorative structure protected the miracle-working image of the Virgin and is inlaid with marble, lapis lazuli, gold and glass.

The 'Rebirth'

The Renaissance refers to a literary, intellectual and artistic movement that flourished in Florence between the 14th and 16th centuries (*see opposite* The Renaissance). Artists, writers and scholars reinterpreted the classical heritage of the Roman Empire, rediscovering its philosophy, art, architecture and literature. The 1401 competition for the east doors of the Baptistery saw **Filippo Brunelleschi** (1377-1446) lose out to **Lorenzo Ghiberti** (1378-1455). Brunelleschi left for Rome in a huff to study the art of the ancients. And he did have the last laugh: on his return to

The Renaissance

The classics that reshaped the world forever

The Renaissance is a massive source of pride for Florence. For centuries, the city has basked in its afterglow, and the world has basked with it.

The guiding doctrine of the Renaissance (*Rinascimento*; literally 'rebirth') was Humanism – the revival of the language, learning and art of the ancient Greeks and Romans, and the reconciliation of this pagan heritage with Christianity. Although the most visible manifestation of the Renaissance in Florence was the astonishing outpouring of art in the 15th century, it was classical studies that sparked the new age.

The groundwork had been done by a handful of men: Dante (1265-1321), Petrarch (1304-74) and Boccaccio (1313-75) all collected Latin manuscripts, which shaped their approach to writing. But it was the mounting Florentine wealth that paid for dedicated manuscript detectives such as Poggio Bracciolini (1380-1459) to dig through neglected monastery libraries across Europe.

A few classical works had never been lost, but those that were known were usually corrupt. The volume of unknown works unearthed during this period was incredible. First came the discovery of Quintilian's *The Training of an Orator*, which detailed Roman education; Columella's *De Re Rustica* on agriculture; key texts on Roman architecture by Vitruvius and Frontinus; and Cicero's *Brutus* (a justification of republicanism). Whereas very few Greek works had been known in Western Europe, suddenly – almost simultaneously – most of Plato, Homer, Sophocles and many other classics were rediscovered.

The Renaissance focus on a pre-Christian age didn't mean that God was under threat. Just as the Renaissance artists had no compunction about enhancing the beauty of their forms and compositions with classical features and allusions, so Renaissance Humanists sought explanations beyond the scriptures that were complementary to accepted religion rather than a challenge to it. Much effort was made to present the wisdom of the ancients as a precursor to the ultimate wisdom of God.

Nor did the Renaissance fascination with things semi-scientific – Leonardo's anatomical drawings, for example, or the widespread obsession with the mathematics of Pythagoras – necessarily mean that this was a scientific age. The 15th century was an era when ideas were still paramount; science, as a process of deduction based on observation and experimentation, didn't really get going until the 17th century. In medicine, the theory of the four humours still held sway. Astronomy and astrology were all but synonymous. Mathematics was an almost mystical art, while alchemy – the attempt to transform base metals into gold – flourished.

It was magnificent while it lasted, but Florence's pre-eminence in art and ideas was abruptly snuffed out on the death of Lorenzo 'il Magnifico' in 1492: the invasion by Charles VIII of France in the 1490s and Savonarola's 'Bonfire of the Vanities' (*see p76*) saw to that. In the early 16th century, the cutting-edge was Rome, where Michelangelo, Bramante and Raphael were in the process of creating their finest works; thence, after Emperor Charles V sacked Rome in 1527, it was Venice, where masters such as Palladio and Titian practised. But the period left Florence with some of the most important masterpieces and artefacts in the world – many of them still in existence, and enjoyed by millions of visitors each year.

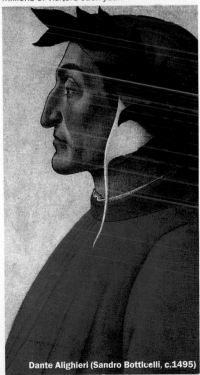

Dante Alighieri (Sandro Botticelli, *c*.1495)

The Procession of the Magi (Benozzo Gozzoli, 1459-1461)

Florence, he was able to build the majestic cupola for the Duomo (1420-36; *see p68*).

As the demand for art grew, so did the number of workshops; here, apprentices learned to paint and sculpt alongside the masters. The workshop of **Luca della Robbia** (1400-82), for example, generated signature glazed terracotta reliefs that grace prominent structures across Florence, such as Orsanmichele, Brunelleschi's Spedale degli Innocenti (*see p136*) and the interior of the Duomo (*see p65*).

As a young apprentice in the workshop of Ghiberti, **Donatello** (1386-1466) worked on the Baptistery doors. Like Brunelleschi, he had studied in Rome, and his Orsanmichele statues of *St Mark* (1411) and *St George* (1416), now in the Bargello (*see p146*),

Brunelleschi's theory of linear perspective became a tool for the realistic representation of distance and depth

demonstrate his ability to create naturalistic drapery over believable bodies.

Commissioned by Cosimo I de' Medici, Donatello's *David* (1430), now also in the Bargello, was the first free-standing life-size nude bronze since antiquity. It was originally designed to stand on the buttress of Florence cathedral, but in 1416, the Priory of the Republic decided that the statue should become a symbol of the Florentine Republic, so *David* was placed in a more prominent position in Palazzo dei Priori.

Andrea del Verrocchio (1435-88) eventually replaced Donatello as the leading sculptor in Florence, and his *Christ and Doubting Thomas* (1476-83) takes on a new dimension as its figures step out of a niche in the exterior of the Orsanmichele (*see p88*). This skilled composition shows an acute awareness of anatomy. Verrocchio, like Donatello, worked for the Medici (*see p263* A Medici Who's Who), creating the tomb of Piero and Giovanni in the Old Sacristy of San Lorenzo (1469-72), as well as the charming *Putto with Dolphin* fountain (1470) in Palazzo Vecchio.

Early Renaissance painting took its cue from sculpture, attempting to create the same sense of naturalism on a two-dimensional scale. Brunelleschi's theory of linear perspective became a tool for the realistic representation of distance and depth. Perspective was first applied to painting by artists such as **Masaccio** (1401-28), particularly in his *Trinità* fresco in Santa Maria Novella (1427; *see p104*) and, with the help of **Masolino** (1400-47), the fresco cycle in the Cappella Brancacci (1425; *see p176*). Similarly, **Paolo Uccello** (1396-1475) experimented with foreshortening and a sense of perspective in works such as *The Battle of San Romano* (1435) in the Uffizi, and the fresco of *John Hawkwood* (1436) in the Duomo.

Piero della Francesca (1416-92) was active in Florence in the 1430s, both as a painter and as an author of treatises on perspective and mathematics. His *Legend of the True Cross* fresco cycle (c1453-65) in Arezzo (*see p216*), reveals his adherence to mathematical order by his treatment of natural and architectural elements, which recede into the distance.

The Dominican **Fra Angelico** (1400-55) also used perspective when creating his sublime frescoes in the monastery (now museum) of San Marco (*see p139*), using them as an extension of reality. His *Annunciation* (1440-41) mirrors the architecture of the monks' cells, adding a new sense of immediacy. The stark style of Fra Angelico reflects the humility of his religious order and the function of the monastery as a place of meditation.

Placing a biblical event in a contemporary Florentine context became acceptable during the Renaissance, providing a new way for lay people to understand and connect with the story. It also became commonplace to depict one's patron in a prominent position. In his painting of the *Cappella dei Magi* (1459-60) in Palazzo Medici Riccardi (*see p120*), **Benozzo Gozzoli** (1420-97) depicts Lorenzo de' Medici as one of the participants in this lavish procession. Gozzoli also painted himself among the crowd, reflecting the growing self-awareness of 'the artist' of this period; another example is **Domenico Ghirlandaio** (1449-94), who looks out from his Cappella Sassetti frescoes in Santa Trinita (1483-85; *see p108*).

Filippo Lippi (1406-69), a Carmelite friar, had little interest in creating an illusion of the real world. In his *Madonna with Child and Angels* (1465) in the Uffizi, he depicts a fantastic background scene behind his pearl-adorned Madonna that disregards the laws of perspective and human anatomy.

Filippo passed his linear style on to his pupil, **Sandro Botticelli** (1445-1510). The figures in both *Primavera* ('Allegory of Spring'; c1482) and *The Birth of Venus* (1476-87), commissioned by the Medici and now in the Uffizi, are infused with grace and idealised beauty, seeming to float just above the ground.

ART

Putto with Dolphin (Andrea del Verrocchio, 1470)

Pinnacle of achievement

The artists of the 15th century developed the tools and methods that would characterise the artistic activity in the century that followed. These artists surpassed their own masters in their quest for ideal beauty, balanced proportions and structured compositions.

Leonardo da Vinci (1452-1519) emerged from the workshop of Verrocchio when he helped his master paint the *Baptism of Christ* (1469-80), now in the Uffizi. A true 'Renaissance man', Leonardo was not only a skilled painter but also a sculptor, architect, engineer and scientist. His exploration of the natural world as a scientist manifested itself in his art, which reflects his sensitive observation of nature. Da Vinci experimented extensively with oils, developing the *sfumato* technique, which creates atmospheric and subtle shading. This can clearly be seen in the carefully structured *Annunciation* (1472) in the Uffizi. The Salone dei Cinquecento in Palazzo Vecchio may hide his lost portrayal of the Battle of Anghiari (*see p80*).

Another quintessential Florentine Renaissance artist was **Michelangelo Buonarroti**, better known simply as Michelangelo (1475-1564). He was catapulted to fame with his idealised male nude statue, *David* (1501-04), quickly lauded as the greatest work of sculpture ever created. Though a copy remains in piazza della Signoria, the original is now in the Galleria dell'Accademia (*see p134*), along with the *Slaves* (1527-28) – half-finished sculptures that reveal Michelangelo's method of removing excess stone to reveal the 'pre-existing spirit' of the statue.

Mind your Mannerism

The prevailing style of the late period of the High Renaissance, from 1520 until 1600, is known as Mannerism. The term originates from the Italian *maniera*, meaning 'style' or 'manner', and it is characterised by complicated compositions, garish colours, exaggerated forms and a heightened sense of drama. To a certain extent this art movement symbolised the anxiety and confusion that was widely felt in Italy as a result of the Protestant Reformation and the weakening power of the Catholic Church. Mannerism is also considered to be a violent

Abduction of a Sabine Woman (Giambologna, 1582)

reaction against the order and harmony of Renaissance art.

One of the leading artists of this style was **Andrea del Sarto** (1486-1530). A contemporary of Michelangelo and Raphael, del Sarto was an equally graceful painter and skilled draughtsman. His *Madonna of the Harpies* altarpiece (1517) in the Uffizi is a fine example of Mannerist painting, as is his *Last Supper* (1526-27), in the refectory of the monastery of San Salvi.

Giorgio Vasari (1511-74) also belonged to the Mannerist circle and was the court architect of Cosimo I (*see p267* A Medici Who's Who). Cosimo was in charge of redecorating the Salone dei Cinquecento in Palazzo Vecchio (*see p78*) and the interior of the Duomo's Cupola (*see p68*), of creating the Uffizi (*see p82*) and the corridors that bears his name. However, he is perhaps best remembered as a chronicler for his book *The Lives of the Artists*, a collection of biographies.

Florence is also home to a number of pieces of outstanding Mannerist sculpture – some on public display in the piazza della Signoria and the Loggia dei Lanzi – reflecting the military strength of the Medici administration under the Grand Duke of Tuscany, Cosimo I de' Medici. **Benvenuto Cellini's** (1500-71) life-size *Perseus* (1545-54) is a chilling reminder of the Duke's authority, combining his appreciation for Renaissance sculptors with the elegance of Mannerism. **Giambologna** (or Giovanni da Bologna; 1524-1608) created the statue of Cosimo I on horseback (1598), as well as *Hercules and Centaur* (1599) and *Abduction of a Sabine Woman* (1582), both also to be found in the Loggia dei Lanzi.

Modern masters

Apart from a few Florentines, such as **Ludovico Cardi** ('Cigoli'; 1559-1613), **Cristoforo Allori** (1577-1621) and **Carlo Dolci** (1616-87), the most important artists were working in Rome in the 17th century. The Medici family, however, invited several artists to their court. **Pietro da Cortona** (1596-1669), for instance, decorated the state apartments in Palazzo Pitti in the 1630s. During this time the Florentine *pietra dura* technique of decorating with inlaid marble was developed.

By the 18th century, Florence was an essential stop on the Grand Tour. The Accademia delle Belle Arti (1784) became the centre of artistic activity during the 18th and 19th centuries, when Romantic and Naturalist styles prevailed.

Throughout the Napoleonic occupation of the city (1799-1814), Florence followed the French neoclassicists, but a group of artists known as the Macchiaioli and united by social, political and artistic discontent, frequented Florence's Caffè Michelangelo. Their name, 'stain-makers', or 'splatterers', refers to their style, comprising patches of colour and inspired by French Impressionism and the Barbizon school. Leading Macchiaioli include **Giovanni Fattori** (1825-1908), **Telemaco Signorini** (1835-1901) and **Silvestro Lega** (1826-95), and their works are in the Galleria d'Arte Moderna at Palazzo Pitti (*see p168*).

Perhaps the most representative local artist of the 20th century is **Marino Marini** (1901-80), whose work can be seen both in Florence in the former church of San Pancrazio (*see p106*) and in his hometown Pistoia (*see p205* Fondazione Museo Marino Marini). Marini devoted himself to sculpture around the 1920s, experimenting with terracotta, bronze and plaster.

A number of artists still work in the Florence area. Among them is **Roberto Barni** (born 1939), formerly known for large monochrome canvases but in recent years more attracted to sculpture; **Paolo Staccioli** (born 1943), whose ceramic sculpture focuses on human figures and animals on the move; and Tuscan sculptor **Enzo Pazzagli**, who specialises in outdoor sculptures with multiple layers, superimposed on each other. Much of Pazzagli's work can be seen at his Art Park on via Sant'Andrea a Rovezzano.

Over the last few decades, a number of contemporary artworks have been placed in strategic points around the city. To name but a few, you will find **Michelangelo Pistoletto**'s (born 1933) *Dietrofront* just outside the Porta Romana; **Fernando Botero**'s (born 1932) *Paloma* just outside the Airport; **Giuliano Vangi**'s (born 1931) *San Giovanni* in the little square of Santa Maria Soprarno (where via dei Bardi meets Lungarno Torrigiani); **Giampaolo Talani**'s (born 1955) large fresco *Departures* above the west entrance to the Santa Maria Novella train station (*see p107*), and a dozen works by Belgian sculptor **Jean-Michel Folon** (1934-2005) in the delightful Giardino delle Rose just below piazzale Michelangelo (*see p188*). The new Museo Novecento (*see p103*) now hosts the vast majority of 20th-century artworks belonging to the Comune.

Contemporary art fans who cannot sate their hunger in Florence, can visit the recently revamped **Centro per l'Arte Contemporanea Luigi Pecci** in nearby Prato (*see p204*). Elsewhere in Tuscany, the town of Pietrasanta in the Versilia Riviera at the foot of the Apuan Alps is home to a remarkable community of Italian and international sculptors.

Plan

Mille Miglia

Accommodation

From boutique hotel to B&B, there's a bed to suit (almost) everybody

While room rates remain among the highest in Italy, the positive side to accommodation in Florence is the sheer variety of options. Whether your bed of choice lies in a boutique hotel with a sharp design edge or a cosy B&B on the top floor of an ancient *palazzo*, chances are that you'll find something appealing. Book a bunk in a youth hostel, a penthouse suite with terrace views or a frescoed boudoir looking on to a private garden: the choice is yours.

Location, location, location

While every city neighbourhood has its merits, you should factor in the length of your stay, your budget and the size and age of your party when choosing where to stay. If you're only visiting for a few days, you may want your lodgings to be central in order to maximise the time available. Although Florence is fairly compact and best navigated on foot, you may not want to drag your luggage too far from the station on cobbled streets and crowded pavements.

While everyone may dream of staying in the **Duomo** area, this location, with its iconic views and the convenience of being able to drop your shopping bags and change your top on a whim, comes at a price. **Santa Maria Novella** has a diverse range of hotels, ranging from seedy one-star holes in side streets to the design gems overlooking the main square. **San Lorenzo** is where you'll find the widest choice of budget accommodation, with just as affordable eating

In the know
Price categories

Our price categories are based on hotels' standard prices (not including seasonal offers or discounts) for one night in a double room with en suite shower/bath. Breakfast is included unless otherwise stated. Given the potential for off-season discounts, it's always worth trying to negotiate a better deal.

Luxury	€300+
Expensive	€200-300
Moderate	€100-200
Budget	up to €100

Suite Dreams

Fancy an alternative to a conventional hotel?

Most significant in recent years has been the huge increase in the number of B&Bs, *affittacamere* (rooms to rent including those found on sites such as Airbnb) and *residenze d'epoca* (listed buildings with no more than 12 rooms), but as these categories lie outside the star rating system (see p289), it can be difficult to judge what you're likely to get. They range from spartan, gloomy rooms with threadbare towels and no breakfast (yes, B&Bs with no breakfast) to homely pads furnished with antiques where you start the day with warm brioches. Good online resources include www.bedandbreakfast.it, www.bbitalia.it and www.caffelletto.it.

Case per ferie are religious institutions that offer a number of beds. The majority are cheap, but they're often single-sex and operate curfews; try www.monasterystays.com for listings. If you are young (or young at heart) and prefer camping or staying in a hostel, www.hostelworld.com is your go-to website.

There are very few *agriturismi* (farm stays) within the municipal boundaries of Florence, but neighbouring areas offer some very attractive ones, so you may want to check www.agriturismo.it (Italy-wide listings) and www.agriturismo.net (Tuscany only) for comprehensive lists. These are privately operated services; the official booking channel is maintained at regional level at http://book.intoscana.it.

Apartment rentals

While some high-end serviced apartments are still available through letting agents, websites such as Airbnb, Booking.com, Wimdu.com and Holidaylettings.co.uk are making it easy to rent directly from property owners at attractively low rates. Renting a room or a flat is an enticing option for stays longer than a few days, but besides location, amenities and previous guest feedback, don't forget to double-check cancellation policies, security deposits, check-in and check-out times and any hidden extras (linen, utilities, final cleaning).

options on your doorstep, but the neighbourhood can be noisy. **San Marco** is probably the most peaceful neighbourhood and offers some exciting options in historic *palazzi*, but its nightlife and dining scene can be on the quiet side. **Santa Croce** has some classy hotels and B&Bs interspersed with a high concentration of genuine residents. Meanwhile, **The Oltrarno** is better known for its nightlife than for its hotels, but some new exciting properties have entered the scene – just make sure your room doesn't overlook a busy street or a piazza where revelries continue into the small hours. Finally, staying outside the city gates can be an attractive option if you don't mind the bus commute. However, until the tramway lines are completed it's wise to avoid the traffic chaos of the area west of town.

When to go

If you're staying in the centre of the city during the long hot summer, a private terrace or balcony – or some kind of outside space – can make a big difference. Easter and the spring holiday weekends (for dates, *see p305*) can be both busy and expensive, but late September and most of October combine pleasant temperatures with thinner crowds. November and March may be rainy, and Florence in winter can be cold by Italian standards. If you don't mind the shorter daylight hours and much reduced nightlife scene, a winter break can actually be a cheap and relaxed option – you may even take your chances on last-minute deals, or hope for a room upgrade.

Bookings & prices

Accommodation prices can fluctuate a great deal depending on the time of year, last-minute vacancies and online special offers. Peak season for Florence's hotels runs roughly from Easter (the busiest weekend of the year) until October. It also covers Christmas, New Year, Italian public holidays and the Pitti fashion fairs in January and June. Hotel rooms at these times are at their most expensive and much in demand, so book well in advance.

On the other hand, low season (roughly November to February) offers great potential for accommodation bargains, especially among the upper-end establishments; budget hotels and B&Bs are less likely to lower their rates significantly. If you are willing to take your chances and are travelling off-season, it's worth doing the rounds to see what kind of bargain you can negotiate.

Details of hotels, *affittacamere* (rooms to rent), apartments, campsites and hostels in Florence and its province can all be found online through www.firenzeturismo.it. Unaccountably, prices and website links are not provided.

One sour note for both hoteliers and travellers is an accommodation tax (*tassa di soggiorno*) ranging from €1.50 (for one-star hotels) to €5 (for five-star hotels) per person per night, up to a maximum of seven consecutive

❤ **Best hotels with a view**

Portrait Firenze *p290*
Hard-to beat spacious suites overlooking the Arno.

Grand Hotel Minerva *p291*
Stunning views from the rooftop terrace.

Palazzo Magnani Feroni *p290*
A different perspective on the city's landmarks.

La Scaletta *p292*
Rooms and a rooftop terrace overlooking the Giardino di Boboli.

Antica Torre Tornabuoni Uno *p291*
Watch the sunset from the rooftop bar while sipping a glass of prosecco.

La Scaletta *p292*

nights. Note that it is usually not included in the price of your booking and will be charged extra at the end of your stay. For instance, a guest staying for five nights in a four-star hotel would pay an extra €22.50. Children under the age of 12 are exempt.

Star ratings & facillties

Hotels are officially given a star rating from one to five by the tourist board, but the rating is an indication of the facilities on offer rather than the standards. There can be enormous disparity within any given category, so it pays to do your research.

Grand Hotel Minerva p291

Most hotels price their rooms according to size, view, the amount of natural light they receive, the size and type of bathroom and whether rooms have balconies or terraces. Phones, en-suite bathrooms, Wi-Fi, safes and hairdryers are pretty standard for hotels, except some in the budget category, but check before you book if you require something specific. Most hotels will put at least one extra bed in a double room for a fee; many provide cots for which you may have to pay extra. If you don't like the room you've been given, ask to see another one, and don't be put off by grumpy owners. Hotels are required by law to display official maximum room rates in each room; if you feel you've been taken for a ride, there's an office for complaints (*seep299* Consumer).

Very few hotels in the centre of town have their own parking facilities; most have an arrangement with a nearby private garage, though this can be expensive. A law requires new and renovated hotels to have rooms with disabled access – but in some cases, rooms for the disabled are only accessible, absurdly, by a lift that's either too narrow to take a wheelchair or is itself accessed up a flight of stairs.

Luxury

Four Seasons Hotel
Borgo Pinti 99, San Marco (055 26261, www.fourseasons.com/ florence). **Map** *p131 R4.*
In Palazzo della Gherardesca, which has one of the largest privately owned gardens in Florence, this fabulous hotel is the result of a multi-million-euro restoration project. As well as the luxurious rooms, there are all the five-star facilities you'd expect, from the big spa to an outdoor pool. The rooms and suites are located in two buildings – the original *palazzo* and the Conventino – across four acres of garden, surrounded by winding paths, fountains and outdoor seating. If the hotel is out of your price range, the gardens are now open to the public, so you can come for a coffee or cocktail; you won't have access to the original frescoes, friezes and hand-painted reliefs that decorate the suites, mind you.

Gallery Hotel Art
Vicolo dell'Oro 5, Duomo & Around (055 27263, www. lungarnocollection.com). **Map** *p63 K9.*
Florence's original hip hotel opened in 1999, back when its East-meets-West design aesthetic was refreshingly different from the norm. Located in a tiny piazza near the Ponte Vecchio, the place has a cosy library with squashy sofas, thoughtfully supplied with cashmere throws and mountains of arty books to browse. The stylish Fusion Bar serves *aperitivi*, brunches, light lunches and dinners. The public rooms on the ground floor often double as show-space for contemporary artists and photographers. The bedrooms are super comfortable, and the bathrooms are a dream.

Hotel Brunelleschi
Piazza Santa Elisabetta 3, Duomo & Around (055 27370, www. hotelbrunelleschi.it). **Map** *p63 L7.*
It's hard to believe that the hotel's Byzantine tower was once a prison – easier to credit is that this is the city's oldest standing structure. The luxurious rooms are spread through the circular tower and reconstructed medieval church, retaining original features. Part of the restaurant is in the tower, and two penthouse suites enjoy 360° city views. There's even a private

museum in the basement, along with an original Roman caldarium (plunge bath) that was found embedded in the foundations. Comfortable, welcoming and with great service, this place also gets a mention in both *The Da Vinci Code* and *Inferno*.

Palazzo Magnani Feroni
Borgo San Frediano 5, Oltrarno (055 2399544, www. palazzomagnaniferoni.com). **Map** *p164 F9.*
Expect top-class service and facilities, with prices to match, at this grand *palazzo* just south of the river. All but one of the ten big suites have separate sitting rooms elegantly furnished with sofas, armchairs and antiques. The most charming room of all is actually the smallest: a romantic junior suite with floor-to-ceiling frescoes and a little private garden. The fabulous roof terrace – complete with a bar serving light meals – offers views of the whole city.

Portrait Firenze
Lungarno Acciaiuoli 4, Duomo & Around (055 27268000, www. lungarnocollection.com). **Map** *p63 K9.*

Staying with Children
Family-friendly accommodation options for every budget

With a few exceptions – notably family-run **Casci** (see *p293*) – Florentine hoteliers used to be fairly wary of potentially disruptive small guests. More recently however, the scales seem to have tipped in favour of families, with higher-end hotels leading the way.

The **Four Seasons Hotel** (see *above*), the **Westin Excelsior** (see *opposite*) and **Grand Hotel Minerva** (see *opposite*) to name just a few, take pride in advertising child-oriented conveniences such as games, kid-friendly breakfasts and babysitting services, besides the obvious cots and high chairs. The latest luxury establishment to join the scene, **Portrait Firenze** (see *above*), has gone one step further and designed family suites with handy kitchenettes.

Lower-tier hotels have been quick to spot the trend and have renovated or adapted their rooms to accommodate families. Reasonably priced options include **Hotel Davanzati** (see *opposite)* and **Torre Guelfa** (see *p292*). Older children and young teens will love the Camera

dei Giochi at **Soprarno Suites** (see *opposite*) and **Garibaldi Blu**'s (see *opposite*) models of Marvel superheroes.

Short-term rentals with kitchen and laundry facilities – and maybe some outdoor space such as a small garden or terrace – can be particularly suitable for families: just make sure that the property is listed as kid-friendly. Quality (if pricey) options include **Residence Hilda** (Via dei Servi 40, San Marco, 055 288021, www.residencehilda. com) and **Lungarno Suites** (Borgo San Jacopo, Oltrarno, 055 27261, www. lungarnocollection.com).

The convenient ATAF day ticket allowing unlimited bus and tram travel for up to four family members for just €6 means that other alternatives outside the city gates such as **Riva Lofts** (Via Baccio Bandinelli 98, 055 7130 272, www.rivalofts.com) opposite the Parco delle Cascine or the charming **Pensione Bencistà** (see *p293*) in Fiesole are also feasible options.

The latest addition to the Ferragamo-owned Lungarno Collection of luxury boutique hotels is gathering praise across the board for its stunning location overlooking the Ponte Vecchio, its sleek designer interiors in muted hues with gold touches and its 37 huge rooms (including a spectacular penthouse suite), each featuring a fully-equipped kitchenette, which are particularly popular with families. The latest technology is integrated seamlessly and unobtrusively throughout the premises, and an excellent breakfast is served until 11am.

Westin Excelsior
Piazza Ognissanti 3, Santa Maria Novella (055 27151, www. westinflorence.com). **Map** *p101 E7.*
While it still offers an element of old-world luxury, the Westin Excelsior has introduced some contemporary touches. There's now a fitness area, plus two 'Westin Workout' rooms that have been equipped for the health-conscious guest. In addition, the restaurant offers a special menu of low-calorie dishes. All this, however, exists within a very traditional framework: the doormen are dressed in maroon and grey livery, and the grand public rooms have polished marble floors, neoclassical columns, painted wooden ceilings and stained glass. The 171 rooms and suites are sumptuously appointed; some boast terraces with views over the river to the rooftops of the Oltrarno.

Expensive
Antica Torre Tornabuoni Uno
Via de' Tornabuoni 1, Santa Maria Novella (055 2658161, www.tornabuoni1.com). **Map** *p101 J8.*
The roof terrace of this 12-room hotel, which occupies the upper storeys of an ancient tower overlooking piazza Santa Trinita, has arguably the most spectacular view of any hotel in Florence. Breakfast and drinks are served here in summer with a backdrop of just about every monument in the city. In cooler weather, the glassed-in loggia is almost as good. While undeniably

comfortable, the bedrooms (several of which have private terraces) are not terribly inspiring; however, the views that they enjoy certainly are. Aside from the terrace, there are no public spaces.

Garibaldi Blu
Piazza Santa Maria Novella 21, Santa Maria Novella (055 277300, www.hotelgaribaldiblu.com). **Map** *p101 H6.*
Well placed near the train station and just a short walk from the main sights and the via Tornabuoni shopping district, this boutique hotel provides a post-modern setting with a sombre palette of denim, grey and antique rose hues. Quirky palm trees made from recycled tyres rise alongside Pietra Serena Renaissance columns, while life-size Marvel superheroes loom on landings and in corridors. Twenty-two individually decorated rooms and suites mix original 19th-century frescoes and 1970s furniture. Shell out that little bit extra for a front room with a view of the lovely church façade. Some facilities, such as the conference and breakfast rooms, are shared with an adjoining sister establishment.

Grand Hotel Minerva
Piazza Santa Maria Novella 16, Santa Maria Novella (055 27230, www.grandhotelminerva.com). **Map** *p101 H6.*
Once an annex hosting guests to the adjacent convent, the Minerva has been a hotel since the mid 19th century, but is determinedly 21st century, with bright, modern colours and a young, dynamic team of staff. It's one of the nicest hotels in this category; it's also close to the train station. Many of the appealing rooms have sunny views over piazza Santa Maria Novella (it can get noisy in summer), while extras include in-room electric kettles, a kids' package of videos and games, and a shiatsu massage on request. Pet owners get a special deal (a room with a terrace and a wooden floor, cat litter and pet food) as do women travelling alone (room upgrades, special bath goodies, magazines, free room service).

There's a small pool and a bar on the panoramic roof garden.

Hotel Davanzati
Via Porta Rossa 5, Duomo & Around (055 286666, www. hoteldavanzati.it). **Map** *p63 L8.*
The friendly owners know a thing or two about being good hosts: they invite guests to socialise over complimentary drinks and nibbles every day at 6.30pm, and provide free laptops and iPads with daily newspapers, streamed HD films and, of course, free Wi-Fi. Beamed ceilings, fragments of frescoes and chunks of exposed brickwork peep here and there, but the 19 rooms are pleasantly functional, spotlessly clean and offer a rare variety of combinations including family and interconnecting rooms. If you can handle the steep flight of 26 steps to the lift (the staff will help with the luggage) and unless you're hell bent on modern design, it's hard to find any drawbacks to this family-run gem set right next to the historic Palazzo Davanzati.

Hotel L'Orologio
Piazza Santa Maria Novella 24, Santa Maria Novella (055 277380, www.hotelorologioflorence.com). **Map** *p101 H5.*
If you like timepieces, you'll love this rather mad hotel – as the name implies, it's dedicated to great watches. Each of the five floors is themed around one brand – Patek Philippe, Rolex, but oddly no Timex – and each bedroom is themed around one vintage model; the public spaces (a grand foyer and pleasantly intimate drawing-room off it) are full of related art, antiques and furniture. A smart corridor leading to the plush and comfortable bar features a modern sundial on the floor. Breakfast is served on the fourth floor, which provides wonderful views across the city.

Soprarno Suites
Via Maggio 35, Oltrarno (055 0468718, www.soprarnosuites. com). **Map** *p164 H10.*
Located on the first and second floor of a 16th-century building at the heart of Florence's left bank

quarter, Soprarno is a stylish B&B offering ten unique deluxe and superior rooms. The eclectic decor blends original frescoes with custom-made furniture and reflects the owners' passion for design and vintage pieces, ranging from printer's cabinets and clawfoot baths to neon signs. There's a pleasantly relaxed feel to the place, with plenty of books and magazines, vinyl records, an honesty bar and complimentary Wi-Fi. Guests are also welcome to use the first-floor kitchen-library-dining room where breakfast is served.

Mid-range
Art Atelier
Via dell'Amorino 20, San Lorenzo (055 283777, www.hotelartatelier. com). Map p119 J5.
Modern by Florentine standards, this 19th-century building exudes good taste and refinement. The rooms, many of them with vaulted ceilings and original features, use an intriguing mix of materials and decorating techniques – Carrara marble, stone, ceramics, frescoes and wall paintings – to create unusual spaces that are on the austere side, but not without charm, and there's an 'Art Atelier' space where exhibitions are held. Breakfast and service are very good, and the location is excellent – the Cappelle Medicee are within 100m, and the key sites in easy reach.

Il Guelfo Bianco
Via Cavour 29, San Marco (055 288330, www.ilguelfobianco.it). Map p131 M4.
Inhabiting two adjacent 15th-century townhouses, this pleasant, efficiently run hotel lies just north of the Duomo. The 40 bedrooms and one self-catering apartment (sleeping four) have been thoughtfully decorated in traditional style; the more capacious rooms allow for an additional two beds, making them a good choice for families. The walls throughout are hung with the owner's impressive contemporary art collection. The rooms that front on to via Cavour have been soundproofed, but those at the back are still

noticeably quieter. Two attractive courtyards offer respite from the city noise; one is used for breakfast in warm weather.

Hotel dei Macchiaioli
Via Cavour 21, San Marco (055 213154, www.hoteldeimacchiaioli. com). Map p131 M4.
Opened in 2010, this well-placed boutique hotel will appeal to fans of the I Macchiaioli group of Tuscan artists. This was their base for more than two decades in the mid 19th century. Palazzo Morrocchi, as it was then known, was filled with unusual frescoes by the group of artists, and many of them are still visible. The outstanding work is by Annibale Gatti – it covers the entire wooden ceiling of the main hall that looks out on to via Cavour. The rooms, all of them on the first floor, are old-fashioned and comfortable, and as charming as the staff.

Hotel Morandi alla Crocetta
Via Laura 50, San Marco (055 234 4748, www.hotelmorandi.it). Map p131 P4.
This hotel transports you back in time from the moment you enter the beautifully tiled entrance hall. With lovely Persian rugs on warm parquet floors, old-fashioned bedspreads in red and gold, and a sense of peace and calm that permeates the entire space. No wonder: the hotel is located in the former 16th-century convent of the Crocetta. Traces of the convent can be found in many of the rooms, with fresco fragments, vaulted ceilings and brick arches adding real individuality. Some rooms have terraces.

La Scaletta
Via de' Guicciardini 13, Oltrarno (055 283028, www.hotellascaletta. it). Map p164 J10.
A change of management in 2005 swept away the figurative cobwebs of the old-style Scaletta, housed in a grand 15th-century *palazzo* between the Ponte Vecchio and Palazzo Pitti, in favour of cleaner – even stylish – lines. The 11 buttermilk-painted bedrooms have elegant matching curtains and bedspreads, modern wrought-iron bedheads and nice old wardrobes. Most are quiet;

three rooms overlook the Giardino di Boboli, while those on noisy via Guicciardini have effective double glazing. All rooms now have bathrooms. There are no fewer than three roof gardens/terraces that offer breathtaking views of Boboli and the city skyline; one has a bar that's open in the evenings.

Torre Guelfa
Borgo SS Apostoli 8, Duomo & Around (055 2396338, www.hoteltorreguelfa.com). Map p63 K9.
This popular hotel literally started at the top and worked its way down; the original rooms were all on the top floor, but the hotel now occupies the whole of the 14th-century *palazzo*, which incorporates the tallest privately owned tower in Florence. Evening drinks come with stunning views at the tower-top bar. Breakfast is served in a sunny, glassed-in loggia on the third floor, where there's also an elegant sitting room (with Wi-Fi access) with a painted box ceiling. Bedrooms are decorated in pastel colours with wrought-iron beds (including several four-posters); some are huge. Number 15 is a romantic little den with its own roof garden – you'll need to book at least six months in advance for this. The 12 rooms on the first floor are cheaper and simpler; those facing the street are quite dark.

Budget
Black 5 Townhouse
Via Giuseppe Verdi 5, Santa Croce (335 6368862, www. black5florencesuite.it). Map p145 O8.
From the outside, the curiously named Black 5 Townhouse looks like any other unprepossessing Florentine block. But once inside, the snazzy black and mirrored elevator gives a hint of things to come: animal skins on the floor, Pollock-esque art on the walls, and muted greys punctuated by bold splashes of colour. It's young, fresh and engaging, with each of the ten rooms spanning myriad gorgeous colours and styles – some have Pop Art wall coverings, others gloriously rich fabric headboards against lime green

walls, and all come with wooden caisson ceilings, period brickwork and a whirlpool bath. Views are either over a central courtyard or the main road. The attic breakfast room opens on to a sweet little terrace with great views across the rooftops to Palazzo Vecchio and the Duomo.

Casa Pucci
Via Santa Monaca 8, Oltrarno (055 216560, www.casapucci.it). Map p164 F10.
Signora Pucci's ground-floor apartment, not far from buzzy piazza Santo Spirito, occupies part of an ex-convent dating from the 15th century. Three of the five rooms lead off a cool, plant-filled courtyard garden where a huge rustic table is laid in the mornings for summer breakfasts. The whole place has a nice, lived-in feel, from the big kitchen (which guests are free to use) to the spacious, homely rooms furnished with family antiques and paintings. Romantics should go for room no.5 with its four-poster bed and stone fireplace. A faithful clientele of return guests – plus amazingly low prices – means that you need to book well ahead.

Casa Schlatter
Viale dei Mille 14, Campo di Marte, Outside the City Gates (347 1180215, www.casaschlatter-florence.com). Bus 10, 17. Map p186.
This characterful three-roomed B&B, just outside the city walls, was once the home and studio of idiosyncratic Swiss painter and sculptor Carlo Adolfo Schlatter. The conversion has been a wonderfully sympathetic one; the artist's work fills every available space and surface in the house, turning it into a strange but fascinating 19th-century museum that will ensure you get an eyeful of genuine weirdness at every turn, from bronze giant squids and gravestones to elegant canvases set on brilliant rose-coloured walls and unusual antique objects in the rooms. Schlatter's great-granddaughter Alessandra cooks amazing made-to-order savoury dishes and cakes for breakfast (which isn't

Gallery Hotel Art *p290*

included, but is great value at €7.50), serving them in a lovely garden.

Casci
Via Cavour 13, San Lorenzo (055 211686, www.hotelcasci.com). Map p119 M4.
The super-helpful Lombardi family runs this friendly pensione, which occupies a 15th-century *palazzo* just north of the Duomo, where opera composer Giacomo Rossini lived from 1851 to 1855. The open-plan bar and breakfast area has frescoed ceilings and shelves stocked with guidebooks; the 24 bedrooms are comfortable and come with up-to-date bathrooms. Rooms at the back look on to a beautiful garden; two sizeable family rooms sleep up to five. It's closed for three weeks in January.

Pensione Bencistà
Via Benedetto da Maiano 4, Fiesole, Outside the City Gates (055 59163, www.bencista.com). Bus 7.
Housed in a former convent and run as a pensione by the Simoni family since 1925, Bencistà has a

fabulous setting on the hillside just below Fiesole. Public rooms are furnished with antiques; one has a fireplace and shelves stuffed with old books. Bedrooms are off a warren of passageways and staircases. No two are alike – those at the front enjoy unrivalled city views, as does the flower-filled terrace. The restaurant overlooks the city and serves homely, traditional food; half-board rates are available.

Scoti
Via de' Tornabuoni 7, Santa Maria Novella (055 292128, www. hotelscoti.com). Map p101 J8.
If you want to secure a room in the wonderful Scoti, housed on the second floor of a 15th-century palazzo, book well ahead: it's popular with visitors worldwide. The lofty bedrooms are simple but bright and sunny and all are en suite; the frescoed salon has retained its air of faded glory. Breakfast (charged extra) is served around a big communal table or in the rooms.

Getting Around

ARRIVING & LEAVING

By air
Amerigo Vespucci Airport
at Peretola is by far the easiest
way to reach Florence, but only
CityJet and British Airways from
London City Airport and Vueling
from London Gatwick and Luton
fly here. Pisa's **Galileo Galilei
Airport** is a train or coach journey
away from Florence, but it has
frequent flights to and from the
UK, and Delta operates a seasonal
service to New York. A third
choice is Bologna's **Guglielmo
Marconi Airport**.

Florence Airport, Peretola (Amerigo Vespucci)
055 3061300,
www.aeroporto.firenze.it.
About 5km (3 miles) west of
central Florence, Amerigo
Vespucci is linked to the city by
Volainbus (800 373760, www.
fsbusitalia.it), a bus shuttle
service that runs half-hourly
5am-midnight, costs €6 (€10
return) and stops in the Busitalia
station at via Santa Caterina da
Siena 15. Buy tickets on the bus,
at the airport bar or wherever bus
tickets are sold. Tickets must be
stamped on board. Bus season
ticketholders don't have to buy an
extra ticket. The new T2 tramway
(*see opposite*) will run from the
airport to the city centre and is
expected to become operational
early in 2018. A taxi to Florence
costs from €22 (*see p296*) and
takes 15-20 mins. For coaches to
Pisa Airport, *see right*.

Pisa International Airport (Galileo Galilei)
050 849300,
www.pisa-airport.com.
Direct trains to Florence no longer
run all the way from the airport;

you first need to reach Pisa
Centrale by a shuttle bus costing
€1.30 each way (in the process
of being replaced by a faster but
more expensive shuttle train). The
train to Florence's Santa Maria
Novella (SMN) station from Pisa
Centrale takes about an hour and
tickets are €8.40 each way.
A coach service from Pisa
Airport to Florence SMN train
station is run by **Autostradale**
(050 6138469, www.autostradale.
it). It leaves from outside the
arrivals area in Pisa and from
piazzale Montelungo in Florence
(walk all the way down platform
16 inside the train station).
Tickets can be bought from
the kiosk in the airport, from
Autostradale stewards at the
terminus or online and cost €7.50
one way or €13.50 return. The
journey takes 70 mins.
To get to Florence by car, take
the Firenze–Pisa–Livorno road,
which goes to the west of the city.

Bologna Airport (Guglielmo Marconi)
051 6479615,
www.bologna-airport.it.
Aerobus (www.aerobus.bo.it)
stops outside Terminal A
(arrivals) and leaves for Bologna
train station every 11 mins
5.30am-midnight. Tickets cost €6
from the machine in the terminal
building and must be validated
on board. The trip takes about
20 mins in total. A taxi costs
about €15 (€18 at night).
From Bologna Centrale,
trains to Florence are frequent
and take 35-60 mins; prices
vary. A downside of flying in to
Bologna is that you may find
some trains into Florence fully
booked, unless you've bought a
ticket in advance (which means
changing your ticket if the plane
is delayed).

The **Appennino Shuttle** (055
585271, www.appenninoshuttle.
it) operates direct buses every
couple of hours between Bologna
Airport and piazzale Montelungo
(near the Fortezza da Basso) in
Florence. Tickets are €20 online,
€25 on board and the journey is
around 80 mins, but allow plenty
of time for possible delays due to
motorway traffic.
Travelling by car, the journey
to Florence takes about 70 mins,
south on the A1 motorway.

Major airlines
British Airways *199 712266,*
www.britishairways.com
CityJet *064 5236910,*
www.cityjet.com
Easyjet *199 201840,*
www.easyjet.com
Ryanair *895 5895509,*
www.ryanair.com
Vueling *tickets 895 8953333,*
customer service 199 206621,
www.vueling.com

By rail
Train tickets can be bought
online, from the ticket desks, from
vending machines in the station,
from www.trenitalia.com, or from
selected travel agents.
Before boarding any train,
stamp (*convalidare*) your ticket
and any supplements in the
yellow machines at the head of
the platforms; failure to do so
could mean a €50 fine.
The main station is Santa Maria
Novella in the city centre. Some
services go to **Campo di Marte**
station to the north-east of the
city. For train information call
892021 (24hrs daily) or visit www.
trenitalia.com. Information on
disabled access is available at
the disabled assistance desk on
platform 5 at Santa Maria Novella
or by calling the national line

199 303060 (open 7am-9pm daily and English is spoken).

Fast trains to Bologna and beyond (to Turin, Milan or Venice) in the north and to Rome and Naples in the south are also operated by private carrier Italo (892020 information, 06 0708 tickets, www.italotreno.it, app Italo Treno). Trenitalia and Italo tickets are not interchangeable.

Campo di Marte *Via Mannelli, Outside the City Gates.* Florence's main station when SMN is closed at night. Many long-distance trains stop here. The ticket office is open 6.20am-9pm daily.

Santa Maria Novella *Piazza della Stazione, Santa Maria Novella. Open 4.15am-1.30am daily. Information office 7am-9pm daily. Ticket office 5am-10pm daily. Map p101 H4* Taxis serve Florence's Santa Maria Novella station on a 24-hr basis; many city buses also stop there. It's a five- to ten-minute walk into central Florence.

By road
Budget national and international coach travel is making a comeback. In Florence, you'll probably arrive using one of the following operators:
Eurolines/Baltour *(0861 1991900, www.eurolines. it) stopping at the Busitalia bus station in via Santa Caterina da Siena 15 (see p200 Transport in Tuscany).*
Flixbus *(02 94759208, www. flixbus.it) stopping in piazzale Montelungo (viale Filippo Strozzi by the Fortezza da Basso, Outside the City Gates).*

PUBLIC TRANSPORT

Bus services
Public bus company
ATAF *(800 424500, 199 104245 from mobiles, www.ataf.net). Open 6.45am-8pm Mon-Sat.* The ATAF infopoint (Santa Maria Novella station ticket hall, counters 8-9) has English-speaking staff, sells a variety of bus tickets, and has a free booklet with details of major routes and fares. The official app is Ataf 2.0.

Fares & tickets
It's cheaper to buy tickets before boarding buses, but you can now also get them on board from the driver at €2 for 90 mins. Tickets are available from the ATAF desk (*see above*), a few machines, *tabacchi* (tobacconists), news stands and any bars displaying an ATAF sticker. When you board, stamp the ticket in one of the validation machines. Bus tickets are also valid for trams (*see p296*). Be aware that plain-clothes inspectors regularly board buses for spot checks; anyone without a valid ticket is fined €50, payable on the spot or within 15 days at the main information office or in post offices.
90 min ticket *(biglietto 90 minuti) €1.20; valid for 90 mins of travel on all city area buses.*
Multiple ticket *(biglietto multiplo) €4.70; 4 tickets, each valid for 90 mins.*

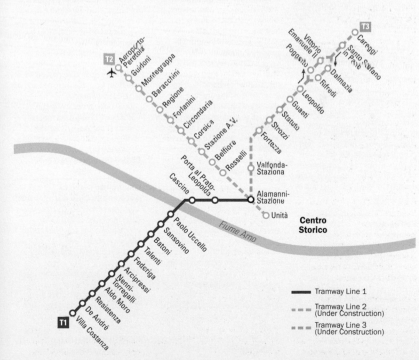

Centro
Storico

Tramway Line 1

Tramway Line 2
(Under Construction)

Tramway Line 3
(Under Construction)

AGILE electronic cards *€10/€20/€30 with 10/21/35 x 90-min tickets respectively (cannot be shared by multiple travellers; swipe once over validating machine).*
24-hr ticket *(biglietto ventiquattro ore) €5; one-day pass that must be stamped at the start of the first journey.*
Daily family *€6; valid for up to 4 family members to midnight on the day of stamping.*
3-day ticket *(biglietto tre giorni) €12.*
7-day ticket *(biglietto sette giorni) €18.*
Monthly and yearly passes are also available.
Most ATAF routes run from 5.30am to midnight with a frequency of 10-30 mins. The orange and white *fermate* (bus stops) list the main stops along the route. Each of the stops has its name indicated at the top.

Disabled travellers
Most buses across Florence are now of the newer design (grey and green) and are fully wheelchair accessible via an electric platform at the rear door. The older orange buses are sadly not.

Useful tourist routes
7 from piazza San Marco to Fiesole.
10 to and from Settignano.
12, 13 circular routes via Santa Maria Novella station, piazza della Libertà, piazzale Michelangelo and San Miniato.
ATAF also runs a network of electric buses, which covers four central routes: **C1, C2, C3** and **D.** Normal bus tickets or season tickets are valid. These routes are detailed in ATAF's booklet and at www.ataf.net.

Rail services
Trenitalia
There are regular local train services from the central Santa Maria Novella station to Campo di Marte in the east and Rifredi in the west (892021, www.tren italia.com). Tickets can be bought online or at the station ticket offices.

Tram services
The T1 **Tramvia** line from central Florence to Scandicci is up and running. Two more lines are due to be operational in 2018; T2 will serve the airport, while T3 will reach the Careggi hospital north of the city centre. A map of the three tram lines is on *p295.* For further information, visit www.gestramvia.it.

TAXIS

Licensed cabs are white with yellow graphics, with a code name of a place plus ID number on the door; 'Londra 6', for example. If you have problems, make a note of this code. You can only get a cab at a rank or by phone. Ranks are indicated by a blue sign with TAXI written in white, but this is no guarantee that any cars will be waiting. Try piazza della Repubblica, piazza della Stazione, piazza San Marco and piazza Santa Croce.

Fares & surcharges
Taxis in Florence are expensive. When the taxi arrives, the meter should read €3.30 during the day, €5.30 on Sun and on public hols, and €6.60 at night. The fare increases at a rate of €0.91/km. Lone women pay 10% less after 9pm, but only if they request the discount when booking. There is a daytime minimum fare of €5; €7 minimum on Sun and public hols; and a nighttime minimum fare of €8.30. Taxis between the airport and anywhere in the city centre have a fixed tariff of €22 in the day, €25.30 at night, plus €1 per piece of luggage.

Phone cabs
Try to book a cab at least a few hours before you need it. When your call is answered, give the address where you want to be picked up, specifying if the street number is *nero* or *rosso* (for an explanation, *see p298*). If a cab is available, you'll be given its code and a time; for example, *'Londra 6 in tre minuti'.* If not, a message or operator will tell you to call back.
Taxi numbers 055 4390; 055 4798; 055 4242; 055 4499.

DRIVING

The centre of Florence is easily walkable and the electric bus service is a good back-up so it's usually best to leave cars at home, particularly given the permanent and expanding Traffic-Free Zones (ZTL), which include the old city centre. Only residents or permit-holders can enter 7.30am- 8pm, Mon-Fri; 7.30am-4pm Sat. This is usually extended in the summer to exclude cars from the centre in the evenings Thur-Sun. In addition, the city is frequently bringing in new restrictions, so if you plan to drive check in the local press or with the municipal police (*see p304*).

Speed limits are currently 50kmph (30mph), or 45kmph (26mph) on motorbikes and mopeds, on urban roads; 70kmph (43mph) on urban highways; 90kmph (56mph) on secondary extra-urban roads (*superstrada*); 110kmph (68mph) on dual carriageways and 130kmph (80mph) on the motorway (*autostrada*).

Superstrada are free roads and have blue signs and a name beginning SS. *Autostrada* are toll roads and are indicated by green signs.

The legal drink drive limit is 0.5g/litre, which as a guide is generally reached or passed with less than a quarter litre of wine or a half litre of beer.

In a traffic emergency call 055 3285 (055 328 3333 for less urgent situations). (*See p298* Emergencies.) For general traffic or parking information, call 055055 (8am-8pm Mon-Sat).

Breakdown services
Automobile Club d'Italia (ACI)
Viale Amendola 36, Outside the City Gates (055 24861/ 24hr emergencies 803 116 or 800 000 116, www.aci.it). Bus 8, 12, 13, 14, 31. **Open** *8.30am-1pm, 3-5.30pm Mon-Fri.*
The ACI charges reasonable rates and will tell you what to do in case of a breakdown. Members of associated organisations such as the AA, RAC or AAA may be entitled to free basic repairs or preferential rates.

Car hire

Avis, Europcar, Hertz and all the usual suspects operate from a car rental hub in via Palagio degli Spini near the airport (shuttle bus available from the airport car park).

Renting an electric car is a very practical option as you can drive them throughout most of the city centre. One conveniently central company offering electric car hire is **ELP** (055 2399231, www.citycarrent.org).

Car pounds

If your car's not where you left it, chances are it's been towed. Call 055 4224142 with the car's registration number to confirm. The central car pound, Depositeria SaS (www.serviziallastrada.it, open 8am-8pm Mon-Fri, 8am-7pm Sat; closed Sun), is in via Allende, behind the Novoli fruit and veg market (bus 23 or 57). The car owner must take proof of ownership and ID to regain possession.

If your car is stolen and found, it will be taken to the Ufficio Depositeria Comunale in via Benedetto Dei 2a (055 3283951). The office is open 8am-12.45pm Mon-Fri, and Thur to 6pm.

Fuel stations

All petrol stations sell unleaded fuel (*senza piombo*). Diesel fuel is *gasolio*. Many offer a discount for self-service. Attendants don't expect tips. There are stations on most main roads leading out of town. Normal hours are 7.30am-12.30pm and 3-7pm daily except Sun. Most stations have 24-hr self-service machines accepting notes and cards.

Parking

Parking in Florence is a major problem and is severely restricted – most main streets are no-parking zones. Parking is forbidden where you see *passo carrabile* (access at all times) and *sosta vietata* (no parking) signs. Beware of white lines, they can mean either free parking, or reserved parking for residents only (check vertical signage to confirm). Blue lines denote pay-parking; there will be either meters or an attendant to issue timed tickets, which you should return to them when you get back. Disabled spaces are marked by yellow stripes and require a permit. *Zona rimozione* (tow-away area) signs are valid for the length of the street, while temporary tow zones are marked at each end. Signs tell you when street cleaning takes place – your car will be towed if parked on a street being cleaned.

The safest place to leave a car is in one of the underground car parks (*parcheggi*), such as **Parterre** and **Piazza Stazione**, which both have surveillance cameras.

Roads

There are three *autostrade* (motorways) in Tuscany that you have to pay a toll to use: the **A1** (Rome-Florence-Bologna), **A11** (the coast-Lucca-Florence) and **A12** (Livorno-Genova). *Autostrade* are indicated by green signs. As an idea of price, it costs around €20 to drive the 270km (168 miles) from Rome to Florence. The dual-carriageway roads from Florence to Siena (RA3) and to Pisa-Livorno (known as FI-PI-LI) are toll free.

CYCLING

There are cycle lanes on the main *viali*, but that's no guarantee they'll only be used by bikes. Watch for doors being opened suddenly from cars parked on the side of the road.

Moped & bike hire

Mille e Una Bici (www.bicifirenze.it) is a council-supported scheme to encourage the use of bikes. There are hire points all around the city including at the three main train stations, piazza Ghiberti, Parterre and Stazione Leopolda. Bike hire costs either €2/hr or €10/day.

The companies below also rent out bikes. To hire a scooter or moped (*motorino*), you need a credit card, ID and cash deposit. Helmets must be worn on all mopeds.

Alinari

Via San Zanobi 38r, San Lorenzo (055 280500, www.alinarirental.com). **Open** *9.30am-1pm, 3-7.30pm Mon-Sat; 10am-1pm, 3-7pm Sun.* **Map** *p119 L2.*
Rental of a 125cc scooter for one or two people is €55/day. A current driving licence is required.

Florence by Bike

Via San Zanobi 54r, San Lorenzo (055 488992, www.florencebybike.it). **Open** *9am-1pm, 3.30-7.30pm Mon-Fri; (9am-7pm Sat; 9am-5pm Sun. Shorter hours in winter.* **Map** *p119 L2.*
Bike hire costs either €3/hr or €14/day. Guided tours are also available, and the majority of staff speak good English.

WALKING

Walking is the quickest way to get around central Florence. Our street maps cover most of the centre, and a good street map is available free from tourist offices. For an overview map, *see p8*.

Resources A-Z

ACCIDENT & EMERGENCY

Emergency numbers
Ambulance *Ambulanza* **118**.
City traffic police *Vigili Urbani* **055 3285** (emergency).
Emergency services & state police *Polizia di Stato* **113**.
Fire service *Vigili del Fuoco* **115**.
Police *Carabinieri* (English-speaking helpline) **112**.

A&E departments
If you need urgent medical care, it's best to go to the *pronto soccorso* (casualty) department of one of the hospitals listed below; they're open 24 hrs daily. Alternatively, call 118 for an ambulance (*ambulanza*).

To find a doctor on call in your area (emergencies only), phone 118. For a night (8pm-8am) or all-day Sun emergency home visit, call the **Guardia Medica** for your area (quartiere 1: 055 6938980; Oltrarno: 055 215616).

Ospedale di Careggi Largo
Brambilla 3, Outside the City Gates (055 794 111, www.aou-careggi.toscana.it). Bus 2, 8, 14C. The main hospital and the best place to go to for most emergencies.

Ospedale Meyer *Viale Pieraccini 24, Outside the City Gates (055 56621, www.meyer.it). Bus 14C.* Children's hospital.

Ospedale Palagi Viale
Michelangelo 41, Outside the City Gates (055 65771). Bus 12, 13. **Open** *8am-8pm daily.* For eye emergencies; outside these opening hours go to Careggi.

Santa Maria Nuova *Piazza Santa Maria Nuova 1, San Marco (055 69381).* **Map** *p101 N6.* The most central hospital in Florence. There's also a 24-hr pharmacy directly outside.

If you need a translator to help out at the hospital, contact:
AVO (Association of Hospital Volunteers) *Via G Carducci 8, Outside the City Gates (24hrs 055 2344567, www.avofirenze.it).* **Open** *Office hours 10am-midday, 4-8pm Mon-Fri; closed Aug.* AVO has a group of volunteer interpreters who help out with explanations to doctors and hospital staff in 22 languages. They also give support and advice.

ADDRESSES

Addresses in Florence are numbered and colour-coded. Residential addresses are 'black' numbers (*nero*), while most commercial addresses are 'red' (*rosso*). This means that on any one street, there can be two addresses with the same number but different colours and these properties can sometimes be quite far apart. Some houses are both shops and flats and could have two different numbers, one red and one black. Red numbers are followed by an 'r' when the address is written, a practice we have followed throughout this guide.

Note that the name on a business's shopfront or awning is quite often different from its official, listed name. We have used the former name wherever possible.

AGE RESTRICTIONS

In Italy, there are official age restrictions on a number of things you can buy and activities. However, it's extremely rare for anyone to be asked to show ID in bars or elsewhere, other than in gay bars and clubs. The age of sexual consent is 14, with an exception for sex between minors who are 13 and have a partner who is less than three years older.

Beer and wine can be legally drunk in bars and pubs from the age of 16; spirits can be drunk by those 18 and over. It's an offence to sell cigarettes to children under 18. Mopeds (50cc) can be driven from the age of 14; cars from 18; only those over 21 can hire a car.

ATTITUDE & ETIQUETTE

In churches, women are expected to cover their shoulders and not wear anything skimpy. Shorts and vests are out for everyone.

Queues are a foreign concept, but in a crowded shop, customers know who is before them and who's after, and usually respect the order. In shops, say *buongiorno* or *buona sera* on entering and leaving, and bear in mind that it's generally considered rude to walk in, look around and leave without asking for what you are looking for or at least greeting the shop assistant.

When addressing anyone except children, it's important to

use the appropriate title: *signora* for women, *signorina* for young women, and *signore* for men.

CLIMATE

The hills surrounding Florence mean that it can be cold and humid in winter and very hot and humid in the summer. Between late Jun and Aug, daytime temperatures often soar to 40°C (104°F) and rarely fall below 30°C (86°F).

During the summer, you should be sure to take the sun seriously: every year, local doctors issue warnings about the number of visitors who are hospitalised with serious burns from spending too much time in the sun and going out in the middle of the day (Italians stay indoors whenever they can during the hottest hours).

The short spring and autumn in Florence and Tuscany can be very warm. They're not without risk of rain, though, especially in Mar, Apr and Sept. Between Nov and Feb, you can't rely on good weather: you could find anything from a week of rain to crisp, bright and sometimes even warm sunshine.

CONSUMER

You can find advice and file complaints at the Sportello Tutela Diritti del Turista desk operated by the *via Cavour* Tourist Information Office (*see p307*). Regione Toscana maintains a list of consumer rights associations. Check www.prontoconsumatore.it/sportelli-di-assistenza (in Italian only) for details.

CUSTOMS

EU nationals don't have to declare goods imported into or exported from Italy for their personal use, as long as they arrive from another EU country. Personal use is considered to be within the limits of 800 cigarettes (and limits on cigars), 10l of spirits, 90l of wine (and limits on other alcoholic drinks). US citizens should check their duty-free allowance on the way out. Random checks are made for drugs (*see p300* Drugs). For non-EU citizens, the following import limits apply:
• 200 cigarettes or 100 small cigars or 50 cigars or 250g of tobacco
• 1l of spirits (over 22% alcohol) or 2l of fortified wine (under 22%)
• 50g of perfume
• 500g of coffee

There are no restrictions on the importation of cameras, watches or electrical goods. Visitors are also allowed to bring in up to €10,000 (or equivalent) in cash without declaring it.

DISABLED

Disabled facilities in Florence are improving. Recent laws stipulate that all new public offices, bars, restaurants and hotels must be equipped with full disabled facilities. Currently, the standard of access still varies greatly, though most museums are wheelchair-accessible, with lifts, ramps on steps and toilets for the disabled.

Pavement corners in the centre of town are now sloped to allow for wheelchair access. New buses are equipped with ramps and a wheelchair area. Trains that allow space for wheelchairs in the carriages and have disabled toilets have a wheelchair logo on the outside, but there is no wheelchair access up the steep steps on the south side of the station: use the east or north entrance, or call the information office for assistance (*see p307*). Taxis take wheelchairs, but tell them when you book.

There are free disabled parking bays all over Florence, and disabled drivers with the sticker have access to pedestrian areas of the city. There are wheelchair-accessible toilets at Florence and Pisa airports and Santa Maria Novella station, as well as in many of Florence's main sights and at several public toilets.

The Tourist Board produces a booklet (also in English, available in print from tourist offices or as a PDF downloadable from www.firenzeturismo.it) with disabled-aware descriptions how many steps on each floor, wide doorways and so on – of venues across Florence Province. The official council website (www.comune.fi.it) also has useful sightseeing itineraries suitable for disabled visitors.

Wheelchair hire is free of charge both from the Misericordia (055 212222) and the Fratellanza Militare (055

Climate

Average temperatures and monthly rainfall in Florence

	Temp (°C/°F)	Rainfall (mm/in)	Sun (hrs/day)
January	8 / 45	63/2.5	2
February	10/46	49/2	2
March	11/50	69/2.7	3
April	18/57	78/3	5
May	20/64	72/2.8	7
June	25/72	50/2	7
July	30/77	31/1.2	7
August	29/75	48/1.8	7
September	25/70	76/3	5
October	17/61	96/3.7	3
November	11/52	102/4	2
December	8/46	72/2.8	2

26021). If they don't have any available, they can refer to paid hire services.

DRUGS

Drug-taking is illegal in Italy and a new law has increased the severity of sentencing and put all drugs, from cannabis to heroin, on the same level from a legal standpoint. If you're caught in possession of drugs of any type, you may have to appear before a magistrate. If you can convince him or her that your stash was for purely personal use, then you may be let off with a fine, have your passport or driving licence confiscated, have your movements restricted or be ordered to leave the country. Trafficking or dealing can land you in prison for up to 20 years. It is an offence to buy or sell drugs, or to give them away. Sniffer dogs are a fixture at most ports of entry into Italy; customs police are vigilant about visitors entering with even the smallest quantities of any banned substances, and you could be refused entry or arrested.

ELECTRICITY

Most wiring systems work on one electrical current, 220V, compatible with British and US-bought products. A few systems in old buildings are 125V. With US 110V equipment, you'll need a current transformer: buy one before you travel as they can be hard to find. Adaptors, on the other hand, can be bought at any electrical shop (look for *elettricità* or *ferramenta*).

EMBASSIES & CONSULATES

There are no embassies in Florence. However, there are some consular offices, which offer limited services.
Australian Embassy *Via Antonio Bosio 5, Rome (06 852721, www.italy.embassy.gov.au).*
British Embassy *Via Venti Settembre 80A, Rome (06 4220 0001, www.gov.uk/government/world/italy).*
Canadian Embassy *Via Zara 30, Rome (06 854442911, www.italy.gc.ca).*

Irish Embassy *Piazza Campitelli 3, Ghetto, Rome (06 6979121, www.embassyofireland.it).*
New Zealand Embassy *Via Clitunno 44, Rome (06 8537501/ www.nzembassy.com/italy).*
South African Honorary Consulate *Piazza dei Salterelli 1, Duomo & Around (055 281863, lnx.sudafrica.it/en).* No office. Call to make an appointment.
US Consulate *Lungarno Amerigo Vespucci 38, Outside the City Gates (055 266951, it.usembassy.gov).* Bus D. **Open** *9am-12.30pm Mon-Fri.* In case of emergency call the above phone number; a message refers you to the current emergency number.
For details of all other embassies, see embassy.goabroad.com.

HAZARDS

In case of an earthquake, flood, fire or other environmental emergency, tourists in Italy should get in touch with the Italian Civil Protection Department's hotline on 800 840840, or its international hotline 06 82888850.

Florence is unlikely to be hit by major earthquakes. However, you can learn more on what to do before, during, and after an earthquake from the Italian Civil Protection website www. protezionecivile.gov.it (English section available). Weather alerts such as warnings for snow, heavy rain, strong winds and extreme heat are issued by the Regione Toscana; please check www. regione.toscana.it/allertameteo (in Italian only, but very visual).

HEALTH

Emergency healthcare is available for all travellers through the Italian national health system. EU citizens are entitled to most treatment for free, though many specialised medicines, examinations and tests will be charged for. To get treatment, you'll need a European Health Insurance Card (EHIC). The card will only cover partial costs of medicines. In non-emergency situations, citizens from countries with a reciprocal agreement with Italy (e.g. Australia) should go to the

state health centre, **Azienda Sanitaria di Firenze** (ASF, www. asf.toscana.it) on the second floor of borgo Ognissanti 20 (open 9am-1pm Mon-Fri). Other non-EU visitors are charged for health care. All foreign visitors are strongly advised to take out private health insurance before travelling.

For hospital treatment, go to one of the casualty departments listed above (*see p298* Accident & emergency). If you want to see a GP, go to the **ASL** (Azienda Sanitaria Locale, local health unit) for the district where you are staying, taking your EHIC with you. The ASLs are listed in the phone book and they usually open 9am-1pm and 2-7pm Mon-Fri.

Contraception

Condoms and other forms of contraception are widely available in pharmacies and most supermarkets. If you need further assistance, the Consultorio Familiare (family planning clinic) at your local ASL state health centre (*see p300*) provides free advice and information, though for an examination or prescription, you'll need an EHIC (*see above*) or insurance. An alternative is to go to a private clinic.

The morning-after pill is sold legally in Italy; it must be taken within 72 hrs, and to obtain it, you'll need to get a prescription (*see opposite*). Abortion is legal in Italy and is performed only in public hospitals, but the private clinics that are listed opposite are able to give consultations and references.

Dentists

The following dentists speak English. Always call ahead for an appointment.
Dr Marcello Luccioli *Via de' Serragli 21, Oltrarno (055 294847).* **Open** *3-6.30pm Mon, Tue, Thur.* **Map** *p164 F10.*
Dr Alessandro Cosi *Via Quintino Sella 4, Outside the City Gates (055 214238/ 335 332055 mobile).* Bus 14. **Open** *9am-1pm, 3-7pm Mon-Fri.* **Map** *p186.*

Doctors

A comprehensive list of English-speaking doctors and medical facilities in Florence, by specialisation, can be provided by the American Consulate (*see opposite*).

Dr Stephen Kerr *Piazza del Mercato Nuovo, Duomo & Around (055 288055/335 8361682, www. dr-kerr.com).* **Open** *Surgery by appointment 9am-3pm Mon-Fri. Drop-in clinic 3-5pm Mon-Fri.* **Map** *p63 K8.* This friendly, knowledgeable English GP practises privately in Florence. Standard charge for a consultation in his surgery is €60.

Arciconfraternita della Misericordia *Vicolo degli Adimari 1, Duomo & Around (055-212221, www.misericordia. firenze.it).* **Open** *7.30am-8pm Mon-Fri, 7.30am-1pm Sat.* **Map** *p63 L6.* An English-speaking GP is on duty 2-4pm Mon-Fri (no appointment needed). Standard fee is €48. For specialist check ups, appointments are given within three days.

Medical Service *Via Roma 4, Duomo & Around (24hr line 055 475411, www.medicalservice. firenze.it).* **Open** *Clinic 11am-noon, 1-3pm Mon-Sat; 5-6pm Mon-Fri.* **Map** *p63 L7.* A private medical service that organises home visits. Catering particularly to foreigners, it promises to send an English-speaking GP or specialist out to you in the city of Florence within an hour for a fee of €70-€200. Clinic visit €50-€60.

Hospitals

See p298 Accident & emergency.

Pharmacies

Pharmacies (*farmacia*), which are identified by a red or green cross hanging outside, function semi-officially as mini-clinics, with staff able to give informal medical advice and suggest non-prescription medicines. Normal opening hours are 8.30am-1pm and 4-8pm Mon-Fri and 8.30am-1pm Sat, but many central pharmacies are open all day. At other times, there's a

duty rota system. A list by the door of all pharmacies indicates the nearest one open outside normal hours, also published in local papers. At duty pharmacies, there's a small surcharge per client (not per item) when only the special duty counter is open – usually midnight-8.30am. Prescriptions are required for most medicines. If you require regular medication, make sure you know their chemical (generic) rather than brand name, as they may be available in Italy only under a different name.

STDs, HIV & AIDS

Ambulatorio Malattie Infettive *Ospedale di Careggi Largo Brambilla 3, Outside the City Gates (055 4279425/6). Bus 2, 8, 14C.* **Open** *7am-7pm Mon-Fri; 9am-12.30pm Sat.* **Map** *p186.* AIDS centre with information, advice and testing. Call ahead for an appointment. Basic English spoken.

Clinica Dermatologica *Ospedale Palagi, viale Michelangelo 41, Outside the City Gates (055 6939654). Bus 12, 13.* **Open** *8am-noon Mon, Wed, Fri; 8-11am Tue, Thur.* **Map** *p186.* Clinica Dermatologica carries out examinations, tests, treatment and counselling for all sexually transmitted diseases, including HIV and AIDS. Some services are free, while others are state-subsidised. Some staff speak English.

HELPLINES

AIDS helpline *800 861061.*
Alcoholics Anonymous *06 6636629.* Regular AA and Al Anon meetings are held at St James Church (*see p305* Religion).
Samaritans *800 860022.* Some English-speakers.
Voce Amica *055 2478666.* **Open** *4am-6pm.* The local Italian version of the Samaritans. Some English spoken.
Women and Children's Rights & Abuse *800 001122.*

ID

In Italy, you're required by law to carry photo ID at all times.

You'll be asked to produce it if you're stopped by traffic police (who will demand your driving licence, which you must have on you whenever you are in charge of a motor vehicle). ID will also be required when you check into a hotel.

INSURANCE

EU nationals are entitled to reciprocal medical care in Italy, provided they are in possession of a European Health Insurance Card (EHIC; *see p300*).

Despite this provision, short-term visitors from all countries are advised to get private travel insurance to cover a broad number of eventualities (from injury to theft). Non-EU citizens should always ensure that they take out comprehensive medical insurance with a reputable company before leaving home.

Visitors should also take out adequate property insurance before setting off for Italy. If you rent a car, motorcycle or moped, make sure that you pay the extra for full insurance and sign the collision damage waiver before taking off in the vehicle. It's also worth checking your home insurance first, as it may already cover you.

LEFT LUGGAGE

There's a left luggage point in Santa Maria Novella train station open 6am-11pm daily on platform 16 (055 9337749, www.kipoint.it). The minimum charge is €6 for the first five hrs.

LGBT

ArciGay *920 17780377, www.arcigay.it.*

Azione Gay e Lesbica *Circolo Finisterrae, via Pisana 32, Outside the City Gates (055 220250, www.azionegayelesbica. it).* **Open** *9am-6pm Mon-Fri. Closed 3wks Aug.* **Map** *p186.* As well as organising parties, this group maintains a library and archive, facilitates HIV testing and provides general community information.

IREOS-Queer Community Service *Center Via de' Serragli 3, Oltrarno (055 216907, www.*

*ireos.org). **Open** 6-8pm Mon-Thur, Sat. **Map** p164 G9.* Ireos hosts social open houses and offers HIV testing, referrals for psychological counselling and self-help groups. It also organises hikes and outings and has free internet access most evenings and Sat mornings. See website for details.

LILA *055 2479013, www.lila. toscana.it. **Open** 9am-noon Mon, Wed, Fri; 5-8pm Tue, Thur.* Not-for-profit gay health advice line.

Queer Nation Holidays *Via del Moro 95r, Santa Maria Novella (055 2654587, www.qnholidays. it). **Open** 9.30am-6pm Mon-Fri; 9am-1pm Sat. **Map** p101 J6.* This tour operator and travel agent can organise individual and group travel. It can also make referrals to other gay and lesbian organisations.

LIBRARIES

Biblioteca delle Oblate *Via dell'Oriuolo 24, Santa Croce (055 2616512, www.biblioteche. comune.fi.it). **Open** 2-10pm Mon, 9am-midnight Tue-Sat. **Map** p145 O7.* The most central and modern city library with a variety of services including a large children's section, a panoramic cafeteria and free Wi-Fi.

British Institute Library & Cultural Centre *Lungarno Guicciardini 9, Oltrarno (055 26778270, www.britishinstitute. it). **Open** 10am-6.30pm Mon-Fri. **Map** p164 H9.* The British Institute's library requires an annual membership fee (€6 daily), but offers a reading room that overlooks the Arno, an extensive collection of art history books and Italian literature, and well-informed staff.

Kunsthistorisches Institut in Florenz *Via G Giusti 44, Outside the City Gates (055 249111, www.khi.fi.it). **Open** 9am-8pm Mon-Fri. **Map** p186.* One of the largest collections of art history books in Florence is held by the German Institute and is available to students. Books are in various languages and there's also an extensive photo library of Italian art. You'll need a letter of

presentation and a summary of your research project.

LOST PROPERTY

Property found throughout the city (including ATAF buses) is sent to the municipal *Ufficio Oggetti Trovati* (Lost & Found Office), Via Veracini 5/5, Outside the City Gates (055 334802). Bus 17. Open 9am-12.30pm Mon, Wed, Fri; 2.30-4pm Tue, Thur. A fee upwards of €3.50 is charged for the service.

The Amerigo Vespucci Airport (*see p294*) uploads a photographic record of found objects on its website www.aeroporto.firenze.it. For more information email oggettismarriti@aeroporto. firenze.it.

MEDIA

Magazines
Many news stands in the centre of town sell *Time*, *Newsweek*, *The Economist* and other glossy English-language magazines. For Italian-speakers, Italian magazines worth checking out include *Panorama* (www. panorama.it) and *L'Espresso* (www.espresso.repubblica. it), weekly current affairs and general interest rags, the full-frontal style covers of which do little justice to the high-level journalism and hot-issue coverage found within.
There are also some useful booklets with listings of events in Florence:

Firenze Spettacolo *(www. firenzespettacolo.it)* A monthly listings and local interest magazine that has an English-language section.

Florence Concierge Information *(www.florence-concierge.it)* Found at tourist offices and most hotels, this freebie gives events, useful information, timetables and suchlike in English.

Florence & Tuscany News Available around town, this booklet is useful for concerts and temporary exhibitions in Florence and Tuscany. (It's also

available as a PDF from www. informacitta.net.)

The Florentine *(www. theflorentine.net)* is a free English-language monthly distributed in restaurants, bars, hotels, language schools and the main squares. As well as news and events, it includes articles on culture, politics, travel and food.

Newspapers
Foreign dailies
Many news stands sell foreign papers, which usually arrive the next day (though sometimes the same evening in summer). The widest range are around piazza del Duomo, piazza della Repubblica, via de' Tornabuoni and SMN station.

Italian dailies
Only one Italian in ten buys a daily newspaper, so the press has little of the clout of other European countries, and the paper is generally a simple vehicle for information rather than a forum of pressure for change. Most papers publish comprehensive listings for local events. Sports coverage in the dailies is extensive, but if you're not sated, the sports papers *Corriere dello Sport* (www.corrieredellosport.it) and *La Gazzetta dello Sport* (www.gazzetta.it) offer even more detail.

Corriere della Sera *(www. corriere.it)* Serious and relatively neutral newspaper. The main news is available in English at www.corriere.it/english, while the local edition for Florence (Corriere Fiorentino) is corrierefiorentino.corriere.it.

Il Giornale *(www.ilgiornale.it)* Owned by the brother of Silvio Berlusconi, Il Giornale takes the expected centre-right line. The Florence edition has a section dedicated to local news.

Libero *(www.liberoquotidiano. it)* Decidedly right-leaning newspaper launched in 2000, with a pull-no-punches, politically incorrect style.

La Nazione *(www.lanazione. it)* Selling some 160,000 copies daily, this is the most popular newspaper in Tuscany. Founded in the mid 19th century by Bettino Ricasoli, it's also one of Italy's oldest. Basically right-wing and gossipy, it consists of three sections (national, sport and local). Each province has its own edition.

La Repubblica *(www.repubblica. it)* Politically centre-left, with strong coverage of the Mafia and Vatican issues. The Florence edition has about 20 pages dedicated to local and provincial news.

Il Manifesto *(www.ilmanifesto. it)* A solidly left-wing intellectual paper.

Radio

Controradio *(93.6 FM/www. controradio.it)* Dub, hip hop, progressive drum 'n' bass and indie rock feature heavily.
Isoradio *(103.3 FM/www. isoradio.rai.it)* Official national radio broadcasting live traffic updates.
Radio Diffusione Firenze *(102.7 FM, www.rdf.it)* Mainstream pop, house and club music.
Radio Montecarlo *(106.8 FM, www.radiomontecarlo. net)* Smooth jazzy sounds and world music.
Rete Toscana Classica *(93.3 FM, www.retetoscanaclassica.it)* Classical music only.
Virgin Radio Italia *(107.2 FM/89.1 FM, www.virginradio italy.it)* Mainstream radio with very little chat and an emphasis on British and US rock.

Television

Italy has seven major networks. Of these, three are Berlusconi-owned Mediaset channels: **Italia 1** shows familiar US series, Japanese cartoons and adventure films; **Rete 4** spews out an awful lot of cheap game shows and *Columbo* repeats but also shows decent nature documentaries; and **Canale 5** is the top dog, with the best films, quiz programmes, live shows and the most popular programme on Italian TV, the scandal-busting, satirical *Striscia la Notizia*. Programmes are riddled with ad breaks and promotions.

RAI, the three state-run channels, are known for their better-quality programming but generally much less slick presenting, and there is still a relentless stream of quiz shows and high-kicking bikini-clad bimbettes.

The last national network is independent **La7**, featuring lots of talk shows and news.

When these have bored you, there are numerous local stations featuring cleaning demos, dial-a-fortune-teller (surprisingly popular), prolonged adverts for slimming machines and trashy late-night soft porn.

Of the many satellite and cable TV subscription channels, the best is Sky Italia. Some packages include BBC and major US channels.

Websites

www.ansa.it/english News in English from the largest Italian News Agency.
www.boxol.it Information and online booking for concerts and shows.
www.firenzespettacolo.it The monthly listings mag website has what's-on information.
www.intoscana.it The official Regione Toscana news site. Updates in five languages.

MONEY

Italy is in the euro (€) zone. There are euro banknotes for €5, €10, €20, €50, €100, €200 and €500, and coins worth €1 and €2, plus 1¢, 2¢, 5¢, 10¢, 20¢ and 50¢ (cents). Credit cards are widely accepted, though AmEx and Diners Club slightly less so than Visa and MasterCard. Travellers' cheques can still be changed at all banks and bureaux de change but are only accepted as payment (in any major currency) by larger shops, hotels and restaurants.

Banks & ATMs

Expect long queues in banks even for simple transactions, and don't be surprised if the bank wants to photocopy your passport or driving licence as proof of ID. Many banks no longer give cash advances on credit cards, so check for the signs, or ask

before queuing. Branches of most banks are found around piazza della Repubblica. To access the cashpoint lobby of some banks, you have to insert your card in the machine outside.

In Italy, ATMs are known as *Bancomat*, which is also the colloquial name for debit cards. Select English as the operating language and, if possible, use ATMs located outside a post office *(postamat)* or a bank branch and do so during banking hours *(see p304* Opening hours*)*, so there is assistance available if needed.

Machines usually dispense €20 and €50 notes. Transaction fees, exchange rates and daily withdrawal limits vary. Mastercard, Visa and Maestro cards are universally accepted.

Bureaux de change

Changing your money in a bank usually gets you a better rate than in a private bureau de change *(cambio)* and will often be better than in your home country. However, if you need to change money out of banking hours, there's no shortage of bureaux de change *(cambi)*. Commission rates vary considerably: you can pay from nothing to €10 for each transaction. Watch out for 'No Commission' signs; the exchange rate at these places will almost certainly be worse. Some large hotels also offer an exchange service, but again, the rate is almost certainly worse than in a bank. Always take ID for any financial transaction.

InterChange *Via Por Santa Maria 35r, Duomo & Around (055 214500, www.interchange. eu).* **Open** *10am-8pm daily.* **Map** *p63 L9.* One of the few exchange offices open on Sun. No commission for cash withdrawal via MasterCard or Visa.

Credit cards

Italians have an enduring fondness for cash, but nearly all hotels of two stars and above, as well as most shops and restaurants (though still surprisingly few museums), accept at least some of the major credit cards.

Lost/stolen

Most lines are freephone (800) numbers, have English-speaking staff and are open 24 hrs daily. **American Express card** *emergencies 06 72282*. **Diners Club** *800 393939*. **CartaSì** *800 151616*. **MasterCard** *800 870866*. **Visa** *800 819014*.

Tax

Sales tax (IVA) is applied to all purchases and services at 4%, 10% and 22% in an ascending scale of luxury, but is almost always included in the price stated. At some luxury hotels, tax will be added on to the quoted rates, but prices will be clearly stated as *escluso* IVA.

By law, all non-EU residents are entitled to an IVA refund on purchases of €155 and over at shops participating in the 'Tax-free shopping' scheme, identified by a purple sticker. On presentation of your passport, they will give you a 'cheque' that can be cashed at the airport desk on your way home at the Tax Free Cash Refund desk at the airport. You'll need to show your passport and the unused goods, and there's a three-month time limit. IVA paid on hotel bills cannot be reclaimed.

OPENING HOURS

Bank opening hours are generally 8.20am-1.20pm and 2.35-3.35pm Mon-Fri. All banks are closed on public holidays.

Most **post offices** open 8.15am-1.30pm, closing an hour earlier on Sat; the main post office stays open 8.15am-7pm Mon-Sat (*see right*).

Food shops generally open early in the morning and close for lunch 1pm-3.30pm (some stay closed till 5pm); then open again until 7.30pm. They are generally closed on Wed afternoons (Sat afternoons in summer). Other shops tend to open later in the morning and are closed on Mon mornings. Many shops now stay open all day (*orario continuato*).

POLICE

Italian police forces are divided into four colour-coded units. The *vigili urbani* and *polizia municipale* (municipal police) wear navy blue. The *vigili* deal with all traffic matters within the city, and the *polizia municipale* with petty crime. The two forces responsible for dealing with crime are the *polizia di stato* (state police), who also wear blue jackets but have pale grey trousers, and the normally black-clad *carabinieri*, part of the army. Their roles are essentially the same. The *guardia di finanza* (financial police) wear grey and have little to do with tourists.

In an emergency, go to the tourist aid police or the nearest *carabinieri* post or police station (*questura*); we have listed central ones below, but others are found in the phone book. Staff will either speak English or be able to find someone who does. If you have had something stolen, tell them you want to report a *furto*.

A statement (*denuncia*) will be taken, which you'll need for an insurance claim. Lost or stolen passports should also be reported to your embassy or consulate. (*See p298* Accident & emergency.)

Comando Provinciale Carabinieri *Borgo Ognissanti 48, Santa Maria Novella (055 2061, 055 27661).* **Open** *24hrs daily.* **Map** *p101 F6.* A *carabinieri* post near the town centre; the best place to report the loss or theft of personal property.

Questura di Firenze Ufficio Denuncie *Via Zara 2, San Lorenzo (055 49771).* **Open** *24hrs daily.* **Map** *p119 N1.* To report a crime, go to the Ufficio Denuncie, where you will be asked to fill in a form.

Police *Via Pietrapiana 50r, Santa Croce (055 203911).* **Open** *8.30am-12.30pm Mon, Wed, Fri; 3-4.30pm Thur.* **Map** *p145 P7.* Interpreters are on hand to help report thefts, lost property and any other problems.

POSTAL SERVICES

Improvements have been made to Italy's postal service (www.poste.it), and you can now be more or less sure that the letter you sent or were sent will arrive in reasonable time.

Stamps (*francobolli*) can be bought at *tabacchi* or post offices. Most post boxes are red and have two slots, Per la Città (for Florence) and Tutte le Altre Destinazioni (everywhere else).

A letter takes about five days to reach the UK, eight to the US. There are now two classes of post (*posta prioritaria*) called Posta1 and Posta4, which generally fulfil the next-day or four-day delivery promise in Italy. A small letter or postcard weighing 20g or less sent to addresses in Italy costs €2.80 by Posta1 and 95¢ by Posta4.

Postamail Internazionale to any EU country costs €1 (estimated delivery 8 days); to the US, it'll cost €2.20 (16 days); sending mail further afield will cost €2.90 (22 days). A faster but more expensive option is Postapriority Internazionale: €3.50 and 3 days to the UK, €4.50 and 6 days to North America, €5.50 and 8 days to Australia.

Mail (20g or less) can be sent *raccomandata* (registered) for €5 for Italy, €6.60 for the EU and €7.80 for the US. *Assicurata* (insured) for up to €50 costs €7.80 in the EU; €8.60 to the US, from post offices only.

Heavier mail is charged according to weight. To send a parcel weighing 1kg to the UK costs €18, €28.50 to the US.

Italian postal charges are complicated, so be prepared for variations. For guaranteed fast delivery, use a courier or the SDA Italian post office courier service.

The Italian post call centre number is 803160. Officially Italian only, though you may strike lucky.

Post offices

Local post offices (*ufficio postale*) in each district generally open 8.15am-1.30pm Mon-Fri; 8.15am-12.30pm Sat. The main post office (Posta Centrale) has longer opening hours and a range of additional services.

Posta Centrale *Via Pellicceria 3, Duomo & Around (055 2736481). Open 8.15am-7pm Mon-Fri; 8.15am-12.30pm Sat. Map p63 K8.* This is Florence's main post office.

Other post offices
Via Luigi Alamanni 14-16 (by the train station), Santa Maria Novella (055 2674931). Open 8.15am-7pm Mon-Fri; 8.15am-12.30pm Sat. Map p101 F4.
Via Pietrapiana 53, Santa Croce (055 2674231). Open 8.15am-7pm Mon-Fri; 8.15am-12.30pm Sat. Map p145 P7.
Via Barbadori 37r, Oltrarno (055 288175). Open 8.15am-1.30pm Mon-Fri; 8.15am-12.30pm Sat Map p164 J10.

Poste restante
Poste restante (general delivery) letters (in Italian, *fermoposta*) should be sent to the main post office (*see above*), addressed to Fermoposta and the code and address of the post office you wish to pick your mail from. You need a passport to collect mail and you may have to pay a small charge if sent from outside Italy (if sent from Italy a charge of €3 is added to the postage). Mail can also be sent to any Mail Boxes Etc. (MBE) branches.

PUBLIC HOLIDAYS

On public holidays (*giorni festivi*) virtually all shops, banks and businesses are shut, though most bars and restaurants stay open so you will be able to eat and drink. Public holidays are as follows:
New Year's Day (*Capodanno*) 1 Jan
Epiphany (*La Befana*) 6 Jan
Easter Day (*Pasqua*)
Easter Monday (*Lunedì di Pasqua*)
Liberation Day (*Venticinque Aprile/Liberazione*) 25 Apr
Labour Day (*Primo Maggio*) 1 May
Republic Day (*Festa della Repubblica*) 2 June
Florence Saint's Day (*San Giovanni*) 24 June
Feast of the Assumption (*Ferragosto*) 15 Aug

All Saints' (*Tutti i Santi*) 1 Nov
Immaculate Conception (*Festa dell'Immacolata*) 8 Dec
Christmas Day (*Natale*) 25 Dec
Boxing Day (*Santo Stefano*) 26 Dec

There is limited public transport on 1 May and Christmas afternoon. Holidays falling on a Sat or Sun are not celebrated the following Mon, but if a holiday falls on a Thur or Tue, many locals also take the intervening day off and make a long weekend of it; such a weekend is called a *ponte* (bridge). Beware of the *rientro* or homecoming, when the roads are horrendously busy.

Many people also disappear for a large chunk of Aug, when *chiuso per ferie* (closed for holidays) signs appear in shops and restaurants detailing dates of closure. These closures are co-ordinated on a rota system by the city council, so there should be something open in each area at any given time.

RELIGION

There are Roman Catholic churches all over the city, and a few churches still sing mass. Catholic mass is held in English in **Santa Maria del Fiore** (the Duomo) on Sat afternoons at 5pm and at the **Chiesa dell'Ospedale San Giovanni di Dio** (*borgo Ognissanti 20*) on Sun and public hols at 10am.
American Episcopal Church (*St James Church*) *Via Rucellai 9, Santa Maria Novella (055 294417, www.stjames.it). Services (in English) 9am, 11am Sun. Map p101 E4.*
Anglican St Mark's Church *via Maggio 16, Oltrarno (055 294764, www.stmarksitaly.com). Services 10.30am (Sung Mass) Sun; 5.30pm (Low Mass) Wed; 6pm (BCP Mass) Fri. Map p164 H10.*
Islamic Moschea di Firenze *borgo Allegri 62-64r, Santa Croce (055 1234567, www.moscheadifirenze.it). Map p145 Q8.*
Jewish Comunità Ebraica *via Farini 4, Santa Croce (055 245252, www.firenzebraica.it). Services 8.30/8.45am Sat. Phone for details of Fri & Sat evening*

services; times vary. Map p145 Q6.
Methodist Chiesa Metodista *via de' Benci 9, Santa Croce (055 288143, www.firenzechurch.com). Services 10.30am Sun. Map p145 N9.*

SAFETY & SECURITY

Crime has slightly decreased in Tuscany in recent years. Serious street crime is rare, and Florence remains a relatively safe city to walk in. Take care at night, when lone women in particular should stick to the main well-lit streets. For visitors to the city, the main risk comes from the numerous pickpockets and bag-snatchers. Buses, shops, bars and other crowded areas are petty criminals' hunting grounds. As you would in any major city, take common-sense precautions:
• Don't keep wallets in back pockets. This is a pickpocket's favourite swipe, especially on buses and public transport.
• Wear shoulder bags diagonally and facing away from the road to minimise the risk of *scippi* – bag snatching from mopeds, which is still common in the city.
• Never leave bags on tables or the backs of chairs in bars.
• Keep an eye on your valuables while trying on clothes and shoes.
• Watch out for 'baby-gangs' of children or teenagers who hang around the tourist spots and create a distraction by flapping a newspaper or card while trying to slip their hands into bags or pockets. If you are approached, keep walking, keep calm and hang on to your valuables.

For emergency numbers, *see p298*. For information on the police, *see p304*.

SMOKING

A law banning smoking in all public places came into force in 2005 and is scrupulously respected and enforced. This includes bars, restaurants and clubs, although there is a clause that allows some venues to set aside a smoking room, as long as it is separated by double doors and adequately ventilated and filtered. Owners who allow customers to smoke are fined heavily; the smoker can also be fined. Cigarettes are on sale at *tabacchi* and *bar-tabacchi*; both are recognisable by the blue/black and white sign outside.

STUDY

With over 20 US university programmes and countless language schools and art courses, many of which have international reputations, the city's student population rivals that of its residents at some times of the year. The courses listed in this section are all generally in English. However, if you don't speak any Italian, double-check before you enrol.

Università di Firenze *Centro di Cultura per Stranieri Via Francesco Valori 9, Outside the City Gates (055 2756938, www. ccs.unifi.it). Bus 8, 10, 11, 17, 20.* **Open** *9am-noon Mon-Fri.* Offers language and cultural courses. Fees are about €800 per term.

Art, design & restoration courses

Il Bisonte *Via San Niccolò 24, Oltrarno (055 2342585, www.ilbisonte.it).* **Map** *p164 P12.* Located among the artisans' workshops in the former stables of Palazzo Serristori, Il Bisonte has specialist courses and theoretical/practical seminars in the techniques of etching and printmaking.

Charles H Cecil Studios *Borgo San Frediano 68, Oltrarno (055 285102, www.charlescecilstudios. com).* **Map** *p164 E8.* The church of San Raffaello Arcangelo was converted into a studio complex in the early 19th century. It now houses one of the more charismatic of Florence's art schools, Charles H Cecil Studios, which is heavily frequented by Brits. It gives a thorough training in the classical techniques of drawing and oil painting, and runs classes for the general public.

L'Istituto per l'Arte e il Restauro *Palazzo Ridolfi, via Maggio 13, Oltrarno (055 282951, www.spinelli.it).* **Map** *p164 H10.* Widely considered one of the best art restoration schools in Italy, the Institute offers a multitude of courses in the restoration of frescoes, paintings, furniture, gilt objects, ceramics, stone, paper and glass. Courses last between one and three years. One-month courses are held from July to Sept.

Università Internazionale dell'Arte *Villa il Ventaglio, via delle Forbici 24-26, Outside the City Gates (055 570216, www. uiafirenze.com). Bus 7.* **Map** *p186.* Based in a fabulous villa, courses cover restoration and preservation, museum and gallery management and art criticism.

Language classes

There are no end of language and culture courses in Florence, including many intensive one- or two-month courses, which should provide an adequate everyday grasp of the language. Prices refer to a standard four-week course with four hours' tuition a day.

ABC Centro di Lingua e Cultura Italiana *Via de' Rustici 7, Santa Croce (055 212001, www. abcschool.com). Price €200 for one week.* **Map** *p145 N9.* ABC offers language teaching at six levels, as well as preparatory courses for the entrance exam to the University of Florence.

British Institute Language Centre *Piazza Strozzi 2, Duomo & Around (055 267781, www. britishinstitute.it). Price €240 for one week.* **Map** *p63 K8.* Short courses in Italian language, history of art, drawing and cooking. For the British Institute's Library & Cultural Centre, *see p302.*

Dante Alighieri Centro Linguistico Italiano *Dante Alighieri Piazza della Repubblica 5, Duomo & Around (055 211211, www.scuola-dante-alighieri.it/ firenze.htm). Price €115-€380 for one week depending on intensity of course.* **Map** *p63 L7.* Eleven language levels; opera and literature courses too.

Istituto Lorenzo de' Medici *Via Faenza 43, San Lorenzo (055*
287203, www.ldminstitute.com). Price €370 for two weeks. **Map** *p119 J4.* Four different courses in Italian as well as classes in cooking, Italian cinema and art history.

Scuola Leonardo da Vinci *Via Bufalini 3, San Lorenzo (055 261181, www.scuolaleonardo. com). Price €110-220 for one week, plus €70 enrolment.* **Map** *p119 N6.* Versatile language courses, plus classes in history of art, fashion, drawing, design, cooking and wine.

Scuola Machiavelli *Piazza Santo Spirito 4, Oltrarno (055 2396966, www.centromachiavelli. it). Price €345-€570 per fortnight depending on intensity of course, plus €40 enrolment fee.* **Map** *p164 H10.* This small co-op offers Italian, pottery, fresco, mosaic, trompe l'œil and book-binding classes.

Useful organisations

Italian Cultural Institute *39 Belgrave Square, London SW1X 8NX, UK (+44 (0)20 7235 1461, www.iiclondra.esteri.it).*

TELEPHONES & INTERNET

Dialling & codes

The international code for Italy is 39. To dial in from other countries, preface it with the exit code: 00 in the UK and 011 in the US. All normal Florence numbers begin with the area code 055. The code for Siena is 0577, for Pisa 050. As with all Italian codes, these must always be used in full, even when you are calling from within the same area, and when dialling internationally. Italian mobile phone numbers begin with 3 (no zero).

To make an international call from Florence, dial 00, then the country code (Australia 61; Canada 1; Irish Republic 353; New Zealand 64; United Kingdom 44; United States 1), followed by the area code (for calls to the UK, omit the initial zero) and individual number. The same pattern works to mobile phones.

All numbers beginning 800 are free lines (*numero verde*).

For numbers that begin 840, you'll be charged one unit only, regardless of where you're calling from or how long the call lasts. These numbers can be called from within Italy only; some only function within one phone district. Phone numbers starting with 3 are mobile numbers; those with 199 codes are charged at local rates; 167 numbers are billed at premium rates.

Mobile phones

Basic pay-as-you-go mobiles can be bought from many phone shops and some post offices from around €20, including the SIM card and €5 of calls. Top-up cards are available from all *bar-tabacchi* and some newsstands; either call the number given on the card, or, if the bar has the electronic top-up facility, tap in your phone number and the amount requested will be credited automatically. One top-up has to be made at least every 11 mths to keep the number active. If your device is unlocked, SIM cards can also be bought without having to buy a phone; prices vary.

The mobile phone shops listed below are located in central Florence.

TIM, Telecom Italia Mobile *Via de' Lamberti 12-14, Duomo & Around (055 2396066).* **Open** *9am-7pm Mon-Fri; 9am-1pm Sat.* **Map** *p63 L8.*
Vodafone *Via de' Martelli 25-31r, Duomo & Around (055 2670121).* **Open** *9am-7pm Mon-Fri; 9am-1pm Sat.* **Map** *p63 L6.*

Operator services

To make a reverse-charge (collect) call, dial 170 for the international operator in Italy. To be connected to the operator in the country you want to call, dial 172 followed by a country code (so 172 00 44 for the UK and 172 00 1 for the US) and you'll be connected directly to an operator in that country.

Wi-Fi

Many restaurants, cafes and hotels offer free Wi-Fi. The city of Florence also offers 500Mb (or 2 hrs, whichever limit you hit first) free internet traffic per user per day in many popular tourist locations across town. Just watch out for the *FirenzeWiFi* network to pop up in your hotspot list, click *Free Internet* from your browser and you're ready to surf. SIM cards with data plans may be purchased from the main mobile operators (*see above*).

TIME

Italy is one hour ahead of London, six ahead of New York and eight behind Sydney. Clocks go forward an hour on the last Sun in Mar and back on the last Sun in Oct, in line with other EU countries.

TIPPING

The 10-15% tip customary in many countries is considered generous in Florence. Locals sometimes leave a few coins on the counter when buying drinks at the bar and, depending on the standard of the restaurant, will drop €1-€5 for the service after a meal. That said, some larger restaurants are now starting to add a 10-15% service charge on the bill automatically. Tips are not expected in small restaurants, although they are always appreciated. Taxi drivers will be surprised if you do more than add a euro or two.

TOILETS

Always visit the restrooms whenever you stop at a bar, restaurant or museum because public toilets are few and far between and cost around €1 to use. Locate the nearest public facilities (including wheelchair-accessible toilets) with the official *Firenze Turismo* app (*see p308*). Of course you can do as the locals do and, for about the same price, purchase a small bottle of water or gulp an espresso from a bar and use the establishment's facilities instead – just make sure the toilet is available before placing your order!

To be sent an information pack in advance of your visit, get in touch with ENIT, the Italian tourist board (UK: 020 7408 1254, www.italia.it; US: 212 245 5618, www.italiantourism.com). Tell staff where and when you're travelling, and whether or not you have any special interests.

In Florence, the tourist information service is operated jointly by the Tourism departments of Comune di Firenze and Città Metropolitana. The official website www.firenzeturismo.it has a useful download area with informative maps and brochures in PDF format. The helpful, multilingual staff do their best to supply reliable information: not easy, since museums and galleries tend to change their hours without telling them. There's no central information service for the Tuscany region; you have to contact the APT in each area. There is a head office in each provincial capital, then local offices in various towns within the province. Details are given in the Day Trips chapter.

Tourist information offices
Via Cavour 1r, San Lorenzo (055 290832). **Open** *Summer 8.15am-7.15pm Mon-Sat; 8.30am-1.30pm Sun. Winter 8.15am-7.15pm Mon-Sat.* **Map** *p119 L5.*
Parco delle Cascine Visitor Centre *piazzale delle Cascine, Outside the City Gates (055 365707).* **Open** *10am-4pm Fri, 10am-5pm Sat-Sun.* **Map** *p186.*
Infopoint Bigallo *piazza San Giovanni 1, Duomo & Around (055 288496).* **Open** *9am-7pm Mon-Sat; 9am-2pm Sun.* **Map** *p63 L6.*
Piazza della Stazione 4a *Santa Maria Novella (055 212245).* **Open** *9am-7pm Mon-Sat; 9am-2pm Sun.* **Map** *p101 H4.*
Run by the City of Florence, these offices provide maps and info. There are also offices in Florence and Pisa airports. Tourist information offices cannot provide hotel booking services. *See p288* Accommodation for more details.

Useful apps

Useful apps that you may want to install on your device before your visit include:

ATAF 2.0 Official app of the bus and tram network. Free.

Firenze Turismo Official app of the Tourist Board. Map-based search of museums, restaurants, facilities, services, accessibility and events. Free.

Florence Heritage Combining historical and contemporary Florence with 12 suggested itineraries. Free.

Inferno Florence Guide Written by editors of local events website The Florentine this app is for Dan Brown fans. Follow in the footsteps of Inferno with a map of locations, 31 listening points around the city, original photos and more. £2.99

Uffizi: The Official Guide Aimed to help you make the most of your Uffizi experience with a guide to exhibition rooms, key artworks, artists and an interactive map allowing virtual access to each room. £3.99

VISAS & IMMIGRATION

Non-EU and UK citizens require full passports to travel to Italy. EU citizens are permitted unrestricted access to Italy to travel (*see right* Work); citizens of the USA, Canada, Australia and New Zealand should check about visa requirements at an Italian embassy or consulate in their own country before setting off for Italy.

WEIGHTS & MEASURES

Italy uses only the metric system; remember that all speed limits are in kilometres (km): 1km = 0.62 miles; 1 mile = 1.6km. Petrol, like other liquids, is measured in litres: 1 UK gallon = 4.54l; 1 US gallon = 3.79l. A kilogram (kg) is equivalent to 2.2lbs (1lb = 0.45kg). Food is often sold in *etti* (sometimes written hg); 1 *etto* = 100g (3.52oz). In delicatessens, ask for multiples of *etti* (un *etto*, due *etti*, etc).

WOMEN

Although it's not one of the worst places for women travellers, Tuscany still has its hassles. Visiting women can feel daunted by the sheer volume of attention they receive, but most of it will be friendly; men are unlikely to become pushy or aggressive if given the brush-off. It's normally a question of all talk and no action, but be aware of who's around you: it's quite common to be followed. If things get too heavy, go into the nearest shop or bar and wait or ask for help. The notorious bum-pinching is actually uncommon but not unknown, especially on buses. As in Anglo-Saxon countries, it's a criminal offence, and recent prosecutions and convictions show that it's taken seriously.

Tampons (*assorbenti interni*) and sanitary towels (*assorbenti esterni*) can be bought in supermarkets, pharmacies and some *tabacchi*. For info on contraception, abortion and other health matters, *see p300.*

Clinica Ostetrica Reparto Maternità *Ospedale di Careggi, Largo Brambilla 3, Outside the City Gates (055 794111, www. aou-careggi.toscana.it). Bus 2, 8, 14C.* **Open** *24hrs daily.* **Map** *p186.* Female victims of sexual assault should go to the Clinica Ostetrica for medical attention. You'll find dedicated specialist operators and a priority path for victims of violence called *Codice Rosa* (Pink Code).

WORK

Finding a job in Italy is not simple. The jobs market isn't known for being mobile and unemployment is fairly high, especially for graduate positions. Most of the jobs that are available are connected to tourism in some way, although there are a few multinationals that occasionally advertise for native English-speakers. The classified ads paper *La Pulce* has job listings; it's also worth checking the local English-language press.

The bureaucracy involved is not easy but has been simplified by recent changes, at least for EU citizens. Since Apr 2007, EU citizens no longer need to apply for a *permesso di soggiorno* (permit to stay). For stays of over three mths, EU citizens should sign up at their local *anagrafe* (Register Office) presenting proof of their work, study or training activities, or providing proof of adequate financial means to support themselves (this is judged by the number of people in the family, from just over €5,000 for single applicants, to just over €15,000 for those with four or more extra family dependents).

Citizens from outside the EU should check about visa requirements at an Italian embassy or consulate in their own country before setting off for Italy. All non-EU citizens who are planning to stay for more than three mths should register with the police within eight days of arrival and then apply for their permits. More details are on the Polizia di Stato website: www. poliziadistato.it/articolo/10617/ (in English).

Administration & permit offices (information, applications and renewals)

Comune di Firenze *Sportello Immigrazione, Villa Pallini, via Baracca 150p, Outside the City Gates (055 2767078, immigr@ comune.fi.it). Bus 29, 30, 35.* **Open** *9am-12.15pm Mon-Fri, plus 2-4.45pm Tue & Thur only.* **Map** *p186.* For residency enquiries, ask for the Ufficio Circoscrizione. Given your address, they will then give you the number you need to call to progress further with your application.

Permits to stay

Immigration Office *via della Fortezza 17, San Lorenzo (055 49771).* **Open** *9.30am-12.30pm Mon-Fri, plus 3-5pm Thur.* **Map** *p119 J2.* To apply for your documents, go here (English-speaking staff are usually available to help).

Glossary

Annunciation depiction of the Virgin Mary being told by the Archangel Gabriel that she will bear the son of God.

Attribute object used in art to symbolise a particular person, often a saint or a martyr.

Badia (also *abbadia*, or *abbazia*) abbey.

Baldacchino canopied structure; in paintings holding an enthroned Madonna and child.

Baptistery building for baptisms, usually octagonal to symbolise new beginnings, as seven is the number of completion and eight the start of a new cycle.

Baroque sumptuous art and architectural style from the 17th to mid 18th centuries.

Basilica in architecture, a large oblong building with double colonnades and a semicircular apse; in Catholicism, a church with special privileges.

Byzantine spiritual and religious art of the Byzantine Empire (fifth-15th centuries).

Campanile bell tower.

Cartoon full scale sketch for painting or fresco.

Cenacolo depiction of the Last Supper, usually found in the refectory of convents.

Chiaroscuro painting or drawing technique using shades of black, grey and white to emphasise light and shade.

Classical ancient Greek and Roman art and culture.

Corbel bracket jutting from a roof.

Cupola dome-shaped structure set on a larger dome or a roof.

Deposition depiction of Christ taken down from the Cross.

Diptych painting made of two panels.

Fresco technique for wall painting where pigments bind with wet plaster.

Giglio a red fleur-de-lis (lily) on white; the symbol of Florence.

Gothic architectural and artistic style of the late Middle Ages (from the 12th century), with pointed arches and an emphasis on line.

Grotesque ornate artistic style derived from Roman underground painted rooms (*grotte*).

Hortus conclusus garden around Madonna and child symbolising their uncontaminated world of perfection and contentment.

Iconography study of subject and symbolism of works of art. For example, in Renaissance art: a **dog** symbolises faithfulness to a master; an **egg** is a symbol of perfection; a **peacock** symbolises the Resurrection; a **lily** is often found in Annunciations to symbolise the purity of the Madonna; and the colour **blue** sometimes symbolises divine peace.

Illumination miniature painted as an illustration for manuscripts.

Loggia covered area with one or more sides open, with columns.

Lunette half-moon painting or semicircular architectural space for decoration or window.

Macchiaioli a group of painters active in Tuscany in the second half of the 19th century, often considered the local equivalent of the French Impressionists.

Madonna of Mercy Madonna with her cloak open to give protection to those in need.

Maestà depiction of the Madonna on a throne.

Mandorla almond-shaped 'glory' surrounding depiction of a holy person.

Mannerism 15th-century art movement in Italy, defined by exaggerated perspective and scale, and complex compositions and poses.

Marzocco heraldic lion supporting the coat-of-arms of Florence with one paw.

Medieval relating to the Middle Ages (from the fall of the Roman Empire in the west, in the fifth century, to the 1453 fall of Constantinople or the 1492 discovery of America).

Modernism (Modernist) the movement away from classical and traditional forms towards architecture that applied scientific methods to its design.

Palazzo (*palazzi*) large and/or important building, not necessarily a royal palace.

Panel painting on wood.

Panneggio style of folded and pleated drapery worn by figures in 15th- and 16th-century painting and sculpture.

Pietà depiction of the dead body of Christ lying across the Madonna's lap.

Pietra dura inlaid gem or coloured stone mosaics.

Polyptych painting composed of several panels.

Putto (*putti*) small angelic naked boys, often depicted as attendants of Venus.

Relief sculpted work with three-dimensional areas jutting out from a flat surface.

Renaissance 14th- to 16th-century cultural movement based on the 'rebirth' of classical ideals and methods.

Romanesque architectural style of the early Middle Ages (c500-1200), drawing on Roman Byzantine influences.

Sarcophagus stone or marble coffin.

Sinopia preparatory drawing for a fresco made with a red earth mix or the red paint itself.

Tempera pigment bound with egg, the main painting material from the 12th to late 15th centuries.

Tondo round painting or relief.

Triptych painting composed of three panels.

Trompe l'œil painting designed to give the illusion of a three-dimensional reality.

Votive offering left as a prayer for good fortune or recovery from illness.

Vocabulary

Any attempt at speaking Italian will always be appreciated. Indeed, it may well be necessary: away from services such as tourist offices, hotels and restaurants popular with foreigners, the level of English is not very high. The most important thing is making the effort, not whether or not your sentences are perfectly formed with an authentic accent. The key is to take the plunge and not be shy.

It's a myth that you can get by in Italy with Spanish: true, you may well understand some Italian (both written and spoken), but try speaking it and Italians generally won't understand you (unless, of course, they speak Spanish).

Italian is a phonetic language, so most words are spelled as they're pronounced (and vice versa). Stresses usually fall on the penultimate syllable. There are three forms of the second person: the formal *lei* (used with strangers), the informal *tu*, and the plural form *voi*. Masculine nouns are usually accompanied by adjectives ending in 'o', female nouns by adjectives ending in 'a'. However, there are many nouns and adjectives that end in 'e' that can be either masculine or feminine.

Pronunciation

Vowels
a *as in* apple
e *like* a *in* age *(closed e), or* e *in* sell *(open e)*
i *like* ea *in* east
o *as in* hotel *(closed o) or in* hot *(open o)*
u *like* oo *in* boot

Consonants
c *before a, o or u: like the* c *in* cat; *before e or*
i: *like the* ch *in* check
ch *like the* c *in* cat
g *before a, o or u: like the* g *in* get; *before e or*
i: *like the* j *in* jig
gh *like the* g *in* get
gl *followed by 'i': like* lli *in* million
gn *like* ny *in* canyon
qu *as in* quick
r *is always rolled*
s *has two sounds, as in* soap *or* rose
sc *followed by 'e' or 'i': like the* sh *in* shame
sch *like the* sc *in* scout
z *has two sounds, like* ts *and* dz
Double consonants are sounded more
emphatically.

Useful words & phrases

hello and goodbye (informal) *ciao*
good morning, good day *buongiorno*
good afternoon, good evening *buona sera*
I don't understand *non capisco/*
non ho capito
do you speak English? *parla inglese?*
please *per favore*
thank you *grazie*
you're welcome *prego*
when does it open? *quando apre?*
where is...? *dov'è...?*
excuse me *scusi (polite), scusa (informal)*
open *aperto*
closed *chiuso*
entrance *entrata*
exit *uscita*
left *sinistra*
right *destra*
car *macchina*
bus *autobus*
train *treno*
bus stop *fermata dell'autobus*
ticket/s *biglietto/i*
I would like a ticket to... *vorrei un*
biglietto per...
postcard *cartolina*
stamp *francobollo*
glass *bicchiere*
coffee *caffè*
tea *tè*
water *acqua*
wine *vino*
beer *birra*
the bill *il conto*
single/twin/double bedroom *camera*
singola/a due letti/matrimoniale

booking *prenotazione*
May I see the menu? *Posso vedere il menù?*
The bill, please. *Il conto, per favore.*

Days of the week
Monday *lunedì*
Tuesday *martedì*
Wednesday *mercoledì*
Thursday *giovedì*
Friday *venerdì*
Saturday *sabato*
Sunday *domenica*
yesterday *ieri*
today *oggi*
tomorrow *domani*
morning *mattina*
afternoon *pomeriggio*
evening *sera*
night *notte*
weekend *fine settimana, weekend*

The come-on
Do you have a light? *Hai da accendere?*
What's your name? *Come ti chiami?*
Would you like a drink? *Vuol bere qualcosa?*
Where are you from? *Di dove sei?*
What are you doing here? *Che fai qui?*
Do you have a boyfriend/girlfriend? *Hai un*
ragazzo/una ragazza?

The brush-off
I'm married *Sono sposato/a*
I'm tired *Sono stanco/a*
I'm going home *Vado a casa*
I have to meet a friend *Devo incontrare un*
amico/un'amica

Numbers & money
0 *zero;* 1 *uno;* 2 *due;* 3 *tre;* 4 *quattro;* 5
cinque; 6 *sei;* 7 *sette;* 8 *otto;* 9 *nove;* 10
dieci; 11 *undici;* 12 *dodici;* 13 *tredici;* 14
quattordici; 15 *quindici;* 16 *sedici;* 17
diciassette; 18 *diciotto;* 19 *diciannove;* 20
venti; 21 *ventuno;* 22 *ventidue;* 30 *trenta;*
40 *quaranta;* 50 *cinquanta;* 60 *sessanta;*
70 *settanta;* 80 *ottanta;* 90 *novanta;* 100
cento; 1,000 *mille;* 2,000 *duemila;* 100,000
centomila; 1,000,000 *un milione.*

How much does it cost/is it? *Quanto*
costa?/quant'è?
Do you have any change? *Ha da cambiare?*
Can you give me a discount? *Mi può fare*
uno sconto?
Do you accept credit cards? *Si accettano le*
carte di credito?
Can I pay in pounds/dollars/travellers'
cheques? *Posso pagare in sterline/dollari/*
con i travellers?
Can I have a receipt? *Posso avere*
una ricevuta?

Further Reference

BOOKS

Non-fiction

Luigi Barzini *The Italians* A dated yet hilarious portrait.

Julia Conaway Bondanella & Mark Musa *Italian Renaissance Reader* An introduction to the major Italian writers and influential thinkers of the Renaissance.

Thomas Campanello *A Defense of Galileo* The life, times and influence of Tuscany's most famous heretic.

Robert Clark *Dark Water: Art, Disaster and Redemption in Florence* The 1966 flood and its aftermath through the voices of witnesses.

Paul Ginsborg *A History of Contemporary Italy: 1943-1980* Italian society and politics.

Frederick Hartt & David Wilkins *The History of Italian Renaissance Art* The definitive work.

Tobias Jones *The Dark Heart of Italy* Fantastic introduction to contemporary Italy.

Ross King *Brunelleschi's Dome: The Story of the Great Cathedral in Florence* A fascinating account of the building of the city's magnificent dome.

Mary McCarthy *The Stones of Florence* A tribute to Florence and its arts.

Caroline Moorehead *Iris Origo: Marchesa of Val D'Orcia* Biography of the intriguing writer who helped to protect refugee children during World War II.

Iris Origo *Images and Shadows: Part of a Life* Autobiographical and biographical accounts of Florence and Tuscany.

Beppe Severgnini *La Bella Figura: An Insider's Guide to the Italian Mind* Find out how Italy and Italia are not quite the same.

Dava Sobel *Galileo's Daughter: A Drama of Science, Faith and Love* A study of Galileo's life in the context of his relationship with his daughter.

Matthew Spender *Within Tuscany : Reflections on a Time and a Place* A witty account of growing up in an unusual family in Tuscany.

Paul Strathern *The Medici: Godfathers of the Renaissance* The remarkable influence of the Medici in Florence and throughout Europe.

Giorgio Vasari *The Lives of the Artists* A collection of biographical accounts, first published in Florence in 1550.

Fiction

Michael Dibdin *A Rich Full Death* An amusing thriller with insight into 19th-century Florence.

Sarah Dunant *The Birth of Venus* Gender and art in Medici Florence.

George Eliot *Romola* A compelling heroine and the turbulent backdrop of Renaissance Florence.

EM Forster *A Room with a View; Where Angels Fear to Tread* Social comedy from the master.

Robert Hellenga *The Sixteen Pleasures* A young American woman in Florence acts out 16 'pleasures' from a book of erotica.

Christobel Kent *The Dead Season; The Drowning River; A Fine and Private Place; A Murder in Tuscany* The investigations of private detective Sandro Cellini.

W Somerset Maugham *Up at the Villa* Temptation and fate in 1930s Florence.

Frances Mayes *Under the Tuscan Sun: At Home in Italy* Year in Provence-style expat dreams.

Magdalen Nabb *The Monster of Florence; Death of an Englishman; Vita Nuova* Just a few titles of the Marshal Guarnaccia mysteries set in Florence.

Michael Ondaatje *The English Patient* Booker-winning novel, partly set in Tuscany.

Food & wine

Giancarlo and Katie Caldesi *Return to Tuscany: Recipes from a Tuscan Cookery School* Recipes, lessons and culture.

Beth Elon *A Culinary Traveller in Tuscany* Recipes and itineraries through lesser known parts of Tuscany.

Claudia Roden *The Food of Italy* A wonderful book of Italian recipes, with a section on Tuscany.

Gambero Rosso *Italian Wines* The English edition of the reliable annual guide to Italian wines.

FILM

The Agony and the Ecstasy
(1965)
Charlton Heston stars as
Michelangelo during the
painting of the Sistine Chapel.

Hannibal *(2001)*
Ridley Scott's sequel to *The
Silence of the Lambs* from the
novel by Thomas Harris.

Inferno *(2016)*
Ron Howard directs Tom
Hanks in the third mystery
thriller of Dan Brown's Robert
Langdon series.

Life is Beautiful *(1997)*
Roberto Benigni's bittersweet
comedy about wartime Arezzo.

Much Ado about Nothing *(1993)*
Kenneth Branagh's
interpretation of
Shakespeare's comedy.

Portrait of a Lady *(1996)*
Nicole Kidman stars as Henry
James's New World woman in
Old World Italy.

A Room with a View *(1985)*
Love and loss in
19th-century Florence.

Stealing Beauty *(1996)*
Bernardo Bertolucci's Tuscan-
based film brought us Liv Tyler.

The Stendhal Syndrome *(1996)*
Detective Anna Manni travels
to Florence on the trail of a
serial killer.

Tea with Mussolini *(1999)*
Judy Dench and Maggie Smith
form part of an eccentric group
of expats.

**The Twilight Saga: New
Moon** *(2009)*
Montepulciano stands in for
Volterra in the second film
based on Stephenie Meyer's
vampire saga.

Up at the Villa *(2000)*
Sean Penn's cynical American
proves innocent in comparison
to his European companions.

MUSIC

Puccini *Gianni Schicchi*
This delightful one-act opera is
set in medieval Fucecchio, west
of Florence.

Tchaikovsky *Souvenir of
Florence* The composer wrote
this string sextet while living in
via San Leonardo in Florence.

▶ *For a selction of useful websites, see p303; and useful apps, see p308.*

Index

INDEX

Credits

Crimson credits
Authors Maddalena Delli, Mary Gray
Contributors Nicky Swallow (History), Sophia Cottier (Architecture, Art)
Editor Lucie Wood
Listing editors Emilie Crabb, Daniela Verma
Proofreaders Liz Hammond, Ros Sales
Layouts Patrick Dawson, Emma Bryers
Cartography Gail Armstrong, Simonetta Giori

Series Editor Sophie Blacksell Jones
Production Manager Kate Michell
Design Mytton Williams

Chairman David Lester
Managing Director Andy Riddle

Advertising Media Sales House
Marketing Lyndsey Mayhew-Dehaney
Sales Molly Keel

Acknowledgements
The authors and editors would like to thank Eike Schmidt, Director of the Uffizi, and the Uffizi press team, plus all contributors to previous editions of *Time Out Florence* whose work forms the basis of this guide.

Photography credits
Front cover Romas_Photo/Shutterstock.com
Back cover left givaga/Shutterstock.com, centre right Christian Mueller/Shutterstock.com, right photogolfer/Shutterstock.com
Inside front cover Simona Bottone/Shutterstock.com
Interior Photography credits, *see p319*.

Publishing information
Florence City Guide 8th edition
© TIME OUT ENGLAND LIMITED 2017
June 2017

ISBN 978 1 780592 47 3
CIP DATA: A catalogue record for this book is available from the British Library

Published by Crimson Publishing
19-21c Charles Street, Bath, BA1 1HX (01225 584 950, www.crimsonpublishing.co.uk) on behalf of Time Out England.

Distributed by Grantham Book Services
Distributed in the US and Canada by Publishers Group West (1-510-809-3700)

Printed by Grafostil.